Schools for Strategy

Schools for Strategy

Education and Research
in National Security Affairs

GENE M. LYONS
LOUIS MORTON

With a Foreword by John W. Masland

FREDERICK A. PRAEGER, *Publishers*
New York • Washington • London

FREDERICK A. PRAEGER, *Publishers*
111 Fourth Avenue, New York 3, N.Y., U.S.A.
77–79 Charlotte Street, London W.1, England

Published in the United States of America in 1965
by Frederick A. Praeger, Inc., Publishers

© 1965, Frederick A. Praeger, Inc.
Library of Congress Catalog Card Number: 65–14056

Printed in the United States of America

Foreword

SOME TIME AGO, two of us at Dartmouth College wrote a study of military education in the United States. Our concern was that the traditional distinction between military and civilian affairs in American life had become less significant. Even under a system of government in which the ultimate authority rests with civilians, military leaders inevitably participate in the formulation of national policy. We undertook to examine the educational institutions of the Army, Navy, and Air Force to determine how well these institutions prepare career officers for participation in the policy process.

For the most part, our friends in the military services responded kindly to our observations, but more than a few suggested that we had examined only half of the problem. If career military officers should have a better understanding of political, social, and economic forces, and be equipped with knowledge with which to deal with an increasing number and variety of scientific and other specialists, what about civilian officials? Given the complex character of questions of national security, are they not judging issues of a military nature, issues that were formerly the prerogative of men in uniform? By what right do these civilians claim competence to deal with such matters? Do our civilian educational institutions adequately prepare leaders for these responsibilities?

It is the task of examining this second half of the problem that

Professors Lyons and Morton have set themselves. This is a larger and more difficult task than we had faced in our earlier book, for we had been dealing with a well delineated professional career group and a highly structured educational system. Civilian policy-makers do not constitute such a homogeneous group, nor are they the products of a common educational experience. Yet, Professors Lyons and Morton have accomplished their purpose well. Their book provides a comprehensive and critical evaluation of the responses of American colleges and universities to the need in our society for leaders, both in and out of public office, who understand national security issues. It analyzes the ways in which the learned professions have adjusted to these circumstances, and it provides for the first time a detailed description of the specialized programs of national security research and training that have been established in certain of the leading universities in the country. It reports also on various in-service educational opportunities that are available to civilian officials of the government.

But the book accomplishes much more than this. It is, indeed, a significant contribution to the intellectual history of the past two decades. Fortunately, Professors Lyons and Morton have gone far beyond the initial goal. They have explored the response of educational institutions in very broad terms, concerning themselves with the response of the intellectual community as a whole to the exigencies of the cold war. They show how members of the intellectual community have sought an understanding of the relationship of force to policy. They describe the development and character of scholarly research and publication on national security matters, the contribution of these activities to public debate, the changing role of the expert in the policy process, and the significant participation by members of the intellectual community in policy formulation.

The result is a book that reveals the dynamic relationship of education and public policy in a free society. It demonstrates that our colleges and universities, as part of the intellectual community, not only respond to needs defined by changing national policies, but that they themselves contribute to the making of these policies.

This volume is the third produced by a small group of scholars at Dartmouth College concerned in their teaching and research with national security policy issues. The first was the study to which I have already made reference: *Soldiers and Scholars, Military Education and National Policy*, by John W. Masland and Laurence I. Radway (Princeton University Press, 1957). The second, a critical examination of the contribution that colleges and universities make to the educational preparation of military officer personnel, was *Education and Military Leadership, A Study of the ROTC*, by Gene M. Lyons and John W. Masland (Princeton University Press, 1959). All three undertakings, as well as continued research by Professors Lyons and Morton, have been supported by grants from the Carnegie Corporation of New York to Dartmouth. As in so many other cases, this support has been most important to the development of national security studies at the College. It is thus an example of the interplay of higher education, the philanthropic foundations, and the government which, as Professors Lyons and Morton point out, has been so responsible for the intellectual response to the cold war.

JOHN W. MASLAND

Hanover, New Hampshire
October, 1964

Preface

THIS BOOK is a study in contemporary intellectual history, about the response of scholars and scientists to the problems of the cold war. In meeting the issues of the cold war, the American Government has found it necessary to call upon the skills and talents of intellectuals to a degree unmatched since the early days of the New Deal. Out of this need a new role for the intellectual has evolved in postwar American society, with important implications for the standards of objectivity and impartiality that characterize the professional life of scholars and scientists. This volume is as concerned with analyzing this problem as it is with bringing order to the wide range of intellectual activities related to the issues of war and peace.

The Introduction to the book sets out the scope and major problems of education and research in national security affairs. Part I defines the field of national security studies, discusses the relation of knowledge and systematic analysis to policy formulation and public debate, and reviews the background to the intellectual response to the cold war. Part II is a broad summation of the approaches taken by scholars, scientists, lawyers, and businessmen, and of how they are developed in programs of public education.

Part III constitutes a study of the institutional response of higher education to the challenges of the cold war. It consists of a descriptive and historical analysis of the major academic centers of teaching and research in national security affairs. In Part IV, we are concerned, in a similar way, with government and private research programs: educational programs for the Foreign and Civil Services; research organizations primarily set up to serve government agencies under contract; and private research groups that link the government and the academic community through a variety of educational and research programs. Finally, in Part V, we try to sum up and evaluate the intellectual response to the cold war and assess, in the light of our findings, the major problems it has raised for higher education and for government.

A primary focus of this book is the wide range of centers and institutes—research and teaching, academic and professional, governmental and private—that contribute most of the intellectual resources available to meet the challenge of the cold war. In dealing with them, our purpose has not been to offer a review of their current operations and activities, which would in any case be outdated by the time this study is published. Rather, in writing a study in contemporary intellectual history, we have sought to gain perspective by examining the development of these centers within the framework of the intellectual response of which they are a part. This examination also provides a firm basis for our generalizations and conclusions.

The research and writing that have gone into this book have been supported by a grant from the Carnegie Corporation of New York to Dartmouth College. During the period of research, we had the opportunity to visit most of the centers and institutes we describe and to discuss the problems involved with colleagues throughout the country. Parts of this book have been published, in different form, in the *American Political Science Review*, the *Bulletin of the Atomic Scientists*, the *Mississippi Valley Historical Review*, the *Journal of Higher Education*, and the *Journal of Politics*. Preliminary drafts were circulated for review to many scholars and practitioners in the national security field, particularly those connected with the centers and institutes we described. During the final stages, Mrs. Joan Safford was a critical and invaluable editorial assistant. We have thus had the help and counsel of colleagues throughout the country. But, as in all such undertakings, the final effort remains our responsibility entirely.

G. M. L.
L.M.

Hanover, New Hampshire
October, 1964

Contents

Schools for Strategy

Introduction

THERE WAS A TIME when military affairs were anathema to American intellectuals. As a social institution, war was conceived to be a triumph of irrationality, and, as a political force, the military establishment was considered an instrument of authoritarian brutality. Regarded in these terms, both were understandably repugnant to that rational, liberalizing spirit which is so important to the intellectual's ideal of the purpose of scholarly research and scientific investigation.

Much of this deep hostility to the idea of armed conflict and to the instrumentalities of war continues to exist. But most American intellectuals, under the pressures of World War II and the unsettled international conditions since then, have learned to live with the realities of conflict and the requirements of security. What is more important, many have contributed to the understanding, and even solution, of some of the difficult problems in contemporary national security affairs.

The involvement of intellectuals in military affairs is the result of changes in the nature of warfare and world politics: the impact of technology on weapons development, and the complexities of the international system created by the rise of Communism and the breaking up of the old colonial empires. These changes have generated new scientific, technological, political, and economic problems that have enlarged the field of military affairs far beyond the traditional

3

area of military expertise. Much of the involvement of scholars and scientists in national security affairs has thus come from the needs of government. But there have been other needs as well.

The intellectual response to the cold war has actually had three major objectives: to contribute to the formulation of national security policy; to contribute to public debate and discussion on issues of war and peace; and to contribute to the preparation of specialists and political leaders. In professional terms, this response has been the work of many disciplines: physics, chemistry, engineering, political science, economics, history, sociology, psychology. In institutional terms, it has been the product of the interrelated activities of government, the philanthropic foundations, and American higher education. There has been some effort at coordination, but little practical success. The directions taken in research and teaching have sometimes been stimulated by specific government requirements, sometimes by the intellectuals' own professional interests, and sometimes by a concern for the national interest as expressed in personal values, social responsibility, and in a variety of other ways.

The intellectual response is evident in the professionalization of political leadership, in the strengthening of career service responsibility, and in the extended use of government contracts. It is also evident in changes and developments in the social sciences, which, through inquiry into new areas of social relations and through experimentation with new methodologies, have begun to view the issues of war and peace as an important intellectual effort. It is evident in the new concern for military affairs among scientists, lawyers, and businessmen, all of whom represent a source of national leadership in a period of national peril, and among organized groups of citizens who are seriously disturbed by the challenges of a revolutionary world and by the strains that these challenges place on the democratic process.

Another measure of this intellectual response lies in the large number of seminars, centers, and institutes concerned with national or defense policy that have been established in the years since the end of World War II. They exist throughout the country: at universities like Harvard, Princeton, Columbia, Chicago, Ohio State, Stanford, California, Duke, North Carolina, and Pennsylvania; at private research centers like the Council on Foreign Relations, the Brookings Institution, and the Stanford Research Institute; and at institutes organized by the government, like the RAND Corporation. Most of the academic programs are supported by one or more foundations; some of them do work for one or more government agencies; other programs, whether independent of or affiliated with a university, derive the bulk of their funds from government contracts. Still others are entirely independent, operating on their own funds but aided by outside grants and government contracts. Some are organizations that exist largely on paper, devices to funnel funds from outside sources into the academic community for the purpose of stimulating research in the problems of national security; others actually possess an imposing array of scholars, with separate working facilities, and research and administrative staffs.

Any precise measurement of the growth of research and teaching in national security affairs is extremely difficult. Not only does the decentralized character of American research and higher education make precise figures hard to come by, but the diverse nature of the programs makes the problem of classification difficult. There is a good deal of research and teaching in international relations, area study programs, diplomatic history, and other fields that are relevant to national security even though they do not directly involve defense studies. All one can hope to achieve by quantitative standards is a sense of the magnitude of the effort. In the spring of 1963, for example, the Bureau of Intelligence and Research of the Department of State compiled a list of more than 400 research projects, planned or in progress, relating to the areas of arms control and disarmament. These projects ranged from long-term group studies to individual scholarly articles. A privately supported compilation made in 1960 listed 21 major research institutions directly engaged on problems of world order and conflict, and, indeed, there are certainly that many and more whose fields of interest overlap with defense problems. Finally, a survey undertaken at the U.S. Air Force Academy late in 1962 indicated that out of 115 colleges and universities responding to a questionnaire, 23 offered courses in national security policy and 25 indicated their plans to do so. All of these statistics need interpretation and qualification before firm conclusions can be stated. But they do give some measure of the response of scholars and teachers to the intellectual demands of the cold war, especially when compared with the almost complete lack of work in the field as late as 1950.[1]

Research programs in national security and defense problems represented an entirely new phenomenon on the American academic scene when they first appeared. Many regarded them with suspicion as alien to the purposes of a college or university, and still do. At the same time, there was a wide difference in approach to the subject. Local conditions, the interests of the participants, and differing objectives continue to contribute to the lack of uniformity. Some programs are oriented to problems of policy and concentrate on issues of current importance; others, in which this approach is considered inappropriate for the scholar, emphasize basic research. The approach also often reflects the disciplines from which leading participants in the program come. Most research programs in national security are interdisciplinary, but in one the impetus may come from political scientists, in another from economists, and in another from social scientists who follow a behavioral approach.

Just as the programs have a variety of approaches, so do they serve a variety of purposes. At some universities, they become a vehicle for the instruction of students. This instruction assumes several forms, the most common of which is the graduate interdepartmental or inter-school seminar. The purpose of this instruction varies, too. Especially in those institutions with a school for public administration or public affairs, the program is distinctly utilitarian and is viewed as a training ground for public servants, present and future. At others, national security is viewed as one element in the international-relations or political-science program and is oriented to graduate students in those fields and to related professions. At most institutions, the national security program serves as a focal point for those interested in research, bringing together men from different disciplines through their common interest in problems of defense. Sometimes, this research is individual and uncoordinated; sometimes, it represents an integrated group program. But no single center in the academic community can be identified as entirely a research one or entirely pedagogic. The difference is one of emphasis, and an interrelation of objectives is almost always present.

In purpose, method, approach, organization, and interest, therefore, the national security programs established in response to the demands of the cold war have varied widely. But all have one common factor —a concern for the problems arising from the revolution in weapons technology and in the dynamics of contemporary international politics. They have had, moreover, one result that may be most significant—the development of a community of experts in national security. Civilian experts in this field are in frequent contact, know each other and each other's work, and have, in fact, developed an informal community of their own. There are meetings, conferences, and study groups through which scholars and scientists working at different institutions meet from time to time to review their work or to focus on a single issue of current importance. This "crossing over" is also carried out through government connections and through publications. Although there is no one journal devoted entirely to studies of national security, despite efforts to establish one, experts in the field play an important role on the staffs of journals like *Foreign Affairs*, *World Politics*, and the *Journal of Conflict Resolution*. Indeed, the development of this community of scholars and scientists may be one of the most important results of the whole effort to apply our nation's resources to the solution of national security issues.

The growth of national security studies has posed a number of distinct problems for American scholarship and higher education, mainly involving questions of focus, financing, and research oriented to policy. Because of the many dimensions of the national security field, the issue of focus raises problems both for research and communication among professionals in different disciplines, and for the integration of military affairs with established areas of study. Financing is an issue because university and private research groups depend for funds on the government and on foundations to expand research and teaching in a field that does not belong within the traditional disciplines. Finally, the trend to policy-oriented research is an issue because of the influence it can have on other major purposes of intellectual life—the pursuit of knowledge for its own sake and the investigation of alternative policies to those that have gained official acceptance.

All national security programs require special financing, and, in the process of providing it, both the federal government and the large foundations play a particularly important role. For an organization like the RAND Corporation, set up by the Air Force, financing comes almost entirely from government contracts. Some academic programs, and non-academic ones like the Council on Foreign Relations or the Brookings Institution, also perform studies for the government. But here the foundations have been more important, although the relation of private organizations to the foundations differs from that of the academic groups. At the Council or at Brookings, for example, studies of national security are part of a larger program in public affairs that is carried forward with an established organization, funds, and staff. They are, moreover, the equivalent, or the agents, of foundations to the extent that they have grant and fellowship programs of their own and can carry out research programs with their own funds.

For the university centers and institutes, foundation support has been vital to giving them their place within the academic community. Without it, few of the programs would have come into existence or survived, for, with only one major exception, all were and still are largely dependent on funds from one or more foundations.* University support has been mainly indirect—through absorbing overhead costs such as office and library facilities, and through providing a general intellectual environment. National security programs have not become a regular part of the university since they are not included in the academic budget and do not fall within the purview of any single department or discipline. Their existence is therefore often precarious and their relation to the university in many cases tenuous.

The nature of foundation support is worth noting. Most of the funds have come from the three leading foundations—Carnegie, Ford, and Rockefeller—and have been given either directly to institutions or to an agency such as the Social Science Research Council that distributes the funds through its own committees. In some cases, the foundations have given direct support to the study of defense policy, but more often they have contributed to international or area study programs in which the problem of national security is an important ingredient.

The Carnegie Corporation of New York has been, perhaps, the most active foundation in the specific field of national security affairs. Between 1956 and 1962, it made grants totaling almost $1.5 million in direct support of research and teaching programs in national security to Columbia, Chicago, Harvard, Dartmouth, and Wisconsin, to the Council on Foreign Relations, and to the Social Science Research Council. The three separate grants Carnegie made to the Social Science Research Council—in 1952 to support a research program in American military policy, in 1956 and again in 1959 for "studies and conferences in national security policies"—have been administered through the Council's Committee on National Security Policy Research. Through conferences and grants to individual scholars, the Committee has been instrumental in encouraging young scholars to enter the field, in creating a forum for interdisciplinary exchange, and in serving as a major focal point for the academic national security community.

The Rockefeller Foundation's contribution to the study of national security policy has also been significant, with foreign affairs as a focal point of its interest. Recipients have included individual scholars, university- and government-affiliated centers, and private institutions; the size of the grants has ranged from under $10,000 to $500,000. Its largest single grant of $500,000 was to the Council on Foreign Rela-

---

* The exception is the Mershon Center at the Ohio State University, described below, Chapter 8.

tions, with substantial support given to the Center of International Studies at Princeton, the Brookings Institution in Washington, and the program on science and public policy at Harvard.

The Ford Foundation, like the Rockefeller Foundation, has emphasized international affairs, and in this broad field has exceeded all other foundations. Among academic institutions, its main support has gone to the Massachusetts Institute of Technology, which received $2.25 million between 1953 and 1959, and to Harvard, which received almost $1 million. Smaller amounts, ranging from $5,000 to $25,000, have gone to Chicago, Princeton, Illinois, and Wisconsin for the study of American foreign policy. The first Ford grant to Harvard in 1955 made possible the expansion and continuation of the seminar on defense policy established the year before, and in 1958, Ford granted Harvard an additional $500,000 to establish the Center for International Affairs. The Council on Foreign Relations has also received large sums from Ford, as has the government-affiliated Institute for Defense Analyses, which received $500,000 to increase the use of the resources of science and technology in the development of defense policy. In 1958, the Ford Foundation also gave $150,000 to a group of British scholars and public leaders to enable them to establish the Institute for Strategic Studies in London, and it has continued to support the Institute.

Ford, Rockefeller, and Carnegie are not the only foundations that have supported or are now supporting programs in national security. The Russell Sage Foundation has made several grants to further the work of sociologists in the field, and the Libby Endowment, the Richardson Foundation, and others have also contributed, as have private unnamed donors. The total amount of this support since 1950 has been considerable, and has been the basis for virtually every university program in the field.

Government support for national security studies has been largely concentrated in specialized institutes set up by the military services— the RAND Corporation, by the Air Force; the Research Analysis Corporation, working almost exclusively for the Army; the Navy's Operations Evaluation Group; and the Institute for Defense Analyses, set up by the Department of Defense. But the government has also contracted with outside institutions for special military studies. For example, from its establishment in 1961 until June, 1963, the U.S. Arms Control and Disarmament Agency, in addition to studies conducted by its own staff, let twenty-five contracts and awarded eight grants to scholars at Princeton, Harvard, and Yale, to groups organized by the Washington Center of Foreign Policy Research, M.I.T., and

Rutgers, to private research agencies like the Hudson Institute and the Stanford Research Institute, and to industrial firms like the Bendix Corporation and Arthur D. Little, Inc.[2] Government-sponsored research is not always limited to specific policy or to technical needs, but also includes broad investigations that are not incompatible with scholarly and scientific inquiry. The government has also made an *indirect* impact on the university and private research groups. The growing need for persons well trained for public service and the attraction, both financial and professional, of a government-sponsored institute like RAND, heighten the competition for well trained scholars and tend to divert them from teaching and from seeking positions in academic institutions.

The infusion of this financial support from foundations and the government has had both beneficial and dangerous results. The benefits obviously show in the development of intellectual resources in a field important to the national interest but one in which there was little scholarly activity. The dangers involve the possible distortion of scholarly development, the imposition of external demands on research and education, the downgrading of teaching in favor of research, and the dependence of educational institutions on outside financing. Centers of research and education in national security affairs have confronted these problems in a variety of ways. A major purpose of this book is to describe the activities of these centers, their contribution to the formulation of government policy and to the intellectual needs of a democratic society, and their response to the particular issues of focus, financing, and policy-oriented research. The measures of success are ambiguous, however. They lie in the wisdom of American policy, in the integrity of American scholarship, and in the American people's understanding of critical and complex issues. Success in these matters, especially in the short run, is difficult to judge.

Any evaluation of education and research programs in national security affairs must be carried out with an understanding of the intellectual challenge of contemporary military affairs, of the developing intellectual concern for these problems, and of the different approaches already discernible in the scholarly disciplines, among scientists and the professions, and in public education programs. To understand these issues is the first order of this book. But they must also be viewed in terms of the role of education and research in a democratic society.

The concept of public service is deeply ingrained in American education. Education was the crucible in which a pluralistic society was unified and the instrument through which the specialized manpower needed for agricultural and industrial development was provided. The response of American scholarship and higher education to the challenges of the cold war needs to be understood in terms of this concept of public service. How could the scholarly and scientific community best help the nation to solve the problems created by the revolution in military technology and the increasing complexity of international relations? On the scientific side, the answer lay in marshalling scientific resources for the research and development of weapons systems and detection devices. On the political, economic, and social side, it lay in the development of national security studies. But public service means more than meeting short-term national requirements. In a democratic society, science and scholarship have an equally important responsibility to remain independent, to extend man's knowledge for its own sake, and to provide a basis for dissent against all that is base, ignorant, and irresponsible. In a field like national security, these can be conflicting obligations, but they are obligations we must live with and deal with.

The Study of National Security Affairs

1

National Security: Challenge and Response

FROM THE EMERGENCE of the United States as a world power at the turn of the century until World War II, the role of civilians in military affairs was governed by a division of labor that left the major problems of defense a monopoly of the military. To be sure, the relationship was subject to the overriding concept of civilian control of the military. But, in peacetime, there was relatively little to control, and, in time of war, civilian direction was limited by the priority given to battlefield requirements that were developed and controlled by military authorities.[1]

Even after World War II, defense organization and planning were largely based on the premise that national security was primarily the responsibility of "military" experts. The concept of civilian control was nonetheless still sacred and took on added significance as the nation was faced with the unusual prospect of maintaining a large military establishment in time of peace. In 1949, for example, the first Hoover Commission asserted that a major reason for strengthening the "means of exercising civilian control" over the defense establishment was to "safeguard our democratic traditions against militarism."[2] This same warning was raised in the Report of the Rockefeller Committee on Department of Defense Organization in 1953. The primary aim of the Committee's recommendations was to provide "the Nation with maximum security at minimum cost," but the Report made clear that there was to be no compromise with "the fundamental principle of civilian control of the Military Establishment."[3]

This concept of civil-military relations has little significance for contemporary problems of national security in the United States. The military services are divided among themselves and are thus unable to present any unified challenge to civilian control, even if they wished to do so. Moreover, the military forces fully accept the principle of civilian supremacy as part of their professional code. Military leaders, however, have been thrown into a political role in the process of developing strategic programs to meet their assigned missions. In this role, their participation in policy formulation is such as to make traditional levels of authority and obedience meaningless.[4] Further, the roles of both civilian and military officers have been changed by revolutionary forces that have greatly complicated the formation of national security policy. Strategic programs are now as much the product of civilian expertise in science and engineering and of civilian decisions on the allocation of national resources as they are of military planning. Under the conditions of the cold war, military planning is also more closely related to foreign-policy planning and thus depends more on political considerations than it has at any other time in American history.

The civilian role in military affairs has also changed with the strengthening of civilian organization for national security and the professionalization of civilian leadership. Civilians are gaining effective authority over military decisions and are concerned with military affairs as a continuing part of their professional careers. A more complex division of labor between civilians and military than has heretofore existed is therefore evolving.[5] But the changing civilian role does not simply reflect a wish to assert control over the military: It is responsive to the new shape of national security, in which military affairs are no longer the monopoly of military officers and there is no clear-cut division between war and peace or between foreign and military policies.

The new role of civilians in national security affairs demands a new kind of professionalism. It is a professionalism requiring knowledge not only of military matters but also of history, politics, economics, law, sociology, technology, and psychology—and of their relationship in terms of human values and social goals. The beginnings of this professionalism were discernible during World War II, but its growth is a postwar phenomenon. In the fullest sense, it involves professional training, scholarly research, and general education, all three inter-related, but each performing a separate function in focusing the nation's intellectual resources on problems of national security. Those problems are complex and their very complexity has helped to shape the nature of this intellectual response. Any assessment of the response of civilian research and educational institutions to the intellectual demands of the cold war thus depends on understanding the nature of those demands.

The Challenge: Problems of National Security

Problems of national security offer a wide variety of policy choices. Alternative policies include, at the extremes, preventive war and unilateral disarmament. The practical range of choices, however, is more limited. For one thing, preventive war would require a fundamental change in the moral attitudes of the American people. While the continuing strain of living under the danger of thermonuclear war could conceivably create such a change, we can hardly imagine that it could come about without such opposition that, in the process, the very nature of American society, and thus of American purpose, would alter. On the other hand, unilateral disarmament is sometimes advocated as the only way to end the existing nuclear stalemate. Without a fundamental shift in Communist attitudes on secrecy and conflict, the risks of unilateral disarmament are certain to temper the actions of American statesmen. Such a shift, moreover, would so change the international system that the barriers to international trust would fall and unilateral action would no longer be necessary in view of the prospect of multilateral agreement. For the foreseeable future, then, the practical policy choices range from deterrence to arms control.

At the pole of deterrence, national security requires a military force capable of imposing decisive damage on any potential aggressor. At the pole of arms control, it requires a system of control and inspection that will deprive nations of certain kinds of military force and, beyond specified levels, compel them to seek nonmilitary adjustments to disputes. A policy of deterrence assumes that no reliable system of inspection is possible and that any relaxation of military preparedness will endanger the security of the United States. A policy of arms control is based on the conviction that military force can no longer be maintained as an unrestricted instrument of national policy without risking the hazards of thermonuclear war.

Between a complete reliance on deterrence or on arms control, there are a variety of intermediate and mixed positions. All of them, however, share several characteristics. They all recognize the practical problems of achieving even the rudimentary stages of an effective system of international arms control. At the same time, they recognize, in varying degrees, the risks of seeking international stability while military force increases in lethal intensity and remains subject to conflicting national interests. They share, in addition, and in contrast to more extreme positions, an evolutionary sense of history. They do not hold that social institutions remain static, but neither do they hold that revolutionary change can be generated without violence unless there is historical preparation for it.

From whichever perspective national security is viewed, the constant element is the management of force in formulating and conducting foreign policy. There is, moreover, no way of dealing with the relation of force to policy except by dealing with the full range of defense problems and with all the complexities of contemporary international politics. This means contending with the determinants of military planning, with weapons technology, and with the economic, human, and organizational factors of military security. It requires an understanding of the impact of science and technology on international relations, of the ideological differences between the Communist bloc and the West, and of the unstable conditions under which the new nations are developing the political and economic foundations for their independence. When the issues shaped by these forces are reduced to the fundamentals of human and social behavior, they are subject to analysis in terms of historical experience.[6] Several factors, nevertheless, appear to be unique in the present situation: the destructive capacity of modern weapons; the precipitous impact of advances in science and technology on the international system; and the widespread and rapid nature of political change.

These distinctive features take on precise meaning when we try to summarize the broad alternatives that are open to the United States in relating force to policy. Perhaps the most clear-cut circumstances are those that involve objectives which are "strategic," i.e., are not subject to surrender or compromise. An attack on what the United States considers a strategic objective would be the first blow in a total war in which both sides would use thermonuclear weapons. But the definition of what constitutes a strategic objective is a difficult practical problem. The consequences are so drastic and the high degree of destruction so inevitable that great care is required in solving it. What aims are so vital to the interests of the United States that no one could question the willingness of a responsible American President to order the use of thermonuclear weapons?

Defense of the United States against overt aggression is certainly a strategic objective and would presumably involve nuclear weapons. Defense of any nation in the Western Hemisphere against direct attack and defense of the NATO Alliance are the only other two strategic objectives that might call forth a thermonuclear response. But beyond these, there is even less assurance that the United States would use the full force of its nuclear stockpile. This was the primary weakness of the concept of "massive retaliation," a weakness which has been accentuated since the Soviet Union demonstrated its capability to launch intercontinental ballistic missiles carrying thermonuclear warheads.[7] Indeed, the Soviet threat to the continental United States is now so great, and the commitment to defend Europe consequently so full of risk, that many statesmen and writers question whether this commitment is completely dependable.

There are a number of objectives that cannot be termed strategic even though the United States might use force in their defense. This is not to say that strategic weapons would not ultimately be employed, but in the initial stages, there would be a strong motivation to use only limited military means. Yet, what is the point beyond which limited war cannot be controlled? This is the essential dilemma. Limited war not only requires limited political objectives, but it may also require a further limiting—that is, a subsequent contraction or surrender of the original aims. Needless to say, any such decision—to retreat to a compromise position in order to avert strategic struggle—could have severe political repercussions both at home and abroad.[8]

The consequences of strategic war and the dilemma of limited conflict emphasize the importance of relating force to policy. It is no less important in areas where the United States and the Soviet Union meet through third parties. In such cases, American policy-makers may seek to establish bulwarks against Communist penetration through political alliances or programs of economic or military aid. In other situations, it may be possible to identify a mutuality of interest with the Soviet Union, thus neutralizing areas through direct agreement. It is in these gray areas that the strategic balance between the NATO and Communist powers and their competition for the emerging nations become related.

This strategic balance is partly determined by the repeated promise of American statesmen that the United States will never be the first to use force. The United States has nevertheless reserved the right to use nuclear weapons first in the event of aggressive action at any level.[9]

Without this qualification, presumably, any self-imposed inhibition not to use force except in defense would rob the United States of flexibility in those negotiations where persuasion without a plausible threat of coercion is meaningless. At the same time, a major characteristic of the new weapons technology is the decided advantage that accrues to the side that strikes first in a strategic exchange. It is difficult to be sure that the command and control of retaliatory forces and the will to decide to hit back will survive the shock of a first strike. The aggressor might therefore achieve his objective without incurring destruction himself.

One way to insure retaliation is to make it automatic. But even if automatic retaliation is technologically possible, it is not certain that it would be wise or prudent. There might be advantages in exposing the offender before attacking. It might also be wise first to calculate the exact nature of the retaliation one will effect, or to seek to ostracize the attacker and to withhold the second strike which, perhaps more than the first, is sure to plunge the world into a war the major industrialized nations might never survive. Any of these alternatives, however, assumes the ability to preserve the processes of government and society after thermonuclear attack. But the payoff of restraint is double, for if the first strike is not decisive, the aggressor must calculate the full consequences of striking again, thus assuring all-out thermonuclear war, or discontinue the attack.

The nature of contemporary weapons technology has made the use of national military forces by the major powers dangerous to the point of catastrophe. In any conflict in which American and Soviet forces are engaged, the chances of avoiding escalation into thermonuclear war are minimal at best. There is therefore a compelling pressure for both nations to avoid direct confrontation and to explore every alternative to the use of military power in pursuing their objectives. The terms under which direct confrontation is to be avoided are, however, difficult to agree upon. Agreement must often be tacit rather than written, subject to the shifting tides of historical circumstances and to the delicate strategic balance between the great powers.

The problem is made more complex by the danger that Americans and Soviets will not be able to control every situation, but will be drawn into the vortex of conflict by other forces. They may thus be compelled to use military force as the only alternative to withdrawal. In the competition for the support of the emerging nations of Asia, Africa, and Latin America, both the United States and the Soviet Union confront forces that are quite independent of the cold war conflict. The cold war is nevertheless ubiquitous, although its impact varies and must be calculated within each situation.

The United States may or may not be able to insulate an area from direct Soviet intervention. It must nonetheless seek to identify American interests with the positive forces of development and progress under all circumstances, or must risk opposing the struggle of men for freedom and better lives. But programs for economic and social development become domestic political issues within the emerging nations, for the instability of most of the new states makes it difficult to offer economic and technical aid without intervening in their internal affairs. It is also often difficult to recognize which factions or groups represent the highest aspirations of the people, or to decide what action to take when domestic dissension turns into civil war. Although the boundaries between international and national politics are breaking down, they cannot be ignored. The ideal of insulating economic and social development from the worst effects of domestic or international politics is devoutly to be wished but rarely to be realized.

As long as the factors of competition between the Communist and Western blocs are unstable, the possibility of nuclear war is ever-present. How can this competition be limited? Two methods of stabilizing the strategic balance between the United States and the Soviet Union have been widely analyzed and discussed: (1) to increase the invulnerability of the retaliatory capacities on both sides; and (2) to devise both multilateral and (where agreement is impossible) unilateral arms-control schemes that would restrict the range and extent of military power used in any major East-West conflict. Neither method is certain to succeed and both present the United States with serious policy problems.[10]

Stabilized deterrence depends on continuing research and development in weaponry. Yet, it can only be expected that the stability of deterrence will always be relative no matter how far research advances, since neither power can be sure of the technological status of the other. Moreover, uncertainty about the leadership's intentions on both sides will continue to be a major issue, for deterrence is based not only on capability but also on intentions, to the extent that they can be reliably evaluated.

The pursuit of absolute invulnerability can blind statesmen to the opportunities that may arise to stabilize relations by arms-control agreements. On the other hand, arms-control measures require a real desire by both powers to limit violence, and even if the United States and the Soviet Union should accept the need to limit violence, they would still be subject to political restrictions. Both now operate within alliance systems that are increasingly pluralistic and in which control of nuclear weapons is becoming diffused. Neither France nor China is likely to abandon its efforts to secure a nuclear capability, whatever agreement the United States and the Soviet Union conclude between themselves.

Problems of national security are thus in one sense the problems of foreign relations viewed in terms of relating force to policy. Clearly, force must not be the dominant factor, but it is present in every major international situation either as a direct determinant of the immediate problem or as a part of the over-all strategic framework within which the problem must be solved. Our purpose in laying out, in broad terms, the array of issues involved in relating force to policy is not to present them as a prelude to advocating a certain solution to them. It is rather to illustrate, at the outset, the nature of the major policy decisions that American political leaders and the American people must make in the area of national security. Their very complexity has been a constant challenge to the development of an organized pattern that can bring men, ideas, and resources together in order to relate force to policy.

Government Organization for National Security

The process of relating force to policy affects the internal as well as the international life of a nation. Indeed, the issues involved in national security affairs transcend boundaries between domestic and foreign programs. Although these boundaries may exist in the formal structure of government and society, they have no relevance to the flow of policy issues.

National security requirements have already been a powerful centralizing force within the government—as a result of the need to coordinate diplomatic and military agencies, the importance of defense spending on the national economy, the need for secrecy and security in the formulation of strategic programs, and the domination of the presidency in the policy process. The institutional response to these requirements has been largely to form presidential and interdepartmental agencies that bring together those who possess the expertise and those who are responsible for the critical areas of national security. There have also been centralizing tendencies within the executive departments—the establishment of the Policy Planning Council and the Arms Control and Disarmament Agency within the State Department, the accumulation of staff and authority in the Office of the Secretary of Defense and of the Joint Chiefs of Staff, and the establishment of agencies such as the Central Intelligence Agency and the Agency for International Development.

These organizational developments reflect the complex character of national security issues. This is most evident in the reorganization that has taken place in the Executive Office of the President. Here, two new presidential instruments—the National Security Council and the Office of Science and Technology—work together with the established agencies to develop budgetary and legislative programs. Each has its own organizational structure, although there are essential differences in their modes of operation.

The NSC is an interdepartmental committee. It is therefore more of a mechanism for reconciling departmental differences than for creating policy. During the Eisenhower Administration, most of its work was actually carried on by the Council's Planning Board and Operations Coordinating Board—the first by preparing plans and programs for Council consideration, and the second by following up on Council recommendations the President had approved. But here, too, the boards were interdepartmental and could only extend themselves beyond the limits of compromise to the extent the President himself projected his initiative through his special assistant for national security affairs.[11] The boards were abolished during the early months of the Kennedy Administration, and greater reliance for planning was placed on the operating departments and for follow-up on informal liaison by key White House staff members.[12]

The Office of Science and Technology is the end result of organizational trends evident since 1957 to upgrade and coordinate scientific activities throughout the government, particularly in departments and agencies involved in national security. The President's Science Advisory Committee and the Federal Council for Science and Technology work closely with the Office, whose Director provides leadership to both groups. As a staff agency, the Office expresses the objectivity and broad view that come with freedom from operating responsibility. These qualities have probably contributed much to the effectiveness of scientists in government,[13] but they also pose potential dangers, since policy can be unreal and power irresponsible unless they are intelligently related to practical operations.

The activities of scientists in government are limited by their actual position and by their reluctance to become involved in political controversy lest they prejudice their effectiveness. Between 1957 and 1961, the Scientific Advisory Committee nevertheless took the lead in several fields (one of them arms control), and for two reasons: first, the State Department's inability to command the resources with which to deal with the problem and the Defense Department's reluctance to see arms control as a phase of military strategy; and, second, the political necessity of reducing negotiations with the Soviet Union to a technical level.[14] At the same time, it is important to remember that technical negotiations are still carried out within the context of situations that can only be resolved by political decisions. Scientists are therefore intimately involved in political problems, no matter how cautiously they seek to tread these troubled waters.[15]

The State Department's response to the demands of national security policy was slow. There were erratic changes to bring the Department into closer relation to economic and military operations and to provide long-range policy planning.[16] Various efforts have been made through reorganization to give it authority over the formulation of policy on economic aid, without burdening it with the responsibility for field operations and foreign-trade activities. All the aid agencies set up since 1947 have been subordinated to the State Department for policy guidance through specified administrative lines. No such lines were established between the State and Defense Departments, however.

The problems arising from the primacy of foreign over military policy and of the State Department over the Defense Department were theoretically but never practically solved, except through the personal relations of their Secretaries or the intervention of the President. Much of the synthesis of politico-military issues might have been carried on by the Policy Planning Council that was established in the State Department in 1947. Throughout the 1950's, however, members of the Council were used for short-term, fire-brigade assignments, and could not fulfill the long-range planning function that was originally contemplated. Moreover, their contacts with Defense officials were only informal, and depended on personal contact. Only in mid-1961, did the State Department take steps to assign a Deputy Under Secretary for Political-Military Affairs and to formalize these contacts.

Within the Defense Department, the organizational pattern has been characterized by a centralization and "civilianization" of authority. Both the centralization and the "civilianization" have developed in response to increased defense costs and to the inability of military officers to agree on the requirements of national security because of their differences over strategic doctrine. (The level of military expenditures has also affected the national economy, the government's tax policies, and a whole range of domestic programs.)

The relationship of technical and political issues to national security has also been a centralizing factor. Work on the military applications of atomic energy was centralized in the Atomic Energy Commission from the beginning. In the late 1950's, the duplication of effort in three competitive programs provoked demands for greater coordination in rocket development. These demands resulted in the establishment of a Director of Research and Engineering in the Office of the Secretary of Defense, and the civilian-directed National Aeronautics and Space Agency.

The political nature of military programs had been recognized early by the first Secretary of Defense, James Forrestal, and he made political-military coordination a responsibility of his immediate staff. Since then, the Assistant Secretary for International Security Affairs has become a key figure in the development of national security policy and in the determination of military requirements to meet policy objectives. In addition to their centrifugal attraction, the demands of financial management, research and development, and political analysis require skills that are essentially civilian and that many high-ranking military officers do not yet possess. They have thus forced "civilianization" as well as centralization across a broad range of defense activities.[17]

The organizational response to national security problems reflects the pragmatic character of the American approach and the presidential character of American government. Within a conservative view of constitutional limits, there has been a general readiness to change and experiment with new arrangements, however strongly vested interests defend the *status quo*. The most convincing motive for organizational change is the necessity to bring to the President the information, analyses, and statements of alternatives he needs to make decisions.

No policy comes up for decision or review without a history. To this extent, the process of determining policy is continuous. Indeed policy is being reassessed constantly at the operational level. A detailed response to a field problem, for example, requires an interpretation of general instructions in the light of specific circumstances. The interpretation can lead to one of several conclusions: that the authorized policy offers sufficient guidance for an adequate operational response; that the policy is not adequate or appropriate to meet the situation in the light of accepted objectives; or that specific conditions bring to light the faultiness of the assumptions on which the policy was based or the need to review these assumptions because of changing circumstances. These possibilities illustrate the link that exists between staff and line, between headquarters and field. This link is tighter than it ever was as a result of new systems of communications that quickly circulate news of major operational obstacles and bring them up to the policy planning level.

The reassessment of policy can also come about without a warning flare from the operational front. Broad policies must be in a constant state of review against changing circumstances and fresh intelligence. Within the American system of government, this review is forced on the executive departments by frequent staff changes, congressional and press inquiries, and the pressures of interest groups. As a result, a policy may be brought up for formal reassessment because of new information or insights that develop in the process of trying to justify existing policy. New alternatives which were not considered earlier or which were not formerly desirable or feasible may emerge. In such a case, the reason for reviewing policy may not be the failure of current policy but the belief that a different policy may bring more desirable results.

The continuous flow of history and the continuous review of policies make it difficult to isolate the beginnings and the endings of individual "cases." Nevertheless, once a policy comes up for review before a high official, such as the President or a high-ranking officer of the Department of State or Defense, and he decides a basic review is necessary, then the processes of data collection and analysis must be carried out. These processes are subject to limitations in time. In an especially urgent case, data collection might be limited to several short oral reports from key officers, and analysis to a brief discussion of the alternative courses of action. Under different (and more normal) circumstances, the process would take longer.

Data—including information on past and present conditions and forecasts about the future—are collected from all available sources. Once collected, they are then set out so as to facilitate analysis. One difficulty in evaluating available information on many national security issues arises from the diversity of the data. Not only are the sources numerous and varied, but the process of relating economic, political, military, and technological factors requires considerable mental dexterity. At the same time, the criteria for evaluation must be adapted to the kind of information available, although the collected data must, in the final analysis, be evaluated in terms of "total" relation to the basic aims of American policy.

Once sufficient information is available to illuminate possible alternatives, there is a general exchange of judgments among the major parties. This exchange may go on at more than one level. It certainly goes on within the separate executive departments and agencies, and it can ultimately lead to a "departmental position" that will be carried into the upper councils where policy recommendations are determined. It might also occur among high-ranking officials in different departments, who come together because of their relation to the President or to a particular approach to national security affairs or because of certain social or intellectual ties. Out of this exchange an influential consensus can evolve that may eventually carry the day. This is particularly so if the exchange is also a "testing" process to determine the broad basis on which the several agencies can agree.

Although this total process of policy formation is usually carried on within the executive branch, it need not be restricted there. Very often, congressional leaders will be consulted, either on instructions from the President or on the initiative of an executive department. Key individuals and private interest groups may also be consulted because of their relation to the problem or their influence on congressional and public opinion. In cases where the cooperation or status of other nations will be affected, diplomatic representatives may be approached. And the press, invited or not, may also be involved.

At some stage—determined by time, external circumstances, internal pressures, executive decision, or a combination of these—the moment for formal presentation, review, and decision must come. It may be *pro forma*, if the President has already been deeply involved and has, through a variety of ways, indicated his own preferred solution and his confidence that he can carry it out. It may be more than that, if divergent departmental positions have developed and a showdown is needed at the highest level of government in order to avoid operational failures after a presidential decision has been made. It may also be essential, even if a broad consensus has developed and has presidential blessing, in order to test all assumptions and estimates one final time in a sharp, perceptive exchange.

While the National Security Council was especially established as a forum for this final exchange, the place and circumstances under which the latter will take place largely depend on what the President wants and on his operating style. President Truman, for example, used the National Security Council infrequently; the elaborate apparatus of planning and follow-up committees was largely developed in response to President Eisenhower's demands for systematic staff preparation; President Kennedy preferred a more flexible system that permitted him to enter the process of policy development at a formative stage if he wished to do so. The method and energy with which an administration attacks the problem of national security reflects both the style and sense of purpose of the President himself.[18]

The final decision and the tenor of subsequent performance are both direct responsibilities of the President. But the complexity of determining policy certainly demonstrates that the President does not carry the burden alone and that he constantly needs help. When the members of the President's Administrative Management Committee first made that plea in 1937, they were responding to the vast new responsibilities that had come to the presidency through the great social-welfare legislation of the first Roosevelt Administration. Today, the same call is sounding in response to the agonizing responsibility of dealing with the issues relating force to policy.

There have been a number of recommendations for strengthening the executive machinery for national security policy.[19] Most of these recommendations have emphasized two needs: (1) better integration of all the elements that go into determining national security policy; and (2) searching, analytical thinking about the national interest with the broadest perspective. Another requirement is that any organizational reform be consistent with the constitutional role of the President. Within these broad limits, any number of operating methods can undoubtedly be devised. But if the needs are to be met, it is important to provide more than organizational change. Three major ingredients are essential: dramatic leadership from the President himself; an adjustment in the administrative environment so that it will be conducive to reflection and study; and a sense of professionalism among government officials and contributing experts.

All of these elements are interdependent. The best will in the world and the best minds in the nation will only be frustrated if there is no response to their efforts from the heights of the presidency. At the same time, a President will have difficulty in exerting his own influence unless he can eliminate a stultifying working climate and attract thoughtful, concerned, and knowledgeable people into his administration. Leadership, organization, and professionalism will produce the kind of information and study required for effective national security policy. This book is principally concerned with the last—the problem of professionalism.

The Expert in National Security Affairs

The expert is not new in American political life. As public policy-making has become increasingly complex, more and more experts have been drawn into government to supply the knowledge needed to make political choices and policy decisions. At one time, engineers and agricultural experts were the only ones required; during the depression years of the early 1930's, trained economists operating at high levels of authority flocked to Washington; and, more recently, top-ranking scientists have been close to the seats of power. Under certain circumstances, the line between the expert and the policy-maker may be very fuzzy indeed. Expert conclusions can be so compelling as to render any policy to the contrary inadmissible. At the same time, when expert opinion offers several alternative choices, it is highly probable that the policy process will be strongly influenced and directed by the logic of the analysis with which the choices are set forth. The primary task of the expert is to study the issues and develop the alternatives for choice; the task of the policy-maker is to participate in the negotiating process in which choices are made.[20]

In the area of national security affairs, the role of the expert is particularly complex. The relationship between the two classes of experts in this area, civilian and military, is itself an issue of importance. The civilian expert not only supplements but, in some cases, *supplants* the military expert at the operational and staff levels. But that is not all; he is also becoming increasingly important at the level where policy choices must be made, because heavy reliance is placed on technical analysis in the choices of objectives and strategies. This is a role that civilian experts have played before, but never to the extent they do now in national security affairs.

The role of the civilian expert in national security is emphasized by trends in government staffing. At the highest level of the executive branch, selection for appointive posts is now characterized by a concern for experience and continuity in government and for specialized knowledge. Appointive posts in the State Department, for example, except for a limited number, are filled by Foreign Service and Civil Service career officers. The Atomic Energy Commission and its General Advisory Committee have always included scientists and experienced scientific and industrial administrators; high-ranking appointive posts in the Department of Defense are now going to men with scientific backgrounds or with long experience in public service who are willing to accept long tenure in office.

The trend toward expertise at the appointive or political level of government is the result of two major sets of factors. First of all, there are a number of variables that go into the choice of political executives: the personal whim and will of the President; the need for geographic, political party, religious, and ethnic balance; the readiness of capable men to be involved in the political maelstrom; and the imperatives that rise out of the conditions of the time. The "mix" of factors that prevail in any particular appointment is itself variable.[21] Nevertheless, the "conditions of the time" will continue to be such that problems of national security will be of considerable, if not dominating, importance in the national life. Each President is and will be compelled to apply standards of competence and experience as well as standards of political balance in filling posts in those agencies that deal with national security.

Secondly, recruitment of political executives below the top level is usually left to the cabinet or other high official, and the qualifications considered in second- and third-level appointments reflect the same concern for continuity and expertise.[22] In national security affairs, these choices are likely to be more insulated from political considerations or other qualifications that are extraneous to the substantive requirements of the job itself. The farther down the heirarchy, the more it becomes necessary to match particular talent to particular position requirements. Thus the tendency is toward greater specialization and greater expertise. While a constitutional or presidential responsibility is emphasized at the top level—where the needs and the will of the President dominate—functional or "program" responsibility is emphasized at the lower levels of political appointments.[23]

The importance of expertise in determining national security policy also enhances the influence of career professionals. This influence has increased both because of the need for continuity and stability, and because of the tendency to seek solutions at a technical level in order to minimize differences at the policy level and to blunt criticism from without. For in the free-for-all of American politics, it is natural that a political leader should refuse to take unnecessary risks in discussing over-all programs involving national survival, when the component parts of programs can be decided on by experts on technical grounds.

Career government officers have not been able, however, to provide the full range of professional competence that current problems of national security demand. The selection and promotion system tends to force them to defend particular institutional interests. At the same time, few yet possess the broad wisdom that high policy demands, or the depth of specialized expertise that is required for technical staff work in areas such as scientific research and engineering systems. A lack of breadth and depth limits the ability of career officers in top planning and program assignments.

Within the special context of American governmental institutions, a series of innovating practices has therefore developed to bring specialized competence and general wisdom to bear on matters of public policy where neither political nor career executives can fully meet the mark. They include *ad hoc* and standing advisory committees, contractual arrangements for consultative services, the assignment of broad investigations or actual operations to nongovernmental institutions, and independent agencies set up outside the bureaucracy but financed by the government.

Such administrative devices serve many purposes. They bring creativity to the public service in areas where it is often discouraged by routine bureaucratic procedures or the dangers of political disagreement. They offer federal executives and Congressmen alternative sources of expert advice. And they permit the kind of experimentation, reflection, flexibility, and deep probing that the complex problems of national security require but that the federal services cannot completely accommodate because of their size, their need for standardization, and their emphasis on current operations.

The need for expertise in the formation and conduct of national security policy is thus being filled in three ways: through increasing continuity and expertise at the level of appointed officials, through the strengthening of executive responsibility among career officers, and through the practice of contracting with private groups. This is in the pragmatic tradition of American society. Many writers and officials have regretted the weaknesses inherent in a system in which there is such a high degree of turnover at the policy-making level. Most frequently, they have looked longingly at the British system of permanent under-secretaries and an administrative class, and have sought to devise a similar system that would be compatible with the American political structure.[24] It is unlikely, however, that any major reforms along these lines will be realized, since the American system is based on a strong executive, a weak party structure, the absence of traditions of public service, and the concept of decentralized power.

At the same time, the transfer of career executives among departments, the development of imaginative in-service training programs, and the encouragement of talent in recruitment, selection, and promotion are efforts to create a stronger public service. But any serious effort to bring the full force of our intellectual resources to bear on the issues of national security needs to include a stronger process of selection of political executives and a refinement of contracting practices.

The civilian expert in national security affairs is both like and unlike experts in other fields. His expertise is based on a definite body of knowledge, but it is a body of knowledge that is much broader than those of the traditional professions and disciplines and includes many of these—history, politics, economics, sociology, law, psychology, military science, physics, and engineering. A characteristic quality is, in fact, the relating of relevant knowledge from many professions and disciplines. The general characteristics of sound methodology—conceptualization, careful collection, evaluation and selection of data, organization of evidence, and analysis—are essential. But there must also be a sensitivity to the variety of methods that can be applied to aspects of national security—where it is possible to apply quantification methods, when model-building is relevant, what is and what is not predictable.[25]

The expert in national security affairs is more than the old "generalist" in new dress. He is a professional in the deepest sense of the word. He must understand the role of force in society, be informed in international politics, and be capable of creative and analytical thought. These qualities can be developed only through rigorous and continuous training. The demands for them underscore the role of education and research with which this book is concerned.

The role of the civilian expert in national security affairs poses a triple challenge to education and research. First, it makes demands on educational institutions to train young men and women in preparation for the duties of formulating and carrying out national security policy, and to provide mid-career and advanced training for those already committed to public service. Unlike military officers, civilians in national security affairs have not entered a single professional career at an early age and progressed in calculated stages to positions of responsibility. They come from a variety of professions, at a variety of points in their careers, and in a variety of capacities— political executive, civil servant, consultant, special adviser, or member of a research team under assignment or contract. The focus, therefore, cannot be on any one educational system. It must include training for those professions that are relevant to the new dimensions of national security policy—history and the social and natural sciences —and for those like law and business that have been continuing sources of political leadership in American society; specialized programs in national security affairs which are interdisciplinary in nature, academic and nonacademic, and privately financed or government supported; and government recruitment and training programs that are geared to develop the professional capacity of civil servants. Only by assessing these varied programs can we measure the response of American education to the requirements of professional training in national security affairs.

The expert in national security affairs presents a second challenge to American democratic government and thus to American education:

Quis custodiet ipsos custodes? As a professional, the expert feels directly responsible to society, but democracy requires more than a sense of social duty. It requires various mechanisms for bringing leaders to account for their actions, and also for supporting them against irrational public pressures. Formal mechanisms, such as elections and a separation of powers, are hardly sufficient. What is needed is a knowledgeable public. This does not mean what is commonly called "informed public opinion." Public opinion is not massive and unitary, but is rather the combination of countervailing interests and a "general mood." Its most responsible element is the attentive public that neither blindly accepts direction nor rejects responsibility, but which has confidence in its own ability to judge and criticize. It goes without saying that there is a correlation between this ability and educational background.[26] In widening the focus of our study beyond the limits of professional training, we thus encompass the education of the "attentive public" as well. Indeed, the "attentive public," in the broadest sense, is also a potential source of expertise: The lawyer or community leader can become a political executive, the laboratory physicist a government adviser, the academician a member of a Presidential task force.

The need for expertise in national security affairs offers a third challenge to American education, the challenge to provide the stimulus and the environment for research. In many ways, this challenge has already been put to American higher education, and, in many ways, it has been met. Government-sponsored research in natural and social sciences not only is being conducted on college and university campuses, but has also attracted academic faculty and administration members into government and industry. College presidents, provosts, deans, and professors are members of hundreds of advisory groups to the government. Areas of government operations that have been contracted out have often gone either to university-based, semi-autonomous groups or to specially established nonprofit corporations run largely by university people and designed to emulate the academic atmosphere of free inquiry. Indeed, so demanding have these obligations become that there is some concern that education may lose the sense of its own purpose in the process of serving the national interest.

These three challenges—in professional training, general education, and scholarly research—are not separate, but closely related in the academic world. Government-sponsored investigations, or fact-finding and commissioned studies produce teaching materials and often provide training grounds for graduate students. Teachers who have sat on consultative boards, spent a year or two in Washington, or joined a research effort are bound to use their own experience with national security affairs to enrich their lectures and course presentation. The interests of students stimulated by the opportunities for public service cause them to ask questions and call for instruction that will support their professional objectives. In all these ways, the needs of professional training, general education, and specialized research in national security affairs are being met. But, perhaps most important, issues of national security are being considered in terms of the profound intellectual problems they raise for our society.

2

The Growth of National Security Research

THE INTEREST OF SCHOLARS and teachers in war is of long standing. As a social institution, war represented too important a phase of man's activity to be ignored. Nevertheless, from the time the United States emerged as a major world power until very recently, American scholars generally regarded war as an aberration in the course of history, and particularly in American history. Except for their acknowledgment of the influence of Alfred Mahan and Theodore Roosevelt in emphasizing the importance of sea power to the United States, researchers and educators treated military affairs as a technical problem quite apart from the process of national development. Military historians were largely concerned with the details of battles and individual campaigns, economists with the techniques of wartime mobilization and peacetime reconversion, and political scientists with the formal constitutional issues and administrative problems of managing a war effort.

To a great degree, these inclinations in education and research reflected the traditional approach to military affairs in American society. Not only was war taken to be an abnormal condition, but the military arm of the government was looked upon as a potential threat to the strength of democratic institutions. Antimilitarism was very much a hallmark of American liberalism, and this liberalism was solidly championed in the universities and colleges. A scholar interested in military matters was presumed to accept the need for military power and to reject the possibility of peaceful settlement of international disputes. To all but the convinced pacifist, moreover, there was no inconsistency in criticizing the military establishment and then supporting the total national effort when war broke out. Broad war aims, expressed in the high moral terms of defending democracy and Western civilization, transcended and justified the immediate and temporary acceptance of the priority of military aims. It was assumed that civilian priorities would reassert themselves once the immediate military objectives were achieved. The institution of war and the role of force in international politics could thus largely be ignored in studying the developing problems of American society.

Precursors in National Security Research

Despite the dominant attitude, there were significant attempts to deal with military affairs as an intellectual problem. One milestone was the publication of Harold Lasswell's *World Politics and Personal Insecurity* in 1935.[1] It was in this book that Lasswell first characterized the essential task of military forces as the "management of violence." Lasswell's work stemmed from his research in the psychological aspects of politics carried on at the University of Chicago, where he was also able to take advantage of the monumental project on *A Study of War*, directed by Quincy Wright. A professor of international relations and law, Wright began his project in 1926 as an effort to clarify the obstacles to peace. This project, which culminated in 1942 with the publication of a two-volume work, provided an apprenticeship for many young scholars who were to become important contributors to the field after the war.[2] Both Lasswell and Wright nevertheless reflected the hostility to war and the military establishment that was prevalent in the predominantly liberal world of academic scholarship.

As the threat of war hovered over Europe in the middle and late 1930's, the military dimension of foreign policy began to draw the attention of a larger group of scholars, many of them refugees from fascist-controlled states. Among these were the members of the "geopolitical" school of international relations who drew their contemporary inspiration from the work of the geographer MacKinder.[3] A leader of this group was Nicholas J. Spykman at Yale; the Yale Institute of International Studies, organized in 1935 to promote research and training in international relations, was a pioneer in the field.

Many of the prewar publications originating in the Institute dealt with military security as an important adjunct to foreign policy, including works by Spykman, George T. Davis, and Arnold Wolfers.[4] An important center of refugee scholars, the New School for Social Research in New York City, organized a faculty seminar that focused on war as a social phenomenon, the results of which were published in 1939.[5]

At Princeton, too, interest in military affairs began to grow under the influence of Edward Meade Earle at the Institute for Advanced Study. In 1940, members of the Princeton University faculty and the Institute for Advanced Study participated in a seminar in military affairs, which two years later resulted in the publication of an important collection of historical studies, *Makers of Modern Strategy*. It was during association with Professor Earle that Harold and Margaret Sprout published *The Rise of American Naval Power* and *Toward a New Order of Sea Power* and Bernard Brodie his first major work, *Sea Power in the Machine Age*.[6] Professor Earle's work at the Institute provided the impulse for a course in "War and National Policy," established at Columbia University in 1941 under the joint sponsorship of the Departments of Public Law and Government and of History, and with the assistance of scholars from other departments and from outside the university. Among the scholars who contributed to the development of a course syllabus were Grayson Kirk, Richard Stebbins, John Herz, Lindsay Rogers, Bernard Brodie, Felix Gilbert, and Alfred Vagts.[7]

The work at Chicago, Yale, the New School, Princeton, and Columbia was principally concerned with military affairs in relation to international relations. But the books by Lasswell and the New School group and parts of the Columbia course were also concerned with the issues that military security raises in a democratic society. This was the theme of E. Pendleton Herring's *The Impact of War*, published as the United States sought to prepare itself for possible involvement in the conflict that had already engulfed Europe.[8] That same year, Herring edited a series of bibliographical notes for the Social Science Research Council on administrative problems of civilian mobilization. The volume included sections on the United States, Great Britain, Canada, Germany, and France, and demonstrated the advantages of the comparative approach in showing how war intensifies problems of political and social organization.[9] In 1940, also, the American Historical Association took "War and Society" as the main theme of its annual meeting. Many of the papers prepared for the meeting were subsequently published in a volume entitled

War as a Social Institution and proved another important source of materials.[10]

In December, 1941, the United States went to war, and military affairs became the preoccupation of the nation. The energies of scholars and teachers, many of them in uniform, were now directed to the war effort on the one hand, and, on the other, to the development of a system of international cooperation that would eliminate war as an instrument of national policy.[11] Economists and experts in public administration flocked to Washington to staff the civilian and military agencies created to mobilize the nation's resources. The State Department remained on the side lines while soldier-diplomats negotiated military agreements, and the President and his immediate staff handled the strategic and postwar arrangements in the great wartime conferences.

In the State Department, however, an impressive group of men, some from academic life and some from the Foreign Service, under the direction of Dr. Leo Pasvolsky, Special Assistant to the Secretary, made plans for the postwar period. They brought together a body of theory and practical experience and applied it to the development of the United Nations system. In 1945, some, like Ralph Bunche and Andrew Cordier, joined the new international secretariat; others stayed at the State Department and on the American delegations to international conferences; still others returned to colleges, universities, and research organizations. Pasvolsky himself organized a continuing research program in foreign policy at the Brookings Institution, and many of his wartime team helped to launch new programs in international relations, international organization, and area studies. The focus of their work was on the problems of developing an organized world system within which national military forces would be contained. Much of their thinking is recorded in the early issues of *International Organization*, a journal founded in 1947 under the auspices of the World Peace Foundation and directed by an editorial board made up of many of the leading scholars of the immediate postwar period.[12]

The plans for international order developed during and just after the war reflected a deep appreciation of the problems of military power. The U.N. Charter recognized the eventual need for an international police force and an interim period of great-power trusteeship for the security of the world. Then, too, the realities of military power were more than dramatized by the advent of atomic weapons. Yet, except within the military establishment itself, the immediate issue was not how to integrate atomic weapons into strategic programs, but how to establish controls over these weapons in the framework of the proposed international system. Any solution, however, depended on a peacetime understanding of basic issues between the United States and the Soviet Union, and the growing mistrust and conflict between these nations forced scholars to study military affairs in terms of national strategy and organization as well.

Stimulants to Postwar National Security Research[13]

Interest in national security, as a field for research distinguished from international organization and area studies, was slow to develop after the war. For one thing, the great changes in the role of force were not yet generally perceived. Also, most scholars were wary of a new field where there were so few guidelines, where access to information was limited by government security classification, and which had still not achieved complete professional respectability. In addition, scholars hesitated to use materials prepared by government agencies when they were unable to criticize their contents. There was constraint, moreover, about even approaching government agencies, particularly military ones, for assistance in gaining access to documents, for fear of being involved in security-clearance problems or of incurring an obligation to defend a particular view.

Some scholarly work in military affairs was nevertheless undertaken. At Yale, for example, the Institute of International Studies had continued its prewar efforts with the publication in 1944 of *The Super-Powers*, by William T. R. Fox, followed soon after the war by Bernard Brodie's *The Absolute Weapon*.[14] Military affairs were the subject of many articles in the *Bulletin of the Atomic Scientists*. More than any single group, except the military men themselves, scientists, stimulated by their knowledge of developments in atomic power and by an increased sense of social responsibility, sought to come to grips with the political and strategic implications of nuclear weapons.

Even before the first atomic bomb was dropped, a group of scientists at the Chicago Metallurgical Laboratory became preoccupied with the political implications of the bomb and sought to influence the decision to employ it against Japan. After Hiroshima and Nagasaki, this same group was instrumental in establishing the *Bulletin* and the Federation of Atomic (later American) Scientists "to meet the increasing responsibility of scientists in promoting the welfare of mankind and the achievement of a stable world peace." Later, through participation on the General Advisory Committee of the Atomic Energy Commission and in major research laboratories, scientists came in touch with new developments in nuclear weapons and the new complexities of American strategy and policy.[15]

The events from 1949 to 1952 marked an important turning point, both in American society's attitude to military problems and in the response of scholars and teachers to national security affairs. These events included the Soviet explosion of an atomic device, the United States' decision to develop a hydrogen bomb, the Communist victory in China, the Korean War, the establishment of NATO, and the presidential election of 1952. The Soviet explosion of an atomic bomb and the loss of China destroyed what was left of America's sense of omnipotence which had been a cornerstone to her approach to war and peace, while the Korean War underscored the complexities of national security in the nuclear age. Almost simultaneously, the moral and political problems that statesmen and scientists had faced in the decision to employ the atomic bomb in 1945 were magnified and multiplied as they were confronted with the Soviet feat and with pressures, at home and abroad, to proceed with the H-bomb. The need to bolster European defense by setting up NATO still further emphasized the loss of independent action as the price for a strong alliance system. A major issue in the 1952 election, when the candidates' debate centered primarily on Korea, was what the strategic response should be to the increasingly dangerous international situation, an issue that was to become central in American political life.

These events dramatized the pressing need to insure that political objectives would prevail over the strong pressures to solve by military means the problems of the cold war. They also directly affected the course of research in national security affairs, forcing attention on national security problems and bringing about the public disclosure of facts and judgments that had gone into the formulation of policy. The publication of congressional hearings on Truman's recall of General MacArthur and on stationing of American troops in Europe under NATO command, and the A.E.C. hearings in the case of Dr. J. Robert Oppenheimer presented scholars with a veritable gold mine of information on which to base theoretical and analytical studies of national security.[16] They also demonstrated the nature of the policy process and the importance for research of access to records. It was now easier to identify the kind of information that was either not available at all or only under prohibitive terms. But, most important, there was no longer any doubt about the relationship between national security and foreign and domestic affairs. Scholars simply could no longer avoid the fundamental social and political problems in national security.

Research in national security was given additional impetus in 1952 and 1953 with the changes in government personnel following the Republican victory in November. Men who had taken part in the determination of policy became free, as private citizens, to discuss, within the limits of security, the determinants of policy. Most prominent in this group were former Secretary of State Dean Acheson and members of the Policy Planning Council of the Department: George Kennan, Paul Nitze, Louis Halle, Charles Burton Marshall, and Dorothy Fosdick. To these might be added former high officials of the Pentagon like John J. McCloy and Thomas K. Finletter.[17] Some took the opportunity to write and others to renew, or begin, teaching careers. Their concern was largely with the role and limits of national power in foreign affairs. In this respect, they differed from scholars and teachers who had returned to research and college teaching in 1945–46. The earlier group was concerned with the problems of establishing the United Nations and fired with the desire to develop needed new techniques of peaceful change. They were not unrealistic about the role of power, but their personal experience had committed them to the success of an international system they had helped create and, in some cases, set into operation. The experiences of this new group had been, in contrast, centered on the dilemma of pursuing national objectives in a divided world that was subject to revolutionary convulsions.

The late 1940's and early 1950's also witnessed the publication of memoirs and biographies of men who had played a leading role in military affairs during and immediately after the war—Secretaries Stimson and Forrestal, Generals Arnold, Bradley, and Clay, and Admirals Leahy and King—and these provided additional sources of important information. By this time, too, a number of volumes had appeared in the Army's broadly conceived World War II history prepared in the Office of the Chief of Military History. Among them were *Chief of Staff: Prewar Plans and Preparation* by Mark S. Watson and Ray S. Cline's *Washington Command Post: The Operations Division*.[18] All these sources provided a new basis for serious, substantial scholarship; they also provided an incentive for such scholarship by posing problems of government that were obviously changing with revolutionary speed.

The Use of Experts by the Government

By the early 1950's, the complexities of military affairs had also led to an expanded use of civilian experts and study groups by the government. These groups can serve a variety of purposes. For one, the study groups make available to the government the expertise of men outside official channels. These men can generally be divided into two groups: first, members of commissions or *ad hoc* committees, usually distinguished citizens who bring a civic-minded understanding of public affairs to the issues, or eminent professional men who have knowledge of the matter at hand; second, staff members who usually work full-time on a project, carry out basic research in the problem area, prepare draft reports for discussion by government officials, and generally draw up a final report and recommendations. Very often these men also come from academic life; they may also be younger colleagues of commission members brought in for an initial baptism in public service, former government employees, or rising young men whose talents and availability have attracted attention. Both groups are linked to significant elements in American society, and their connections, their interests, and the published results of their work have stimulated the study of national security problems by scholars and teachers.

A second function of the expert group has been political. Creation of expert and citizen committees was common during World War II as a practical means of rallying the nation to the war effort, and, immediately after the war, to meet the problems of peacetime adjustment. In the 1950's, the use of such groups increased markedly, in part because of the complexity of national security and the need for expertise in government. But there were other pressures. Some derived from the general public mood in 1951 and 1952, a mood of impatience and frustration—impatience with what seemed to be an inconclusive approach to world politics in general and the Korean conflict in particular; frustration with the new complexities of involvement and the limits of American power.

The cult of the expert is so accepted in the United States that the resort to expert advice is useful as a political maneuver to allay public fears, to lift the issue above partisan debate, and as an attempt to reduce complex problems to manageable proportions. The establishment of a group of outside experts to represent a total national interest may counterbalance, in a legislative struggle, the fragmentary effect of special interest groups. In this way, the President can inject a national perspective into the public debate without committing himself to a position. The Eisenhower Administration, particularly, recognized the advantages of this tactic and also found it useful in fulfilling the President's earnest wish to develop a consensus before a major policy decision was made.

The need for new means of dealing with national issues was emphasized by the change in administrations in 1953. Any new administration must, even before taking office, first survey the problems it faces. This was especially true in the case of the Eisenhower Administration. As the first Republican administration in twenty years, it was subject to great political pressures to make sweeping changes in the personnel of the executive departments, reaching down as far in the bureaucracy as possible. Many Republican attacks on the Truman Administration had been directed against career officers as well as appointed officials, and the Republicans obviously distrusted a bureaucracy developed largely during twenty years of Democratic domination. The general turnover that resulted left the executive branch with limited resources for insuring a flow of information and analysis into the making of policy. The Administration tried to meet this lack in several ways: by bureaucratizing the National Security Council machinery; by relying heavily on individuals, like John Foster Dulles, in whom the President had complete confidence; and by using expert groups, like the Rockefeller Committee on Department of Defense Organization in 1953, the Gaither Committee on civil defense in 1957,[19] and the Draper Committee on the military assistance program in 1958–59.

The military departments and the Atomic Energy Commission had already developed new methods of administration for bringing in experts to cope with special technological problems. Scientific and engineering needs could be met only partially through the development of government laboratories and test stations; the huge capital expenditure involved could not always be justified, in view of the existing available facilities in the private sector; and government salary scales were not competitive with industry's for first-rate scientists and engineers. New contracting techniques were devised to meet these problems: ad hoc and standing advisory committees, arrangements for consultative services with individuals, educational and research organizations, or other private organizations established primarily to provide these services. This last group turned out to be important. Each of the military services and the Defense Department supported a private research organization largely through contract—the RAND Corporation for the Air Force, the Operations Research Office (later, the Research Analysis Corporation) for the Army, the Navy's Operations Evaluation Group (organized by M.I.T.), and the Institute for Defense Analyses for the Defense Department.*

During recent years, the Congress, too, has begun to use expert

* For a full discussion of these agencies, see below, Chapter 11.

groups. Though its role in national security affairs has necessarily been limited largely to reviewing defense programs rather than to formulating policy, the Congress has sought to play a more active role by developing its own expert judgments independent of the executive departments. Through control of the purse and the relations of various committees with the military departments, it has participated in the process of executive policy-making, and many of its members and staff have demonstrated ability in dealing with the complexities of national security. Among these are Senators J. W. Fulbright, Henry Jackson, Hubert Humphrey, and Stuart Symington; Congressmen George Mahon, Melvin Price, Chet Holifield and Carl Vinson; and staff members of the Legislative Reference Service of the Library of Congress, the Senate Committees on Foreign Relations and Armed Services, the House Committees on Foreign Affairs and Armed Services, subcommittees of the Committees on Appropriations and Government Operations, and the Joint Committee on Atomic Energy.

Congress has also reached out beyond its own membership and staff for knowledge and opinion on which to base legislative action. For example, in a general review of foreign policy in 1958, the Senate Committee on Foreign Relations called a number of scholars as expert witnesses in addition to responsible administration officials.[20] Congressional committees also contracted with private research institutes and centers for foreign-policy and defense studies. Perhaps the most ambitious project of this kind was the series of thirteen reports prepared for the Senate Committee on Foreign Relations in 1959 and 1960 by as many private research groups, which covered the whole field of foreign policy—from administrative practices in the State Department to the role of ideology and the military and nonmilitary implications of technology.[21]

The State of National Security Research in the 1960's

The number of expert groups participating in the Senate project testifies to the vigor of research in the national security field by 1960. By then, there was a flow of publication not only from official and semi-official sources, but also from scholars, journalists, retired military officers and statesmen, and other analysts and opinion-makers. Many of these worked individually, but much scholarly work was undertaken in affiliation with existing research organizations, newly established academic centers for national security study, and research groups supported by the government. Many of the research organizations had their roots in the work of early pioneers in national security studies, but others were impelled by the new demands of the postwar period, particularly by the impact of weapons technology on warfare.

The growth of research in national security affairs has been, then, the net result of a series of complex relations between government agencies, higher education, private research organizations, and philanthropic foundations. There has been no regular pattern to these relations; sometimes the initiative has come from one source and sometimes from another, with the national security expert moving freely from college campus to foundation board-room to government office. Together, scholars, scientists, public servants, and politicians have developed into a cohesive intellectual community. They know each other, keep in close touch, and are all thoroughly familiar with research in and out of the government. Highly motivated, articulate, sophisticated, and knowledgeable, they furnish a transmission belt by which ideas are fed into the government and information is funneled out.

Perhaps the climax of this development was the appointment of so many national security experts to high posts following President Kennedy's election in 1960. It became clear that there was an important cadre of men in the intellectual community who had devoted most of their professional lives to problems of national security. Some, like Dean Rusk and Paul Nitze, had served in the Democratic administration under President Truman; almost all, like McGeorge Bundy, Walt Rostow, Charles Hitch, and Roger Hilsman, had served as consultants or advisers or members of government research groups during the Eisenhower Administration; and all, in one way or another, had been involved, as teachers, scholars, or foundation administrators, in contributing to the intellectual response to the cold war.[22]

The contribution of national security research to American policy and strategy cannot be assessed in precise terms. Indeed, the full implications are still to be realized. The influence of intellectuals in the strategic debate of the 1950's and early 1960's is nonetheless evident not only among those who assumed high policy-making posts in 1961, but also among those who continued as "experts": Bernard Brodie and Albert Wohlstetter of RAND; Herman Kahn of the Hudson Institute (formerly of RAND); Arnold Wolfers and Robert E. Osgood of the Washington Center of Foreign Policy Research; Robert R. Bowie, Henry Kissinger, Thomas Schelling, Samuel P. Huntington, and Louis Sohn of Harvard; Max Millikan, William W. Kaufmann, and Lincoln Bloomfield of M.I.T.; Klaus Knorr of Princeton; and William T. R. Fox of Columbia. To Kaufmann, who was then at Princeton, credit must be given for first exploring the concept of credibility in relation to a deterrent strategy. Kissinger and Osgood were the first to develop fully the importance of limited war in the nuclear age. Kahn forced many to think about nonmilitary defense and the unpleasant, even "unthinkable," possibilities of nuclear war. Schelling made arms control part of a broader strategy, and Sohn and others made imaginative advances in developing arms control as a feasible alternative for great-power negotiation.

Most scholars working on strategic studies have accepted the policy of deterrence as a starting point for their work. Their major contribution has been to explore the nature and implications of deterrence and to develop alternative strategies to deter aggressive action and prevent the escalation of conflicts into thermonuclear war. The emphasis has been on the problem of how to control the use of force. Between 1950 and the early 1960's the focus was thus first on maintaining a strategic balance in the international system, and, then, in the wake of political and technological change, on specific issues such as limited war, arms control, and internal violence in underdeveloped areas.

Not all these scholars have accepted a policy based on deterrence or the premises of the cold war, however. Through historical and theoretical analyses, some have sought to clarify the behavioral and social conditions within which conflicts arise and are resolved, and to provide basic knowledge from which a change in policy can be considered—particularly in the light of possible future changes in the Communist bloc and in the international system generally. The work of Charles E. Osgood, a psychologist at the University of Illinois, Kenneth Boulding and others at Michigan, and Emile Benoit and Seymour Melman at Columbia are representative of this approach.

In addition to strategic studies, scholars have also been concerned with the impact of national security on internal political, economic, and social affairs—particularly on the process and organization through which military programs are developed and selected. The most efficient use of resources to achieve the goals decided on has been another concern of scholars. A third area has been the study of the implications of national security for the democratic process. The response to continuing international crises is a strain on a pluralistic system. Scholars have been aware of the difficulties of gaining a national consensus and the temptations to forsake democratic processes under the threat of destruction.

Studies in national security affairs have been the work of many scholars and scientists in different fields. We have already suggested that national security is not an integrated field that can be developed as a separate academic discipline. Rather, it involves a group of problems that should be studied within the traditional fields of scholarship but also in special interdisciplinary programs. In this respect, it bears resemblance to other complex problems that now affect American society, such as urbanization, or the development of new nations.

How to achieve effective collaboration of scholars and scientists is but one of the problems involved in the organization of intellectual resources for national security research. There are a number of others fully as complex and difficult. All of them may be related to three major issues: the proper focus of national security studies; the financing of national security programs; and the role of the scholar and scientist in the determination of policy. It is these issues and the questions that arise from them which we shall treat throughout this book.

II

Approaches to National
Security Affairs

3

History and the Social Sciences

THE HISTORY of national security studies makes one thing clear: The problem of force in international relations is now seriously studied in relation to political, social, and economic developments. The evidence can be found in all the social sciences, though each scholarly discipline has responded differently and in varying degree to the issues raised by national security.[1] Despite this trend, the study of military affairs has never been fully accepted as an important professional concern by historians. Political scientists have been the most receptive to national security studies, both because international relations has developed as a major field within the discipline and because of the political scientist's concern with the impact of national security measures on democratic institutions. Few sociologists, on the other hand, have shown interest in the implications of national security for changes in the social order. The contribution of economists has been uneven and is difficult to generalize about. As a group, economists tend to regard national security as an area of practical application of economic theory, like labor or agricultural economics, yet have not given the field comparable attention. Nonetheless, a few economists, especially those of the RAND Corporation, have applied the techniques of economic analysis to the study of strategic alternatives with great success.

The response of scholars to national security affairs has undoubtedly reflected the traditions and structure of their disciplines. It was perhaps to be expected that historians would be the most reluctant and political scientists the most responsive to a field the importance of which derives largely from current public policy. Similarly, both sociology and economics are more theoretical and empirical and scholars in these fields are thus more inclined to treat national security to the extent that its problems relate to the systematic development of their disciplines. The response of the social sciences may thus be evaluated in two ways: (1) in terms of the application of techniques of systematic analysis to military problems; and (2) in terms of the extent to which problems of war and peace as substantive areas of intellectual concern are included within the separate disciplines.

The Historian and the Study of War[2]

In many ways, professional training in history develops qualities that are most valuable in the study of national security and policy planning—scrupulous objectivity, the reconstruction of past events, orderly presentation, a broad knowledge of society, and an understanding and appreciation of the dynamic forces of change. Despite this potential, historians have traditionally shown a lack of interest in military affairs and the profession itself discourages careers in the public service. This attitude has only modestly changed under the pressures of the cold war.

Before World War II, there were few civilian courses in military history taught at American colleges and universities. Even after 1945, when interest in the war was at its height, the number of courses was still small.[3] A detailed investigation made in 1954 of the teaching of military history in 493 colleges and universities showed that though most of these offered courses in military history as part of ROTC programs, only 37 offered or planned to offer courses on war or military policy in their history departments.[4] The total number of such courses was 46. Those that had no courses or plans for courses in military history gave a variety of explanations: general disinterest in the academic community; lack of student interest; lack of qualified instructors; lack of adequate texts and other teaching materials; and the specialized nature of the subject. A number of institutions (more than half) reported that they offered "quasi-military" courses, that is, courses in general or diplomatic history that included consideration of major wars. The largest number of such courses, as one would expect, dealt with the American Civil War and the French Revolution and Napoleonic Wars. The military content of these courses, it was estimated, varied "from about one-third, at the most, down to practically no emphasis at all."[5]

Among the forty-six courses specifically designated as concerned with "purely military history or policy," three types were identified. The first was largely devoted to either military or naval history and concentrated on military techniques and organization. A second type was devoted to a study of specific wars, such as the Civil War or the two world wars. Finally, there were courses that dealt with military affairs in terms of society as a whole, either in relation to Western society or the United States alone. Enrollment figures for these latter courses were not given in all cases, but in the twenty-two cases that were reported, the total enrollment was about 1,700. Significantly, three of the courses accounted for over 1,000 of the student enrollment, but all three were required ROTC courses, though taught by civilian instructors.[6]

The ROTC program remains the largest single source of students for military and naval history. Except in special cases, as at Princeton and Dartmouth, instruction in military and naval history ROTC courses is in the hands of officers. The Navy maintains this practice on the ground that the primary purpose of the course is service indoctrination rather than general education. In 1960, the Army relaxed its rules to permit civilian instruction in the military history course, but the invitation has gone largely unanswered. Only a few schools have indicated any desire or interest in assuming responsibility for the course in one term. In a large state university where ROTC is compulsory, there might be as many as 800 to 1,000 students. No instructor could handle this many students effectively, nor would he want to do so. To lecture to a minimum of several hundred students whose only text is the official Army manual is hardly a satisfactory arrangement for any professionally trained historian, no matter how interested he may be in military history. Moreover, few college or university history departments have men qualified to teach the subject. Often, members of a history department do not wish to be identified with military history or the ROTC because of the general attitude toward the subject and the low intellectual status of the ROTC program. Even when competent military historians have been willing to teach the subject and to accept ROTC students in their course, they have naturally been reluctant to teach the course as the Army prescribes or to use the official text. As a result of all these factors, both Army and Navy ROTC history courses are most often taught by military and naval officers who are neither qualified historians nor good teachers.

Interest in World War II, together with Americans' intense preoccupation with their Civil War and with the threat of war in the nuclear age, is nevertheless evident in the increased attention historians give to past wars and to the impact of military institutions on American political, economic, and social development. A recent two-volume history used widely as a text devotes three chapters to the Civil War, one of which deals in detail with military operations and two with such problems as war economics and finance, manpower, military resources, and wartime politics.[7] Three more chapters are assigned to World War II, two of which are concerned largely with military operations and the conduct of the war. An additional chapter is entitled "Nuclear Diplomacy" and includes an account of the Korean War and a discussion of the strategy of massive retaliation and of the arms race with the Soviet Union. Comparable space is given to military problems in other standard texts in American history.[8]

The same trend can be noted in diplomatic history, where the relation between international events and military developments is even more striking. Thus, in the 1959 edition of his *A Short History of American Foreign Policy and Diplomacy*, Samuel Flagg Bemis, the dean of American diplomatic historians, sums up the impact of the last twenty years by stating that "the new and foreboding picture of power and politics produced a *diplomatic revolution* in the history of the United States."[9] The element of military force has been so pervasive during these years that some historians have begun to re-examine the role of military affairs in shaping the nation's foreign policy in earlier periods of American history. In *A History of United States Foreign Policy*, Julius W. Pratt includes a chapter on "The Tools of Force," and explains the inclusion in these terms:

> The average reader . . . may or may not be aware that military force, whether used or held in reserve, is an indispensable instrument in the prosecution of foreign policy. The chances are that he knows little of the past practice of the United States in the maintenance and use of armed force as a support of its diplomacy. Since an acquaintance with this subject seems highly relevant to an understanding of foreign policy, [this] chapter summarizes the history of the military and naval policy of the United States.[10]

Despite this kind of recognition, military history can hardly be expected to gain general acceptance as a subject for academic study until historians accept it as a desirable field for research and until they train students to work in the field. On the first of these needs, appreciable progress has been made in recent years with the rapid increase of historical writing on military subjects. Much of this literature deals with World War II and is written by professionally trained historians who are employed by the governments of the major powers, rather than by military men, as had been the case before. The British have their official history, prepared largely by civilians, as do the Australians, the Dutch, the Canadians, the Russians, and others. In the United States, also, the official historians are mostly civilians. So voluminous is the literature on World War II only twenty years after its close that the student is hard put to keep up with it.[11]

On the other hand, the graduate schools that supply most of America's college and university teachers have not kept pace with this research and writing. The attitude of history professors discourages young historians whose interest in military affairs may have been aroused by their personal experience in World War II and Korea from specializing in this field. And those who are sympathetic feel constrained to point out to Ph.D. candidates that military history is not a recognized specialty and that opportunities in the field are likely to be limited. In his 1954 survey of instruction in military history, Professor Richard Brown found only five schools with graduate courses on military affairs and five with courses open to both graduates and undergraduates.[12] The total enrollment in the graduate courses was between 40 and 45, but not all of the students in them were candidates for advanced degrees. Since 1954, some of these courses have been discontinued, but others have been established, so that the total number remains about the same.

What other opportunities exist for a graduate student in history, if he wants to specialize in a field for which there is so little demand in the academic world? Can he do research and still hope for academic advancement? If not, can he turn to the government? And if he does so, will he risk loss of status in his profession? There are no clear-cut answers to these questions, but it is fair to say that there is virtually no recognition in university history departments—as there is, for example, in political-science departments—of public service as a legitimate aim of graduate training. Perhaps more than in any other discipline except the study of literature, the purpose of graduate instruction in history is to train students for teaching and research.[13] Only rarely does a promising student from a reputable institution go into the government, and there are few professors who would advise their students to do so. The values of the profession tend to divert from government employment all but those who cannot be placed elsewhere.

The values of the historical profession also tend to make it conservative, although historians as individuals are generally liberal in their political outlook.[14] There are recognized fields of specialization, and change comes slowly. Other disciplines may respond somewhat more readily to contemporary needs of society if they emphasize current problems and if their training includes preparation for careers other than in teaching. This awareness of public needs may also be reflected in their graduate programs, more rapidly in some than in others. The absence of this pressure on the historical profession as a whole has meant that there has been little response to the intellectual challenge of the cold war in terms of research and training. Few military historians are being trained, simply because the graduate centers see no need to do so. Those who enter the field often do so by accident or despite the pressures of the profession, which remains, on the whole, unresponsive to the contributions it could make to the study of war and to the search for solutions to contemporary problems of national security.

There is little doubt that historical training provides both the skills and outlook that are needed by the professional in government service. Whether the study of military history has any relevance to the problems of the nuclear age is, apparently, not so certain. There are some who argue that the character of war has altered so radically since World War II that military history has no lessons for us today and may even be harmful if it continues to be used as it has in the past to train military men in the exercise of their profession.[15] This view is based on a conception of military history as the account of battles and campaigns written primarily to instruct military men. Most historians would view the study of war in much broader terms and seek to show how war is related to society and how it affects and is affected by political, social, and economic institutions. Viewed in this way, military history represents a potential field of specialization in which the historian can contribute to the better understanding of the problems of our own age.

There is some basis for the suspicion and skepticism with which the historical profession has regarded the study of war. Military historical writing and instruction since the early nineteenth century stems not from intellectual developments in the academic world, like other branches of history, but from the needs and interests of the general staffs of Europe. Its purpose was to derive practical lessons from the study of past wars that would educate soldiers, and its preparation was the job of staff officers. Only later, in the late nineteenth century, was its purpose broadened to include the enlightenment and education of the reading public.[16] It is not surprising, therefore, that the academic historian deeply rooted in the traditions of his profession should regard military history as an alien branch of his discipline, narrow and technical in approach, didactic in character, and unrelated to the broad stream of historical writing. Suspicion of this type of history, associated as it is with the military profession, was, perhaps, well founded in an earlier day. It is doubtful that it can be justified in our own time, in view of the broadened conception of military history and the role of civilians in military affairs.

There is still another reason for the negative attitude of many historians toward the study of war. Modern American historiography is heir to the strong antimilitary stream of American political philosophy and to the liberal tradition of the late nineteenth century. Both combined to produce among historians a tendency to minimize the role of the military forces in the development of the nation, and to regard the professional soldier as an alien, if not hostile, element in American society. The net effect was to create so unfavorable a climate for the serious study of military history that few historians have wished to enter the field.

The Study of Politics and International Relations

Dealing as they do with contemporary problems of society, social scientists would be more likely than historians to analyze the problems of national security. The response of the social sciences has nevertheless been uneven, more having been accomplished in political science than in economics and the behavioral sciences.

The study of politics has several purposes: to prepare specialists for teaching, research, and public service; to prepare "generalists" for both public and private vocations; and "citizen" education. Various faculties will emphasize one or another of these aims. But, in the aggregate, the multiple purposes of politics courses (public service and "citizen" education especially) result in considerable concentration on problems of current public policy. In economics and sociology, the emphasis, even at the undergraduate level, is more on model-building and on training specialists. Courses thus concentrate on theory and methodology. Some, of course, think that undergraduate courses in these disciplines should be part of a general education and, in business schools, economics courses serve an essential, if "servicing" role. But a review of academic courses in national security affairs indicates less activity among economists and sociologists than among political scientists, the reasons bearing on the differences in their purposes and methods.

Political scientists are concerned that the several functions they perform are dissipating their resources and diluting their scholarly contributions. Not only that, but political scientists themselves are being called upon to serve as publicists and experts at every level of political life. The criterion for a reasonable objection to these activities is the extent to which they do or do not contribute to scholarship and teaching. Few political scientists do not agree that experience in government provides the invaluable and almost indispensable insights into politics that good scholarship and teaching require. But the inevitable questions about the degree of participation and concern always arise, and there is no satisfactory yardstick against which to measure what is beneficial or what is excessive.[17]

One important advance in the methodology of political science has been the introduction of new methods of quantification of political behavior, a development accompanied by controversy between those with a "behavioral" approach to politics and those with a more traditional approach to political theory and institutions.[18] Many political scientists accept the validity of the behavioral position but object to the fact that extreme "behaviorists" deny the validity of other approaches. They contend that it is impossible to dissociate the study of political theories and institutions from that of political behavior. Theories and institutions have a primary identification quite apart from "actors" and must be studied for themselves as well as in relation to each other and to human behavior. All these concerns are legitimate ones for the student of politics, they argue.

The variety of perspectives from which political scientists view government and politics is reflected in their response to the issues of national security. One has been to study the impact of national security on political institutions and organization. National security affairs have precipitated important changes, for instance, in executive-legislative relations, in the role and power of executive departments, and in the relations between national and international agencies. These changes have received considerable attention and been extensively written about. For example, the theory of presidential influence advanced by Richard E. Neustadt in his book *Presidential Power* is supported by case studies, several of which involve national security issues. Although in no single book has there yet been an analysis of the full effect of national security affairs on the role of the Congress, at least three books cover special congressional problems: *The Purse and the Sword*, by Elias Huzar; *Congress and Foreign Policy*, by Robert Dahl; and *The House of Representatives and Foreign Affairs*, by Holbert N. Carroll.[19]

Because a key factor in national security affairs is the rational relation of means to ends, the field is a rich area of application for public administration. In response to the demands for efficient and honest government, students of public administration early in the twentieth century argued that to separate politics from administration was the best way of eliminating corruption and waste. But the New Deal and war experiences helped to re-establish the unity of policy-making and administration. This unity has been emphasized by new problems in national security. Public administration studies have ranged from general books on the administration of foreign affairs to specialized studies of defense organization. Perhaps most impressive in its foresight was Herring's The Impact of War, published in 1941.[20]

Out of the study of political institutions and organization has developed the study of the process by which political decisions are made and action taken. A major reason for focusing on the process was that political scientists realized the inadequacy of studying only formal or constitutional governmental mechanisms. By the postwar period, their own practical experiences had reinforced their sense that it was essential to understand the effect of noninstitutional factors on policy formulation and implementation. Their interest was whetted by developments in administrative science and sociology that emphasized the interaction of formal and informal systems and the notions of "role" and "actors" in political situations,[21] also by the work, both theoretical and descriptive, on "decision-making." This theoretical work reveals one instance of the influence of the behavioral approach on the study of politics and is exemplified by the studies directed by Richard C. Snyder first at Princeton and later with Harold Guetzkow at Northwestern University. Individual decisions have also been the subject of a series of descriptive case studies published under the Inter-University Case Program, several of which deal with national security issues.[22] Most pertinent to the field, however, have been the case-study projects in civil-military relations of the Twentieth Century Fund, directed by Harold Stein, and of the Institute of War and Peace Studies at Columbia, directed by William T. R. Fox.[23]

The focus on the "actors" in national security affairs also highlighted the need to analyze the changing role of military forces in American politics and society. Studies in military politics have shown that civilians have now moved into commanding positions where military expertise once dominated, while military officers, by necessity or default, have often taken the initiative in political affairs.[24]

The impact of these various scholarly activities on the teaching of politics is difficult to measure. In undergraduate courses in American government, national security is one of several topics that must be covered. The emphasis given to it will depend on the faculty's interest. Most often, basic courses are planned by departmental committees, and they tend to reflect a compromise in which the special interests of each teacher are given "equal time." The new emphasis on national security affairs is nevertheless indicated in two of the most frequently used texts on American government.

In the first edition (1951) of *American Democracy in Theory and Practice*, by Robert K. Carr and associates, the final section was entitled "National Security and Foreign Policy." In terms of space, it was about as long as the sections devoted to the judicial system and to civil liberties, but somewhat less than that on public administration and considerably less than that on economics and welfare. Moreover, the discussion was focused on the diplomatic aspects of foreign policy, and only a brief six pages was devoted to the "organization of national security" and the "role of the military in foreign policy."

Subsequent revisions to the Carr textbook gave increased attention to national security affairs. In the 1961 edition, problems of foreign and military policy were brought together in a section entitled "Providing for the Common Defense." Again, the material took up about the same number of pages as that on the judicial system. But, in addition to the problems of diplomatic representation and of determining foreign policy, the authors now discussed "The Nature of the Strategic Problem," "The Technological Race," "The Shape of Future Wars," "The Battle of the Pentagon over Roles and Missions," "Organization for National Security," "The Cost of National Security," "National Security and the Economy," "Industrial Mobilization for Defense and War," "Civil Defense Against Attack," and "National Security and Individual Liberty."[25]

In contrast, the 1952 edition of the textbook by James M. Burns and Jack W. Peltason, *Government by the People*, included three chapters on national security affairs. The fourth edition (1960) retains and brings up to date these same chapters on the position of the United States in world affairs, and executive and legislative roles in the formulation of foreign policy; on the administration of the State Department; and on the problems of defense. But there has been no expansion of the material. In both cases, national security affairs are covered in approximately seventy-five pages in volumes that run to 800 and 880 pages.[26]

In one way or another, then, there is certainly an increasing concern with national security affairs in basic government courses. But the greatest attention to the subject is given in courses on foreign policy and international politics. Three important trends have developed in the study of foreign affairs in recent years which relate to the impact of military factors: the interrelation of domestic and foreign affairs; the dominance of a concept of power, rather than law and organization, in international relations; and the increasing study of other societies. Domestic considerations affect foreign policy at several levels, for the "ends" of foreign policy will depend on the available "means." The "means," moreover, consist of more than merely goods and services: In a democratic society, they also consist of a general will and determination to use the available material means so as to meet designated ends. National security is as much involved with the domestic affairs of a people as it is with the country's international position.

The second development in the teaching of foreign affairs concerns a change in the concept of power. In the period after World War I, theories of international relations were dominated by the quest for world order through law and organization. But, by the mid-1930's, the concept of national power began to find its way back into the literature. In the first edition of *International Politics*, Frederick Schuman held out the hope of world order but also analyzed the power struggle among nations that was to become so evident within a few years. The work done at the Yale Institute under Nicholas Spykman and the American publication of E. H. Carr's *The Twenty Years' Crisis* in 1939 added to the interpretation of the international arena in terms of power politics.[27]

After World War II, the building of a stable world order was still a major topic for analysis in undergraduate courses in international relations. The complexities of the process were, however, underscored in other topics: "the nature and operation of the state system, factors affecting the power of the state, the international position and foreign policies of the great powers [and] the history of recent international relations."[28] By 1959, a survey of education in international relations indicated important changes in emphasis and method:

> Courses today stress power and the complexity of world affairs rather than the state system; they probe deeper into the elements of national power, and in so doing take account of the theoretical and practical results of research in economics, psychology, and sociology. In debating the position of the realists and idealists and presenting the cold war, instructors now pay more attention to theoretical presuppositions; and in presenting accurately the picture of world politics today, they have had to give a larger place than before to Africa and Asia.[29]

The most significant postwar text on international politics has been *Politics Among Nations*, by Hans J. Morgenthau.[30] Morgenthau's key idea is "that statesmen think and act in terms of interest defined as power." In response to criticisms that his concept of national power is too ambiguous and puts too much emphasis on the military aspects of national power, Morgenthau sought to clarify his concept of power in a preface to the third edition of his book.[31] He explains that "against the misunderstanding of the central element of power, which, after having been underrated to the point of total neglect, now tends to be equated with material strength, especially of a military nature, I have stressed more than before its immaterial aspects, especially in the form of charismatic power, and have elaborated the discussion of political ideologies."

Under the assault of political events since 1939, few teachers have been able to ignore the element of power as a central theme in international relations. But the problems of interpreting the full complexity of that power and of maintaining power as a central theme without making it the central value of the international system remain. The quantitative "factors" analysis of power—adding the geographic, population, industrial, and military factors—has long since been discarded. Nor is it sufficient merely to take cognizance of the "immaterial" factors such as morale, leadership, and social cohesion. One must consider all the factors of power in their dynamic interrelation, in their projection in time, and in comparative terms. The vast range of data and phenomena with which the study of international relations is concerned and the variety of ways they can be analyzed and ordered make it difficult to establish a single unifying concept.[32] Yet, even though Morgenthau's concept of power has been regarded as less than completely satisfactory, it has encouraged a realistic view of international politics that gives due respect to the uses and limits of military force.

Changes in the study of international relations since World War II have been accompanied by the growth of area study programs. In 1946, there were thirteen such programs (six on Latin America, four on the Far East, and three on Russia); six years later, the number had grown to twenty-nine, distributed among nineteen institutions, involving 375 faculty members and almost 700 students.[33] In 1952, a survey of seventy-five political-science departments revealed that 300 out of 800 research projects undertaken at that time by members of these departments dealt with international relations, and that 200 of these were area studies.[34] A survey made by the Department of State in late 1960 listed 109 research projects concerned primarily with foreign societies and regions. Most of these were being carried out at universities, but a few were conducted by private research organizations such as the Council on Foreign Relations or the Twentieth Century Fund. The largest number dealt with areas in which American interests were most involved and where the requirements of national policy were greatest. There were about twenty projects on the Soviet Union and Eastern Europe, about forty on parts of Asia, and twenty-one on Western Europe and the British Commonwealth; the smallest number were concerned with Africa and the Near East, not because these areas were less important, but because the number of scholars in the field was so small.[35]

The relation of area studies to the study of national security problems is direct and close. In addition to the direct contribution they make by training specialists in particular regions, area studies focus specialized skills and knowledge in many disciplines on a single area. The result is a picture of a way of life that makes each society more meaningful to those who must relate events in the area to American security interests.

Few national security research or training programs fail to use the products of area-studies programs. It would be difficult to study Soviet strategy, for example, without utilizing the work of a Russian-studies program. Conversely, the materials used in a national security program, whether it be concerned with the problems of emerging nations or the economics of Communist China, can hardly fail to be of interest in any program concerned with those areas. If survival of the nation depends as much on understanding other nations as on the strength of our arms and the resolution of our people, then area studies constitute an important element in the total contribution of the universities to national security issues.

All the issues of national security that have been integrated into established courses in political science and international relations have also, occasionally, been brought together in specialized college courses on national security affairs. These courses are ordinarily given at the advanced undergraduate and graduate levels, usually by scholars who have contributed to the development of research in the field themselves. The courses offered by Samuel P. Huntington at Columbia and Harvard and by Fred Greene at Williams College are illustrative, the first being principally concerned with military affairs in relation to American government and the second in relation to foreign-policy problems. Both nevertheless covered much of the same ground.[36] Huntington's course at Columbia was entitled "American Government and National Security" and was limited to graduate students. The first subjects considered in it were historical and analytical: "National Defense Policy and American Society," "The Pattern of Policy, 1946–1958," "The Uses of Force," "The Strategy-Making Process," "The Great Equation: How Much for National Security?" and "The Competition of Military Programs." The following weeks were devoted to an analysis of several important policy issues: "The Arms Race and Mutual Deterrence," "Continental Defense and Weapons Selection," "The Defense of Europe," and "Limited War and Defense of the Gray Areas." Huntington concluded with a discussion of the budgetary process and of organizational and manpower policies, returning to the introductory emphasis on the relation of national security to American governmental processes.

The course offered by Fred Greene to upperclassmen at Williams was more concerned with policy issues, although the dominant theme was the complexity of strategic planning. In contrast to Huntington's approach, Greene's historical background included an analysis of several non-American cases of strategic planning—Great Britain before 1914, Germany and France between the wars—and of American military planning before World War II. Unlike Huntington's course, the purpose here was to demonstrate the interrelation of foreign and military policies rather than to summarize the history of the American experience. Most of the course was an analysis of the current strategic issues—"Gradations of Warfare: From Limited to Total War," "The Quest for a Reliable Strategy," "Organization for Defense: The Armed Services and the National Security Council," "Diplomacy, Alliances and Security," and "Arms Control."

Both courses used the full range of national security literature written after 1950. Neither used a textbook of the traditional kind. Professor Huntington assigned his own book *The Soldier and the State* and Henry Kissinger's *Nuclear Weapons and Foreign Policy* for general background, while Professor Greene had his students read *American Foreign Policy Since World War II*, by John Spanier.[37] Specific reading assignments included selections from other books in the field, from *Foreign Affairs*, *World Politics*, and the *Bulletin of the Atomic Scientists*, from congressional hearings, and from official executive and congressional reports. Both courses required papers on specific problems of national security with research in primary as well as secondary sources.

Political scientists, then, have begun to re-analyze political institutions and processes in the light of the impact of security requirements on domestic and foreign affairs, and these investigations are increasingly reflected in courses on American and comparative government. The greatest impact, however, has been in the fields of foreign policy and international relations, where it has become essential to clarify the complexities of the military dimension of the current international scene. But the discipline is highly fragmented into competing specializations and the major response has been made by the scholars who have both written about and established courses in national security affairs. However small their number, these scholars stand out in contrast to those in other disciplines as the major single professional group to devote themselves to problems of national security.

Economics and the Behavioral Sciences

There is a logical sequence of development in the introduction of a new area of specialization into an established discipline. What is first needed is a body of knowledge and a literature that relates the field to the basic objectives of the profession, and a method of circulating this knowledge within the profession. This may be done through the presentation of papers at professional meetings and their publication in scholarly journals; through the informal exchange of research information; and through special conferences sponsored by informal groups of interested scholars, private research organizations, foundations, or universities. Progress from this point needs the support of prominent senior members of the profession. Their participation on panels, their authorship of a book or article in the field, or their sponsorship of research projects indicates the professional legitimacy of the field.

To a greater or lesser degree, the field of national security has advanced to this point both in the study of government and politics and in the study of economics. But economics, like history, has not advanced to the next step, which is the development of young economists whose graduate training and early research work focus on issues of national security. In political science, there are now scholars who have made national security their career specialization, like federalism, or international law and organization. No such group is emerging to give the economics of national security the status that more traditional specializations, like agricultural economics and labor economics, enjoy.

Like the politics of defense, the economics of defense has changed in character. The new economic problems of national security are different from the problems of mobilization and reconversion that were familiar at the time of the two world wars. They involve the allocation and efficient use of resources to meet national security requirements on a continuing basis, and the impact of defense and foreign aid on national economies and world commerce. In all these problem areas, the line between economics and politics is vague. For example, the size of the defense and foreign-aid budgets is determined by the international commitments undertaken by the United States and the strategies decided on to meet these commitments, but earlier decisions as to what the economy can afford may limit the policy alternatives open to an administration. Moreover, it is difficult to distinguish between purely economic factors and political or personal preferences in determining the potential output of the economy and the priority given to competing demands on it. Under conditions of total war, there are no competing demands other than the objective of unconditional surrender or total victory. There are usually alternative means, but the choice of means is less difficult when there is a single overwhelming objective. Within the cold war situation, the economic choices are more complex and more political.

Much of the recent research by economists in the field has reflected the multidisciplinary nature of national security. For example, in the preface to his book *The War Potential of Nations*, Klaus Knorr, Director of the Princeton Center of International Studies, states that, "instead of confining itself to 'economic' or 'industrial' war potential, this study is equally concerned with the administrative and 'morale' components of war potential and attempts to throw some light on their interrelations." To carry through this broad approach, Knorr noted that "to the best of his ability," he had to draw on "the methods and researches of political scientists, sociologists, psychologists, historians, and economists."[38] A similar approach is followed at the Center for International Studies at M.I.T., where the leadership comes from a strong economics department. An over-all study of the emerging nations, which the Center undertook in 1960, was described by the Director, Max Millikan (himself an economist), as "an exercise in interdisciplinary analysis" in which "the varied insights" gained from earlier studies are woven "into a reasonably integrated account."[39]

Other economists have also contributed to the study of national security. Arthur Smithies, of Harvard, devoted a substantial portion of his book on *The Budgetary Process in the United States* to the complexities of the military budget.[40] Kenneth Boulding, of the University of Michigan, and Emile Benoit have done important work on the economics of disarmament.[41] Thomas Schelling, of the Center for

International Affairs at Harvard, has applied game theory to military strategy and thus extended to national security the pioneering efforts of John von Neumann and Oskar Morgenstern in applying game theory to economic behavior.[42] Economists working for the Committee for Economic Development and the National Planning Association have contributed to the studies on the economics of national security made by these groups. Among these economists are Gerhard Colm, Charles Hitch, Klaus Knorr, Edward S. Mason, and Herbert Stein. Finally, the SSRC Committee on National Security Policy Research sought, in 1958 and 1959, to encourage economists to further research in the field through a program of grants and through a special conference.[43]

Economists have also been foremost among social scientists in applying techniques of systems analysis to problems of military strategy. This has been especially evident at the RAND Corporation. Charles Hitch, Director of the Economics Division before his appointment as Defense Comptroller in 1961, described the method as "economizing . . . a certain kind of rational choosing and behaving . . . making the most of one's resources in achieving one's objectives, in whatever kind of institutional framework."[44] The ability of economists to work in this area depends both on their capacity for advanced mathematics and on their habits in dealing with quantifiable data— skills that are helpful not only in handling problems related to military weapons and equipment, but also in facilitating communication with physical scientists and engineers.

Despite these impressive research gains, national security has had little impact on the study of economics. In a few cases, economists have decided to give special courses on the economics of national security, but these have been exceptional. At Ohio State University, for example, Professor Meno Lovenstein emphasized the World War II mobilization experience and contrasted it with the new problems that would face the nation today in case of an outbreak of war. Thomas Schelling, in a course at Harvard, discussed the economic problems of a situation with a stabilized deterrent force and the application of economic techniques to problems of strategy and military organization. But both courses, different as they are, were isolated cases. For the most part, elementary economics courses emphasize theory and economic institutions, and advanced courses make only incidental reference to problems of national security, in connection with public finance and international economics. The impact of national security affairs on economic issues has yet to be reflected in teaching, even though many first-rate economists have been drawn to study the application of techniques of economic analysis to military strategy.

The lack of courses in the economics of national security is undoubtedly due to economics' generally theoretical and empirical orientation, to a reluctance to add another field of specialization to an already long list, and to economists' resistance to teaching courses on public policy issues. A report of the American Economics Association in 1950 indicated that teachers of elementary courses in economics aimed principally at "the development of analytical thinking and method of analysis." The report concluded that college teachers of economics did not give enough attention to "citizen" education. Moreover, graduate work in economics is highly specialized and emphasizes economic theory and statistics. In recent years, graduate students have had to give increasing time to work in mathematics in order to deal with advanced work in statistics and the use of computers.[45]

The specialized nature of economics courses has raised questions about their relevance for students of international relations. In 1947, Klaus Knorr urged that economics teachers develop courses for international relations students so that the latter would not be forced to take courses designed to train professional economists. Knorr based his argument on the need to understand "the interaction of economic and political problems and policies" within the context of international studies.[46] In almost all cases, the areas of economics that are important in the national security field have political and psychological implications—not only in the determination of defense budgets, for instance, but also in the complexities of economic growth in both advanced and underdeveloped countries. In the emerging nations, particularly, problems of economic development are at the very heart of politics, internal and external, and to isolate the one from the other is certainly to distort the picture. It is nevertheless also true that one must analyze economic data objectively, even though ultimate choices about the economic system are in essence political, for objective analysis helps to clarify the alternatives and sometimes offers a guide for decision. A balance between "pure" economic analysis and awareness of the social context of the economic system is vital in relating the study of economics to national security.

To the extent that college teachers are concerned about their responsibilities beyond teaching more "experts," it is becoming increasingly difficult to ignore national security issues. In *Economics*, one of the most successful economics textbooks, Paul A. Samuelson states that he was forced to change his emphasis "away from the problem of mass unemployment and toward this next decade's problems of inflation and a national security economy."[47] Immediately after the war, the practical problems for professional economists had been related to the general problems of economic growth and the maintenance of full employment within a mixed economy. The problem of growth remains but, as Samuelson noted, the circumstances under which it needs to be studied have changed, particularly since the Korean War. It is now connected with the requirements of national security, which can be expected to extend beyond the 1960's and into the 1970's. Economists' contribution to solving these and other questions is vital, and the range of problems on which they can work is wide. Charles Hitch listed the following issues: the analysis and measurement of economic strength for war; determining the size of the defense budget; efficiency in using and managing defense resources; military research and development; the economics of military alliances; civil defense and recuperation; and disarmament and arms control.[48]

The situation in the behavioral sciences—sociology and psychology —is not unlike the situation in economics. Indeed, behavioral scientists, even more than economists, devote most of their advanced studies to theory and methods of empirical research. The contributions of behavioral scientists to the study of national security affairs are nonetheless several—ranging from research on information and propaganda activities to the application of theories of change and conflict to social crises.

Behavioral scientists were involved in the psychological-warfare and intelligence agencies during World War II and have continued to serve as staff experts and consultants in such work.[49] During the war, they also directed research on morale and personnel management in the armed services, work that is summarized in *The American Soldier*, a many-volume work written under the direction of Samuel A. Stouffer. The statistical material available in the personnel records of the wartime Army and Selective Service was also later used in a military manpower study undertaken at Columbia, which resulted in the three volumes of *The Ineffective Soldier*, edited by Eli Ginzberg and designed to provide lessons in the utilization of manpower that would be useful in any large-scale organization.[50] At the same time, psychologists and sociologists under contract with the military services continued to work on specific personnel management problems.

Despite this activity, sociologists—again, like economists—have neglected many areas of national security affairs, particularly those involving the impact of military affairs on American society. Although political scientists have adopted many of sociology's research methods, sociologists have responded in only a limited fashion to the systematic study of the military establishment. A major exception is the work of Morris Janowitz in *The Professional Soldier*. Yet Janowitz himself noted that, "the absence of a sustained interest in military institutions is manifested in all phases of sociological effort, including the standard introductory text." This neglect is especially notable when compared with "sociological literature . . . on industrial and factory organization." Much of the reason, Janowitz suggests, lies in the "understandable but fundamental tension between the professional soldier and the scholar, who seeks to apply the scientific method to the human side of military organization and armed conflict."[51]

Under Janowitz's leadership, a program of research and teaching in the sociology of military organization has nevertheless been established at the Center for Social Organization Studies in the Department of Sociology of the University of Chicago. In the program, graduate students may select military institutions for special study and have access to the work of an inter-university seminar on military organization sponsored by the Russell Sage Foundation. Participating in the seminar in 1961–62, in addition to Janowitz, were sociologists such as Maury Feld, of the Defense Studies Program and the Center for International Affairs at Harvard, Kurt Lang, of Queens College, and Peter Rossi, of the University of Chicago. Research papers were prepared on the problem of succession in military organization, the role of military elites in new nations, trends in professional identity in the officer corps, the commitment to military careers among enlisted men, etc.[52]

The focus for Janowitz and his colleagues has been the military establishment as a social order. A number of behavioral scientists, including economists and political scientists as well as sociologists and psychologists, have concentrated their efforts on the applications of the methods of social sciences to the problems of conflict. They have advanced the proposition that while scientific investigation of international conflict is complex and difficult, studies at lower levels yield more accurate data which may be used to develop a general theory that would at least shed light on the international situation. This has been the premise behind Kenneth Boulding's work in his *Conflict and Defense*, and the work done at the Center for Research in Conflict Resolution at the University of Michigan.[53] Boulding acknowledges certain peculiarities of the international system that necessitate the modification of generalities based on experience at other levels of human conflict—the persistence of war as a social phenomenon, the distinction between offensive and defensive armaments and actions, the importance of geographic boundaries, and the complexities of national power. He also acknowledges the special nature of the present conflict, which is not only political in character but ideological as well, and which thus poses another set of problems of correlation.[54]

The behavioral approach to the study of conflict contrasts with the more traditional approach of historical analysis in a work like Quincy Wright's *Study of War*.[55] The major distinction is in the former's use of empiricism and mathematical reasoning, and in the resulting development of general theory. But both approaches have been related to the mathematical work of the physicist Lewis F. Richardson, whose generalizations on war and peace are based on an exhaustive compilation of historical statistics on conflict situations. Indeed, in an introduction to Richardson's *Statistics of Deadly Quarrels*, Wright notes that "the comparison of conclusions" between his own and Richardson's work "shows few inconsistencies, though Richardson's method often made the proof more convincing."[56] Richardson's work has also been used by Boulding, and has served as well as a starting point for the book on *Fights, Games and Debates* by Anatol Rapoport, an associate of Boulding's at the Center for Research in Conflict Resolution.[57] In his preface to his own book on statistics, Richardson cited two "motives for writing this book . . . a prejudice that the moral evil in war outweighs the moral good . . . [and] my prejudice that scientific method is more trustworthy than rhetoric." While the two motives could potentially conflict, Wright remarked on "the scrupulous honesty with which [Richardson's] methods have been applied to eliminate bias and prejudice. . . ."

Schelling, as we noted, has followed the behavioral approach in his effort to apply game theory both to the development of military strategy and to the relation of arms control to strategic thinking.[58] It has also been the basis for the research by the psychologist Charles E. Osgood, Director of the Institute of Communications Research at the University of Illinois, in developing a program of "graduated unilateral disengagement."[59] Schelling's work derives from his study of bargaining and negotiation in economic situations. Osgood is clearly seeking to find a policy based somewhere between a complete reliance on deterrence and the unknown risks of unilateral disarmament—thus suggesting a program in which each initial step can be taken unilaterally, awaiting a response from the adversary, so that no one step upsets the strategic balance. Both approaches, quite different in purpose, nevertheless anticipate reaction patterns that are based on behavior in other kinds of social situations. In game theory, the expectation is that behavior will follow the demands of rational self-interest; Osgood's work is based on the thesis that internal behavior is conditioned by external threat. Both approaches nevertheless run into complications when projected into the context of the cold war, since, in the one case, there are a variety of interpretations of "the rules of the game," and, in the other, the practices of propaganda and the absence of any mutual trust make it difficult to distinguish real from imagined threats.

The behavioral sciences are very much in a state of ferment. In 1960, the National Science Foundation undertook major support to the behavioral sciences, and, in 1962, a panel of the President's Science Advisory Committee called for expanded support from government and private sources.[60] The stimulus for the report of the PSAC derived from the recognition both of new contributions to social problems and of new possibilities of investigating behavioral phenomena by scientific methods. The latter include survey and sampling techniques, the use of mathematical models, the availability of high-speed computers, the accumulated data on the study of cultures, and advances in the study of knowledge and how it is acquired. The Committee did not suggest any direct contribution of the behavioral sciences to national security and cautioned that "behavioral scientists have 'no miracle solutions' to problems of international relations." Nevertheless, the relevance seems clear, particularly in relation to organization theory, manpower utilization, communications, and the nature of foreign culture and societies.

The President of the Social Science Research Council noted, in his report for 1960–61, two major trends in the social sciences: One was "the more intensive application of scientific methodology with the expectation that techniques that have led to so great a mastery over physical phenomena may force more obdurate human problems to yield"; and the second, "an increasing concern on the part of social scientists in questions of public policy."[61] Both these trends, as we have seen, have contributed to the intellectual response to the cold war. But the response of the several disciplines has been uneven: In political science, national security affairs is more accepted as a field of specialization than in economics or the behavioral sciences, yet scholars in all of these disciplines have contributed to research in the field. The difference in response, moreover, is related as much to differences in professional development as to different emphases on public policy. It is possible that a pattern of professional development similar to that in economics and sociology will develop in the study of politics, as the behavioral aspects of the discipline strengthen.

All the scholarly professions are basically conservative and resist becoming so involved in the demands of contemporary society that the core and structure of their own disciplines are neglected. This is particularly true of history. Yet the imperatives of our time are also demanding; the contemporary problems of national security affect every aspect of the social order, and the resolution of these problems demands the full application of our intellectual resources. The answers extend beyond the disciplines themselves, beyond the development of methodologies and skills or the application of knowledge to public policy and action. They extend to the broadest obligations of scholarship to society, and to the effort to judge rationally the exceedingly difficult problems our society faces.

4

Scientists, Lawyers, and Businessmen

MILITARY OFFICERS involved in policy-making have at least one advantage over their civilian counterparts: They have been specifically trained for the jobs they do. It is possible, of course, to be critical of military training and education because of their rigidity, narrowness, and emphasis on military force. But military officers rise through a career hierarchy in which advanced education is related to future assignments in a reasonably rational way. In this regard, the federal Civil Service is far behind, and comparatively few political appointees receive the same kind of preparation for their jobs as do military officers.

An increasing professionalization of civilian leadership in national security affairs has come about, however, through changes in the criteria for appointment to high office, strengthening of the public service, and special contracting methods. Nevertheless, many political leaders, who may be considered professional, have been trained in fields quite apart from military affairs, and, while they may become expert in national security affairs through study and experience, their behavior is certain to be conditioned in varying degrees by their primary professional training. This is especially true of scientists who are new to government and politics, and of lawyers and businessmen, the two traditional sources of political leadership in the United States.

Scientists, lawyers, and businessmen all bring distinctive habits and attitudes to their consideration of national security policy. They are shaped by a complex of professional, experiential, and educational factors which are, in turn, influenced by the demands of the professions and by their perceived relationship between the professions and the rest of society. These perspectives have been changing since the end of World War II; the changes influence the approaches that scientists, lawyers, and businessmen take to national security.

Scientists and National Security

The impact of science and technology on the nature of war, international communications, and the timetable of economic growth and development is a dynamic feature in the new problems of national security. Certainly, two of the most revolutionary events of modern times have been the explosion of the first atomic bomb by American scientists in 1945 and the launching of the first artificial earth satellite by Soviet scientists in 1957. Both events underscored the need to bring scientists into government and into close relation with the process of determining national policy.

In the field of national security, the scientist in government, like any other expert, actually operates on three levels. At one, he is the pure technician working on the technology of military systems but unconcerned with their relation to strategic or policy issues. At a second level, he is involved in the operations of a system of which technological components are only one part. At this level, together with military officers, financial and logistics experts, and social scientists he plans and develops strategic programs to support national policy goals. Finally, the scientist serves as a policy adviser to cabinet officers, congressional leaders, and the President himself. Here, his role is most ambiguous. For it is at this level that the distinction between technical advice and opinions on policy is vague, the results of technical studies inconclusive, and final decision made almost always on the basis of partial knowledge projected in terms of both calculated probability and reasonable expectation.

Historically, there has always been a place for the scientist in American government, particularly in public programs devoted to the development of national resources.[1] But, since 1945, scientists have come to play a political role in the determination of national security policy for which they had no previous experience. Immediately after

World War II, they were particularly influential in determining the administration's program for the international control of atomic energy and the "civilianized" character of the Atomic Energy Commission.[2] They were able to influence policy through their expertise and through the prestige they carried over from their wartime accomplishments, and they continued to be influential in the field of atomic energy through their powerful position on the General Advisory Committee of the AEC.

As a group, scientists responded sooner than other civilian professional groups to the new complexities of strategic doctrine. First, they had had to deal with the tactical use of new and improved weapons during the war and had developed methods of systematic analysis that they effectively applied to military operations. This experience brought them into cooperation with the military establishment, where they dealt with the use, as well as the development, of weapons. And second, many scientists had a sense of responsibility, if not of guilt, for the development and use of the atom bomb, even though the ultimate decision to use it had been President Truman's. Out of this sense of responsibility came their desire to tackle problems that were essentially outside their own fields, but which might be responsive to their discipline and training.

Scientists were also among the key protagonists in the debate over the decision to proceed with the hydrogen bomb after the Soviet atomic explosion in 1949—when a major review of American policy was undertaken, in terms of integrating nuclear weapons into strategic plans. The scientists' arguments over the H-bomb involved not only the problem of technical feasibility; the scientific community was also divided over the strategic and security implications of the bomb's production. Many scientists feared that a decision to proceed with the H-bomb would give impetus to a spiraling arms race from which there would be no return. They also believed that American strategy in general was suffering from inflexibility, because of the United States' heavy concentration on high-yield nuclear weapons, and therefore argued for an American response over a wide range of atomic weapons rather than the single "super-bomb."

The need for greater strategic flexibility was also the focus for the "Project Vista" study on the feasibility of low-yield atomic weapons and their tactical use, an investigation carried out in 1951 by scientists and engineers at the California Institute of Technology. Between 1951 and 1953, scientists also participated in three projects—Project East River, Project Lincoln, and the Lincoln Study Groups—that lay the groundwork for the development of a continental defense system to meet the threat posed by new Soviet advances in weapons and delivery systems. In these latter instances, the scientists were particularly intent on insuring that new technical possibilities were taken into account in strategic planning. But they found themselves attacked by Air Force partisans who feared that the high cost of developing warning systems would result in a reduction of the strategic air budget. Under this Air Force attack and within the political process in which these strategic programs were developed, they were also forced to deal with controversial estimates of Soviet capabilities and intentions, and with the politically volatile issue of how to allocate national resources.[3]

Despite their powerful position on the AEC General Advisory Committee, the scientists' political position in government was weak. In some cases, they were brought into the inner councils in the military establishment, and military support was given to basic research as well as to development (particularly in the Office of Naval Research). But scientists had no representation in the State Department and for the most part were buried in the military bureaucracies. Although they operated on the old Research and Development Board and, after 1953, in the Office of the Assistant Secretary of Defense for Research and Development, neither of these bureaus had real authority over the military departments. Until the Reorganization Act of 1958, the Department of Defense itself could neither effectively initiate scientific research nor exercise authority over the services' research programs. Nor was there a role for scientists at the level of the Joint Chiefs of Staff, even though the Rockefeller Committee report of 1953 had recommended that civilian scientists be brought into the Joint Strategic Survey Committee, a group of senior officers that advises the Joint Chiefs on strategic matters.

It was the Soviet Union's launching of an artificial satellite in October, 1957, that precipitated the decision to strengthen the role of scientists in government. In the Defense Department, a Director of Research and Engineering, third in command under the Secretary of Defense and his Deputy, assumed responsibility (under the wide authority given the Secretary in the Reorganization Act of 1958) for the transfer of weapons systems from one service to another and the maintenance of centralized direction of all military research and development. At the same time, an Advanced Research Projects Agency (ARPA) was created under his aegis to undertake basic research projects that had no immediate military application. Primary responsibility for research on outer space and its exploration was vested in the civilian National Aeronautics and Space Administration. In the State Department, an Office of the Science Adviser was established, and scientific attachés were posted to major foreign capitals.[4] Finally, the President appointed his Special Assistant for Science and Technology and raised the Science Advisory Committee in the Office of Defense Mobilization to the rank of a presidential committee directed by the Special Assistant.

These organizational arrangements were more than stopgap measures. While they have already changed and will continue to change under the pressure of political and technological forces, these arrangements have established a pattern that will probably remain for some time to come. Scientists are now strategically placed at both the operating and policy-making levels of government, and their expanded role in national security affairs raises a range of complex intellectual issues.

Political pressures pose risks for all experts who are called to government service. To this extent, the problems of the scientist are not unique. But scientists are experts *par excellence*, because the facts they deal with must ultimately be consistent with the laws of physical nature. That is to say, the sanctions that control the actions of scientists and other experts in government are largely professional. But while social scientists rely on intuition and experience, the standards of natural scientists are based on a very high reliance on empirical proof. It is true that as great a variety of opinion can be found on scientific issues as on political ones, but a scientist's testimony on the technical feasibility of defense against surprise attack compared with, let us say, that of a political expert on developments in the Communist bloc shows three things: There will be less basis on which a non-expert can question the scientist; the spectrum of possible scientific opinions is likely to be narrower than in the case of political analysis; and the testimony of opposing experts can be subjected to more objective evaluation. The scientist in this sense is the most "authoritative" of experts.

But no matter how authoritative they are, scientists run into trouble when they have to make public judgments and choices about future or as yet inconclusive scientific and technological advances. Although they may be duly cautious and insist on qualifying their remarks by pointing out unknown factors, political pressures may nonetheless force them to predict on the basis of incomplete technical data or to discuss issues that do not really turn on scientific or technological matters. More important perhaps, scientific knowledge is, at best, only tentative, the next step in a continually unfolding continuum.

Scientific investigation continues, and new developments can easily upset or make obsolete the basis of an original decision.

Politicians, diplomats, and scholars are accustomed to the rigors of reassessing original theories in the light of changing conditions or new information. And, indeed, so are scientists. They check and double-check hypotheses every day in their laboratories, where the elements of chance, intuition, and accident play an important part. In the words of Albert Einstein, "There is no logical way to the discovery of . . . elemental laws. There is only the way of intuition, which is helped by a feeling for the order lying behind the appearance."[5] But this is not to say that scientists rely on intuition alone. On the contrary, the scientist is ultimately tied to the discipline of empirical proof, and without it, the decisions he reaches are either not conclusive or not scientific.[6]

Scientists themselves have recognized their special problems in government service. They have expressed their fear that "the integrity of science is beginning to erode under the abrasive pressure of close partnership with economic, social and political affairs."[7] Some have refused to participate in defense projects.[8] Others have urged their fellow scientists to support active lobbying and information programs to influence public policy as the only way to protect their own interests and standards.[9] On the other hand, many scientists have sought to separate scientific from nonscientific considerations in the formation of policy and to restrict their participation to the former.[10] But this separation is artificial. Not only is the fragmentation of a problem in policy unrealistic in the final analysis, but like other specialists, the scientist has been drawn into the process of determining policy as issues have become more complex and as decisions have come to depend more and more on systematic analysis and substantive knowledge.

The approach of many scientists to national security policy is influenced by their contributions to military strategy and operations. Scientists had begun to devise operational programs for the improved and more efficient use of weapons during World War II and had played an important role then in the development of tactics and strategy. In working out these programs, scientists used methods of quantitative analysis that substituted logic and mathematics for the traditional rules and responses of military command. Much of this effort was pioneered by the British in connection with antiaircraft and antisubmarine warfare.[11]

Weapons development and operations research were both major objectives of the armed services when they established or sponsored scientific research groups immediately after the war.[12] In the early stages, the groups were geared primarily to respond to questions put to them by the military services about such problems as the tactical implications of new weapons or the feasibility of designing new weapons to meet a changing combat environment. Then, the research groups expanded in two ways. First, political, psychological, and social considerations became increasingly important in devising strategic programs. The services often looked to their civilian colleagues in the research agencies to bring these factors into the analysis and to supply the expertise they themselves did not have. Secondly, the scientists often questioned the way a problem was presented to them. Military requests, as noted, were usually very precise and tied to a particular problem for which a specific technological or operational solution was wanted. The scientists, on the other hand, sought a broader mandate. Their very method of analysis forced them to examine the circumstances out of which the problem had developed, in order to determine whether the most efficient solution could be found within the limited context of the problem itself or in prior conditions. Of all the research groups, the RAND Corporation developed along the broadest lines. RAND not only worked out a relationship with the Air Force that provided increasing opportunities for broadly conceived studies, but it also encouraged its staff to engage in research oriented to military affairs and based, not on a request made by a service, but on their own professional evaluation of national security requirements.[13]

Scientists' work on problems of military operations has often brought them into disagreement with the military. However closely he may be related to a particular service, the civilian scientist does not operate with the same devotion to service mission and traditions as his military colleagues do. His conclusions may thus be contrary to accepted service doctrine and may even provide the grounds on which a higher civilian authority will overrule service judgment. Indeed, the establishment of increasingly strong scientific groups for weapons evaluation in the Defense Department has been a major reason for the increasing civilian authority over the military departments. At the same time, the civilian scientist has to "sell" new ideas to the military services in a field where the latter continue to be major managers and operators. This also becomes a point of tension, especially when scientists emphasize nonmilitary means, such as international control systems. Just as the military are committed to a prescribed service mission, scientists may become wedded to a particular weapons system. But, just as often, the civilian scientist may be motivated by the larger purpose of maintaining a stable strategic balance, and have no overriding professional preference for any one means to do so.

Whatever tensions exist between military officers and civilian scientists, they are both devoted to the maintenance of maximum military efficiency. This objective has, in many ways, split the scientists oriented to military affairs from those who give a lower priority to military means in the development of international stability and whose primary focus is on the creation of a new world order. Inevitably, this split involves more than an appraisal of what science can do. It involves the scientists' beliefs in what the role of science in society is and their interpretations of the contemporary international situation.

Scientists, no more than other professional groups, do not fall into precise categories. Some, like Linus Pauling, advocate radical policies of unilateral disarmament, based on a passionate conviction that an enlargement of military preparedness will result in armed conflict in which thermonuclear weapons will inevitably be used. They accept neither the premise that a policy of deterrence can be effective nor the theory that wars can be limited. Other scientists, however, give greater weight to the difficulties of understanding the intentions of Communist leaders and acknowledge the dangers of weakening the military guard of the Western Alliance. They are nonetheless concerned about the risks of war, and many deeply believe in using both the authority and the method of science to reduce tensions and develop a more stable international system than they believe a policy of deterrence can achieve.

The editorial policy of the *Bulletin of the Atomic Scientists* reflects a viewpoint shared by many scientists, which contrasts with that of scientists closely related to the military services.[14] They assume that it is possible to use the same systematic approach to political and social problems that the scientist ideally uses in approaching scientific problems, and they seek to promote an openness of spirit and a dedication to knowledge and human values that transcends narrowly defined national interests. Their premise is that the contemporary revolution in science and technology has in fact created the pressures to achieve such a fundamental change in the international community. For one thing, the very destructiveness of modern weapons has constrained major nations from using force except under the most extreme conditions. For another, advances in science and technology have necessitated a high degree of international cooperation in such fields as space exploration and nuclear research—a degree of cooperation all the more remarkable in the light of tense political antagonisms. Finally, the application of technology to the needs of new nations has advanced the timetable of development, hastening the building up of new nations and changing the existing power configuration.

The policy recommendations that stem from such an analysis seem clear: to maintain the *status quo* in existing areas of tension, to insulate new areas of instability, and to bring new energy and imagination to those programs that will change the international system and thus the basic relations among the major powers.[15] This approach is evolutionary rather than radical. It is, in fact, more evolutionary than it would have been just after World War II, when many scientists assumed that changes in the Soviet Union and in the intentions of Communist leaders could be achieved more directly. This viewpoint has changed primarily because of continual frustrations in dealing with the Soviet Union on problems of disarmament and arms control. There is, nevertheless, a conviction that direct communications between the Soviet Union and the West must be continued, both to avoid catastrophic miscalculations of the other's intentions and to emphasize that changes in the world situation are important for the Soviet Union as well as for the West.

Scientists have thus been in the forefront of programs of cultural and technical exchange. Most significant have been the Conferences on Science and World Affairs, the so-called "Pugwash" meetings, which have been held regularly since 1957.[16] The meetings were begun after Bertrand Russell's appeal in 1955 for greater cooperation among scientists. Their popular name comes from the locus of the first conference—the home of the American industrialist, Cyrus Eaton, near Pugwash, Nova Scotia—though in recent years the meetings have been held in Austria, the Soviet Union, the United States, and Great Britain. American participants in the Pugwash conferences have always emphasized the nonpolitical, private nature of the meetings, although American observers with official government connections have on occasion attended.[17] The participating Soviet scientists have, of course, had close official relations with their government.

The accomplishments of the Pugwash meetings are difficult to measure. It is particularly difficult to know what influence the Soviet scientists have in the formation of their government's policy or to what extent they are free to express their views on important issues. Certainly, the repeated statements issued from the conferences calling for a halt to the arms race have had little perceptible impact on the policy of either the United States or the Soviet Union, and it would be difficult to relate the recommendations of the conferences to the nuclear test ban treaty. The meetings may, on occasion, have given the Americans new insights into the forces at work in the Soviet

Union, but here, too, interpretations of what the Soviet participants meant have varied. For example, after the meeting of November, 1960, in Moscow, the American physicist Jay Orear remarked that he was encouraged by the impression that "these Soviet scientists, who are the highest ranking in their country, sincerely want disarmament and would now agree to any reasonable kind of inspection . . . as long as the inspection is associated with an explicit program leading to complete disarmament." On the other hand, Thomas Schelling stated that, "My own impression of the conference was different. . . . There was no evidence that the Soviets had given serious thought to the problems raised by their own disarmament proposals."[18]

The differences among scientists were dramatically exposed with the publication of Herman Kahn's *On Thermonuclear War*, in 1960. Kahn's book was an outgrowth of his work at RAND on deterrent systems and civil defense. Accepting the impossibility of establishing in the foreseeable future any kind of a world government that could control nuclear weapons, Kahn argued that a nuclear war was a possibility that could not be ignored. Projecting present technological and political trends into the future he made specific recommendations for a maximum system of deterrents, and argued that this method was the only way of stabilizing the strategic balance as it appeared under present circumstances. His recommendations concerned principally a mobile and invulnerable striking force and a major civil-defense program, the latter being both part of the deterrent system and a practical precaution.

Kahn was attacked on several grounds. First, in his description of what future wars might be like, he clearly disturbed certain persons, who portrayed his willingness to discuss clinically the catastrophic consequences of thermonuclear war as almost inhuman. Second, his calculations of the relative effectiveness of civil-defense measures were disputed, and he was accused of creating a deceptive illusion of safety under conditions of nuclear warfare. Finally, Kahn's agenda for action, it was asserted, would so embitter the international atmosphere that it would be impossible to find any opportunity for nonmilitary cooperation, let alone for a continuance of the efforts, however slow and halting, for some kind of limited arms-control agreement.[19]

The first charge against Kahn was irresponsible in that it attacked Kahn while failing to deal with his argument; the second was clearly a genuine and debatable point; and the third rested on a certain order of priority in national-security measures—how much risk should we take to maintain the opportunity for possible accommodation? The controversy was raised to an hysterical level, and his critics forgot

Kahn's own limited goal "of anticipating, avoiding, and alleviating crises." Kahn himself at this point acknowledged the danger of dealing with the material as he had, remarking that "any book that treats deterrence objectively may encourage the Soviets toward experiment." The truth is that deterrence is, among other things, a psychological phenomenon, and any system of international relations will be complicated by the enigmas of human behavior. In response some scientists have insisted that if only a more vigorous methodology were applied, human behavior could become as predictable as natural phenomena. Some have even called for a "science of human survival" to mobilize "the power of science to illuminate the self-destructive nature of modern war and to discover new social inventions to replace it."[20] Most scientists, while acknowledging the limits and complications of studying human behavior, encourage the behavioral sciences to seek to develop systems of quantification and model-building in the study of politics and society.

The division among scientists has been no less seriously joined by the intellectual division between scientist and nonscientist. This division has also been emphasized by the crises in national security affairs since 1945. There has been concern about the scientists' political naïveté, considering that they may occupy a position of political influence in the government, and about the scientific illiteracy of political leaders and the general public, considering that science depends on public support and a favorable cultural climate of understanding. There has also been concern about the inability of scientists and nonscientists to communicate meaningfully about the issues of national security at the policy-making level and in private debate. Out of these concerns has evolved a series of moves to broaden the educational base of scientists and to educate the nonscientist in science.

The split between science and a liberal-arts education has been recognized for some years. Hiroshima and Sputnik I did not create the problem: They dramatized its existence. As the understanding of scientific phenomena has increased and the rate of discovery become more rapid, science has become more and more specialized. At the same time, scientific training has become longer and more concentrated. Basic science courses are now mere stepping stones in the training of scientists and engineers. In the process of this development, the scientific component of a liberal education has been neglected by the scientists themselves. Conversely, scholars and professional men in other fields have had neither the time nor the inclination to educate themselves beyond the most elementary stages in the basic principles of modern science. They, too, have had to cope with the problems of specialization in their own fields.

Educational programs designed to close the intellectual gap between the scientist and nonscientist have taken several forms: imaginative, experimental college courses in science for the future nonscientist; programs in the humanities and the social sciences designed for schools of science and technology; and an increased emphasis on the history of science, both in order to teach science and to deal with science as a part of intellectual history. In addition, there have been advanced research and teaching programs directly related to the scientific and technological dimensions of public policy, which have been motivated and shaped largely by developments in national security affairs. These programs include the Council for Atomic Age Studies at Columbia University, the Science and Public Policy seminar at Harvard, and a doctoral program in political science at the Massachusetts Institute of Technology.[21]

The interrelation of science and society—in its broadest context as well as in the field of national security affairs—is also reflected in an increasing variety of programs sponsored by professional organizations. In 1960, the American Association for the Advancement of Science abandoned its traditional "no politics" position by undertaking a series of projects involving the relation of science to politics.[22] The Association, for example, held a series of dinner meetings at which scientists and members of Congress were invited to discuss the problems of science and public policy, and it has included in its annual meeting a number of joint sessions with the American Political Science, Sociological, and Economic Associations. The *Bulletin of the Atomic Scientists* also continues to perform an invaluable service as a magazine of "science and public affairs." Among social scientists, the President of the Social Science Research Council, Pendleton Herring, has called for more attention "to science as a social phenomenon."[23] There are also the beginnings of a specialized literature in the field, in addition to a wide range of books on the history of science, now more and more available in inexpensive editions.[24]

The study of the relation between science and public policy seems likely to expand as a separate focus of attention as well as in relation to national security affairs. It was nevertheless the issues of national security that brought it to the fore as a subject of intellectual concern. For the problems of national defense have thrust the scientist into public life, as an expert and as a citizen. As a citizen, the scientist has much to offer as a highly intelligent, informed, and concerned individual. As an expert, he has much to offer in his ability to apply disciplined methods of thinking to problems of war and peace. Still, the question remains of how exactly science and the scientific method relate to the basic dilemmas of national security. The uniqueness of each historical act limits the validity of generalizations and often defies the demands of empirical testing. Moreover, the values that affect one's approach to the problem rest on another plane entirely. It is true that we have hardly stretched the limits of scientific methodology in learning about social and individual behavior; indeed, the search has only begun. But there are many issues that still must be understood and met through intuitive insight and wise experience—by scientists and by others as well.

The Education of Lawyers and Businessmen

The entry of scholars and scientists into a policy role in national security affairs marks a shift in leadership away from the traditional monopoly held by lawyers and businessmen to a more broadly based group of statesmen, scholars, scientists, and public servants whose interest in national security is a primary concern of their professional lives. The shift is, in essence, an enlargement in the base of leadership, not a displacement of one group by another. Lawyers and businessmen also participate in the new civilian expertise in military affairs, but they usually come from a special sector of their own professions. Generally speaking, they are members of large New York, Washington, or Chicago law, investment, or banking firms, or are men who have climbed to important positions in complex commercial and industrial organizations. Very likely, their firms and companies have important connections with government agencies and in international operations, and they themselves have become interested in national security affairs as a result of these activities.

But members of the practical professions of law and business also become involved in national security affairs in other roles than that of "expert." Their social and financial position makes them leaders in their communities, and their professional interests often make it important for them to engage in local and state politics. These activities lead in many directions—to elective office at the local, state, or national level, to a high appointive post in a political party, to nomination to a citizens' advisory board, or to an influential role in an organized pressure group. Law and business are still the main stepping-stones to the Congress, state legislatures, local political groups, and national organizations representing important domestic interests.[25] These institutions are bases of considerable power in American politics, but they are different bases than the research laboratories, study groups, and special task forces from which the new civilian expert operates. The lawyers and businessmen who operate from the traditional bases of political life are more likely to emphasize the internal problems of the country than the external, more apt to rely on intuition and practical experience than on empirical analysis and conceptualization, and more likely to reduce problems to the level of known realities than to dwell on uncommon complexities. In these respects, they differ in perspective and approach from the expert.

The role of the lawyer and the businessman in society is an old theme in professional education. As the values and needs of our society have been affected by international and defense affairs, so the professions have responded by developing educational programs designed to broaden the exposure of lawyers and businessmen to these problems. Legal education, for example, is being brought into closer relation to the social sciences and coming to include serious work in economics, politics, and sociology. This trend reflects not only a broad concept of the function of law in society, but also special recognition of the traditional role of the lawyer as a public servant. But the response of law schools is uneven and programs in "nontechnical" fields often conflict in the increasing demands on student time with ever-growing areas of legal interest.[26]

The role of the businessman in society is treated at two ends of the educational process. At one end, the bachelor's degree in business administration, with the requirement of a high percentage of vocational courses, is being discouraged. It is giving way slowly to a broad graduate program of one or two years, based on three or four years of liberal-arts or engineering education. Business recruiters increasingly move away from those students with a narrow orientation around cost accounting and office management to those with a broad view of administrative method and liberal education. At the same time, the importance of technology in industrial development makes the combination of engineering and business education an attractive package.

At the other end of the educational process, there has been a proliferation of programs for business executives in mid-career. Many of these are geared to the study of advanced management techniques, but others devote some, or even most, of the course to instruction in the humanities and social sciences. These courses are designed to confront executives with the changing environment of their own profession, and they often cover problems of international economics and politics and their relation to complex military and social issues.[27] They are important not only because of their content but also because

the students are at an age when they might make an important contribution to public service. The concept of service is nevertheless an
issue over which there are great differences of opinion, and these
differences are reflected both in the business community and the legal
profession.

The objectives of legal education are to train lawyers, to improve
the law, and to provide public leaders at all levels of authority. All
law schools readily accept the first two of these objectives. Some
question the third. The problem of training public leaders is so difficult to come to grips with that it could dissipate the law schools'
limited resources and energies. There is no way of knowing which
student is a future public leader, nor is it possible to cover all the
issues that political leaders will deal with a generation hence. Moreover, the objective of providing public leaders is often subsumed in
the general objective of training lawyers. In almost all law schools,
there is a working assumption that most of their graduates will become public leaders by the nature of their calling. It is therefore
thought sufficient to train lawyers and unnecessary to embark on ill-
conceived and ill-defined public-service programs. Indeed, it is fully
accepted (though not always with grace) that many students study
law because it is a stepping-stone to leadership in business or government.

Legal education deals with two elements: with the law itself and
with the development of skills. Both these aims are pursued through
the "case method," a system of study in which the student is presented with the facts of a specific case and is forced to sort out the
relevant from the irrelevant, determine the principles of law that
apply, and come to a decision on how he would advise a client to
argue a position. In dealing with a wide variety of cases, the student
is exposed to data of different kinds—medical, political, psychological,
economic. If he is well trained, he develops an ability to handle a wide
range of information with relative ease and to make up his mind in a
systematic way. Throughout this process, his guide is the law—a
system of rights and duties designed to resolve conflict in human relations.

Stated in abstract terms, this system of professional education
would seem to be excellent training for a future policy-maker in national security affairs. National security policy involves both a great
number of factors and the problem of conflict. But policy-making also
means relating these factors to an over-all strategy and projecting
them into a future situation, even transforming their very elements.
Under such conditions, a tendency to "settle the case" under generally

equitable terms is not always possible or desirable. "Settlement" of the immediate problem is not so important as the relation of the problem to the changing international environment and to an abstract system of world order that corresponds to one's ultimate goals. This is a less tangible guide than "the law," however flexible and adaptable that may be. The skills of the lawyer can be profitably fitted to the issues of public policy, but there must be recognition of their limitations when there is little knowledge or sense of perspective on the material at hand. Knowledge and perspective can develop with greater training in the social sciences. But the three years of law school are short for all that must be accomplished. If a student has not had a substantial grounding in the social sciences during his undergraduate years, he may miss this connection between legal techniques and the substance of social problems.[28]

A number of law schools have developed programs in the social sciences in order to meet this deficiency. Most of these are the so-called "national" law schools whose students come from all over the country, and are likely to enter law firms in the large centers of governmental and industrial activity. At one of these, the University of Chicago, the infusion of the social sciences into the curriculum began in the mid-1930's, when the Law School assumed the task of preparation for the public service as a major objective of legal education. While the early emphasis at Chicago was in economics, a program in law and the behavioral sciences was more recently inaugurated.[29]

Yale Law School also introduced the social sciences into the law curriculum in the mid-1930's. The results were noticeable by 1951, when a curriculum committee recorded that critics of the Law School had objected that a disproportionately large number of its courses were concerned primarily with "economics, sociology, government, and philosophy" rather than with the "fundamentals of the common law." But the committee found the balance to be a healthy one and the courses oriented to the social sciences to be justified on the grounds that they gave students the full intellectual exposure they need to perform their function as lawyers in modern society, and the broad intellectual base they need for entry into other fields—such as teaching, business, and government, and public service in general.[30]

The time factor is often a problem in adding social-science material to an expanding professional curriculum. An alternative available at several major law schools is to offer a four-year graduate program in law and one other area in philosophy or the social sciences. At Yale, this program "is intended for those who plan to become law teachers, or who wish to acquire the specialized skills of some body of knowledge related to law as preparation for certain branches of law practice, or for other careers." Of the four years, the student spends the first and last at the Law School, divides the second and third between the Law School and his graduate department, and, on completion, receives a Master of Arts as well as Bachelor of Laws degree.[31] At the Columbia Law School, four-year programs can be arranged with either the School of International Affairs or the Graduate School of Business, while law students may also participate in the International Fellows Program, which permits graduate students to acquire a knowledge of world affairs while pursuing their special field of study.[32]

But these programs, particularly those that include international studies, are not typical. Both the Yale and Columbia law schools profit from their place in universities with a strong international flavor, from faculties continually engaged in government research and diplomatic activities, and from geographic locations that put them close to the center of international political and financial operations. These are exceptional assets. The study of international law in most law schools in the United States is considerably different, as is evident in the results of a survey made in 1960 by the Special Committee on World Peace Through Law of the American Bar Association. Of a total of 124 law schools, 49 had no courses at all in international law and related subjects, 37 had one course, 14 two, and 24 had three or more. The survey indicated "that a large number of law schools have added their first course or expanded their offerings in this area during the last year." This marks some progress, but where one or two courses in international law are offered, they are not usually part of the required program, but one of a number of elective courses attracting only a few students. Among the reasons for neglecting the study of international law, according to the ABA survey, are lack of funds, lack of student interest, and a "tendency to concentrate on the 'bread and butter' courses to assure adequate preparation for the bar examination and for domestic practice."[33]

These figures indicate the high degree of parochialism in all but a few law schools in the country. And this lack of exposure to international issues during the course of their legal training may very well have an effect on the approach lawyers take to problems of foreign and military policy. The Ford Foundation sought to stimulate the development of international studies in law schools by a series of grants in the 1950's.[34] While the grants were offered to major institutions, the objective was obviously to spur a general movement through example, the dissemination of literature, and the preparation of teachers.

The Harvard Law School program of International Legal Studies is an important example of the kind of program the Ford Foundation grants sought to stimulate. It is conceived and carried out "as an organic part of the normal course of teaching and research," on the grounds that the world position of the United States affects not only "the policies and conduct of our government, and the questions of war and peace, but also the daily processes of American industry, agriculture, trade and finance."[35] The director of the program, Milton Katz, also emphasized this plurality of purpose. A former chief of a Marshall Plan mission in Europe, Katz explained that "when the law students of today reach their maximum level of professional opportunity, whether in law practice, government, or teaching and scholarship, [international] problems may be expected to constitute a significant part of their active daily concerns."[36]

Other attempts have been made to stimulate a broad law-school curriculum encompassing materials in international affairs. At the World Rule of Law Center established at the Duke University Law School in 1958, the director, Arthur Larson, developed a program that tries to improve the teaching of international law by preparing and publishing new textual and source material. In contrast to traditional international law, Larson's concept of "world law" stresses the maintenance of peace, uses other legal systems besides those of the Western world, and provides for continual development in response to such international problems as the exploration of space, the control of atomic energy, and international propaganda. An active program was also launched through the American Bar Association's Special Committee on World Peace Through Law, headed by Charles Rhyne, a Washington lawyer and former Bar Association president. The committee held a series of regional conferences throughout the country in 1959, established contact with local bar associations, assigned tasks to lawyers and law students throughout the country in preparation for international conferences, helped to form a counterpart committee in the American Law Student Committee, and carried out the aforementioned survey of the teaching of international law. By February, 1960, it reported that its efforts had encouraged law schools to expand their international legal studies.[37] Although results of this kind are difficult to measure, the committee is clearly in a position, particularly through the bar associations, to influence those smaller law schools that, out of necessity, are still wedded to the "bread and butter" approach.

The slow pace with which most law schools have responded to the problems of a changing world has not gone unnoticed by members of the profession. Many years ago, the profession was admonished by one of its most distinguished members, himself an eminent public servant, Elihu Root: "Unconsciously, we all treat the business of administering justice as something to be done for private benefit instead of treating it primarily as something to be done for the public service."[38] More recently, the Dean of the Harvard Law School, Erwin Griswold, translated this same problem into contemporary terms: "Even in the international field, where our activities have broadened so extensively in recent years, the . . . tendency toward commercial areas is evident. . . . We have not yet sufficiently oriented ourselves when dealing with the laws of other countries to approach them in terms of helping the people of those countries rather than from the point of view of Americans who may want to be doing business there."[39]

This conflict between private and public interest is also evident in the way businessmen approach the issues of defense and diplomacy. When Charles Wilson, Chairman of the Board of General Motors, testified at the Senate hearings for his confirmation as Secretary of Defense in 1953, he discounted any conflict of interest on his part by making the now-famous statement, "For years I thought what was good for the country was good for General Motors and vice versa." In one sense, Wilson expressed the conviction of most American businessmen (and labor leaders) that the honest pursuit of personal interests cannot fail to be in the public interest, a conviction based on the valid assumption that a strong economy will insure continuing and profitable development for industry and thus a solid base for government programs. Wilson was also recognizing the close relation of private and public enterprises. But he also expressed the continued priority that American businessmen (and labor leaders) give to private interests. This priority is understandable, but one nonetheless should take into account the complex relation of private to public interests.

The relation of government to business has been in a constant state of change and is taking new forms under the pressures of economic, scientific, and political developments. Until recently, government was both regulator and umpire among competing economic interests. The role of regulator was first established in relation to entrepreneurial interests with the establishment of federal regulatory commissions, with antitrust legislation, the establishment of federal food and drug standards. It was expanded during the New Deal, when labor became an independent force in national economic life and when the government interposed itself as umpire between labor and management. But interpretations of the federal government's role continued to focus on private interests, with the public interest being conceived largely as a check on private excesses rather than as a positive factor in the relationship.

The changing relation between government and business is due in large part to the indispensable role of government in the development of new international economic arrangements and in the research on and development of scientific, technological advances. Government laboratories for years have played an important part in agricultural advancement and in the field of conservation. In many ways, the federal and state governments have also helped to build transportation systems and train skilled manpower. But none of these compares to the government's influence in developing atomic energy, aeronautical and space technology, and the many areas of application that branch out from these basic advances.[40]

To some extent, government involvement in the development of new areas of technology is necessitated by the huge initial investment and the high order of risk involved. But the stronger motive, by far, is the close connection between technological advances and the requirements of national security. Not only are developments in atomic energy and space technology crucial to military strength, but they are also symbols of power and competence. The early Soviet exploits in the space race were of critical importance in shifting the world strategic balance. They indicated more than a mere new technical ability on the part of the Russians and a new vulnerability on the part of the United States. They also broke the illusion of American technological and industrial pre-eminence and demonstrated the ability of a Communist society to apply resources and skills to industrial objectives with amazing results. This ability is of prime importance to the leaders of the new nations, who are preoccupied with the application of modern technology to the development of their countries in as short a time as possible and under revolutionary political conditions.

In the light of these considerations, it was deemed impossible to leave the exploitation of atomic energy and space technology to the laws of supply and demand of a market system. Some objectives can be gained through a system of tax laws and subsidies designed to offer incentives for investment in areas of public interest. But the stakes are too great to depend on speculative results, and the positive involvement of the government in the development and exploitation of national resources has become a virtual necessity. The techniques vary, and include the use of tax laws and licensing authority, the operation of government-owned laboratories and other research facilities, and the contracting of programs of research and development to private institutions. In one way or another, all these methods contribute to a system of interdependence between government and industry that is primarily based on the furtherance of the public interest rather than the pursuit of private gain.

But it is not just the requirements of national security that change the relation between government and business. New sources of power and new probes into outer space are creating a need for regulatory authorities at an international level. American proposals on disarmament and arms control since 1946 have been tied to the development of a system of inspection that would subject certain national industries to international regulation. The full development of space communications will have to be related to the complex issue of national air and space rights, and an international law of space will need to be developed. As leader of the free world, the United States has been forced into economic arrangements that subordinate certain domestic interests to the needs of world economic growth and stabilization. Thus far, the Congress has refused to authorize American membership in any international organization with authority to regulate domestic trade practices. Nevertheless, American involvement in the General Agreement on Trade and Tariffs, in basic commodity agreements that seek to protect "one-commodity" countries from a "feast or famine" cycle, and in efforts to stimulate regional common-market systems implies at least partial acceptance of institutions that are primarily concerned with the conditions of the world economy. The immediate application of these developments may be exercised through the national government, but this in no way disguises the fact that the origin of the authority lies at an international level and has roots in a broad sense of public interest.

American industry is thus on the threshold of a new phase of development, and the environment in which businessmen operate is changing fundamentally. This change relates to many of the immediate problems of national security and the nature of the future world order. In many ways, American business has begun to respond to this changing environment. Industry has contributed greatly, on its own initiative, to the "research revolution."[41] It has also developed new techniques of administration and management, often based on the use of highly advanced computers and designed to synchronize the operations of unusually large and complex systems. These new techniques have imposed new requirements in the education of executives. They have put a priority on scientific and engineering talent and on advanced knowledge of the "science of management." At the same time, an important segment of the business community has started to develop a new sense of perspective on its role in society. This is evident in the work of a group like the Committee for Economic Development, which is devoted to economic research "from the standpoint of general welfare and not from that of any special political or economic group."[42] It is also evident in the increasing tendency to relate executive advancement to liberal learning.

Recent improvements in business education have developed in several directions: in the strengthening of business education in relation to the liberal arts; in increasing the opportunities for a business education within an engineering context; and in the development of rigorous programs in management theory. These improvements are particularly evident in graduate education in business administration which has also been strengthened by the development of research programs. Several research programs have included national security projects—such as a study of weapons acquisition at the Harvard School of Business Administration, and a study of the "Strategy, Organization and Economics of Research and Development" at the University of California School of Business Administration at Berkeley.[43] These trends, taken together, have several advantages: They place business within its broadest social context and expose students to courses in the humanities and the natural and social sciences; they give a business-administration program unity in terms of either liberal education or management theory; they emphasize educational programs for full career development rather than preparation for one's first job; and they relate business education to the technology that is the key to changing industrial patterns. These advances have been made largely in response to the changing nature of business organizations under the impact of specialization, the separation between ownership and management, the rapidity of technological innovation, and also the changing environment within which businessmen operate.[44]

Unlike law schools, business schools make no assumptions about the leadership potential of their students and no great effort to tailor the curriculum as a preparation for public life. Such efforts are almost wholly restricted to the major graduate schools that try to attract and produce potential top executives. But the career pattern of business executives is such that they do not begin to emerge as community leaders until they have reached high levels of executive responsibility, in contrast to lawyers who, by the nature of their profession, become involved at an early age in matters of public policy.

Business leaders have now recognized the pattern of advancement in their careers and the advantages of a system of continuing education that coincides with this pattern. Indeed, the continuing education of businessmen contrasts sharply with that of lawyers. Executive-management programs, varying from company-run courses in advanced management to academic courses in the humanities and the social sciences, are far more imaginative than the continuing programs of legal education, more theoretical, and more concerned with the development of the individual's potential and with his future role in his company and in society. It is in these more broadly based academic programs that business executives are exposed to the complex issues of national security. Their preparation for the courses varies since some will not have been concerned with national or international problems; others will have had close contact with defense programs in their positions in the aircraft, electronics, or automotive industries; still others may, as well-informed citizens, be concerned about national security affairs.

One pioneering effort in mid-career education is the Sloan Fellowship Program in executive development at the M.I.T. School of Industrial Management. Initiated in 1931, the program runs a full year, leads to a Master of Arts degree, and includes courses in American foreign policy and international trade, as well as the major ones on administration and management.[45] M.I.T. also conducts a ten-week senior executive program. The Bell Telephone System carries out a series of programs, including one of ten months at the University of Pennsylvania, and eight-week summer courses at Dartmouth, Williams, and Northwestern. The Stanford University Graduate School of Business has also established a nine-month program for Business Executive Fellows with the aid of a grant from the Sloan Foundation, as well as a Ph.D. program for six Sloan Fellows. The Harvard Business School has an eight-month middle management program and a thirteen-week advanced management program. Others are conducted at Pittsburgh, Northwestern, Indiana, Columbia, Cornell, Carnegie Institute of Technology, Case Institute, Michigan State, and Chicago.[46] In one way or another, these programs seek to help future business leaders work out new management theories required by increasingly complex industrial problems and understand the changing environment of American business. Sometimes one, sometimes the other aim is emphasized. The Stanford programs, for example, concentrate on research and the development of managerial techniques.

The Bell programs, on the other hand, are based on the thesis that an understanding of the interdependent world within which business operates could be best gained through a broad program of liberal education.

This new kind of business education, at both the graduate and executive levels, reflects in many ways the attitude and perspective of the civilian expert in national security affairs. The professionalization of management involves the application of rigorous analytic techniques to problem-solving and substitutes a systematic process of data collection and evaluation for hunch and instinct. It also involves an attempt to unify the diverse parts of modern business operations. At the same time, increased recognition of the changing relation of business to society might eventually change the American businessman's concept of service. Businessmen are apt to emphasize the personal hardships they endure in agreeing to serve in a public capacity —the cut in salary, the loss of company benefits, the risks of poor publicity—and they are likely to think they have cleansed themselves of possible conflicts of interest by the mere sale of stocks and rights and by their resignation from policy positions in private companies.[47] But these are superficial actions. They do not really change attitudes or habits of mind, for all the good intentions they indicate. A true concept of public service is difficult to develop. Yet, it might someday evolve within the business community out of the increased exposure of businessmen to problems of world affairs and to analyses of the interlocking nature of public and private interests. There are encouraging signs that these concepts are already considered in programs of advanced academic preparation for business careers.

It is not unwarranted to compare the process of political preparation of leadership groups in the United States to the processes in other countries. The American process is less rational than the British or Russian, for example. In Britain, a long and rigorous apprenticeship in the political party system and in the government ministries usually precedes important responsibility. In the Soviet Union, the preparation is even more arduous, given the tight and closed nature of the Communist Party hierarchy. Although political leadership is increasingly professionalized in the United States, the loose party structure, the popular distrust of politicians and bureaucrats, and the demands to reduce complex issues to recognizable terms tend to produce a more open system, in which relative amateurs are assigned to positions of responsibility. For this reason, the education and training in those professions from which political leaders are drawn is of critical importance, especially in national security affairs.

5

The Education of the Public

THE PROBLEMS of national security are volatile subjects for public debate. Few issues, for example, have provoked so spirited a discussion at every level of American society as civil defense. Soviet achievements in weaponry and delivery systems in the late 1950's gave notice of the United States' vulnerability to attack and brought the question of civil defense into every American home. The Soviet Union's ICBM capability, moreover, came at a time when civilian analysts like Herman Kahn and Bernard Brodie of RAND were beginning to emphasize the relation between civil defense and a strategy of deterrence. It was necessary, they said, in order to insure continuous political and economic activity after attack, not only to protect U.S. strategic military bases in the United States but to provide shelter for the civilian population. They also argued that an unprotected public was a source of weakness in political negotiations with the Soviet Union, since American leaders would be under pressure to seek accommodation for fear of provoking open conflict; a defenseless public would be a kind of hostage in exchange for which the Soviet Union could demand otherwise unacceptable concessions.[1]

The public debate was, unfortunately, confused by government policy. Civil defense was, and remains, a highly expensive program, and it always had low priority because of the precedence of "active" military requirements while pressure existed for reduced expenditures. Questions were also raised about the kind of civil defense that could be developed. Defense against direct blast and against heat was considered virtually impossible. Nothing less than a complete underground community would suffice for this purpose, and such a plan raised problems of time and psychological adjustment, as well as of expense. Nevertheless, by the late 1950's, a consensus had developed in government circles that protection against radioactive fallout could be achieved through various precautionary measures and shelter arrangements. The full measure of protection possible was, however, a matter for continual disagreement among scientists and laymen. And the disagreement was exacerbated by the Eisenhower Administration policy that provision for a fallout shelter was a personal responsibility, and that the government's role was largely limited to coordination and information.[2] There was thus little guidance for the individual citizen in deciding what to do.

The debate was renewed during late 1961, when President Kennedy, under the tensions of the Berlin crisis, gave a new sense of urgency to the shelter program. He transferred major responsibility for it from the Office of Civil and Defense Mobilization to the Department of Defense and ordered that a full review be made of the federal government's responsibilities and that full information on the nuclear-fallout question be made available to the public. By December, both orders had been carried out. A pamphlet on *Fallout Protection: What To Know and Do About Nuclear Attack* was available to the public at all post offices, and the Pentagon issued a new policy statement emphasizing community rather than individual responsibility for shelters and including provisions for a survey of national shelter facilities, the identification and marking of available shelter space, the preparation and dissemination of shelter plans, the modification of federal buildings to provide shelter space, and a program of federal grants to provide incentives to construct shelters in schools, hospitals, and welfare institutions.[3]

The Administration's shelter proposals, though they included a larger role for the federal government, nonetheless left much of the initiative to local communities. Indeed, Kennedy's more positive approach posed the problems of civil defense more pointedly than ever before. Communities were faced, in practical terms, with the full range of issues that had been studied for several years by experts in national security affairs. How much protection would a shelter program afford? What is the probability of thermonuclear war? Could the costs of a shelter program be used better in alternative programs designed both to deter aggression and build institutions for world order? Would a shelter program provoke rather than deter Soviet attack? Would a shelter program tempt American statesmen to make dangerously assertive demands of the Soviet Union? In short, would a shelter program bring on the very war the policy of deterrence was designed to prevent? Where could the public turn for answers to these questions?

The civil-defense issue illustrated how numerous are the sources of information on issues of defense and diplomacy in the United States. The problem for the public was not so much where to find information, but rather of how to distill the truth from the stream of facts and opinion on issues of national security that came pouring out through the instruments of mass communication. Arms control, test bans, civil defense, inspection systems, and defense expenditures were featured in mass circulation magazines like *Time, Life* and *The Saturday Evening Post*, in special programs on television and radio networks, and in regular public-service programs like the President's televised news conferences and Sunday afternoon interviews with congressmen, cabinet members, scientists, and pundits. They were also analyzed in numerous pamphlets and bulletins devoted to national or international issues and prepared and distributed by professional, political, and social organizations. Yet, for all this information, the problems of analysis and judgment remained for anyone who was not content to accept opinion uncritically, who questioned his sources as well as his data, and who realized the difficulties of coming to grips with the complexities of national security affairs.

Citizen Education and National Security

Public discussion of issues such as civil defense and test bans may often isolate these issues from the broad problems of foreign policy and defense of which they are a part. When this is the case, popular opinion arrives at a consensus on the basis of oversimplified and frequently emotional assumptions about the relation of defense to diplomacy, the intentions of Communist leaders, and the determinants of American policy. The consequences are several. Public debate may become irresponsible by ignoring the complexities and posing the questions in unrealistic terms, but may nevertheless influence public policy by creating pressures that neither the President nor the Congress can ignore. The influence of public opinion on the United States Government limits the freedom to respond to challenges rather more than it encourages changes in policy. For this reason alone, the education of the public in international affairs, as well as defense policies, is directly significant in meeting the problems of the cold war.

There has been a growing awareness since World War II of the need for public education to provide a basis of knowledge for understanding world affairs. The original motives were related to the commitments the United States had undertaken first in the United Nations and later in the network of regional and bilateral arrangements that followed the Truman Doctrine and the Marshall Plan. Not only did the democratic process demand a public understanding of these commitments, but there was also a practical need for public support of the high costs that the military and economic programs would entail. In 1961, the Foreign Policy Association published a directory of over 350 organizations either "wholly concerned with world affairs . . . [or] engaged in major programs of world affairs education." These organizations represented "a wide range of religious and political belief, all trades and professions, special interests and general interests. There are advocates of specific policies and techniques and organizations whose programs are based on a belief that an informed public can be depended upon to come to . . . sound conclusions."[4] The means through which these organizations sought to educate the public were also diverse; they ranged from lectures, debates, and forums to organized series of lectures or discussion meetings that required a considerable preparation and participation.

The privately organized adult-education program is an institution peculiar to democratic society. Where the program is designed to support a particular cause, its continuance depends on the rights of free assembly and expression. When its aim is to educate the general public to a greater understanding of world affairs, it reflects an optimistic view of human nature that is also characteristic of democratic society. Whether or not such programs are effective—either in influencing public policy or in increasing public responsibility—is problematic. But one thing is certain: They are an important channel through which many people are exposed to problems of national security in a systematic way.

In the period between the two world wars, adult-education programs reflected a traditional division in the way Americans thought about war and peace. On the one hand, general adult education in world affairs was preoccupied with the issue of international organization and cooperation and with attaining a broad knowledge of the culture of other nations. But as in academic programs of the period, there was little analysis of the means of carrying out national foreign policy—political or economic, let alone military.[5] Organizations that dealt directly with problems of war fell usually into one of two loosely organized categories—a preparedness movement and a peace movement. Within the preparedness movement were nationalist groups like the Liberty League, the Daughters of the American Revolution, and the American Legion, and organizations sponsored by the military services, like the Navy League. An equally diverse mixture could be found in the peace movement, which included organizations such as the scholarly World Peace Foundation and the National Council for the Prevention of War.[6] But since World War II, almost all groups concerned with public education or action have reflected the more complex nature of world affairs.

The Foreign Policy Association is a major adult-education group and a pioneer in the world-affairs field. Founded shortly after World War I, the Association was originally formed as a pressure group to influence American foreign policy along liberal, internationalist lines; but, in 1922, it began to emphasize education and research rather than political action.[7] Today, the Association—financed by foundations, corporations, and individuals—provides a variety of services for community and educational organizations: a World Affairs Book Center in New York with a wide range of material on world affairs, a bimonthly "Headline Series" of booklets on foreign-policy topics in the news, and a periodic information report, *Intercom*, a review of world-affairs activities undertaken by governmental and nongovernmental agencies. All these services are available to any group at a small fee, as is material for community discussions and debates, organized around the "Great Decisions" before the American people that year.

The president of the Association from 1953 to 1962 was John W. Nason, a former president of Swarthmore College. In 1962, the post was assumed by Samuel P. Hayes, a former government official and professor of economics at the University of Michigan. The Board of Directors of the Association has, over the years, included men such as Dillon Anderson, former Special Assistant to the President for National Security Affairs; Robert R. Bowie, Director of the Harvard Center for International Affairs; Roswell L. Gilpatric, who has held several defense positions; former U.S. representative to the U.N., Henry Cabot Lodge; and scholars like Dexter Perkins and David B. Truman. During the year 1961–62, operating expenses for the Association ran to slightly more than $1 million with all but $170,000 covered by grants from foundations, corporations, and individuals. Major expenses included the costs of publications and program materials and the staffing and coordination of the activities of the Association. In its New York headquarters, located directly opposite the United Nations, the Association runs special conferences and makes its facilities available to other world affairs groups. In 1961–62, these included the fifth annual program of "U.N. briefings" for nearly 1,000 community leaders from all parts of the country, special conferences for executives of World Affairs Councils, and public meetings and luncheon lectures for groups in New York. The Association also has regional offices in Boulder, Colorado, in Atlanta, and in San Francisco, where its representatives are responsible for stimulating and assisting community activities in their areas.[8]

National security has become a major theme of several of the studies in the Association's Headline Series and of much of the material prepared for the annual Great Decisions programs. Many of the Headline Series booklets have focused on American policy in a particular area of the world—Western Europe, Eastern Europe, the Middle East, China—and have discussed the military aspect of policy problems. Several issues have been devoted exclusively to studies in the national security field: *The Future of Nuclear Tests*, by Hans Bethe and Edward Teller; *Disarmament: Atoms into Plowshares* by William R. Frye; and *The U.S. and Armaments* by Mark S. Watson. Each Headline Series publication contains a discussion guide so that it can be used as a basis for group discussions as well as for general reading. *The U.S. and Armaments*, by Watson, military correspondent for the *Baltimore Sun*, is an example. Watson sets out, in a relatively uncomplicated way, the relation between foreign policies and military preparedness and between military strategy and proposals for arms control. His discussion is then followed by a series of questions for discussion and bibliographies on topics such as the "Character and Cost of a Defense Program," "The Weapons Debate," and "Government Organization and Defense."

The importance of national security in foreign policy has also been emphasized in the Great Decisions program, in which some 300,000 people in more than 1,000 communities participated in 1962. (Additional large numbers were reached in the extended coverage given the program in the mass media.) Once a year, a series of fact sheets are published on the "great decisions" and, taken together, are used by community groups as a unifying theme for a series of meetings. Discussion questions and references to further reading follow the analysis of each problem area. Every year, defense policy has been one of the themes marked for discussion. In 1962, for example, there were seven topics: "Vietnam—Win, Lose, or Draw?"; "Red China—Which Way Half a Continent?"; "Nigeria—Democracy in a New Climate?"; "Iran—Middle East Pivot?"; "Berlin—Test of Allied Unity?"; "United Nations—Independent Force?"; and a summary, "United States—

New Directions in Foreign Policy." Each issue was presented in its full complexity, with the problems of defense and security thus presented in a broad context of world politics.[9]

The Great Decisions program is but one of several nationally organized discussion series. A Great Books program, for example, touches often upon the issues of war and peace, as do programs financed by the Fund for Adult Education and sponsored by colleges and universities.[10] Among the organizations the Fund supports is the American Foundation for Continuing Education, one of the most successful of the adult-education programs that began after World War II and one whose activities bear comparison with those of the Foreign Policy Association.[11]

Organized in 1947 by a group of young men at the University of Chicago, the Foundation's purpose is to provide "education in international affairs." It encourages the formation of small, seminar-type groups to discuss the problems of foreign policy over a sustained period; it finds discussion leaders, helps train them in special leadership institutes, devises discussion methods that can be adapted by the groups themselves to meet their particular needs, and prepares reading materials. These activities are financed through registration fees, sales of publications, and grants from organizations like the Fund for Adult Education.

Until 1962, the Foundation's President was Jerome M. Ziegler; that year, he was succeeded in the post by William J. Trainor. As in the Foreign Policy Association, contact with community groups is made through regional representatives with program materials developed by a small research staff at headquarters. General guidance on the program is available from two groups, a Board of Directors largely made up of businessmen and lawyers, and an Advisory Board made up of scholars and educators. Among those who have served on the Advisory Board are McGeorge Bundy, former Dean of the Faculty at Harvard and now Special Assistant to the President for National Security Affairs; Thomas H. Hamilton, President of the State University of New York; Joseph E. Johnson, President of the Carnegie Endowment for International Peace; Professor Elting Morison of M.I.T.; and Dr. Harold Taylor, former President of Sarah Lawrence College.

By 1960, the number of community groups participating in the Foundation's programs had increased from 45 to more than 600 and participating individuals from 1,000 to more than 10,000. The groups were located in 445 communities in 31 states and several foreign countries. Although the Foundation expanded the area of its activities, the major emphasis is still on world affairs. Several anthologies of readings prepared by the Foundation have now been published and are being used as texts in college courses, including those on *World Politics, American Foreign Policy, Russian Foreign Policy,* and *American Democracy.* The Foundation has also sponsored and published a series of case studies in politics as supplementary reading for discussion groups, among them studies of the decision to use the atomic bomb and of American policy on the Hungarian revolution. It also prepared a volume on *Arms and Foreign Policy in the Nuclear Age* including selections by Herman Kahn, Hans Morgenthau, Henry Kissinger, and Robert E. Osgood.[12]

The programs of the Foreign Policy Association and the American Foundation for Continuing Education are illustrative of adult education in world affairs. They differ sharply, however, from the program of an organization like the National Committee for a Sane Nuclear Policy, which is oriented to political action and committed to a particular position on specific issues, but is also educational in a variety of ways. SANE is one of the most important organizations in the peace movement that has emerged since World War II. Just after the war, many peace organizations rallied around the cause of world government, but, as the cold war developed and as world government seemed less and less feasible, peace groups began to focus on specific issues, such as the international control of atomic energy, the dangers of radioactive fallout from nuclear testing, and civil defense. In dealing with these issues, some peace groups espoused unilateral action by the United States to reduce the possibility of the use of armed force to resolve international disputes. In doing so, they found themselves in opposition to the advocates of the strategy of deterrence.

Founded in 1957, SANE has had the sponsorship of men such as Norman Thomas, the respected Socialist Party leader, Norman Cousins, the editor of the *Saturday Review,* the physicist David Inglis, of the Argonne National Laboratory, the psychologist Erich Fromm, Clarence Pickett of the American Friends Service Committee, and David Riesman and H. Stuart Hughes of Harvard. Until the formation of SANE, the peace movement had been made up largely of devoted pacifists and various individuals and groups who, at least by the nature of the issues and times, found themselves advocating a policy that seemed to parallel the Soviet Union's position on security and disarmament. SANE's objectives were to shift the aims of the movement from the idealism of world government to more limited goals, and to divorce it from any tendencies to follow Communist leadership. In seeking an objective base from which to operate, SANE precipitated a crisis within the movement and alienated a number of more radical groups, many of which were opposed to totalitarianism but convinced that the peace movement required cooperation with Communists. The controversy also involved the complex problem of defining what the Soviet position was and judging the motives of individuals.[13]

SANE's program includes both political action and education. The National Committee attempts to be a clearinghouse on research, particularly on current issues in the disarmament field, and to issue policy statements for the guidance of local chapters. For example, at the time disarmament talks began again in March, 1962, SANE, together with the American Friends Service Committee, convened a small meeting of experts from several disciplines to discuss the negotiations. From this meeting came a signed statement analyzing the positions of the major powers and making recommendations for limited unilateral actions on the part of the United States. Signers of the statement included Fromm, Riesman, and Norman Thomas, as well as the chemist William C. Davidson, SANE's Executive Director, Homer A. Jack, Professor Seymour Melman of Columbia, and the physicist Jay Orear. The statement was published in SANE's newsletter, *Sane World*, and circulated to chapters and members, thus making it available for discussion in local groups and as guidance for political action.[14]

Despite its very real efforts to be objective, the focus of SANE's criticism is almost inevitably the United States rather than the Soviet Union, since the organization is devoted to influencing American foreign policy. While SANE groups protested the resumption of nuclear tests by the Soviet Union in the fall of 1961, the demonstrations seemed to some no more than a gesture when compared with its attacks on official acts of the American government. The very nature of the issues makes much of the SANE program often seem an apologia for the Soviet Union. Leaders of SANE have recognized this problem and have worked to counteract it. In the early summer of 1962, they refused to send an official delegation to a disarmament rally held in Moscow on the grounds that Communist domination of the rally would prevent a full and free exchange of views.

SANE's membership includes a high percentage of people in academic life, underscoring the interest of scholars and scientists *as citizens* in issues of national security. But there is one interesting distinction among the professors and scholars working in the peace movement. Few leading historians and social scientists can be found in the movement; rather, it seems to have attracted proportionately more natural scientists and some psychologists. The controversy over civil defense in the summer and fall of 1961 provided the impetus for an effort to bridge this division.

In many colleges, faculty members had signed petitions protesting any civil-defense program; they argued that civil defense offered only an illusion of safety and could be interpreted as a provocative act, possibly preparing the way for a first-strike strategy. Many had then considered it worth while to continue to discuss and argue the broad issues of national security. Almost all these groups were only loosely and informally organized, and were often joined by colleagues who were not prepared to sign the civil-defense petition but who were nonetheless anxious to study the problems of defense and disarmament together with men from other disciplines and other persuasions.

From these beginnings, discussion groups and seminars in national security appeared at various colleges and universities throughout the country in 1961 and 1962. While there is no uniformity to their work (although a good deal of professional contact), they all, in one way or another, are concerned with examining alternatives to a complete dependence on a strategy of deterrence, alternatives that could open the way to disarmament without upsetting the strategic balance between the Soviet Union and the United States. Several also adopted the so-called "gradualist" program, outlined by Amitai Etzioni in *The Hard Way to Peace*; these are formally organized as the American Faculty Council for the Gradualist Way to Peace. Etzioni, a sociologist at Columbia and research associate at its Institute of War and Peace Studies, advocates an effectively safeguarded arms reduction system, together with a broadening of the functions of international organization and an acceleration of the modernization of new nations. The "gradualist" groups reject simple panaceas and demonstrate a deepening awareness of the complexities of national security issues, and, at the same time, generally hold that peace can be maintained without sacrificing either security or the values of American society. The gradualists circulate their views in "position papers" on such topics as inspection, nuclear testing, and general disarmament.

All these discussion groups—from the Foreign Policy Association's Great Decisions series to local SANE chapter meetings to seminars of scholars and scientists—make a real impression on American society. In all of them, the problems of war and peace are studied in a systematic way and, whatever the objective, one ultimate achievement is better public understanding of the issues involved. But no matter

how broad and numerous such groups become, the number of participants will be small in comparison with the potential audience. Their
most important asset is the participation of a high portion of the
"attentive public" whose influence is wielded in a myriad of ways in
an open society. The challenge is not one of mass education so much
as the encouragement and education of public leaders.[15]

Communism as a Focus for Adult Education

The nature of the cold war has given rise to a number of special
adult-education programs in which the focus is almost exclusively on
problems of Communism. The issue of Communism is as complex
and disquieting as is that of the impact of nuclear weapons and long-
range delivery systems on military policy or the international implications of political, economic, and social change in the new nations.
Moreover, a background of emotionalism constantly threatens the
objective study of the history, aims, and methods of the Communist
movement. Any rational assessment of Communism by the public is
confused by the secrecy that surrounds the Communist leaders' decisions, by the ideological antagonism between Communism and the
West, by the bewildering history of alliance with the Soviet Union
during the war, by well-known instances of espionage practiced by
the Russians since the war, and, finally, by the hysteria and irrespon-
sibility that characterized the McCarthy period in our own struggle
to cope with the full meaning of the Communist challenge.

Immediately after World War II, Soviet affairs became an area of
intensive study in many major colleges and universities. Institutes of
research and training were set up at universities like Columbia,
Harvard, and Indiana, almost all of them following the area-study
approach, including work in language and literature as well as history
and the social sciences.* The study of Russian became one of the
most important languages in the curriculum and, following the Soviet
launching of the first Sputnik, became a principal subject in the
secondary schools. By the fall of 1960, Russian-language study was
offered in 593 colleges and universities, and Russian or Soviet studies
was an accepted field of concentration at 48 colleges and 21 graduate
schools.[16] Soviet history became an important area of specialization,
and social scientists and specialists from all disciplines found a common forum for professional development in the American Association
for Advancement of Slavic Studies.[17] This expansion of intellectual

* For a discussion of the relevance of area-study programs to national security
in general, see Chapter 3.

interest in Russian and Communist affairs reflected both the power of the Soviet Union and the importance of this power to the United States. The objectives of Soviet studies, as of the study of national security, were to train specialists for government, teaching, and research, to contribute to scholarship and policy-making, and to enrich general education in an important area of international relations.

In terms of national security, the most pressing problems were those that involved Soviet military capabilities and doctrines, on the one hand, and Soviet political motives and objectives, on the other. For the former, a small but excellent body of literature appeared. Some of the major books in this area were *Soviet Military Doctrine* and *Soviet Strategy in the Nuclear Age*, both by Raymond L. Garthoff, *War and the Soviet Union* by H. S. Dinerstein, *Atomic Energy in the Soviet Union* by Arnold Kramish, and *The Red Army*, edited by the British military historian B. H. Liddell Hart.[18] All these academic programs and literature were thus available to adult-education programs on Communism which, for the most part, were concerned with the nature and intentions of the Communist states and the Communist movement.

At least two programs on Communism have been sponsored by important national organizations, one by the American Bar Association and another by the U.S. Chamber of Commerce. The ABA program was planned by two committees: the Special Committee on Communist Tactics, Strategy and Objectives, and the Special Committee on Education in the Contrast Between Liberty Under Law and Communism. Early in 1962, the ABA held a series of seminars designed to inform lawyers and the general public on Communist strategy and objectives. The ABA seminars were announced as an alternative program to extreme right-wing movements that were gaining increasingly large audiences. At the ABA meeting held in St. Louis in January, 1962, for example, there was harsh criticism of irresponsible charges of Communist infiltration and influence made by radical groups like the John Birch Society. What was needed, said one speaker, was "to do enough 'homework' on Communist strategy and objectives to become informed."[19]

Early in 1962, the ABA published a handbook on "Instruction on Communism and Its Contrast with Liberty Under Law." Its purpose was to provide guidelines not only for seminars, but also for the work of local bar associations in encouraging "instruction in schools and colleges on the subject of Communism."[20] The handbook called for the development of forums and institutes at state and local bar associations to "stimulate lawyers to assume active roles in creating public awareness and acceptance of the broader program." Like most projects on Communism, the ABA's emphasized the need to create a greater awareness of the true nature of what it described as "a new and fanatical movement, with characteristics of repression and tyranny almost unintelligible to the American mind." While the pamphlet emphasized the external threat, it also noted that "a study of the facts as to Communist tactics and strategy will show the importance attributed by Red leaders to internal subversion in America and other Western countries."

Like the ABA program, the program on "Freedom vs. Communism" sponsored by the U.S. Chamber of Commerce urges a reasonable approach and emphasizes that its course is "not a highly emotional, Communist 'witch-hunting' exercise."[21] It is actually a series of eight weekly workshops (of one-and-a-half to two hours), each session designed for 16–20 participants and conducted by a discussion leader who follows a specially prepared manual. A set of eight pamphlets and a series of problems and exercises are also available. The course is subtitled "The Economics of Survival," and it is largely a comparative study of the free enterprise and Communist economic systems. The course materials are made available (with charge) to business and community groups who organize and run the course themselves.

The Chamber of Commerce program is similar to the ABA program in its general approach to the Communist issue. In varying degrees, both are concerned with the internal threat, despite the overriding importance of the external challenge. The Chamber's course material notes, for example, that despite a decline in membership in the American Communist Party, "the Communist menace in the United States has continued to increase, due partially to the mistaken impression that Communists are few and, therefore, need not be feared." Both programs urge private citizens to pass information on internal subversion to the FBI, whose director, J. Edgar Hoover, is frequently quoted. Both groups view the external challenge of Communism as a fight to the finish, because of the Communists' unambiguous goal of world domination. Communist strategy is seen as one of "controlled conflict" in which each move follows a pre-arranged formula taking full advantage of weaknesses in the armor of the Western alliance.

The tone and perspective of both programs raise doubts about the validity and realism of this view of the Communist problem. Not only is the internal threat unduly stressed, but the picture of a monolithic Communist movement does not explain the dynamics within the Communist system. The "master conspiracy" concept gives Communist leaders more unity of purpose, sagacity, and power to insure concerted action than recent history suggests they have. It is nevertheless significant that both programs stress the need for objectivity and take pains to dissociate themselves from radical movements. This disavowal demonstrates, perhaps, that the radical right-wing movement that erupted in the late 1950's was disconcerting for conservatives as well as liberals.

The radical right is not a centrally controlled movement but a number of groups of varying size with an extreme approach and program in dealing with the problems of Communism. Broadly speaking, it interprets Communism as an atheistic ideology whose followers are all puppets of the central command; it blames the setback and the frustrations of the cold war on subversion by liberal State Department officers, social reformers, and weak and dishonest political leaders; and it advocates, either explicitly or implicitly, a "hard line" in national security policy that verges dangerously on the brink of preventive war. One of the most extreme of the right-wing groups until 1964 was the John Birch Society, whose president, Robert Welch, in his now famous *Blue Book*, questioned the loyalty of President Eisenhower and John Foster Dulles. No less extreme but with a much broader base was the Christian Anti-Communist Crusade, headed by an Australian doctor, Fred C. Schwarz.

Schwarz' organization is primarily devoted to the running of "schools" on anti-Communism.[22] Beginning in 1953, when the Crusade showed an income of $23,356, the schools were conducted throughout the country, and the Crusade expanded to a point where, in 1961, income amounted to $1,273,492. The Crusade does not take a stand on contemporary issues or try to influence policy; its purpose is entirely related to public education on the meaning of Communism and the strategy of the Communist movement. The "schools" normally run for five days and usually employ as "faculty" former FBI investigators, retired military officers, and writers whose views coincide with Schwarz' own. Guest lecturers also speak, but the major presentation is always by Schwarz, who was described by *The New York Times* as "an earnest soft-spoken man [who] is transformed on the platform into an arm-waving thunderer." Income for the Crusade comes from tuitions for the schools, from private contributions, and from the sale of Schwarz' book, *You Can Trust the Communists*. Among the contributors have been industrialists and corporations who also assist by sponsoring television and radio broadcasts by Schwarz and his staff.

Schwarz contends that, in Communism, "we are confronted with a movement which is frightening in its superb organization, strategic mobility and universal program, but which is perfectly understandable and almost mathematically predictable." The way to "understand" and "predict" what the Communists are up to is to study the ideology and techniques of the movement. Schwarz describes Communism in terms of "a cancer cell" that obeys "the laws of its lawless growth." By studying "the Communist mind, motives and techniques . . . we can see clearly in the murk of the Communist dialectic, detect the tactics of the enemy and devise a program to abort his plans." With this premise, there is no need to take a stand on specific issues or criticize the acts of specific individuals. Like the fundamentalist that he obviously is, Schwarz concentrates on "the word." He has thus stayed clear of the slander that has characterized other rightist groups though he bases his approach on a similar interpretation of Communism. There is, moreover, an evangelical zeal to the Crusade, rooted in Schwarz' fundamentalism and in the dictum that "Communism . . . should be taught with a moral directive." It is dramatized by the calls to "smite the Communist foe and if necessary give up our lives" (which *The New York Times* quotes as a typical Schwarz exhortation).

All the anti-Communist programs demonstrate the dangers of approaching the Communist issue apart from the total context of world affairs. Communism becomes the cause of all the ills of the world, all the troubles of the United States, and all the tensions of contemporary politics. It is also pictured as omnipresent, which tempts the unknowing to see programs of social legislation or public regulation as part of a large and hostile Communist conspiracy. In this kind of atmosphere, the admonitions of the American Bar Association and the Chamber of Commerce are hardly sufficient to insure responsible action. Responsible and intelligent approaches to Communism would seem difficult when the basis for interpretation of Communist activity is a static view of history and social institutions.

These same approaches are noticeable in courses in anti-Communism in high schools throughout the country. The increase of such courses is undoubtedly attributable in large degree to the participation of educators and community leaders in adult-education programs that take anti-Communism as a focus for their study of defense and foreign affairs. By mid-1962, a Soviet specialist for *The New York Times* concluded that "the anti-capitalist and anti-American indoctrination given Soviet pupils in all Soviet schools is being matched by anti-Communist and anti-Soviet indoctrination in many American schools."[23] The pressures for establishing such high-school courses are often powerful at adult anti-Communism meetings, and anyone opposing them can easily be accused of being "soft" on Communism. Like the American Bar Association, the National Education Association and the American Legion jointly issued a guide on "Teaching about Communism" in 1962 which cautioned against taking an extreme approach,[24] but emphasized Communism as an enemy, suggesting a kind of black-and-white comparison of Communism with American democracy and asserting that only the tactics, not the goals, of Communism have changed over the years. All these assertions are common to those who take the study of Communism out of a broad historical and political perspective.

The rise of adult-education programs on Communism is thus a matter of considerable concern. The programs do not, by and large, fully utilize the scholarly resources that have been developed in the field of Communist affairs since 1945. Books by men like Philip Mosely and Henry Roberts of Columbia University, and Marshall Shulman of the Fletcher School of Law and Diplomacy, are occasionally cited in bibliographies, but the main material is highly oversimplified exposés, and their major source of information and expertise ex-FBI investigators, retired military officers, ex-Communists, East European emigrés, and the reports and hearings of the House Committee on Un-American Activities. A common element in all the programs is a sense of frustration, hysteria, and desperation that makes it difficult for their followers to apply rational judgment to the complex problems of national security.

The Military Services and Adult Education

In a period of crisis, threats of war, and heavy military expenditures, the military services become a highly influential group in society. No discussion of adult education in national security affairs can therefore ignore their role. The services conduct active and reserve training programs and seek to inform the public or influence national security decisions through a network of private and military-sponsored organizations.

The use of information and education programs to instruct troops on the nature of the cold war was intensified after the experience of the Korean War. Many American prisoners of war in that conflict were subjected to psychological pressures from their Communist captors to a point where they collaborated with them and signed statements in which American motives and methods were violently criticized.[25] The reactions in the U.S. armed services to these "brain-washing" episodes were several. A new Code of Conduct was circulated which pledged troops to ideals of duty and honor and bound them to answer no more than the straightforward "name–rank–serial-number" response in case of capture. Admiral Arthur Radford, Chairman of the Joint Chiefs of Staff during the first Eisenhower Administration, sought to go further and spread a program of Militant Liberty, in which the closed Communist society was analyzed and compared in raw, naked terms with a democratic society.[26] Realistic training was also adopted to stiffen the resistance of troops. In one case, soldiers were placed in a simulated prisoner-of-war compound and subjected to treatment similar to that experienced by prisoners in Korea. The exercise was described as follows: "They receive a Communist-type reception and are exposed to a propaganda speech delivered in a foreign tongue and translated into English. The reception and propaganda speech are accompanied by harassment and torment to create a feeling of shock and a frame of mind similar to that experienced by actual prisoners of war." They are then submitted to "trained interrogators."[27]

The use of military information and educational services as a means for indoctrination on Communism derived from a secret National Security Council directive of 1958 that authorized the military services to participate in an intensified effort to increase public awareness of the dangers of the Soviet threat. The directive itself—though not its details or background—was disclosed during 1962 congressional hearings, called, in part, to inquire into the dismissal of Major General Edwin A. Walker, who had been charged with seeking to influence the voting of troops under his command. While there was unanimous military agreement that Walker had overreached himself, the hearings showed a wide divergence of opinion among the services as to their role in cold-war education.[28] Both the Air Force and Marine Corps spokesmen rejected the suggestion that military officers play a major role in informing the public about the Communist threat. The Chief of Naval Operations, on the other hand, positively asserted that the military forces should "contribute our knowledge of communism toward the goal of seeing to it that not only our Navy men but all Americans understand the origin and nature of the peril our country faces today." Similarly, the Army's Vice Chief of Staff disclosed that, under broad guidance, all Army commanders had authority to participate in activities "to help spread an awareness of communist stratagems and to gain public support for national security objectives." His justification was that "we are at war. This is a cold war we're in and anything that the military can do to help win this war, we should be ready and willing to do."[29]

The argument over the proper role of the military forces in nonmilitary education involves three major questions: Should the education of troops in cold-war issues be part of the military training programs? Are military officers competent to teach such courses? Should military officers attempt to reach the civilian public with their information programs and should they become involved in programs sponsored by private organizations? The development of information and education activities during World War II and the Korean War had made nonmilitary education an accepted part of troop training, partly because it was felt that, in a democratic society, soldiers must know why they are in service, and partly because it was believed that there was a direct relation between indoctrination and high morale. But military services had also assumed that nowhere else in American society, in no other educational program, did recruits receive any education concerning the basic issues of the cold war—a generalization about American secondary-school and college education that is difficult to substantiate completely.

Since training is an essential function of command, it was natural that troop information and education was undertaken by military commanders.[30] In mid-1961, Senator J. W. Fulbright raised serious doubts about the ability of U.S. military officers to deal with the full range of national security issues and to bring military solutions into balance with political requirements.[31] Senator Fulbright's expression of doubt was received with anger by the military services. Among those who came to the armed forces' defense was President Eisenhower, who reminded a Senate subcommittee "that the aims, objectives, and methods of communism and its aggressive threats to our system are probed more intensively and more pragmatically in [the service and joint war colleges] than in virtually any civilian university in the Nation"; and that, as a result, "senior officers in the Armed Forces are qualified to develop among their units the necessary understanding concerning potential aggressors, and their purposes and tactics."[32]

The military education system has indeed expanded its horizons considerably during the past fifteen years. There is still the question, nevertheless, whether the education in nonmilitary issues is sufficiently deep and penetrating to qualify officers for the sensitive task of troop and public education. Instruction at the war colleges continues to be part of a career system in which the military element is of prime importance, no matter what weight is given to political and economic considerations in the deliberation of broad national security issues. Service education, of course, must contend too with a more practical problem: selection and promotion of officers normally are decided in favor of those officers who, throughout their development, strengthen their loyalties to their services' role in the national defense posture.[33]

So long as troop information and education remains a function of command, military officers will nonetheless continue to play an important role in the development of popular attitudes about cold-war issues. Their education and the organization of the central information services on which they rely for teaching materials therefore need continual reassessment in the light of implications that extend far beyond the immediate troop-training function. This does not, however, answer the final question: Should military officers be involved in programs sponsored by private organizations? Unfortunately, the distinction between private organizations and regular training programs often breaks down, since many reserve officers receive training credit for participating in privately sponsored programs. Indeed, the whole system of reserve training provides a bridge between the military establishment and the public that no other government agency enjoys.

Most reserve units operate under broad training directives in which technical instruction is spelled out in considerable detail but in which nonmilitary education is left to local commanders. The local commanders often try to make maximum use of the resources available in their areas, including meetings and other gatherings sponsored by universities and private organizations. But they are nevertheless guided by military headquarters in a variety of ways: through regular contacts through the command structure, special instructions and general information bulletins, the distribution of educational materials, and the attendance of reserve leaders at high-level educational programs at the Industrial College of the Armed Forces (which includes civilians) and the National War College. The latter programs are particularly important, since they serve as models that ranking officers and civilian community leaders can follow in courses for reservists and local civilian groups.

The Industrial College programs, conducted since 1948, were first called National Defense Resources Conferences and then National Security Seminars. Authority for the programs came from a Joint Chiefs of Staff directive to offer courses for officers of the National Guard, Army, Navy, and Air Force reserve officers, selected executives of industry, educators, and other prominent citizens.[34] Arrangements are made by local civilian groups, such as the local Chamber of Commerce with the cooperation of local reserve officers. In any one year, there are about fourteen conferences, two a month from October through May, in cities throughout the country. Attendance by reservists is limited to approximately 200, with an equal number of civilians from business and other organizations in the area. In this way, the seminars perform the functions of reserve training and adult education both, and involve the joint cooperation of the military and private groups. They run over a two-week period and are conducted by teams of officers on the staff of the Industrial College. By the fall of 1963, it was estimated that the Industrial College program had reached approximately 70,000 men and women.

The seminars are highly capsuled versions of a year-long course run at the College. Although the Industrial College was originally organized to concentrate on the economics of defense, its curriculum now includes the study of political and organizational problems, as the issues of national security have become more complex and interrelated. Reflecting this aim, the Industrial College justifies the seminar on the ground that "this 'age of peril' demands the attention not only of Reserve officers, but equally of civilian leaders." It therefore emphasizes the interdependence of civilian and military organizations and resources, especially in the area of economic mobilization, and seeks to demonstrate "the Communist threat to world peace . . . in its full magnitude." All participants who attend a required percentage of lectures, seminars, and discussion periods during the two weeks are presented with a Certificate of Completion, and reservists also receive active-duty training credit.

The reserve training programs operating through the National War College are of more recent origin, having started in 1959 when the first Defense Strategy Seminar was held there. Like the Industrial College program, the strategy seminars have involved cooperation between military and private organizations, in this case the Reserve Officers Association and the Institute for American Strategy.

The strategy seminars were only one of several projects sponsored by the Institute for American Strategy in its program of promoting public awareness of the Communist challenge.[35] The Institute originally grew out of a symposium on the utilization of technical and scientific manpower held in Chicago in March, 1955, and sponsored by the Chicago Association of Commerce and Industry, the Society of American Military Engineers, the Illinois Institute of Technology, and various branches of the armed forces. Called the National Military-Industrial Conference, the symposium brought together leaders of industry and government, and also enjoyed the sponsorship of some of the largest corporations in the country. In 1958, the organizers decided to continue it on an annual basis and to broaden its scope to include all matters affecting the security of the United States. At the same time, plans were made for a "permanent year-round program" to awaken the public to the "all encompassing nature of the Soviet-Communist challenge," with the Institute for American Strategy, originally financed by the Richardson Foundation, established to carry out this objective.[36]

The activities of the Institute began to expand in 1959, when, with the Reserve Officers Association, it served as joint sponsor of the National Strategy Seminar. The Seminar was held at the National War College in Washington under the authority of the Joint Chiefs of Staff and was attended by more than 200 carefully selected reserve officers from all branches of the service. The students assembled at Fort McNair, site of the Industrial College and the National War College, and included two state governors, three congressmen, seventy educators, and a number of newspapermen, radio and television executives, lawyers, and writers drawn from all the states in the Union and Puerto Rico. All were reserve officers and as such were on active duty for the two-week period of the course and under military orders providing transportation, housing, and pay appropriate to their rank.

What was particularly striking about the Seminar is that through the authorization of the Joint Chiefs of Staff, the Institute for American Strategy in effect took over from the services the responsibility for training reserve officers on active duty, even though the National War College, whose facilities were used, had been giving courses on strategy to senior officers of the three services as well as senior government civilians for ten years before. At the same time, while the government paid for allowance, travel, facilities, and services, the Richardson Foundation provided the funds for other expenses— including the cost of developing a curriculum for the Seminar, hiring a staff, securing speakers, and purchasing books and other materials to be distributed to the students without charge. The task of developing the curriculum was turned over to the Foreign Policy Research Institute of the University of Pennsylvania and the Institute's Director, Robert Strausz-Hupé, brought his own staff to the National War College to serve as the staff for the Seminar.* The Director of the Seminar was Brigadier General Donald Armstrong (ret.); Colonel William Kintner, a member of the Foreign Policy Research Institute

---

* For a full description of the Foreign Policy Research Institute, see below, Chapter 9.

and an Army officer then on active duty, served as Associate Director. The Seminar, now retitled "Defense Strategy Seminar," has become a regular summer program. The locus and general procedure remain the same, although the Director changed in 1960 when the Commandant of the War College assumed control of the course. Since then, neither the Institute nor the Pennsylvania group has been involved, although Mr. Frank Barnett, formerly program director for the Institute and research director for the Richardson Foundation, continues to be a member of the Seminar faculty and to offer a keynote address at the close of the course. The small faculty is supplemented by a group of moderators for the discussion groups into which the students are formed. Moderators are drawn from previous classes, and the student body continues to include political and business leaders. The program has remained constant, treating a broad sweep of national security issues, with special emphasis on the challenges and techniques of Communism. At the end of each session, participants have been urged to start seminars in their own communities.

The War College seminars have thus been a catalyst for regional seminars held throughout the country. In many of these efforts, the sponsors could look to both the Institute for American Strategy and the military services for support. Indeed, these seminars demonstrate the close relation between the military services and privately sponsored adult-education programs, with reserve training providing the link between the military establishment and the public.[37] In this respect, they contrast sharply with adult-education programs like those of the Foreign Policy Association and the American Foundation for Continuing Education. While both kinds of programs use similar techniques—meetings, discussion groups, lectures, publications, and services for conferences and study groups—the military-connected programs can call on greater resources and sometimes on material support from the military services. They also have more specific purposes than general enlightenment and debate, and are thus more sharply focused—on the one hand, on the dangers of Communist expansion and on the other, the development of broad public support for a strong military establishment.

The military services have gone even further in seeking popular support by actually helping to set up private organizations whose only purpose is to further the programs of the services with which they are connected. The Association of the U.S. Army, established in 1955, is a case in point. In a memorandum informing major commands about the formation of the Association, the Secretary of the Army made clear that one of its main objectives was to gain public support and understanding for Army activities. He pointed to the "independence of the Association" but nevertheless stressed that "the relationship between the Department . . . and the Association . . . , although unofficial, must be close and cooperative." He also called upon "commanders at all echelons" to "render the Association the maximum support and encouragement." He made it clear that "by support," he meant "assistance in connection with the organization of membership, the provision of meeting places, the provision of qualified speakers, and the attainment of local recognition."[38]

The Association's position is broadly spelled out in a policy statement, *The Security of the Nation*, originally published in 1957 and revised in 1959. In general, the policy may be described as support of and belief in the Army's vital role in the nuclear age, both as a deterrent to local or limited aggression and as the military force that would ultimately have to occupy "key enemy areas" and control "the enemy peoples" if war should break out.[39] This support of the Army was to be achieved through the Association's annual convention, through the publication of a monthly, *Army*, through a Washington staff in contact with the Pentagon and Congress, and through a system of nationwide chapters (now numbering well over a hundred) whose activities include "AUSA Weeks, . . . speaking programs in cooperation with other organizations, publicity, in local news media, television, [and] information to Members of Congress." The Association also "sponsors classified symposia and briefings designed to bring together the key industrial leaders with the top officials of the Department of the Army to discuss plans, problem areas, and future programs."[40]

The Air Force Association, like the Association of the U.S. Army, is devoted to a military service program, in this case to "obtaining and maintaining adequate airpower for national security and world peace." Likewise, it operates through a national headquarters, through a monthly publication, *Air Force*, and through a network of regional, state, and community organizations. Of particular importance is the relation between the air industry and the service. The broad basis for the Air Force Association's activities is usually set down in a policy statement adopted at the annual convention. The fifteenth convention was held in 1961 and passed a statement that called for "complete eradication of the Soviet system" as "our national goal—our obligation to all free people—our promise of hope to all who are not free." To meet the requirements of "this crusade," the Association recommended that a "National Alert" be declared by the President and that "the overriding priority of the day . . . be the unquestioned credibility of our nuclear deterrent." Specific military programs were then urged in order to strengthen the credibility of American posture; these included hardening of strategic bases, expansion of both manned-bomber and long-range missile systems, protection of command and control systems, and accelerated research and development in the "aerospace" field.[41]

The educational program of the Air Force Association mainly concentrates on what is called "aerospace education," an understanding of revolutionary changes in science and technology as they apply to aviation and space exploration and as they contribute to the security requirements of the nation.[42] The program actually operates through an affiliate, the Aerospace Education Foundation, and under the guidance of an Aerospace Education Council. Both groups include distinguished educators, industrialists and community leaders; the Foundation, for example, is chaired by Dr. W. Randolph Lovelace, Director of the Lovelace Foundation and chairman of the NASA Life Science Committee, and the chairman of the Council for 1960–61 was Dr. Lawrence G. Derthick, former U.S. Commissioner of Education. The method is to organize a series of major seminars for educators, and to encourage participants to undertake new programs on their return to their schools. In 1961, a series of such "Aerospace Education Seminars" were held in major cities. At these meetings, "educators . . . heard briefings from an Air University team . . . on national space programs," and "panels and discussions [were] held at which conferees . . . discussed . . . the problems of upgrading the school curriculum to meet space-age requirements." The Association counted educational programs in twenty-four states that, by mid-1961, had been affected as a result of the work of its Education Foundation.

The programs of the Army and Air Force Associations, added to those of the Navy League, reserve training programs, cooperative enterprises with private organizations like the Institute for American Strategy, and active troop information and education activities make up a tremendously powerful force in adult education in national security affairs. It is inevitable, of course, that the military establishment should have great influence in shaping popular attitudes about defense and diplomacy. In sheer size and resources for reaching the public, there are few institutions in American society that can today compete with the military establishment. Considerable research needs to be done to evaluate fully its impact on our society, but it is possible, on the basis of existing evidence, to suggest certain tentative conclusions.

The programs sponsored by or related to the military services take a limited view of international politics. They naturally emphasize military means rather than diplomatic, economic, or cooperative international efforts to achieve international stability. This emphasis on the use of military force leads to a marked preoccupation with Communism as an enemy, and this tendency has, in several instances, led into dangerous partnerships with movements of the radical right.[43] To attribute this relationship to reactionary tendencies of the "military mind" is an oversimplification, however. Not only does it ignore the complexities of the "military mind" and the frequent aggressiveness of the "civilian mind," but it also shows a lack of understanding of the pressures under which the military establishment lives in an era of cold war.

Military officers are playing an expanded part in American society under the compelling requirements of defense, and their role often exceeds the narrow limits of military expertise. This, indeed, is one of the bases for the new system of civil-military relations that we have already discussed. But whatever their new role in society, neither military officers nor civil servants should become actively involved in programs that seek to influence public views about vital matters of public policy. Education at any level is explosive. However factual and objective educational programs may be, they inevitably have an impact on habits of mind and attitudes about the world. This is a sensitive area that is already affected in a myriad of ways by governmental activities—by the regulation of the information flow from government agencies, by the sense of authority with which high ranking officials speak, and by the impressive facilities that government agencies possess for publicizing their programs and policies. Under these conditions, military officers, like other government officials, have a special responsibility to exercise restraint and responsibility, since they cannot nor should not isolate themselves from the society of which they are very much a part.

Restraint of the military and civilian bureaucracy nonetheless begs the question: How to develop an "attentive" public in the area of national security affairs? We posed the dilemma early in this book: "*Quis custodiet ipsos custodes?*" In the final analysis, public officials might well be the most effective agents for stimulating discussion in the field of national security affairs—their role extending far beyond the raising of purely military issues. It involves the enormous impact of the President as a "teacher" as well as political leader, in using the communications power of the mass media to explain a crisis in Berlin or the significance of an arms build-up in Cuba. It also involves the educational effects of well-articulated political controversy on issues such as arms control, the sharing of the nuclear deterrent within NATO, and the allocation of funds for competing weapons systems. It involves far more than a strong sense of restraint and responsibility in the federal bureaucracy, and particularly in the military establishment. It also involves the preservation of a political process that encourages the open expression of all views and opinions, and an educational system that prepares men to cope with the complexity of contemporary political issues.

III

Academic Programs in National
Security Affairs

6

The Pattern of Early Programs

IN ANALYZING THE INSTITUTES, centers, and seminars that are primarily devoted to research and teaching in national security affairs, our purpose is *not* to provide a complete catalogue of current activities. It is rather to develop a sense of perspective on how the national security field has developed in the years since World War II and how major institutions that have made the most important contributions have responded to the problems of focus, financing, and policy-oriented research. This development involves more than an accumulation of information; it involves the ability of institutions in a free society to adapt to the intellectual needs of public policy and, in the process, to preserve both diversity and freedom in intellectual life.

The academic programs to which we turn first play a particularly important part in the intellectual response to the cold war. The response, as we have seen, derives from beginnings made before the war —from Wright and Lasswell at Chicago, Spykman and his colleagues at Yale, Earle at Princeton, and Herring and his work at the Public Administration Clearing House. Intellectual involvement in national security studies has spread throughout the country, producing an often overwhelming but impressive literature and, perhaps most important, providing a core of knowledgeable men who could be called into public service at the highest echelons of government. But the field's roots—and its future—must lie in the colleges and universities.

For no area worthy of intellectual inquiry can be strong without good teachers.

The first universities to rise to the intellectual challenge posed by America's position in the postwar world and by the changed nature of war were those that already had an interest in national security and military affairs, either because of an existing program, as at Princeton, or because of the interest of faculty members. The work done at Princeton, Columbia, and the University of Chicago illustrates the continuity in the study of military affairs from the earlier period to the changed conditions of the cold war. In all three cases, programs in national security were closely related to the comparatively new study of international relations and were headed initially by scholars in the latter field. They were also generally similar in organization, funding, objectives, and method of operation. All were largely supported by funds from outside sources, and the primary objective of all three was to do research in problems arising from the changed nature of international relations and military technology. In one important respect they differed. At Princeton and Columbia, the national security programs were organized in close relation to broad public-service training programs in international affairs. At Chicago, no comparable program existed, and research in national security affairs was less closely related to the university itself.

The relation of national security studies to public-service training programs is important, and the reasons are not difficult to suggest. The development of national security as a field of academic interest has largely been in response to the needs of the government and the policy-maker, needs which, in a broader sense, schools of public and international service, such as those at Princeton and Columbia, were established to meet. At such institutions, there is a tradition and environment in which a new policy-oriented field like national security can be accepted. It is more difficult to develop a program of national security studies where this tradition is absent and where the institutional character is dominated by the traditional social-science departments.

Princeton University

The Center of International Studies forms the focal point for Princeton's response to the intellectual challenge of the cold war. Founded at Yale in the mid-1930's by Nicholas Spykman as a pioneer program in international relations, the Center moved to Princeton in 1951 as the result of a difference in policy between its director and the Yale administration. By that time, the Center, under direction of the late Frederick S. Dunn, had achieved an enviable reputation. It had trained a number of young scholars who were assuming leading positions in the field, pioneered in the study of strategic problems, and made a notable contribution to an understanding of the relationship between military force and foreign policy.

At Princeton, Professor Dunn and the scholars who accompanied him were able to carry forward the work begun at Yale.[1] As an institution with a strong tradition of public service, Princeton furnished both an intellectual and institutional environment favorable to the study of national security problems. There were already scholars at Princeton—including Edward Meade Earle, at the Institute for Advanced Study—who were interested in national security affairs, and the social-science departments offered courses in military and related subjects. At the same time, the Woodrow Wilson School of Public and International Affairs provided a natural base for the Center's work.

Professor Dunn continued to develop the Center of International Studies at Princeton until his retirement, when Professor Klaus Knorr, who had been Associate Director, replaced him. Dunn was appointed Professor of International Law in the Woodrow Wilson School and Knorr a professor in the university's Economics Department. The scholars who came with them from Yale—William W. Kaufmann, Roger Hilsman, and others—received no comparable appointments on the regular faculty, but remained for several years as Research Associates. Members of the Princeton faculty work at the Center, but the only permanent members of both the Princeton faculty and the Center have been the Director and Associate Director.

The organization of the Center has remained substantially unchanged since its transfer from Yale in 1951. The affiliation with the Woodrow Wilson School is a link between the Center and the University. A concrete expression of this relationship is the Faculty Committee that provides general policy guidance for the Center and helps to integrate its activities with those of the University. The Committee is presided over by the Director of the Woodrow Wilson School (in the absence of the President of the University) and includes the chairmen of the History, Politics, and Economics Departments, and the Director of the Center. It approves the Center's budget and program but exercises no direct control over its activities or personnel.[2] Support comes from a number of sources, including the Milbank Memorial Fund, the Rockefeller and Ford Foundations, and the Carnegie Corporation of New York. In addition, there is some income from the Center's publications, and, for special purposes, from other sources. Some funds, in addition to the physical facilities, come from the University.

The relationship between the Center and the University is further promoted through Faculty Associates, a group of senior members of the Princeton faculty who are interested in national security problems and who from time to time engage in research sponsored by the Center or participate in its activities in other ways. Moreover, wherever possible, the Center utilizes the Princeton faculty. Not only does this policy provide it with first-rate scholars, but it also creates a favorable attitude toward the Center on the part of the faculty in the College's departments.

The Center also appoints Research Associates—who may or may not be members of the Princeton faculty and who have short-term appointments, usually for one or two years. They may be established authorities from other universities and research organizations or young scholars still to establish their reputations. Each has a research project that is usually related to a central theme the Center has selected for intensive study. In addition, there are a small number of research assistants, usually students still working for their doctoral degree. The number varies with the funds available each year and the nature of the research in progress, but there are always several associates and assistants in residence. Occasionally, the Center supports nonresident associates, when their research must be performed elsewhere. Altogether, it is a very flexible and loose organization, particularly appropriate to scholarly research in an academic community.

The position of the Center has been strengthened, and conflicts with the College and between the faculty and the Center's research associates avoided, by limiting the number of research associates and refraining from seeking university appointments for them. But this practice has also limited the Center's effectiveness in recruiting promising young scholars. The fact that an appointment to the Center is a short one, with little likelihood of a permanent appointment to the Princeton faculty, limits the attractiveness of the Center. The University's departments also pay a price by not strengthening their own staffs with scholars from the Center, although possibilities of doing summer research at the Center may make departmental appointments more attractive. As in other universities, the departments at Princeton are thus in the stronger position in their relation with the Center, being free to take what they need and give only what they wish.

Despite the fact that the Director holds a faculty appointment and the associates may be involved in various teaching activities, the Center is essentially a research organization. Its aim is to develop systematic and comprehensive studies in international relations—including those that are particularly relevant to American national security and defense policy. The Center has staked out various broad areas in which to carry out its research programs; national security, it should be noted, is only one of them.

In a very real sense, the Center is a community of scholars. There are no closely directed programs and little hierarchy. Every member's work is subject to review and criticism, but he is free to work in his own way, formulate his own research, and come to his own conclusions. At the same time, he enjoys and profits from close association with other scholars working on similar or closely related problems. The virtue of the Center as a research organization lies in its capacity to bring together a group of scholars to work on a given topic, free them from teaching duties, and provide them with funds and with every facility for research, criticism, and, finally, publication. Early in 1960, for example, the Center selected the topic "Internal War"—military conflicts within a state rather than between states. Professor Knorr organized the project, established the conceptual framework for it, secured the funds, and recruited the scholars to work on it. By the summer of 1961, less than a year after the group had begun work, the Center had published several research monographs and policy memoranda, and the following fall held a conference on the subject. Since then the program has been greatly expanded.[3]

The Center's record is also impressive when measured by the number and quality of its publications. It publishes *World Politics*, a quarterly journal of international affairs and a leading publication in the field;[*] it has published or materially assisted in the publication of more than a dozen books and a large number of short studies. Not all the books relate directly to national security problems, but of those that do, one can count *Military Policy and National Security*, a pioneer work of its kind edited by Kaufmann; *Deterrence and Defense*, by Glenn H. Snyder; and *Limited Strategic War*, edited by Knorr and Thornton Read.[4] The shorter publications of the Center are organized into two series—memorandums and research monographs. At the end of 1963, there were more than forty of these, with the series continuing to grow each year.[5]

But the Center's contribution is not confined to its research facili-

* See below, Chapter 13, p. 304.

ties and its publications. Many of its members engage in other activities through which the Center's work is made available to public officials and other scholars, and through which the Center, in turn, receives information and ideas helpful in its own projects. These include conferences, professional meetings, and consulting.

While it is primarily a research organization, the Center has undoubtedly strengthened both undergraduate and graduate instruction at Princeton. The College had already offered courses in military and related subjects before the advent of the Center in 1951, most of them having developed as a result of efforts to improve ROTC instruction. The History Department assumed the obligation for teaching military history, initially to all three services, in a course emphasizing the broad role of the military forces in society and problems of organization, policy, and strategy.[6] Similarly, the Politics Department gave a course on "Military Strategy and National Security Policy," the Economics Department on "Economics of National Security," and the Psychology Department on "Military Psychology." All these courses were undergraduate ones open to non-ROTC students as well as ROTC cadets. Thus, while they were initiated to meet a particular need of the military services, they were integrated into the broad undergraduate program.

The Center has also contributed to the teaching program of the Woodrow Wilson School in which it is physically housed. The School, established in 1934, is a joint enterprise of several departments, primarily those of History, Politics, and Economics, with both undergraduate and graduate programs. The former, designed to provide a broad understanding of public issues, is in effect a departmental "major," beginning in the junior year and limited to about fifty students in each class. Most of them go on to law schools, where they retain a strong interest in public administration, and subsequently enter government service; others enter the Foreign Service; some go into business; and a few become teachers.

The graduate program, begun in 1948, is specifically designed to train men for the public service rather than for teaching and research. It is a two-year program designed to give the students integrated social-science training for responsible policy-making positions.[7] On the theory that a public official requires not only a certain knowledge but also the conceptual tools to apply this knowledge, the curriculum seeks to develop the ability to analyze and to approach problems critically, and an understanding of the interrelation of historical, political, economic, and social aspects of modern society. Students are required to take courses in four separate fields: Economic Analysis,

Applied Social Science Analysis, American Institutions, and Political Processes with a major concentration in one of these fields.

Among the courses the School offers are two seminars: "Economic Growth and Social Change in Underdeveloped Areas," and "National Security." The first is a comparative analysis of the processes of economic growth; the second, taught by Professor Knorr, deals with resource allocations, international alliances, arms control, strategic doctrines, and civil-military relations. The course stresses the use of concepts in the study of defense problems. In the fall term of 1962, there was initiated, in addition to a new seminar by Professor Knorr on "Military Power in International Affairs," a bi-weekly "forum" on the national defense establishment, which was addressed by such distinguished officials as Allen Dulles, Carl Marcy, and Livingston Merchant, each of whom spent a full week at the Center.

Just as the Center strengthens the teaching program, so does it, in turn, draw strength from the graduate programs in history, politics, and economics. Though none of these departments offers national security or defense policy as a field of specialization, the interest of several senior faculty members and their association with the Center have the effect of attracting students into the field and sometimes into the Center as research assistants. At the same time, military officers assigned to the Woodrow Wilson School for advanced work in public administration or international affairs, or for preparation for teaching at West Point, have sometimes chosen to take the Ph.D. with one of these departments, and they have usually decided to write dissertations on military topics.

The Princeton programs illustrate a number of trends and problems that are found in many other universities. The work in national security affairs is principally concentrated in the research program of the Center which, in turn, is linked to the rest of the university primarily through the public-service programs of the Woodrow Wilson School. While relations with the University departments have been good and a variety of interlocking arrangements have been established, the departments, assured of support, maintain an autonomy the Center itself cannot afford. Not only must it rely largely on outside financing, but it must also staff its projects in part with faculty from the departments.

As in other universities, national security studies vie for support against the new substantive areas as well as the more traditional fields and against new methodological advances in the social sciences. As a result, the response to national security affairs within the College varies greatly, and the Center can only partially influence the work done in the various departments. Whether national security will be established as a special field in history and the social sciences at Princeton is a major open question in what is otherwise one of the more comprehensive programs in the country. It is, indeed, the acceptance of national security studies by the established disciplines that is the most serious objective to be achieved in the goal of a total intellectual response to the cold war.

Columbia University

The program at Columbia bears comparison with that at Princeton in a variety of ways. As at Princeton, it is related to the early work done in national security—through the seminar Grayson Kirk and his colleagues organized in 1940 and through the Director of the Institute of War and Peace Studies, William T. R. Fox, who worked under Wright at Chicago and was an associate under Dunn at Yale. At Columbia, as at Princeton, national security is emphasized as a field for scholarly research. This research is carried out in a university supporting many activities designed to meet the growing intellectual needs of the United States in world affairs—the School of International Affairs, the several area-studies institutes, and the International Fellows Program.

The School of International Affairs and several of its associated area-studies institutes were established immediately after World War II, with the objective of training men and women to "provide a reservoir from which experts capable of handling the increasingly complex and intricate problems of international affairs can be drawn."[8] The first area-studies program was the Russian Institute, to which were added the East Asian Institute, the Near and Middle East Institute, the European Institute, the Program on East Central Europe, the Program of Studies on Africa, and, most recently, an Institute of Latin American Studies. Each of these regional programs provides a focal point for scholars from different disciplines to coordinate investigations on areas of the world that are now of crucial importance to American policy and security. They also offer a two-year graduate program in cooperation with the School of International Affairs or the Graduate Faculties. A student in such a program receives his graduate degree and also a certificate from the area-studies institute.

The newest program at Columbia is that of the International Fellows, initiated in 1960. The program permits a limited number of students in the graduate and professional schools to combine their studies with courses in international affairs.[9] It differs therefore from the School of International Affairs in that it is not specifically a training program in international affairs.

Supporting and reinforcing these programs are three research programs closely concerned with national security affairs: the Institute of War and Peace Studies, the Council for Atomic Age Studies, and the Research Institute on Communist Affairs. The last program, established late in 1961, is in many ways an extension of the Russian Institute—one that reflects a recognition of the growing complexities and variety within the Communist bloc. Indeed, it is one of the first efforts to broaden the study of Communism beyond its central concern with the Soviet Union. The relation of such broad research in Communist affairs to national security policy is clear: The validity of the basic assumptions of this policy depends to a great extent on a realistic appraisal of Communist societies. The presence and strength of the two institutes concerned with these societies is extremely important for that program at Columbia which is most directly concerned with national security policy: the Institute of War and Peace Studies.

The Institute of War and Peace Studies had its origins in General Eisenhower's interest in the area while he was President of the University. In the Gabriel Silver Lecture of 1950, he had stressed the need for a better understanding of the causes and nature of war through historical studies, and had proposed the establishment of a chair for such a purpose.[10] Efforts were then made at Columbia to meet the needs he had outlined. Friends of the General and of the University contributed funds for the chair, but no appointment was made. (There was also discussion of a possible arrangement with the American Military Institute, which was then in financial straits, by which the University would assume responsibility for and direction of *Military Affairs*, the Institute's journal. For several reasons, this proposal failed.[11]) The final decision was to create an Institute of War and Peace Studies, a form of organization for which there was precedent at Columbia. Professor Fox was chosen to direct the Institute. At the same time, Fox was active in the School of International Affairs, thereby, in his own person, providing a link between the Institute and the expanding program of that School and the area-studies institutes.

The program inaugurated at Columbia was, then, quite different from what President Eisenhower had envisaged. Instead of a single chair, the University created an institute bringing together a number of scholars. Moreover, since Professor Fox was a political scientist, there was to be more emphasis on theory and political process than on historical analysis, as Eisenhower's lecture had suggested.

The Institute began in 1952, from the start functioning entirely as a research organization. Unlike the area-studies institutes at Columbia, it neither offers nor sponsors courses, but seeks rather to encourage scholars to do research in problems of war and national security by furnishing funds and facilities to free them from teaching duties and to publish the results of their research, and by providing the intellectual stimulation that comes from association with other scholars. The Institute's funds can also be used to support publication of research in the field done elsewhere than Columbia. Professor Fox also stipulated that research done at the Institute was to be of a scholarly nature and not the kind that could be carried out more appropriately by journalists, publicists, or government officials with access to information unavailable to the scholar. In short, the Institute was to avoid current policy issues and confine itself to the kind of research appropriate to private scholars working in a university—that is, basic research affecting long-range policies.

The idea behind this approach was that the function of the scholar was to search for knowledge, for the underlying principles and long-range trends that affect current issues; certainly, the point was not to try to do the work of the policy-maker, but simply to throw light on the choices open to him. The value of this kind of research lay, it was felt, in its power to alter "the climate of opinion" so that even under the pressure of immediate crises, responsible officials might make their decisions with a broader understanding of the problems involved.[12]

The research program of the Institute, like that of the Center at Princeton, encompasses more than national security policy. During its first ten years, members of the Institute worked in three areas: international relations, civil-military relations and American national security policy, and political change and comparative politics.[13] One aspect of the studies in international relations is based on interdisciplinary efforts within the social sciences. It stems from an earlier project begun by Grayson Kirk, one of the first to concern himself with the postwar relation of military force to national policy. When Dr. Kirk became President of the University, Professor Fox assumed direction of this earlier project—a series of studies relating demography, international organization, political sociology, and military history to the study of international relations—and it became part of the Institute's program. Two volumes published as a result of this program are *Man, the State and War*, by Kenneth Waltz, and *De-*

fense and Diplomacy, by Alfred Vagts. Institute members also do research in the theory of international relations, research that reflects Fox's own interest in the subject.[14]

Research in defense and national security problems performed at the Institute has varied widely, reflecting the members' interests rather than any preconceived program. This is not to say that Professor Fox has not provided intellectual leadership in suggesting subjects that required study or that he has failed to interest scholars in these subjects; on the contrary, he has done this more successfully than most, exerting a real influence on the field as a whole. But he has also maintained great flexibility in the Institute program and has encouraged research in any problem that seems worthy of support. Each of the research associates has been free to pursue his own studies and to consult his colleagues without the formal coordination and direction characteristic of other, more highly organized research programs. The result, as at Princeton, has been a community of scholars interested in the same field but working independently, and in an environment that encourages frequent interchange of views and mutual criticism.[15]

A major project of the Institute, supported initially by a grant from the Carnegie Corporation, was Professor Fox's "Civilian and Military Perspectives on National Security Policy"—a study dealing with "the characteristics of those civilians and soldiers whose activities have to be related to each other at policy-making levels." By analyzing the public statements and remarks made in interviews by political and military authorities, Fox's aim was to assess their "distinctive predispositions, beliefs, intellectual skills, and problem-solving techniques."[16] Professor Fox also planned a number of case studies to provide a basis for testing the operational significance of his findings. Three of these were published in 1962, written by associates of the Institute who had begun their work under Fox's direction.[17]

Another major part of the Institute's work has been concerned with the processes by which national security policy is formulated. The study of processes is more traditionally a concern of the scholar than policy-oriented issues. The case studies in Professor Fox's project fall into this category, as does *The Common Defense*, by Samuel P. Huntington; *Organizing for Defense*, by Paul Hammond; and a study by William and Annette Baker Fox on the impact of the North Atlantic Alliance on American policy-making processes and institutions. The Institute has also sponsored work in comparative civil-military relations and comparative politics in general. Here, a number of books and studies were undertaken: *Changing Patterns of Military*

Politics edited by Huntington; a study of praetorianism by David C. Rapoport; an analysis by Kenneth Waltz of the foreign policy process in democratic countries; a joint study by Huntington and Zbigniew Brzezinski, director of the Research Institute on Communist Affairs, comparing the political systems of the United States and the Soviet Union; and a sociological study by Amitai Etzioni on the evolution of supranational communities.[18]

As in the case of the Princeton Center, members of the Institute are active in the national security field not only as authors. Professor Fox, for example, has served as chairman of the Social Science Research Council's Committee on National Security Policy Research since its establishment in 1952, where he has done much to further research in the field and has gained an influential position that has given added prestige to the Institute. Though membership in the Institute does not automatically provide admission to the small group of scholars who influence policy, some do belong to this group, of which Professor Fox is certainly a leader. These men serve as consultants, offer advice, prepare papers, and maintain informal contact with responsible officials in many government agencies.

The Institute has been closely linked to the Council for Atomic Age Studies at Columbia through a mutual interest in the relation of science and technology to national security affairs. Several of the Institute's projects have focused on this relationship. For example, at the invitation of the Institute, Seymour Melman assembled a series of technical studies on problems of arms control and detection and summarized and interpreted the principal findings in non-technical terms for his volume *Inspection for Disarmament*.[19] Warner Schilling, Associate Director of the Council as well as a member of the Institute, has been concerned in much of his teaching and research with the relation of military technology to strategy, an interest illustrated by his study on the decision to proceed with development of the hydrogen bomb.[20] Moreover, the Council is also linked to the Institute through Professor Fox, one of the original faculty members on the Council and now its co-chairman with I. I. Rabi.

The idea of the Council for Atomic Age Studies grew out of a study, undertaken in 1956 by the Legislative Drafting Research Fund of the Columbia Law School, on insurance problems resulting from atomic hazards. Late in 1956, a group of faculty members proposed a council that would have a continuing interest in similar problems where advances in science and technology have social and political implications. In January, 1957, the Council for Atomic Age Studies was formally established, made up of ten faculty members representing a variety of disciplines and serving renewable three-year terms. The Council meets four times a year to review the total program and to plan new activities. Professor Philip C. Jessup served as co-chairman with Professor Rabi until he was elected to the International Court in 1960 and was replaced by Professor Fox. Financial support came first from the Rockefeller Foundation and then from the Carnegie Corporation of New York. The Council staff, consisting of a full-time Executive Director, Christopher Wright, and part-time Associate Directors as well as clerical help, serves as a clearing house for Columbia groups interested in atomic-age problems, and as a point of contact for outside groups and individuals seeking information or interested in the possibility of cooperating with the Council.

The task of the Council for Atomic Age Studies is described in general terms as "the identification and study of the new and awesome problems facing society in our era as a result of major scientific and technological developments—symbolized by the atom."[21] One of these, of course, is national security. The work of the Council falls into several major categories. The first includes projects and programs that the Council assists or specifically encourages—conferences on the international control and administration in outer space, or the organization of science in government; staff services for the meeting on "Atoms for Power" held by the American Assembly late in 1957; and co-sponsorship of the annual Advanced Science Writing Program at the Graduate School of Journalism. Carnegie Corporation funds also permit the Council to make small grants to individuals or groups at Columbia for "research on selected aspects of the impact of science on the social order." In 1962, in cooperation with the Social Science Research Council's Committee on National Security Policy Research, the Council undertook a study project on the role of the scientist in the policy-making process.

A second broad category covers general surveys and analyses of atomic-age problems. Here, the Council's staff is continually engaged in drawing up an inventory of all scientific research and development being carried out or planned that could effect significant changes in the social order. Through this inventory, the Council hopes to expose problems that have been neglected, prepare the way for scholarly research, and provide a central storehouse of information on atomic-age issues.

Finally, the Council has recently turned to teaching programs in an effort to bring the results of its research directly to the student. Undoubtedly, it has indirectly affected the academic program at Columbia. But, in 1961, the Council sought a direct approach when its Executive Director offered a seminar on "Science and Society" for undergraduate seniors.

The impact of research on the curriculum is more evident in the independent activities of the Institute of War and Peace Studies, for its presence on the campus has greatly contributed to the Columbia curriculum. In a sense, such teaching has been a by-product, a sort of bonus, of the Institute's research activities, since the scholars it brings to Columbia often assume teaching duties as well. (In this respect, the Columbia program differs markedly from that at Princeton where a sharp line has been drawn between the departments and the Center.) The result is that the research associates of the Institute share teaching duties with their faculty colleagues.

The courses that Institute members give, whether standard departmental offerings or not, invariably reflect an interest in national security problems and in their research projects. Because most of the men appointed to the Institute have been trained in political science, most of the courses have been in the Department of Public Law and Government. In addition to Professor Fox's own courses in international relations, which devote a good deal of time to military subjects, and other courses dealing with Communist ideology and policies, Glenn Snyder has taught a course on "Military Power and National Security Policy"; Warner Schilling, a member of the department as well as of the Institute, teaches courses in the College and in the School of International Affairs, in both of which he devotes considerable time to national security problems and to his special interest, military technology; Samuel P. Huntington, before he returned to Harvard in 1963, taught two courses in American government and national security, one in the department and one for the International Fellows.

Though national security is not identified as a separate area for graduate work, the presence of men such as Fox and his associates has led students who wished to do their Ph.D. dissertations with them to select topics in the field. Of course, some of the students, especially those sent by the military services, are predisposed toward such topics, as are some from the School of International Affairs. But this does not diminish the importance of the faculty supervisors; in universities that have no professors in the field, such students would select other topics. Most of these dissertations at Columbia are in Public Law and Government. In contrast, the History Department at Princeton is at least as active as the Politics Department. But the same basic problem exists at Columbia as at Princeton: Despite a strong research program in national security affairs related to a whole series of other research and teaching programs, there has been commensurately mild expansion of graduate work in national security affairs as a recognized area of specialization.

The University of Chicago

The University of Chicago's interest in the study of war and military problems goes back to the decades before World War II. It will be recalled that the project headed by Quincy Wright at Chicago was perhaps the first effort after World War I to study war systematically on a large scale, through the cooperative efforts of scholars in many fields. It produced not only the two-volume *The Study of War* and supporting monographs, but also scholars like William T. R. Fox and Bernard Brodie, who were to make major contributions to the study of national security policy.

With this background, the University of Chicago seemed to be one of the more favorable locations for establishing a center of research in this new and rapidly expanding field. There were other reasons to expect the University of Chicago to become an important center for the study of national security. It had made many contributions to the war effort, it had large resources, a distinguished faculty, and a strong tradition for undertaking bold and challenging experiments in education. In the field of social sciences, it had made interdisciplinary work a regular feature of the curriculum, and had initiated programs in international relations, public administration, and other fields related to national security. The Law School was broadly based in the social sciences and could contribute to the public service through the study of the practical and theoretical legal aspects of national security. Finally, as the home of the Argonne Laboratories and the Fermi Institute, the University of Chicago was one of the leading centers of scientific research in nuclear physics, and its scientists had been among the first to recognize the political and social consequences of the atomic bomb. Some had helped to found the *Bulletin of the Atomic Scientists*, and they continued to maintain a strong interest in these problems.

The program established at Chicago in 1950 for the study of America's changed role in the world was a modest one, concentrating almost entirely on international relations and having as its objective the systematic analysis of American foreign policy (later broadened to include military policy). The purpose of the program was twofold: to provide the public, as well as government agencies, with a clear understanding of the historical background and the objectives of

American foreign policy, and to explore the means required to achieve these objectives. The Center for the Study of American Foreign Policy (its original name) was meant to encourage studies that would throw light on the sources of American policies and relate these traditional definitions of national interests to contemporary problems.

In a very real sense the Chicago Center is the creation of one man, Hans Morgenthau, and it reflects his own view of international relations. German by birth and a graduate of European universities, Professor Morgenthau joined the Chicago faculty in 1943 and has been Director of the Center since its establishment. A leading authority on international relations, he is chief exponent of the view that national foreign policies are based ultimately on national interest. His books deal mostly with this theme and its application to current foreign-policy issues.[22]

Professor Morgenthau viewed the Center primarily as a means of supporting the research and writing in which he and several other scholars might be engaged. Its broadly stated objectives permitted almost any project the Director might wish to undertake, so long as it was related to American foreign or military policy. In this respect, this Center—like those at Princeton and Columbia—has a high degree of flexibility. It is also virtually unstructured, with a Director whose duties are nominal and only a small administrative staff consisting of a secretary and several research assistants. Research associates attached to the Center are few, never numbering more than four at a time, and each is free to work as he chooses. Research assistants are employed as the need arises. The entire operation is marked by an informality and absence of direction appropriate to mature scholarship.

Financial support of the Center comes entirely from foundations. The initial grant was from an educational trust, the Libby Endowment, which provided for a small staff (a historian, a political scientist, and two research assistants) for a limited period. Subsequent support came from the Carnegie Corporation of New York, the Rockefeller Foundation, and, indirectly, the Ford Foundation. In 1957, Carnegie renewed its grant to the Center for five years. It was then that the name was changed to Center for the Study of American Foreign and Military Policy, presumably to indicate that its scope of inquiry included military problems, in which Carnegie had shown a strong interest.

The principal activity of the Center is the preparation of studies for publication, and its work can be evaluated largely on the basis of the books prepared or published under its auspices. By late 1962, it had nine volumes to its credit.[23] Taken together, these studies are a major contribution to the study of American foreign and military policy and more than justify the Center. Each book is a solid and scholarly achievement, and several have had an important and widespread influence. Robert E. Osgood's *Limited War* has made a great impact on the study of the problems of limited war, and certainly Morgenthau's ideas are accorded the utmost respect wherever questions of foreign policy are discussed.

The interdisciplinary approach that typifies other programs in international relations and national security is absent from the Chicago Center. The emphasis is clearly on international affairs and political science. In the first ten years, the Center had only one senior associate who was not a political scientist, and of the first nine studies originated there all but one—by Gerald Stourzh, a diplomatic historian—were by scholars in international relations.

The purpose of the Center is to facilitate research by providing funds to relieve its associates from part of their teaching duties, and to assure continuing research and secretarial support. It employs research assistants, but awards no fellowships. It does not establish projects or set up elaborate programs into which each man must fit his own work, nor does it set deadlines or require reviews of preliminary drafts. The associates set their own pace, teaching part of the time and joining other programs when the opportunity arises.

Like other research centers affiliated with universities, the Center at Chicago contributes to the academic program of the University through the teaching activities of its associates. The contribution is, however, smaller than it is in the cases of Princeton and Columbia. Nor, again in contrast to the situations at Princeton and Columbia, has the Center at Chicago either sought or desired close association with other groups working in the same field. The reasons are undoubtedly partly organizational, partly personal. There is, for example, little at Chicago to compare with the Council for Atomic Age Studies at Columbia, despite the scientific installations there working on defense projects. Indeed, the Center at Princeton and the Institute at Columbia are both, in a sense, more a part of their universities than is the Center at Chicago, for at both there has been a conscious effort to integrate them—an effort that has been noticeably lacking at Chicago.

At the same time, all three centers exist largely on grants from the foundations and if the foundations decided for some reason that they could no longer support them, all three would have to seek funds elsewhere or greatly curtail their activities. In short, the centers must secure their own funds in order to survive. This fact affects every aspect of their activities and their relationship to the university. They can offer no permanent posts to research associates except through the university faculty and can make no firm plans beyond the period of each grant. Their only hope for permanence depends on a non-terminal grant by a foundation, or action by university trustees. Neither is likely. Nevertheless, it is unlikely that any of these centers will be unable to secure outside support, for they have all made a real contribution to the study of war and peace. It might well be said that continued support largely rests on the presence of certain individuals—especially at Columbia and Chicago, where Fox and Morgenthau have dominated the centers. The Center at Chicago is probably more vulnerable in this respect, since it has fewer ties to the University and there would be less likelihood that it would be continued in its present form if Morgenthau left. This kind of situation points up the problems of focus and financing and demonstrates the importance of integrating national security studies into the traditional disciplines if they are to be more than a temporary research fad.

7

The Cambridge Complex

CAMBRIDGE, MASSACHUSETTS, is a strategic location in American higher education. At the core of the expanding network of research facilities near Boston are Harvard University and the Massachusetts Institute of Technology—the first, the oldest and proudest of American universities, and the second, the most highly developed of the specialized schools of science and technology. The response of both to the intellectual requirements of national security was naturally determined by the impressive resources they possess—their research facilities and their faculties—but also by a sense of the university's service to society. At Harvard, this concept of service is rooted in the traditional idea of the educated elite's responsibility to the world around it and in the example of Harvard men in high public office. At M.I.T., it is based on the school's deep concern to put science and technology at the service of mankind.

Harvard and M.I.T. are more than geographic neighbors. Together, they form an intellectual community, acting with and upon one another. Scientists and scholars at both institutions frequently collaborate—formally, in cases like the Cambridge Electron Accelerator and the Joint Center for Urban Studies, and informally, through the social and intellectual ties that bind men of similar interests and qualities of mind. There has also been frequent collaboration in the field of national security affairs, particularly a series of joint meetings and studies on arms control in 1960–62. But the development of defense studies has taken a different form and different perspective in each case.

Harvard University

Research and teaching in national security affairs at Harvard is centered in three separate programs: the Defense Studies Program, the Center for International Affairs, and the program in Science and Public Policy. These programs developed separately to meet different needs in scholarship, teaching, and the public service. But together they represent a total institutional response that has had an important effect on research and training in the whole field of national security affairs.

The first of the Harvard programs to deal directly with national security was a Defense Policy Seminar inaugurated in September, 1954—largely through the efforts of W. Barton Leach, Story Professor of Law. Convinced that civilians should be trained in military matters if they were to participate constructively in policy-making, he proposed that Harvard institute courses in this field.[1] The university authorities accepted his recommendations and granted permission to conduct an experimental graduate Seminar in "Defense Policy and Administration" under the joint auspices of the Graduate School of Public Administration and the Law School.[2] Participants included not only the students and instructor, but also other faculty members and guest lecturers, civilian and military, who held or had held positions of responsibility in national security affairs.[3]

This experiment in graduate education proved immediately successful, and, as a result, the Ford Foundation provided funds to continue and expand the Seminar in June, 1955. This grant, made initially for a three-year period, set the pattern for the future development of the Seminar and its place at Harvard. Specifically, it called for the establishment of a Defense Studies Program, which included the Seminar, to be administered by the Graduate School of Public Administration.[4] General policy problems were determined by an Advisory Committee, appointed by the President of the University, consisting of the Director and representatives from the School of Public Administration, the Law School, Business School, the Science Faculty, and the Government and History departments.[5] The staff of the Defense Studies Program was drawn from various parts of the University. The few members who served full time did not, however, hold permanent positions on the University faculty, while regular

Harvard faculty members participated only on a part-time basis. The quality of the Harvard faculty did much to ensure the success of the Seminar during its first years. There were, however, basic weaknesses—dependence on outside financial support, lack of permanent faculty members on its full-time staff, and a weak position within the organizational structure of the University. Under the administrative control of the Graduate School of Public Administration, sponsored jointly by it and the Law School, and staffed by men with no departmental affiliation, the Seminar was in an anomalous position on the periphery of several parts of the University, belonging fully to none. Yet this position had certain elements of strength. It enabled the Seminar to draw on the support of the Law School and the graduate departments, and gave it a degree of flexibility and freedom it might otherwise not have had. Nonetheless, it left the program vulnerable if it lost its outside financial support.

The loss of this support became a reality when the initial grant from Ford expired in 1958 and was not renewed. During the 1958–59 academic year, the Seminar existed on funds remaining from earlier grants supplemented by other contributions. When no outside support was forthcoming for the following year and it seemed as though the program would come to an end, Don K. Price, Dean of the Graduate School of Public Administration, took steps to raise funds from University sources to continue the program during 1959–60. By this time, the Seminar had also been made a regular offering in the Government Department, and was under the direction of Henry A. Kissinger, who received a tenure appointment in that department in 1958. Dean Price's decision to continue the Seminar was also supported by the Carnegie Corporation, which made a three-year grant to the Defense Studies Program in 1960. But, even without this kind of support, the Seminar would probably have been continued since it had become a regular part of the graduate curriculum. Thus, the Seminar is no longer entirely dependent on outside aid, both because of the commitment of Dean Price and because of Professor Kissinger's departmental position, and is in a much stronger position than in 1958.

The basic objective of the Defense Policy Seminar—to provide training for civilians who might later be involved in the formation of defense policy—continued, though there have been shifts in emphasis in recent years. "Demands for informed, perhaps specifically trained civilians in the military establishment will increase, not diminish," wrote Professor Leach in 1955. "There must be an academic source from which such personnel can be drawn and to which they can return for refresher courses as military officers return to their staff schools and war colleges."[6] From this point of view, the purpose of the Seminar was at first distinctly professional. It emphasized teaching rather than research, and was oriented to current policy issues; this naturally determined the kind of students who were attracted to the course.

The grant from the Ford Foundation in 1955, as we have said, broadened the frame of reference of the original Seminar by creating the Defense Studies Program. This program had three purposes: "to carry out experimentation in courses dealing with defense policy as a problem in public administration"; to prepare teaching materials and "guidance" for other universities that might wish to establish courses in defense policy; and to make available a program for those already in the public service or those interested in entering government agencies concerned with problems of national security.[7] This last objective was close to the original aims of the Seminar, and fitted in perfectly with that of the Graduate School of Public Administration to provide advanced training under the direction of a faculty actively engaged in the study of public policy or administration.

The terms of the Defense Studies Program had the effect of enlarging the objectives initially set, making possible additional activities on the part of the staff and encouraging additional courses in military affairs. Thus, the objectives of the Seminar in succeeding years included both the increase of civilian knowledge of military affairs, and the development of resources for academic study and the practical application of such work in the formation of military policy.[8] The requirements of the Seminar, reinforced by the terms of the Ford grant, led to the preparation of a large body of teaching materials in the absence of any suitable text. These materials, prepared during five years, were distributed to universities with programs in national security affairs and to other interested groups providing a stimulus to the growth of the field. The staff also maintained a complete file of news clippings and other current materials—a unique, specialized library offering convenient working tools for both teaching and research.

The staff's contributions in research and participation in government projects have been equally important to the broadened aims of the program. Professor Kissinger's works have probably been as widely distributed and as important as any in the field. Timothy W. Stanley, one of the first teaching fellows in the program, in 1955–56, wrote one of the early standard works on defense organization, *American Defense and National Security*. During his association with the program, Dr. Harry Howe Ransom wrote his full-scale study on the *Central*

Intelligence and National Security, and his successor, Morton Halperin, has written extensively on problems of arms control and limited war.[9] The staff of the Defense Studies Program has also served as special advisers and consultants to government agencies, participated in conferences and meetings, and lectured frequently at the war colleges. Lastly, members of the staff have served the public interest and contributed to the formation of national security policy through participation in public discussion. By appearing regularly on radio and television, lecturing at colleges and universities, and talking to civic groups of all kinds, they have increased public knowledge on matters of national defense and thrown light on issues of current importance.

The attempt of the staff members to teach courses on national security affairs within the regular departments has been less successful. Early in the program, two such courses were offered, "Government and Defense," by Professor Samuel P. Huntington of the Government Department, and "History of Civil-Military Relationships," by Professor Ernest May of the History Department. Both were discontinued, however, as was a course in comparative defense policy given for two years by Edward L. Katzenbach, Director of the Defense Studies Program from 1956 to 1958. The program also supported a history course on the "Emergence of the United States as a World Military Power," but it was offered only once.[10]

To a certain extent, the failure to continue these courses was the result of the departure from Harvard of both Huntington (who later returned) and Katzenbach, and the somewhat experimental nature of the history course. But the departments were little inclined to integrate the work in national security affairs into their traditional disciplines. This is characteristic of national security policy studies not only at Harvard but at other institutions as well. Despite the fact that the Seminar has now become an accepted and integral part of the professional program of the Graduate School of Public Administration and a regular offering of the Government Department, national security is not on a par with the traditional fields of concentration.

The major activity of the Defense Studies Program was and remains the Defense Policy Seminar. Since its inception, the course has become less oriented to professional training. Reflecting the interest of its present Director, the course now focuses on the relation between foreign and military policies, a relationship considered in terms of organization, strategic doctrine, and strategic and foreign policy. The specific problems discussed may vary from year to year as policy issues change, but an effort is made to concentrate on fundamental problems of continuing importance. The Seminar has thus moved from its original emphasis on the "viewpoint of the appropriate Congressional Committee" to recognition, as Dr. Ransom put it earlier, that "concern with today's or tomorrow's public policy should not overshadow the quest for answers to basic questions and for meaningful generalizations or attention to theory."[11]

The shift in orientation from training to basic analysis and inquiry is due in part to the effect of the Center for International Affairs, established in 1958. The Center is related to the Defense Studies Program through its directorship and to the Graduate School of Public Administration of which all but one of its faculty are members. Organized and directed by Robert R. Bowie, formerly Assistant Secretary of State for Policy Planning, it combines basic research in foreign affairs with a seminar for students drawn from government agencies of the United States and other nations. These students are Fellows— mature officials designated by their agencies or governments to spend from six months to two years at the Center to improve their knowledge in a particular field by reading, research, and discussion with their colleagues and faculty advisers.

The central idea of the Center is to achieve a sustained and systematic analysis of fundamental issues of foreign policy. In recognition of the fact that the study of foreign affairs "stands at the confluence of many disciplines" and requires the cooperation of government officials and agencies, the Center has designed an interdisciplinary program utilizing the knowledge of scholars in various fields, officials of the U.S. Government, and of the governments of nations in Western Europe, the Middle and Far East, and Latin America.[12] Its program is focused on basic, long-range problems rather than immediate policy issues, which are better studied, it is felt, by the appropriate government agency rather than by a private group. Private scholars in a university are probably able to do a better job on the basic, long-range problems because they are not under pressure from immediate crises, have more time to work, and combine the knowledge of various disciplines. Moreover, the lack of classified material is less important for such problems than for current issues. The Defense Studies Program has, of course, the same approach now.

Though the Center holds no formal classes, its research activities provide the basis of a seminar system. Each faculty member conducts regular seminars not only for the Fellows but also for visiting officials, scholars, and interested persons. By providing a forum for criticism and discussion in an atmosphere of free inquiry, the seminars fulfill an important objective of the Center—to develop analytical skills and broaden the Fellows' perspectives. But they also give the faculty an opportunity to instruct and test the critical ability of their students, and the participants the opportunity to exchange ideas and to discuss issues openly and freely from the point of view of their own national interests.

The organization of the Center for International Affairs is unusual in several respects. The faculty is small and only the Director, Professor Bowie, serves full time. Members include Professor Kissinger, who serves as Associate Director as well as Director of the Defense Studies Program; Edward S. Mason, Lamont University Professor and former Dean of the Graduate School of Public Administration; Professor Thomas C. Schelling of the Economics Department, and, most recently, Professor Huntington. All these men, including the Director, have been and continue to be active in government affairs. There are also Research Fellows, Associates, and Visiting Scholars, drawn from the Harvard faculty and from other universities in the United States and abroad. It draws on all of Harvard's resources—its libraries and special programs as well as its faculties. (In addition, the Center maintains its own specialized library.) Moreover, the area-studies programs, the Defense Studies Program, and other programs in the Law, Business, and Public Administration Schools contribute the experience and the experts who can provide strong support to the Center.

The work at the Center is in three main areas: the economics of underdeveloped areas, political-military problems, and the political problems of Europe. The first of these, which Professor Mason directs, is concerned with factors affecting the economic development of the new nations of Asia, Africa, and the Middle East. The political-military research, under Professors Kissinger and Schelling, concentrates on problems of disarmament, the policy of alliances, and the relation between American foreign policy and national security—the last of which forms the theme of Defense Policy Seminar. The European research group, directed by Professor Bowie, deals with two broad problem areas—the Communist bloc and the unity of Western Europe.

In the spring of 1962, the Center received an additional grant of $750,000 from the Ford Foundation to expand its activities in economic-development studies. Under the aegis of a Development Advisory Service, established to direct this program, the Center was to provide professional personnel to assist foreign governments concerned with economic development in setting up their own planning agencies, economic staffs, and research and training institutes. These men, recruited by the Advisory Service, were to work on the staffs of foreign governments and then return to the United States, where their firsthand experience would presumably prove valuable to the government, and to research and training programs.[13]

The Center has undoubtedly added to the strength of the Defense Studies Program since the Fellows of the Center regularly attend the Defense Policy Seminar; the two programs share a building and a library; and participants in the Center, especially those working on political-military relations, cooperate actively in the Seminar. The directorships of the two interlock through Kissinger's dual appointment, and both receive support and cooperation from the Deans of the Graduate School of Public Administration and the College of Arts and Sciences. Taken together, they constitute an important response to the need for national security studies. They are, moreover, joined by a third program at Harvard, the program in Science and Public Policy, inaugurated at the School of Public Administration in 1959, with a grant from the Rockefeller Foundation.

The triple attack that Harvard makes on the study of national security can be characterized in the following way: The Defense Studies Program moves directly into the field; at the Center, national security is viewed as an aspect of international studies; finally, in the program in Science and Public Policy, the focus is the interrelation of advances in science and technology and changes in public policy and government organization. Major problems considered are the revolution in weapons technology, its effect on government and society, and the increasingly important role of scientists in the formation of national security policy.

The Science and Public Policy program is largely the work of Dean Price, who came to Harvard after a long and rich experience in government and with the Ford Foundation. As a member of the Bureau of the Budget shortly after World War II, he was closely involved with the legislative plans for establishing the Atomic Energy Commission and the National Science Foundation. Later, he served as Deputy Chairman of the Research and Development Board of the Department of Defense, extending his experience not only in science and public policy, but also in the total range of problems involved in relations between the federal government and the universities.

In 1953, Price was given an opportunity to develop his views on science and public policy when New York University invited him to deliver the James Stokes Lectures on Politics. Subsequently published under the title *Government and Science*, these lectures provided a solid background for the program of research and training Price undertook at Harvard. In his concluding chapter, Price expressed particular concern for strengthening the career services in government for science, and underscored what he considers a special "opportunity for the American university—to educate in the humanities and the social sciences men who have an understanding of the role of the natural sciences in government and society, and to educate natural scientists who can appreciate the problems faced by the politician and the administrator, and who will, some of them, shoulder the burdens of the direct administration of national affairs."[14]

Besides Dean Price, other senior faculty members have at different times assisted in the program, among them Jerome S. Bruner, Professor of Social Relations, I. Bernard Cohen, Professor of History of Science, and Carl Kaysen, Professor of Economics.[15] Each senior staff member has an assistant; other faculty members, visiting scholars, and scientists participate as consultants and research associates.

While the program brings together diverse faculty members and consultants interested in research in the field, it is brought into focus by an advanced seminar in science and public policy. The first year was wholly devoted to research by the faculty, with the seminar beginning only in 1960–61. The seminar is open to a limited number of students, most of whom have had a number of years of experience in government. Of the twenty-one participants in 1961–62, all but six were connected with government agencies in the United States or abroad. The composition of the seminar is thus highly professional, in keeping with the tenor of the School and resembling in many ways the Defense Policy Seminar.

The first year of the seminar was, by intent, a time for experiment. The general approach reflected the background of all of the directors. The first four topics, for example, focused on the history of science and technology in the United States, reflecting Professor Cohen's work. The interests of Dean Price were evident in the study of the contemporary organization of science in the United States. The interests of both Price and Kaysen were reflected in the topics that followed—industrial research, government-university relationships, and the role of government agencies and private philanthropy in financing laboratories and research centers. Finally, the seminar undertook a review of the international aspects of science, the problems of scientific manpower, and a study of the scientist in the laboratory and in the political process.

During its second year, the seminar covered many of the same topics, with faculty and consultants leading the discussions during the first half of the year and student participants the second. One major change was the introduction of comparative material, contrasting the organization of scientific enterprises in a number of countries. The seminar thus took advantage of both the expanding interests of the faculty members and the practical experience of many of the participants.

The training aspect of the program is its unique feature. Nevertheless, it has already had an effect on at least one other department in the University. An undergraduate course in science and public policy was offered jointly in 1960–61 by J. Stefan Dupre, a member of the Department of Government, and S. A. Lakoff—both of them associates in the program and co-authors of *Science and the Nation*. Indirect effects may have been felt in other departments as well. Indeed, one of the advantages of the interdisciplinary approach is to stimulate interest in several directions.

Taken together, Harvard's three programs described above constitute a significant response by a major university to some of the problems posed by the cold war. Each approaches national security from a different point of view, but the total contribution can be weighed in terms of scholarly research and theoretical analysis of public issues as well as of education for public service. As in the case of earlier programs at other institutions, Harvard's efforts absorb only a small part of the University's resources, with most of the financial support coming from outside sources. Though there is evidence that faculty and graduate students from the College of Arts and Science are becoming more interested in national security studies, such studies are not important within the academic disciplines at Harvard. The enrichment of teaching and scholarly resources is thus an objective still to be met.

Nevertheless, the Harvard experience suggests possible lessons for study. Professional training and policy-oriented research have been pressing immediate needs of the United States Government. The acceptance of national security affairs as a major field within traditional disciplines is a long-range commitment and requires a genuine conviction about the continuing significance of issues of defense and security. It is this conviction that is still lacking. It may, however, develop under the persistent pressures put on universities by the government, not only for assistance in resolving current crises, but in clarifying the long-range aims and responsibilities of the United States in world affairs.

Massachusetts Institute of Technology

The development of national security studies at M.I.T. contrasts with the others we have discussed not so much by the direction it has taken—there have been similarities as well as differences—but by two institutional factors: the nature of the original stimulus and the special environment at M.I.T.

Schools of science and technology have become indispensable resources in an age when national security is closely allied to weapons technology, and when technical changes are frequent and often revolutionary. Their relations to the military forces have nevertheless posed serious questions. As early as 1949—before the Korean War and the expanded defense budgets of the 1950's—M.I.T. had already undertaken more than $15 million in research each year for the military services and the Atomic Energy Commission.[16] M.I.T. had done considerable work for the military services during World War II, but after the war some expressed concern about the implications of government research for the Institute. Indeed, a faculty committee warned in 1949 that "we must learn now how to incorporate research sponsored by a variety of external agencies into our plan in such a manner as to strengthen and sustain the educational program, without placing in jeopardy the freedom of thought and liberty of action that lend to academic life its very special flavor."[17]

Sponsored research is, of course, a manifestation of the broader problems raised by the relation of science and technology to public affairs. M.I.T.'s case is special, however. Not only is M.I.T. the major school of its kind in the country, but it has elevated work in the humanities and the social sciences to a level approaching the work it does in the primary fields of science and engineering. And it is also the seat of the Center for International Studies, which has as one of its central interests the area of national security.

M.I.T. is neither a college nor a university, yet it has the characteristics of both and sees itself as a university polarized around science. In establishing the School of Humanities and Social Sciences as one of its five schools, M.I.T. recognized the contribution of the liberal arts to an understanding of man's role in society and to the preparation of scientists for leadership in government, education, and industry.[18] Organized into three departments, the School offers an undergraduate program in the liberal arts, and a graduate program leading to a Ph.D. degree in Economics and in Political Science.

Research is of primary importance at M.I.T.; it is fully integrated into the graduate program and to a lesser extent into the undergraduate program. Most of the organized research is related to science and engineering (there are more than seventy special laboratories on the campus), and there is a considerable amount of work on military problems of all kinds. M.I.T. offers courses in weapons systems and operations research; it participates in the operation of the Brookhaven National Laboratory, and it runs the Lincoln Laboratory, which is supported by the three armed services, and the Center for Communication Sciences; and, with Harvard, it operates the Cambridge Electron Accelerator, made possible by a grant from the Atomic Energy Commission. So extensive are M.I.T.'s operations in military and related fields that it has established a special office called Defense Laboratories. Headed by Vice President James McCormack, a former general officer, and consisting of the Directors of the Lincoln Laboratory, the Instrumentation Laboratory, and the Operations Evaluation Group (operated by M.I.T. for the Navy), this office coordinates many of M.I.T.'s defense projects.

But research and teaching programs at M.I.T. are not confined to science and engineering. The undergraduate and graduate courses in the School of Humanities and Social Sciences seek to relate science and society, and research is conducted in various areas of the arts and social sciences. It is in the Center for International Studies that most of the social-science research on international affairs, defense, and national security problems is conducted; and it is in its new graduate programs in political science that it has had its most important effect on teaching.

A meeting of natural and social scientists and public administrators —held at M.I.T. in November, 1958, to discuss the issues involved in the relation of science to public policy[19]—led M.I.T. to establish a graduate program in government and science. The natural scientists evidently were most concerned with their inability to influence government policy and with the ambiguities and irrationalities of the political process. At the same time, they seemed somewhat fearful of losing their own integrity through political contact, even though they realized that politics would never be as orderly as scientific inquiry. The social scientists seem to have attempted to urge the natural scientists to accept the distinct character of the political process, to seek to understand it, and to equip themselves to make their contribution to the formation of public policy more effective. One of the *rapporteurs* reduced the issues to three major areas, each of which suggested a number of fruitful problems for a teaching and research program: the first concerned the broad objectives of science in public policy, and how to relate science to particular issues such as national security, foreign affairs, and social welfare; the second concerned the organization of the scientific community and of scientists in government and politics; finally, there were the special contributions of the social sciences in advancing public policy in areas affecting science and in developing effective communications between the natural and the social scientists.

The Center for International Studies has, however, been M.I.T.'s most important catalyst for research and teaching in national security affairs. It was established in 1951 as a result of the experience of faculty members on a project in electronics and overseas broadcasts that M.I.T. had undertaken at the request of the U.S. Government. Solution of the scientific problems posed in that project depended on a knowledge of the country to which the broadcast was directed, the objectives of the information program, an understanding of how public opinion is formed and national behavior influenced, and many other nonscientific issues. There was ample academic talent at M.I.T. but no research organization to utilize it effectively. When the project was completed, the Center was formed to meet the need for new institutional arrangements for social science research.[20]

The Center is formally a part of the School of Humanities and Social Sciences. In most respects, its status is equivalent to that of an academic department, the major difference being that it offers no courses, operating essentially as a research organization. It is headed by a Director, Professor Max Millikan, and has a research and administrative staff and an Advisory or Visiting Committee appointed by the M.I.T. administration and responsible to it. Funds for its operations come from foundations and from contracts with government agencies.

The Center is exceptional among university-affiliated research centers in several respects, and one of them is its size and method of operation. It is perhaps the largest of the centers, with more than fifty scholars doing research, its own library, an administrative staff of eight, and a supporting staff of about twenty clerical workers and technical assistants—about one for every three professionals. The Center also has its own editors, librarian, and administrative officer, and has recently begun to publish its own studies. The professional staff includes senior associates, both full- and part-time, research assistants, and Guests of the Center, a title usually reserved for distinguished scholars from other institutions and countries.

Associated with the Director are a number of scholars in many fields. At first, most of the associates were economists, economic historians, and statisticians, perhaps because M.I.T. already had a strong economics department. But the number of political scientists, sociologists, and psychologists has increased, and occasionally, for a specific project, men from other disciplines (including science and technology) come to the Center. Drawn to M.I.T. by its vigorous research center, political scientists of high caliber have so strengthened their discipline at the Institute that, in 1959, M.I.T. was able to launch a Ph.D. program in political science. This, in turn, has made it possible to attract other political scientists of reputation; today, the Center for International Studies has a roughly equal number of economists and political scientists.[21]

As a research organization, the Center's principal aim is to contribute to an understanding of human behavior and "to the solution of some of the long-term problems of international policy which confront decision-makers."[22] For this reason, the Center emphasizes basic research on issues that are important to the public official and of concern to an informed citizenry. The Center's method of operations is based on a carefully articulated philosophy of research. Starting with the conviction that original contributions to basic knowledge are usually the result of individual rather than group effort, the Center has avoided highly organized, directed research and left the individual scholar free to pursue his work in his own way, believing that only in this way can the imagination, insights, and synthesis necessary for creative scholarship come into play. Any attempt to impose a pattern on research, to channel and direct the efforts of the individual into a common product, is likely to represent the lowest rather than the highest level of the group. Originality and creativity, Professor Millikan points out, "are the attributes of individuals, not of organizations."[23]

But this is not to say that the Center does no more than provide housing, administration, and support, or that its program consists of a group of unrelated projects. The intellectual leadership of the Director and senior associates of the M.I.T. faculty, the common focus on specific problems in carefully delineated areas, the close association fostered by proximity and shared interests produces a distinctive point of view and characteristic approach. The products of the Center have been marked by an internal consistency and unity that make them more than a series of independent or unrelated projects.[24]

The Center has shown a strong preference for research in areas of interest and importance to policy-makers. The dangers in such an orientation were clear from the start, and the Center has sought to focus its research on basic problems affecting these issues rather than the issues themselves. This, it has felt, is the appropriate job of the scholar in the study of national security policy. The unique advantage of an academic institution lies in its ability to perform fundamental research; the problem is to relate this research to current issues—in short, to bridge the gulf between the scholar and the policy-maker.[25]

The Center has sought to accomplish this by concurrent work of basic research on fundamental questions with little or no applicability to current issues and research on those dealing with urgent questions of international import.

The research philosophy of the Center is marked by three other characteristics: an interdisciplinary approach, concentration on the process of change, and the conviction that the behavior of nations is conditioned by their "internal dynamics." The first of these has already been noted. The focus on processes that produce change in society rather than a static analysis of that society stems from a concern with the patterns of evolution in a rapidly changing world. The Center is less interested in the institutions and behavior of a state than it is in the direction in which that state is moving, its rate of change, and similar questions. In the internal dynamics of states, the Center believes, lie the roots of international behavior, and its research program of "micro-studies" of social and economic institutions is designed to achieve an understanding of the action of units such as castes, families, business communities, and pressure groups in order better to predict the behavior of societies.

Viewed in these terms, most of the projects at the Center are part of an integrated whole rather than of a series of separate and unrelated studies. They usually fall within four broad areas: underdeveloped countries, international dependence and communications, U.S. military and foreign policy, and the Communist bloc—the largest of these areas being the study of underdeveloped countries. This study began with research on India, Indonesia, and Italy, and was later extended to include Burma, Latin America, and Africa. Much of the work was supported by generous grants from foundations and involved many of the staff members of the Center, some of whom did field work in connection with their studies and wrote extensively about it.

In the field of international communications—defined as "the ways in which influential citizens in various countries acquire and respond to information about other countries and about international affairs in general"—the latest techniques of the behavioral sciences are employed by political scientists, sociologists, and social psychologists. Various studies have already been completed on a number of subjects, among them: the image Americans and Africans have of each other and the ways in which these images affect Afro-American relations; interpersonal contacts in acquaintanceship networks; European attitudes toward unification; the impact of educational television (done with the cooperation of WGBH-TV in Boston); the communication process in India; and the impressions of American scientists visiting the Soviet Union.

American military and foreign policy is the third major area of research. Two of the studies in this field dealt with American society in its world setting and the relation of the United Nations to the foreign policy of the United States. The former project was directed by Walt W. Rostow, in connection with which he wrote *The United States in the World Arena*.[26] The United Nations project, directed by Professor Lincoln Bloomfield, has produced a number of studies exploring such different issues as the attitude of American defense officials to the United Nations, and presidential statements from 1945 to 1958 dealing with the national interest in the U.N. Professor Bloomfield's *The United Nations and U.S. Foreign Policy* also resulted from this topic.[27]

In 1960, the Center began to increase its activities in military and security affairs—first with a seminar on arms control conducted in cooperation with the Harvard Center for International Affairs under a grant from the Rockefeller Foundation. Staff members of the Center wrote papers, memoranda, and articles on arms control for the seminar. In addition, some served as consultants and members of governmental boards, and Professor Bloomfield taught an undergraduate political-science course and a graduate seminar on problems of disarmament and arms control. Under a grant from the Rockefeller Foundation, the Center staked out a program of research in arms control and foreign policy, which is also directed by Professor Bloomfield.

Expansion of the Center's work in national security affairs was furthered by the appointment in 1961 of William W. Kaufmann, formerly with the RAND Corporation, as Professor of Political Science. Professor Kaufmann's first task was to prepare a series of courses in defense policy and strategy for the Political Science Section and an outline for a research program for the Center. Professors Daniel Lerner and Ithiel Pool also moved actively in this field, undertaking a series of studies for the Naval Ordnance Test Station at China Lake on the implications of foreign political attitudes on American military and arms-control policies.

The fourth part of the Center's program, the study of Communist societies, has interested the Center from the start. (Among its earliest studies were those done under Walt Rostow's direction on contemporary Russia and China.) More recently, the Center has been engaged in research on problems related to the Communist bloc. The first of these, which has resulted in many published works, is a comparative analytical survey of the process of change in the satellite countries by William Griffith, formerly political adviser to Radio Free Europe. Dr. Edgar H. Schein and two colleagues published a study of the techniques and effectiveness of persuasion by coercion, as well as Communist society's need for such persuasion; and Alexander Korol, after completing a study of Soviet scientific and technical education, undertook a study of Soviet scientific research and development, with emphasis on the basis for allocation of resources.[28] The National Science Foundation was interested in this study and furnished funds as well as assistance for it through an advisory panel.

The total impact of the work of the Center, as in most cases, is difficult to estimate. Measured in concrete terms, it adds up to a formidable list of publications consisting of more than eighty volumes and more than 400 articles and preliminary studies.[29] All the books were published commercially and available to a wide reading public, while some were noted in the nonscholarly press both at home and abroad. In this sense, the Center has certainly contributed to public discussion and broader understanding of the problems of national security.

But the Center has tried to do more than this. It has tried to reach the policy-maker and has focused on problems of immediate relevance to him. As far as one can tell, it has been successful in this effort also. For undoubtedly the Center's studies have been carefully read by government officials, and a number of studies have been specifically prepared for executive agencies and Congressional committees. Moreover, the Director and other members of the staff have often given advice, testified before Congressional committees, lectured to small but influential audiences, and served as government consultants here and abroad. Certainly, Millikan and several of his research associates can be considered members of the small band of academicians whose advice is frequently sought by policy-makers and who, by personal prestige and knowledge, exert an influence on the formulation of policy. Of the M.I.T. group, Walt Rostow, Counselor of the State Department and Chairman of the Policy Planning Council since 1961, is the best known.

The Center for International Studies has been more successful than most in gaining financial support, but it was not able to free itself from the limitations inherent in the method of financing. Recognizing this fact, Professor Millikan campaigned to raise funds for the Center, basing his appeal not only on the needs of the Center, but on the importance of strengthening the social-science program in international affairs at M.I.T. The first result of this campaign was a grant in the spring of 1959 from the Ford Foundation for $850,000. With these funds, Dr. Millikan was able to support two more professorships in international affairs and to provide security for several other faculty members when they were not working on other projects. With two other professorships in international communications made possible by an earlier grant from the Ford Foundation, and appointments from regular departmental funds, the Center is now assured of a small senior staff for an indefinite period. The later Ford grant also provided for graduate fellowships in the fields of economic development, international communication, and international politics, thus strengthening the graduate program of the Department of Economics and Social Science while training young scholars in those fields in which the Center was most interested.

These measures have done much to assure the Center's future and to enrich M.I.T.'s academic program. But the Center's plans go further—not only to have a permanent senior staff, but to provide them with research and secretarial help, to secure sufficient funds to enable it to undertake its own research, and to seize unusual opportunities when they arise without having to go through the time-consuming steps to secure foundation support.

Already the Center has been able to assure the stability and flexibility of its program more than has any other comparable academic organization. It has been a prolific source of published research on a broad range of subjects related to national security; it has exerted influence in government circles and stimulated public discussion; it has strengthened greatly M.I.T.'s academic program. It has, in sum, met the problems of focus, financing, and policy-oriented research in a most effective way. But its success is due not only to the direction the Center has received, but also to the special circumstances at M.I.T.: the concept of basic research and the commitment to build a strong faculty in the social sciences. These factors have given the Center the power and stability that, in other institutions, resides in the traditional departments.

8

The State University

NATIONAL SECURITY PROGRAMS in state universities vary as much among themselves as they do with programs in private colleges and universities. The one thing they have in common is the aim of public service—an important responsibility of the American system of public higher education. Certainly today's large state universities are far removed from the land-grant colleges established in the second half of the nineteenth century to provide the country with agricultural specialists and industrial technicians. Just as the nation's needs are more complex, so are the tremendous educational enterprises that are the heirs of the land-grant movement. It is sometimes said that the future of American higher education no longer rests with the private colleges and universities that so long had led it, but with the great state universities that are expanding to absorb the increasing number of young men and women seeking advanced education. The state universities already house some of the most important scientific and technological facilities sponsored by the federal government. Here, their contribution to national defense is manifest. Their contribution in intellectual and educational terms can perhaps be measured by a description of several of the principal national security programs that have grown up since the Korean War.

Two State Universities: A Comparison

Wisconsin and California boast of two of the best state university systems in the country. Both possess major intellectual resources and both have made efforts to develop programs in national security studies. Although they are alike in purpose, these programs differ in important respects that are less the result of geography, institutional objectives, or problems of financing than of individual faculty motivations and administration interest.

Work in national-security affairs at the University of Wisconsin is centered in the National Security Studies Group, organized in 1957 largely through the efforts of Professor Carlisle P. Runge, then Assistant Dean of the Law School.[1] This Wisconsin program actually owed its initial stimulus to the Harvard Defense Studies Program, which it greatly resembled during its formative years.[2] It has had both University and foundation support, an original grant of $75,000 for a three-year program by the Carnegie Corporation of New York having been matched by the University.

The aims of the Wisconsin program were modest and realistic, and its founders tried to build it mainly from the Wisconsin faculty rather than from outside sources. Viewing the study of national security as essentially an interdisciplinary one, Professor Runge avoided any effort to organize "a separate and distinct academic entity." He sought to build up instead a small staff to support and coordinate, rather than direct, work in various disciplines at the University, and to secure the cooperation of qualified members in various departments. As a part of a public university with a long tradition of public service to the state and close ties to the state government, the program also provided advice and assistance to the Governor and state legislature on national security matters such as civil defense.

The staff of the National Security Studies Group was housed in the Law School, which provided its administrative support, but organizationally it was in the Division of Social Studies. The then Vice-President of the University (now President), Fred Harvey Harrington, maintained a close personal interest in it and, in 1960, formed a committee to supervise its program. Harrington's personal interest gave the program a standing on the Madison campus it might otherwise not have had.

The major activity of the National Security Studies Group in its early years was a seminar on "Military Policy and Administration," a two-semester graduate course whose twenty students came mostly from the Law School, with some representation from the College of Arts and Sciences and the military forces (these last being instructors in ROTC units and officers sent to Wisconsin for graduate work—usually in the School of Journalism). The seminar attracted few of the regular graduate students in the University, which was disappointing, since the group had set as one of its goals the training of graduate students and the recruitment of a faculty capable of supervising doctoral dissertations in national security affairs.

An important part of the Wisconsin program, though not its central focus, was the research activity it sponsored, which was conducted by members of the staff, its research associates, and by interested faculty members in various departments and in the Law School. The program also provided financial assistance to graduate students whose theses were on issues relating to national security. One major project was an historical study of U.S. defense organization, prepared by Captain Francis N. Laurent, USN Ret., for use by the seminar but also distributed to a limited number of institutions and agencies. Runge's main interest was in the implications for strategy of the obsolescence of Army equipment. Other projects were a study of political consultation in NATO, a study of West German rearmament, and an analysis of the legal and constitutional aspects of civil defense.

In the area of public service and discussion, the Studies Group participated in the formulation of state legislation, worked closely with the University's adult-education program, and cooperated actively in planning and conducting various conferences and meetings on defense issues. During 1958–59, the Group prepared a series of eight bills on civil defense designed to provide continuity of government in Wisconsin in the event of nuclear attack, and, in 1959, it sponsored a three-day conference on state civil defense. Dean Runge also served on the panel of lecturers of the Wisconsin Extension Division, and spoke on national strategy to adult-education groups in various parts of the state. In addition, Runge was active in the reassessment of the ROTC program at the University.

Outside the National Security Studies Group, there was little work done at Wisconsin in defense policy or related fields. Except in the natural sciences, where members of the faculty were active in government research and as consultants for government agencies and committees, there were, at first, few faculty members with active professional associations in the field or interested in teaching national security courses of their own. Certain departments, such as Political Science, obviously had a greater interest than others and members would lecture to the seminar and cooperate with the Group. In 1959, moreover, the department took a major step by adding to its staff Bernard Cohen, former research associate of the Center of International Studies at Princeton, and managing editor of *World Politics*.

During his first year at Wisconsin, Professor Cohen participated to only a limited extent in the seminar. He did, however, teach a departmental course in "Problems of American Foreign and Military Policy." When Dean Runge left for Washington in February, 1961, to become Assistant Secretary of Defense for Manpower, Cohen became director of the Studies Group. Since he was scheduled to be on leave during 1961–62, it was decided to continue on the existing basis under Professor James McCamy of the Political Science Department while preparing plans for the following year. The Carnegie Corporation then gave funds for continuation of the program for an additional three years; thus, on Professor Cohen's return, the National Securities Studies Group took on a new vigor. It was moved out of the Law School to the Department of Political Science, and came under the direction of an executive committee composed of the Director and Professors McCamy and Leon Epstein—all political scientists. It broke away also from the early Harvard model and became, in effect, a broad social-science program. Professor Cohen initiated a graduate seminar on "Military Policy and Administration" replacing the earlier seminar; in addition, he continued his undergraduate course in "American Foreign and Military Policy." This increased activity was bolstered when the History Department took on a military historian and the Economics Department appointed a junior faculty member interested in national security and offered a course on the economics of defense.

With its greater resources and larger aims, the Defense Policy Seminar at Harvard had reached more students and received more attention. But, like Wisconsin, it had drawn heavily on the Law School for students. Neither Wisconsin nor Harvard was initially successful in attracting the best students from the graduate departments, though both developed in this direction later. The potential success of the Wisconsin program now rests on the decision of the administration to develop the field as a regular part of the academic offerings of the University.

The work at Wisconsin bears both comparison and contrast with the work done at the University of California. On the Berkeley campus, there is an outstanding faculty in history and the social sciences and a full awareness of advances in national security affairs— just as at Wisconsin. But the similarity ends here, for Berkeley has no developed program of research and training, despite the fact that there already exist a number of organizations working in international relations upon which the University could build such a program.

One of these organizations is the Bureau of International Relations, established in 1919 to coordinate various activities of the University in international studies after World War I. The Bureau is responsible for the special International Relations Library; it conducts conferences and meetings and works closely with outside agencies and groups such as the World Affairs Council; it assists students interested in entering the Foreign Service; it takes care of foreign visitors, handles University contracts with foreign governments, and arranges an orientation program for families going abroad under University auspices. Since 1955, the Bureau has been part of the Institute of International Studies and serves as the administrative office for that body.[3]

The Institute of International Studies, which operates under an interdepartmental faculty committee, is a clearing-house for information on international studies at the University, supports faculty research, and coordinates the various approaches to research in the field. The actual research is carried out usually within the centers, committees, and projects that are component parts of the Institute. The organizations served by the Institute are concerned for the most part with regional or area studies, which receive support from one or more of the foundations, have their own directors, and conduct research and training. (They include centers in Far Eastern, Slavic, and Latin American affairs.) Much of the work done at these centers is relevant to the national security field, but there is no single operation that focuses on the defense area.

At the University of California at Los Angeles, there has been a more concerted effort to develop a national security program. As at Berkeley, area-study programs at UCLA were placed under the general supervision of a central organization, the Institute of International and Foreign Studies, in 1958. Headed by Professor R. G. Neumann of the Political Science Department, the Institute began in 1959 to plan for the establishment of a national security program. The original impetus for this effort seems to have come from Najeeb E. Halaby, a Los Angeles attorney and former Assistant Secretary of the Army. Advice was solicited from people who had had experience in organizing such programs, and, in 1960, a National Security Studies Program began in the Institute of International and Foreign Studies.

At the start, the National Security Studies Program was largely limited to the sponsorship of meetings and lectures (that, it was hoped, would stimulate interest in and support for the program) on disarmament, NATO, and science and public policy, by men like Edward Teller, Paul Nitze, Denis W. Healey, I. I. Rabi, and Sir Solly Zuckerman. UCLA also had the advantage of being a neighbor of the RAND Headquarters in Santa Monica, and many RAND experts participated in the program. RAND scholars also became part of the expanded activities, when a series of graduate seminars were organized in 1962 and 1963 with Professor Richard N. Rosecrance of the Department of Political Science serving as Coordinator. The RAND relationship was formalized through the annual appointment of a RAND Senior Fellow in the National Security Studies Program, and demonstrated by the heavy reliance on RAND lecturers in the series of colloquiums and lectures sponsored under the program. The first RAND Senior Fellows were Albert Wohlstetter, Amrom H. Katz, and Malcolm Hoag. The collective volume on *The Dispersion of Nuclear Weapons*, edited by Professor Rosecrance and based, in most cases, on seminar reports and discussions in 1961, 1962, and 1963, was the first published result of this relationship with RAND.[4]

The outstanding institutional characteristic of the UCLA program is, indeed, its dependence on RAND. In many ways, this dependence reveals a lack of initiative on the part of the University administration and faculty. Nevertheless, UCLA has an incentive to develop strength in the social sciences, and it can now build on the basis of an organized program. No such basis exists at Berkeley, even though for several years the Political Science Department has been interested in developing national security studies as an area for specialization and in taking the initiative with a research and teaching program in all of the social sciences. Other departments such as economics, history and sociology, it was hoped, would follow this lead and persuade their own specialists to participate in such a program, but it has evidently been difficult to make the major appointments essential to progress.

In this respect, the example of Wisconsin is instructive. The program is modest, manageable, and practical within the framework of the University. But what is most important, national security affairs is being integrated into the curriculum as an important educational and intellectual field.

A State University and a Private University Collaborate

The program in national security affairs set up by Duke University in Durham and at the University of North Carolina at Chapel Hill is of particular interest for two reasons: It is the only academic effort in the field conducted jointly by two large universities; and it is the only program in the South.[5] Initiative for the program came from a small group of faculty members from different disciplines at both institutions. Some were already teaching courses in the field, some were engaged in research, and others were interested in working on some aspect of national security studies. They included Professors

Theodore Ropp and Robert H. Connery from Duke, and political scientists S. Shepard Jones, Andrew Scott and Keener C. Frazer from North Carolina.

The initial idea was to provide a forum for those interested in national security affairs to discuss mutual problems. There was also the hope that these meetings would develop into a more formal program utilizing the faculty and facilities of two of the largest universities in the South. Cooperative ventures between the two, one a state university, the other private, were not uncommon. An arrangement had long existed for the exchange of library resources, and there were precedents for joint graduate courses. Thus, the first meetings of the group in the fall of 1959 led easily to the organization of a joint National Security Policy Seminar.

The primary objective of the Seminar was to stimulate interest among faculty and graduate students and to discuss work in progress. No formal organization was established, but Dr. Robin Higham, a young historian at North Carolina, was designated executive secretary to handle the details of the meetings. Meetings were held monthly, alternately at Duke and Chapel Hill, to discuss a paper presented by one of the members, with occasional meetings for outside speakers when the public was invited. The Seminar had virtually no funds, and in its first year had only two guest speakers—General James Gavin and Michael Howard, a British military historian visiting the United States under the auspices of the Ford Foundation. Support from the participating departments made it possible to invite additional speakers in subsequent years, but the number was small. Lack of funds also prohibited those other activities, such as conferences, fellowship programs, grants, etc., that were usually employed in national security programs to create interest and attract students and scholars.

What the Duke-UNC Seminar lacked in financial resources, it made up in seriousness of purpose. Each of its members, whether graduate student or faculty, was engaged in research, and meetings were devoted to a critical examination of each other's work. Not only did they profit from this interdisciplinary criticism, but each carried over into other activities the insights and points of view of his colleagues.

The experience of the first year, which was largely experimental, convinced the members of the Seminar that the project should be continued and, if possible, expanded. They were also encouraged to hope for financial support from a foundation, and began in the spring of 1960 actively to plan a five-year program.

The objectives of the program reflected a sound and realistic appraisal of what a university could contribute to the study of national security affairs. The emphasis was on graduate work and scholarship rather than training for the public service, for all the members belonged to regular departments with strong graduate offerings, and they conceived of national security studies in terms of an interdisciplinary graduate program. The Duke-UNC proposal represented a traditional approach to graduate study; the differences were the interdisciplinary nature of the field and the joint character of the effort. Their approach may also be related to the fact that neither institution has a school of public administration nor trains public officials as Harvard does at Littauer and Princeton at the Woodrow Wilson School. There is also no relation to the law schools, despite the fact that Duke has one of the best law schools in the South, which is involved in one aspect of national security studies through Professor Arthur Larson, Director of the World Rule of Law Center. At Harvard and Wisconsin, the law schools had played an important role in the establishment of the national security programs; at Duke and North Carolina, they played none, though the existence of the World Rule of Law Center was noted as a resource on which the program could draw.

By pooling their resources, the universities are able to put together a strong basis for their program. The Duke History Department includes men like Professor Ropp, a leading American military historian, Professor I. B. Holley, author of *Ideas and Weapons*, a pioneer study on the development of air doctrine, and Professor Richard C. Watson, one of the authors of the Air Force history of World War II. Among the political scientists at Duke is Professor Connery who has been consultant to the Navy Department, the Secretary of Defense, and the Hoover Commission, and who collaborated on a book on James V. Forrestal. North Carolina's Political Science Department, in addition to Jones, Frazer, and Scott, also recruited one of its former graduate students, Raymond H. Dawson, to strengthen its position in the national security field. Dawson, who had spent a year at Ohio State University working on a study of air defense policy since World War II, has, since 1960, given a graduate course on "Defense Policy and National Security" and a graduate seminar in "National Security Policy." By 1963, two Master's theses had been written on defense studies in the Department of Political Science at North Carolina, and three doctoral candidates were writing their dissertations in the field.

Duke and North Carolina have other resources to support the existing Seminar and the proposed expanded program. Their combined library holdings are particularly strong in European, diplomatic, and military history, and at both institutions there are additional programs to supplement the work of the Seminar: at North Carolina, the Institute for Research in Social Science and the Psychometric Laboratory of the Institute of Statistics (which does work for various government agencies); at Duke, the Commonwealth Studies Center, an International Studies Program, and an Office of Ordnance Research (which monitors basic research projects at more than a hundred institutions).

The Duke-UNC National Security Policy Seminar is interdisciplinary, in order "to take cognizance of the manifold and inter-related factors contributing to national security." The teaching program, however, is organized within the existing departmental structure. Graduate students work in one of the established departments and meet all the requirements of that department, but if they specialize in national security affairs and write a dissertation in that area, they can work under one of the faculty members of the group, apply for research grants, and profit from the interdisciplinary approach of the Seminar. In this way, it was hoped to combine research and teaching in an integrated program.

Lacking outside financial support, the Duke-UNC program is necessarily limited. Nevertheless, the Seminar has continued, operating without a budget or administrative staff. From 1960 to 1962, it held thirteen meetings devoted to discussion of papers presented by members of the Seminar and by visiting scholars, and, jointly with the Air Force Historical Foundation, it sponsored a symposium on the History of Air Power. Lacking financial support, the Seminar cannot expand its activities, but there is every indication that it will continue to provide a forum for faculty members and graduate students of the two universities interested in national security studies. The strength of the program lies in its maintenance of an interdisciplinary program of teaching and research built on the traditional courses in participating departments. It is thus possible to develop national security as an area of specialization within the existing educational programs of both institutions, even if lack of outside financing makes it impossible to expand special activities.

A Special Case: The Ohio State University

In the field of national security policy studies, the Ohio State University is unique in two important respects: It defines national security affairs more broadly than other educational institutions; and it enjoys independent funds for work in the field and is thus not obliged to seek support from foundations or government contracts. The broadened concept of national security policy studies is mainly reflected in the support given to specialized scientific and technological projects. Where scientists and engineers are involved in national security research and teaching programs elsewhere, it is usually in terms of the "policy" role they play as consultants and advisers or in terms of the political and military implications of advances in science and technology. But at Ohio State, grants in a program of "education in national security" have been made to studies on subjects like the biosynthetic potential of fungi or infrared astronomical photometry.

This support of science *qua* science may not be unrelated to the fact that the University has at its disposal considerable funds for national security studies—an estimated annual income of approximately $300,000 in the early 1960's. For a variety of reasons, there has been little opportunity to spend anything like this amount on research and teaching in the recognized areas of national security studies. Major grants have thus been made for scientific and technological projects that would normally not be included within the limits of the field.

The Ohio State program began when Colonel Ralph D. Mershon, an alumnus and former Army reserve officer, left the bulk of a large personal fortune to the University on his death in February, 1952. Not less than half the income of the bequest was to be used to "promote, encourage and carry on civilian-military education and training in the United States and its territories," with the decision as to what constituted such education and training left to the "judgment and discretion" of the University.[6]

Colonel Mershon had been a staunch advocate of a strong reserve system and had been instrumental in establishing the Reserve Officers Training Corps after World War I. Reserve affairs, therefore, plainly fell within the scope of the bequest, and, in the initial Mershon program, heavy emphasis was placed on ROTC activities. Between 1955 and 1960, Mershon funds supported a pioneer program in cooperation with the Air Force ROTC to test the feasibility of civilian instruction in ROTC courses. At the inception and again at the end of the program, conferences on ROTC problems were held, and, in the summer of 1957, the Mershon Fund supported a short Air Force ROTC Instructor Training Course.[7] In addition, Mershon funds made possible, in 1956 and 1957, a training program for Army ROTC instructors in American Military History, a required ROTC course that lent itself to civilian instruction.[8] Since then, the Committee has continued to support other ROTC programs.

But the improvement of ROTC instruction was only one of many activities sponsored by the Mershon Fund. The plan was to avoid long-range commitments and to support only limited ventures with a minimum of faculty direction and participation. Under the aegis of a Defense Studies Committee composed of faculty members and headed by Professor H. F. Harding, the Fund supported a number of diverse projects—a seminar in National Security Policy on the Harvard model, related courses in the History, Political Science, and Economics Departments, a scholarship and fellowship program, public lectures and conferences.[9]

At the same time, problems of definition, purpose, and focus were the subject of a continuous inquiry by faculty members. One difficulty was the lack of specific guidance in the bequest and the nature of the field itself; the other was the large amount of money available. The first made it possible to justify almost any project in the name of "civil-military education"; the second to support a great number of projects. Aware of these problems, the Defense Studies Committee attempted to frame a concept of national security studies and a program to meet the special needs of Ohio State.

In February, 1958, the Committee submitted a report to the President and the Board of Trustees proposing a broad program to develop trained minds—"High Talent Manpower" was the phrase used—and create ideas and imaginative proposals. The Committee envisaged the development of this program on three levels, to be carried forward concurrently: "*one*, the immediate task of organization for defense; *two*, the intermediate task of developing High Talent manpower; and *three*, the task of creating a flow of ideas that will guarantee our long-range security."[10]

At the same time as these general goals were articulated, the organization of the program was given new form. The Defense Studies Committee was dissolved and a new twelve-man committee with enlarged powers was created. Known as the Mershon Committee on Education in National Security, this group was composed of nine voting members (appointed from the faculty by the President for staggered three-year terms) and three corresponding members—the Dean of the Graduate School and the Assistants to the Vice Presidents for Curriculum and for Research. Appointments to the Mershon Committee included representation from many departments and schools of the University—Engineering, Medicine, Law, Agriculture, Chemistry, Political Science, History, and Economics. The chairman of the

Committee was Robert J. Nordstrom, Associate Dean of the Law School.

The Mershon Committee does not itself direct any of the activities in the program, but is rather a supervisory board establishing general policy and controlling the purse strings. It has no staff of its own, and when it requires expert advice, it calls in consultants. In the sense that it defines the conditions to be met by those requesting support and passes on the merits of their proposals, the Committee acts like a foundation. Following this example, it adopted initially the "seed money" principle—it supported projects for a limited period of time, after which the projects had to become self-supporting or receive support through regular University channels or outside sources.[11]

Whether the "seed money" principle, utilized so effectively by the foundations in opening up new areas of research and stimulating interest in selected fields of study, was applicable to the situation at Ohio State was not at all certain. Indeed, the Committee reconsidered its position after the first few years. For it had become clear that no outside agencies would support such activities so long as the University itself had the means to do so. But the "seed money" principle had committed the Mershon Committee to a series of experimental projects and weakened the possibility of a continuing large-scale integrated program with a guarantee of permanence that independent resources could provide.

Both educational or instructional and research activities have been conducted under the auspices of the Mershon Fund. Probably the longest-lived is the National Security Policy Seminar, established on a five-year trial basis in 1955 and then continued. It is a three-term course for graduate students and advanced undergraduates, and is not listed under a particular department. The Director of the course has changed several times. For a period it was Professor Harding, who was also Acting Director of National Security Studies. Professor Harvey C. Mansfield, formerly chairman of the Political Science Department, was director for a year, and since then the course has been headed by a member of the Law faculty and by an economist appointed as a Mershon Professor in 1961.

The Seminar has followed the pattern of the Harvard Seminar in many ways. During the initial years, for example, extensive use was made of visiting lecturers, with members of the staff serving as chairmen, panel moderators, or discussants. No effort or expense was spared to bring to the Seminar the most distinguished speakers; in one year, General Arthur Trudeau, Paul Nitze, Eric Goldman, Gerhard Ritter, Albert Hill, Henry Kissinger, Dean Acheson, and V. K. Krishna

Menon, among others, attended. However qualified the speakers, there was considerable doubt whether such a roster actually constituted a course. The same question had been raised at Harvard, it will be recalled, and the decision there had been to reduce the number of speakers. Under Professor Mansfield's direction, there was a similar reduction, and the Seminar was conducted more like a college course than a series of public lectures. This general tendency has continued.

In addition to the Seminar, the Mershon Fund supported a special national security course entitled "Minor Problems in National Security Policy," offered only once, in 1959–60. The course was largely an experiment undertaken by John Phelps, a physicist, who was himself working under a Mershon grant on research on deterrence and arms control. (Phelps later left to join the staff of the Institute for Defense Analyses.) The students numbered seven, five of them supported by Mershon funds. Each student selected a topic and prepared a paper for discussion; occasionally, outside scholars, such as Albert Wohlstetter, were invited to meet with the group, not to lecture but to participate in the discussion. In organizing the course after the first term, Phelps limited the theme to "Accidental War" and had the students write research reports on various aspects of the subject.[12] These papers on accidental war have been widely cited in the expanding literature in the field and constitute one of the few published contributions of the Mershon program.

The Mershon Committee also supported certain departmental courses, and was willing to support more if a member of the faculty or a department desired to add them. The criterion for Mershon support was that the courses make a "demonstrably substantial contribution" to national security studies; the method, on the "seed-money" principle, was to pay for released time for the instructor to prepare the course and teach it for one or two terms. After that, the department was to budget for the course as it did for all others. One could expect, therefore, a certain unwillingness on the part of departments to encourage experimental courses that they would have to fund later on, and a reluctance on the part of younger instructors to become involved in a project that lacked strong departmental support.

Under these conditions, the impact of the Mershon program on the social sciences was at first limited. In the History Department, for example, the Committee supported a course in "American Military Policy," taught by Professor Harry L. Coles, and, in 1959, also supported a proposal to bring visiting professors in military history to the campus for several months. One was the German scholar, Gerhard Ritter, and the other Norman Gibbs, Chichele Professor of the History of War at Oxford University. The visiting program was not continued beyond these two, however, nor did the department utilize Mershon support to expand its work in military history beyond the course taught by Professor Coles.

Interestingly enough, the most positive response to Mershon support came from the Department of Economics. For some years, the Committee supported a basic course in the Economics of National Security taught by Professor Meno Lovenstein. In 1961, with Mershon support, the department appointed Richard M. Sherman, Jr., a former staff member of the Army-affiliated Operations Research Office, Mershon Professor of Economics. Professor Sherman teaches a graduate seminar in problems of national security economics and ran the National Security Policy Seminar from 1962 to 1964. The Economics Department also voted in 1962 to make the economics of national security a recognized area of specialization for its graduate students, thus making Ohio State one of the few universities where national security is a major field within a department of economics.

In developing a Mershon program, Ohio State largely relied on its own resources. The University has been slow in adding new strength to its faculty, even though the Mershon Committee was at first willing to support the appointment of Mershon Professors specializing in national security affairs in different departments. Not until 1961–62 did any of the social-science departments appoint professors in this field. The reasons for this reluctance are not entirely clear, but may be related to these factors: a conviction that the existing faculty was adequate to the task; doubts about the relevance of the program to the University's aims; unwillingness of traditional departments to enter new fields of study; the competing rivalries among departments and schools for a share of the funds; and, finally, an inability to attract men from the top universities or from important posts in the government.

Some members of the University had always recognized the need to add to the faculty recognized authorities in national security affairs, and a few abortive efforts were made to do so; not until 1960, however, was the early proposal to appoint Mershon Professors seriously pursued. These men were to have a dual appointment, in a department and in the Mershon Center, to teach courses and participate in the Center's activities. Initially, their salaries were to be met from Mershon funds, but would later be paid from the department's regular budget, although no definite time was set for this change. It was expected that these Mershon Professors would not only strengthen the departments but also the Mershon program, and presumably would carry on their research and direct graduate students in the field. Various departments were asked whether they were interested in this arrangement, and if so, to nominate candidates. Not all responded affirmatively. But Professor Sherman was named a Mershon Professor of Economics in 1961 and, in 1962, Edgar Furniss, formerly of the Politics Department of Princeton, was named Mershon Professor of Political Science. By the end of 1962, two other Mershon professors had been appointed, but in fields that could only be included in a national security program within Ohio State's broad definition of it. One was in Engineering and the other in Chemistry.

Strengthening the faculty was only one problem faced by the Mershon Committee; the other was how to arouse student interest in courses and specialized fields in national security affairs. An extensive scholarship and fellowship program was initiated with the expectation that the recipients would not only add to the strength of national security studies on the campus but attract competent young scholars from other universities to Ohio State. In the three years of 1958–61 alone, there were sixty-six such awards on the predoctoral level and six more on the postdoctoral level. Of the predoctoral scholars, forty-two were undergraduates and twenty-four graduates, all of them required to attend the National Security Policy Seminar. (Many of the awards were made to students in the physical sciences—another reflection of the broad definition of national security studies held by the Mershon program.) The postdoctoral fellowships, carrying a stipend of $7,500, were for mature scholars, who were required to remain in residence for a year and participate in the Seminar and other Mershon activities, while doing their own research.

In addition to trying to strengthen faculty and student participation in national security affairs, the Mershon Committee sponsored a series of public lectures and conferences. The conference program included meetings on the ROTC, an important Civil-Military Relations Conference held in 1959, and two meetings focused on international law, one being the Fifth Annual Regional Meeting of the American Society of International Law. The Committee also supported a large gathering in February, 1959, to consider the logistical implications of changes in military technology; conferences on the role of military forces in the Middle East and Latin America; and a meeting in October, 1962, on the economics of research and development, initially organized by the University's College of Commerce and Administration.[13] In addition, in 1960, the Committee inaugurated an annual competition (for a prize of $2,500) for the best book-length manuscript on national security "to create an awareness of the prob-

lems of our national security and to stimulate ideas which will contribute to their solution." In the first three years, three books were
accepted for publication, although only in 1961 was a volume
deemed sufficiently broad in scope to warrant the full prize.[14]

All of these activities added up, by 1963, to a considerable amount
of experimentation, but not to an effective program. The program at
Ohio State cannot be said to have made a major contribution to
the development of research and training in national security affairs,
even though it had the financial resources to make the program a
success. Research failed to produce a single significant publication
by a member of the Ohio State faculty; the volumes published were
submitted by outside scholars for the Mershon Award, or consisted
of papers most of which had been written by outside scholars. The
National Security Policy Seminar was uneven, and had few students
who had not been attracted by the promise of scholarships and fellowships. There were many public lectures and conferences, but the
tangible results—in terms of publication and student interest—were
small. Finally, efforts to strengthen the faculty through the appointment of Mershon professors were minimal in the first seven years of
the program. In short, Ohio State failed to realize its potential in
national security studies.

This failure seems to have confirmed the "haunting fear," expressed
by Vice President Frederick Heimberger in 1959, at the time the
Mershon Committee was reorganized, that the faculty "might fail to
take full advantage of this opportunity to do things which are bold
and productive and which will add to the strength and prestige of this
University."[15] This fear must have also been felt by the Mershon
Committee, when its first efforts to secure more faculty participation
brought little response. But the Committee continued to explore the
ways that it could contribute significantly to the study of national
security. Under its broad definition of that field, it was supporting a
variety of research projects in physical sciences, but it clearly needed
to do more in the social sciences.

In mid-1960, a committee of the social-science departments and
the Law School actually prepared a detailed study for a Social Science
Center for National Security Policy Studies.[16] It defined the field of
national security studies in terms of the development and use of
national power and noted the interdisciplinary character of the field.
Carefully studying existing centers, seminars, and institutes concerned
with national security problems, it concluded that the Ohio State
program had failed "because of the lack of a proper organization,
adequate resources, and the necessary encouragement from the right

places."[17] It found that there were a number of teaching and research activities at Ohio State in national security affairs, but thought they were uncoordinated and unfocused. What was needed was a center, under a single director, to serve as a "catalyst and clearing-house," which would develop the three major fields—graduate studies, advanced specialized training, and faculty research.

This proposal for a center with a full-time director and an integrated program was not adopted. A modified social-science program in the form of a Graduate Institute for World Affairs was established in 1961 by the Mershon Committee, with a member of the History Department, Professor Sydney Fisher, a specialist in the Middle East, serving as Acting Director. The Institute was based on an "interdisciplinary approach" and was set up "to stimulate and facilitate . . . studies of the development of national strength, the threat of force in international relations and the diminution of such threats, and the impact of these phenomena upon world society as well as upon individual national communities." Major efforts at the Institute were made in two directions: to encourage graduate students to participate in interdepartmental seminars (in addition to meeting their departmental requirements); and to hold conferences on specialized topics in which both graduate students and faculty could participate. The Institute activities still did not comprise a national security program as envisaged in the report of the social-science committee, but it offered certain institutional arrangements that could eventually prove useful.

It was not until 1963 that an integrated social-science program was set up. It is significant that the program was put under the direction of Professor Furniss, who had been named Mershon Professor of Political Science the previous year. For Furniss was a teacher whose special qualifications were what Ohio State had been lacking all these years; he was an established scholar whose research had been done primarily in national security affairs. Of all the members of the Ohio State social-science departments, only Professor Mansfield had been able to bring similar stature to the program; but, in Mansfield's case, national security was not of primary interest. While at Princeton, Furniss had participated in the Center of International Studies, contributed to several of the Center's studies, completed an important research project on contemporary France in connection with a study group at the Council on Foreign Relations, and contributed some of the earliest textual materials for national security courses. Furniss brought to Ohio State what Bernard Cohen, James McCamy, and Leon Epstein brought to the Wisconsin program and men like Theodore Ropp, Robert Connery, Andrew Scott and Raymond Dawson added to the Duke-UNC program.

The social-science program at Ohio State does three things: It coordinates previously approved Mershon projects; it expands some of these projects; and it offers a conceptual basis for all Mershon activities. For example, the program serves as a "home" for both predoctoral and postdoctoral fellows, assumes coordinating responsibility for Mershon Professors in the social sciences, and sponsors special seminars and general and scholarly conferences. In an attempt to expand its activities, it also offers research support to scholars outside the Ohio State faculty through cooperative projects, visiting Mershon Professorships, and direct grants—if a "substantial portion of the research" can be carried out at Ohio State.

The conceptual basis for the program is both interdisciplinary and comparative—comparative because "the United States cannot pursue security for itself alone, in disregard of what is taking place beyond its borders." Within this context, the program "is interested . . . in the subnational setting within which official policy-makers must operate, in *patterns of national policy* within the international environment, and its rudimentary *institutions* designed to protect the security of the members, even while affecting the particular pattern of their statecraft." Without attempting to cover all the issues posed by "these large, inter-locking areas," they nevertheless provide the intellectual framework on which "to determine the support of particular projects." This kind of framework had been sorely needed at Ohio State.

The development of the Ohio State program is particularly instructive for it demonstrates that even when financial support is assured, focus and a strong, experienced faculty are essential. Indeed, the Ohio State program stands in sharp contrast to the Duke-UNC activities. In the latter case, a group of first-rate scholars with clear objectives have been able to make national security affairs a meaningful intellectual and educational activity at two major institutions even though they have received no special financing for their program. With the appointment of Professor Furniss and the establishment of the social-science program, Ohio State made the first major step in making up for much lost time. The over-all Mershon program continues to cover a broad area, including scientific and technological projects, and it thus continues to differ from other academic centers. But in its support for the Social Science Program, the Mershon Center set up the base from which it could make its real contribution to the development of national security studies.

9

Policy and Behavior

THE EARLY PROGRAMS for national security studies, with their origins in the years before World War II, established a general pattern for later ones, but, within this pattern, there was wide variation. The institutions discussed in the present chapter have developed programs that have common characteristics with the programs we have already discussed, but that in certain respects differ in approach, objective, and method. These differences can be explained in part by the institutional setting and local conditions at each university—the external environment that determines in large measure the organization, methods, materials, and size of a program. But more important, perhaps, are the approaches and objectives of the scholars who were responsible for establishing the programs. Their approaches and objectives have resulted in programs of two general types: those with a policy orientation and those oriented toward behavioral studies.

The Pragmatic Approach

We have already suggested some of the perils of research oriented to current national policy issues: the temptation to step over the line from policy clarification to policy determination, the impatience of the policy-maker, the problems raised by classified information, and the restrictions on objectivity and academic freedom that may be involved. These are risks that scholars must recognize if they are to deal with contemporary issues of national security. Recognition of the risks can affect the decision of which issues a scholar will choose to investigate, the research methods he will adopt, and the ultimate objectives he will set for himself.

One of the academic centers oriented to current national policies is the Washington Center of Foreign Policy Research, established in 1957. Its objectives and methods of operation are quite distinctive, both because of its location in the nation's capital, and because of the close relations many of its members enjoy with government agencies. Indeed, the Center serves in many ways as a convenient research arm to which both the State and Defense Departments (as well as other agencies) can turn. During both the Eisenhower and Kennedy Administrations, for example, the Center was a base for a small number of men whose advice and counsel were valuable to the government, but who either by preference or political ineligibility held no official governmental position. At the same time, a major aim of the Center is to provide a forum where the policy-maker, in confidence and candor, can test his thinking and planning against the uncommitted and objective reasoning of the scholar. Through both these methods, and through special studies conducted under government contract, the Center serves as an important transmission belt between the academic world and the government. Indeed, the Center's purpose was to bring about a marriage between theory and practice, between the scholar and the policy-maker, so that each might profit from the skills and experience of the other.[1]

The combination of scholars and practitioners was only one method the Center used to achieve its objective. It also sought to establish an atmosphere free from academic and operational pressures. Members of the Center are carefully selected for their ability and interests and left free to work on projects of their own choice, with ample opportunity for mutual assistance and criticism. The advantages of group criticism and discussion are carefully provided for by a weekly round-table that has become one of the distinctive features of the Center. These round-tables deal with theoretical and practical problems with which the members of the group and invited guests are particularly concerned. Thus, the Center combines individual research with group discussion as the most effective means of stimulating its members and developing their understanding of the different approaches to international problems.

The Center is affiliated with the School of Advanced International Studies of the Johns Hopkins University. The School, which forms an organization quite distinct from the rest of the University in Baltimore, was founded in 1943 by the Foreign Service Educational Foundation, a private organization formed to establish a training center in international affairs and to further mutual understanding between government and business in their activities abroad. In 1950, the School became a graduate school of Johns Hopkins, but it remained in Washington—to take advantage of the special opportunities there for the study of international affairs. The Foreign Service Educational Foundation, whose Board of Trustees constitutes the Advisory Council to the School, continued to provide most of the funds required for its operation.[2]

Like other schools of Johns Hopkins University, the School of Advanced International Studies has its own administration, staff, and endowment. It offers both the M.A. and Ph.D. degrees, although between 1943 and 1961 only about a dozen Ph.D.s were awarded. Since then, under Dean Francis O. Wilcox, formerly an Assistant Secretary of State, the faculty has been enlarged and the program expanded, with more emphasis on Ph.D. work. But the School is still predominantly oriented to training for government, industry, and private organizations in the international field.

At first, the Washington Center of Foreign Policy Research was only loosely related to the School of Advanced International Studies. General supervision over the Center was exercised not by the Dean of the School but by a committee appointed by the President of the University. (The chairman of this committee until 1961 was the present Secretary of the Navy, Paul H. Nitze, former head of the State Department Policy Planning Staff and a member of the Research Staff of the Center until his appointment as Assistant Secretary of Defense for International Security Affairs in 1961.) More recently, the School and the Center have grown closer, and the Dean has taken over the duties of the committee, acting for the President of the University in most matters. The Center continues, however, to have its own funds, director, and professional staff. Like most organizations in the field, the Washington Center receives its financial support largely from the foundations. The grant to establish the Center came from the Rockefeller Foundation; in 1960, the Ford and Rockefeller Foundations, the Carnegie Corporation, and others made substantial grants to Johns Hopkins for both the School and the Center.

The regular staff of the Center is small, consisting of the Director, eight or ten research associates, research assistants, and secretarial help. The Director is Dr. Arnold Wolfers, one of the original members of the pre–World-War-II Yale Institute of International Studies. Research associates from academic life and government join the Center for varying periods—six months to two years or more—to devote their time to research that ultimately results in a published work. (Such volumes may be published under the auspices of the Center, but need not be.) In addition, the Center normally has a group of research consultants, who are not necessarily in residence or working on individual research projects, but who attend most of the weekly round-tables and are available for consultation with the associates. The entire arrangement is flexible and informal, permitting the staff to profit from close contact with consultants, government officials, visiting scholars, and others who join the group from time to time.

As a research organization oriented to current policy issues, the Washington Center is one of the most effective and influential groups in existence, its influence based in part on its scholarly work, and in part on the activities and extensive contacts of its members. Professor Wolfers, for example, is a trusted adviser to several government agencies. Two early members of the Center, Paul Nitze and Roger Hilsman, held high positions in the government, the first in the Defense Department and the second in the State Department. And even before their appointment to the government, both Nitze and Hilsman, as well as others—such as James E. King, Charles B. Marshall, and Robert E. Osgood—played a major role in the development of national security studies as consultants to government and through their writings. Former Secretary of State Christian Herter and former Ambassador Livingston Merchant became associated with the Center on their retirement from government service, but are often called back for special assignments in the government—Herter in connection with foreign-trade negotiations and Merchant in connection with the NATO multilateral nuclear force.

The Washington Center of Foreign Policy Research also influences teaching programs in national security in several ways. Not only do associates of the Center lecture at many academic and military institutions, but the Center also provides a Washington base for scholars from major colleges and universities whose research is related to national security affairs. Among these scholars in past years have been Max Beloff, Hans Morgenthau, George Liska, Robert W. Tucker, and Paul Y. Hammond. Several associates of the Center are also involved in the School of Advanced International Studies: Professor Wolfers is on its Academic Board; Paul Nitze has continued to serve on its Advisory Council. In this way, the faculty of the School has been strengthened and its relationship with the Center has become closer.

Publications that stem from the Center's work are three in kind: government reports, some never made public; special studies that come out of the round-table discussions; and scholarly works that were completed by scholars in residence at the Center. Outstanding among the government reports is the one done for the Senate Committee on Foreign Relations in 1959 on the impact of military technology on U.S. strategy and foreign policy. Others have been prepared for the Weapons Systems Evaluation Group, the Draper Committee on Foreign Aid, and the Departments of Defense and State. Of the publications resulting from round-table meetings, one was a collection of papers prepared in 1957 on *East-West Negotiations*, later published as a brochure distributed to about 400 persons in and out of government. The following year, the same procedure was used with a publication entitled *Military Policy Papers*. Among the other published volumes prepared at the Center are *Alliance Policy in the Cold War*, edited by Arnold Wolfers; *Discord and Collaboration*, a series of essays by the same author; *Nations in Alliance* by George Liska; and *Arms and Arms Control*, edited by Ernest W. Lefever.[3]

In terms of its objectives, the Washington Center has been extremely successful. Its relation with Johns Hopkins gives it an academic base, but its separate financing gives it the autonomy needed for the particular function it was designed to fulfill. This autonomy permits organizational flexibility and makes it possible to secure first-rate people from universities and the government. It also means, of course, that the Center must continually rely on outside support and therefore cannot expect any long-range security, except through its relation with Johns Hopkins. Nonetheless, it is an exceptional case of a research center, based in an academic institution that profits from its independence but that also enhances the quality of the university to which it is attached.

Perhaps the greatest success of the Center has been that it has maintained a high level of scholarly impartiality while closely connected with policy formulation in the government. This success is, to some extent, a measure of the progress government agencies have made in working with scholars, but it is also a measure of the deep concern that the Center, and particularly its Director, Dr. Wolfers, has in maintaining high standards of objectivity.

The Ideological Approach

The Foreign Policy Research Institute at the University of Pennsylvania is also oriented to current policy problems, but it differs in style and operation from the Washington Center. Its government connections are more with the military departments than the civilian agencies, and it has a further aim of working with and influencing important private groups, particularly in the business world. Virtually all the work done in national security studies at the University of Pennsylvania is conducted at the Institute. At Harvard, Princeton, Columbia, and elsewhere, there are a number of research and instructional activities that add strength to the national security programs and which, in turn, draw on these programs for their own support. But at the University of Pennsylvania, there is no major program other than the Foreign Policy Research Institute that is concerned with defense or national security policy. At the same time, the relationship of the Institute to the University, in terms of staff and curriculum, is more distant and formal than such arrangements at most other institutions.

The Foreign Policy Research Institute is primarily a research organization concerned with the problems arising from the cold war. It is interdisciplinary, with the largest representation from political science and international relations, and cooperative in its techniques of staff research. Established in February, 1955, with the announced purpose of studying "fundamental and long-range problems in U.S. foreign problems" and producing "imaginative and constructive concepts" for the guidance of future policy, the Institute set as its goal a research program built around three broad problem areas: the worldwide Communist movement; the revolution in the underdeveloped areas of the world; and the Western alliance.[4] Since 1955, it has conducted research in all three areas.

The Institute's statement of purpose emphasizes basic research on long-range problems, like the Columbia Institute and the Harvard Center, and it explains this emphasis with similar statements on the proper scope of academic inquiry into national security policy or any other policy area of current importance. The scholar's contribution, the Institute Director wrote, should be in the field of *"long-range policy formation."*[5]

The actual work done at the Institute, however, is concerned more with immediate policy responses than this statement suggests. It reflects the belief that the security of the United States and the free world is threatened by international Communism and the revolutionary forces in the new nations in underdeveloped areas. Thus, the Institute has been primarily concerned with the nature and techniques of Communism—which it defines as an ideological power movement dedicated to the achievement of world domination. "Forceful measures and new initiatives" are needed to meet this threat, and it is these that the Institute hopes to uncover in its studies. In this sense, the Institute is more interested in policy determination and in the practical results of its research than are most scholarly programs.

The Institute's organization also differs somewhat from most university-affiliated centers. It is incorporated separately as a nonprofit organization, but is attached to the University, which contributes administrative support without the customary overhead charge. Financial contributions for the operation of the Institute are made to the trustees of the University, and come from foundations and from contracts for research made with the government and industry. The initial grant establishing the Institute was made by the Richardson Foundation of North Carolina and New York, a private philanthropic organization created by the founder of the Vicks Chemical Company. More recently, other foundations have contributed, sometimes for special projects.[6]

The Institute program is planned by the Director and associates, subject to review by an Advisory Committee composed of trustees and friends of the University. (The members of the Committee have included a judge, three attorneys, four bankers and businessmen, a former Under Secretary of State, a university official, and Admiral Radford, former Chairman of the Joint Chiefs of Staff.[7]) The Director of the Institute is Robert Strausz-Hupé, Professor of Political Science at the University and an authority on geopolitics. Strausz-Hupé operates under the administrative supervision of the Dean of the Graduate School of Arts and Sciences. Appointments to the Institute are made by him, subject to the approval of the Dean and the University Committee on Appointments, even though such appointments do not carry faculty status.

This formal structure, more closely resembling that of a private research institute than an academic body, is carried over into the organization and active direction of research. Both are theoretically in the hands of a group of senior associates, scholars selected for their competence in the field, usually with experience as consultants to government agencies. These associates form the Staff Conference that supervises the activities of the Institute; although some of them are on the faculty of other universities and busy with their own affairs, they are asked to attend monthly meetings at the Institute and to read the research papers sent to them for comment.[8] The Director may also call on the services of contracted consultants from time to time; for this purpose, the Institute carries on its rolls such men as Gerhart Niemeyer of Notre Dame, John S. Reshetar of the University of Washington, and Richard B. Foster and Francis Hoeber of the Stanford Research Institute. The actual staff of the Institute is small in comparison to the group of advisers, associates, and consultants, numbering in 1962 only eight research assistants. In addition, the Institute annually grants several graduate research fellowships in international relations at the University.

Much of the work of the Institute is performed on a cooperative basis, unlike the procedure at Harvard, Columbia, Princeton, Chicago, and, to a lesser extent, M.I.T., where individual scholars select their own topics, do their own research and writing, and produce independent studies. At Pennsylvania, a group headed by the Director and consisting of several research assistants and one or more associates and consultants is organized for a specific project. A plan is worked out, an outline developed, assignments made, and each senior member of the group directs the research of teams working on the portion for which he is responsible, but the final product bears the names of all the participants. The senior associates participate by reviewing and analyzing the draft chapters, each on the basis of his own special competence and "all bound by a common interest in bringing to light the most meaningful basic truths,"[9] but they bear no responsibility for the conclusions reached in the completed studies.

The methods used at the Institute are illustrated by the best-known work produced by the group, *Protracted Conflict.*[10] The project that resulted in this book was begun in 1955, shortly after the Institute was established, when each associate was asked for his views on the nature of the Communist challenge. Research was directed by Strausz-Hupé, William Kintner, and Stefan Possony, and preliminary draft papers were circulated among the associates. After a year, members of the group visited a number of nations, mostly in Asia and Africa, under a grant from the Richardson Foundation and with the cooperation of the State Department, to "discuss critical problems confronting American foreign policy" with American political and military officials in the area.[11] Reports of these trips were published separately and distributed to selected groups. In April, 1958, when most of the research had been completed, a full statement of the thesis of the study was submitted to about forty officers on the staff and faculty of the Army War College, Carlisle, Pennsylvania, and their views on it were solicited; these were discussed at some length at a two-day seminar held at Carlisle. The final draft of the manuscript was written that summer and fall, after nearly three years of study and discussion. The aid of the Institute associates throughout, wrote the Director, was of "incalculable" benefit.[12]

Protracted Conflict and its companion volume, *A Forward Strategy for America*,[13] illustrate the strong thematic quality that characterizes the program at the Foreign Policy Research Institute. This quality stems, apparently, from its conception of the nature and techniques of international Communism, and its dedication to the task of providing "imaginative and constructive concepts" to apply to policy issues. No one issue, in the view of the Director and several of his associates, is more important than the threat of Communism. Thus, they write in the preface to *Protracted Conflict*, it is their hope that the book "will help to establish a conceptual consensus among American policy-making groups and opinion elite on the protean nature of the Communist challenge."[14]

The theme of *Protracted Conflict*, a phrase taken from Mao Tse-tung's writings, is the pervasive and increasing struggle between the Communist and the Western world. Communism is viewed as a doctrine and technique of total conflict aimed at world conquest, and all intercourse between Russia and the West, the authors hold, must be understood as part of this conflict. Deception and the use of all means (including psychological warfare) to confuse, throw off balance, and wear down resistance until the proper moment—these are the essential elements in the Soviet strategy of protracted conflict. *A Forward Strategy for America* is concerned with the response to this strategy, with the measures the West must adopt if it is to survive. These measures range from political subversion and propaganda to limited war, or, if necessary, larger conflicts. The danger of negotiation with the Communists is emphasized, and the possibility of effective limited agreements with the Soviet Union minimized.

The Institute has undertaken several studies at the specific request of outside groups, employing the same methods of team research. As a matter of fact, the Director has attributed the growing number of such requests to the advantages of this method.[15] The list of government agencies and private corporations for which the Institute has prepared studies is extensive: the President's Committee to Study U.S. Military Assistance (the Draper Committee), the Senate Committee on Foreign Relations,[16] the U.S. Information Agency, the National Broadcasting Company, and the Metropolitan Education Television Association—the last two in connection with educational television programs. The members of the Institute have thus not only made their views known on the highest levels of government in the executive and legislative branches, but also reached out to a larger audience than is ordinarily available to a working group of scholars.

Moreover, Institute members have been unusually successful in presenting their work in popular journals that ordinarily do not publish scholarly writings, such as *U.S. News and World Report, Esquire,* and *The Saturday Evening Post,* as well as in influential journals of opinion and professional scholarly and military journals. In the spring of 1957, the Foreign Policy Research Institute began publication of its own quarterly, *Orbis;* the editor is Strausz-Hupé, and a special feature of each issue is a leading article in which he interprets key international developments of the preceding three months.

The Foreign Policy Research Institute offers no courses of its own and sponsors no teaching program at the University of Pennsylvania. But many of the associates and a few of the research assistants hold faculty positions at Pennsylvania and elsewhere, and Professor Strausz-Hupé teaches a seminar in "International Relations" in which members of the Institute participate. Various associates have been appointed visiting professors at Pennsylvania, though there is no indication that their teaching activities involved more than participation in Strausz-Hupé's seminar.

The range of the Institute's influence goes beyond the University to a broad spectrum of public opinion and to certain government agencies, mainly military ones. Its publications are on the reading list for most courses dealing with defense problems, and *Protracted Conflict* is one of the basic works that every student of national security policy should read. Government agencies also use the publications of the Institute—especially the military departments, since the War Colleges of all three services, as well as the joint military colleges, make wide use of this material, and frequently invite members of the Institute to be regular lecturers. In addition, Institute members are in demand as speakers at "strategy seminars" and other meetings held throughout the country. In 1959, moreover, the Institute prepared the curriculum and conducted a two-week National Strategy Seminar for 200 reserve officers at the National War College—a unique instance of military reserve instruction by a private civilian agency.* The course continued to reflect the initial conceptual design during the following years.

The dominating theme of the Institute is shared by two other centers of research—the Hoover Institution on War, Revolution, and Peace, at Stanford, and the Center for Strategic Studies, at Georgetown University. (Among the Institute's closest collaborators is Dr. Stefan T. Possony, who, in 1961, was appointed Director of International Political Studies at the Hoover Institution.) Founded by Herbert Hoover in 1919 as a special library of materials on World War I,

* See above, Chapter 5, pp. 118–19.

the Hoover Institution has expanded its holdings greatly since that time and has become an important center of research and study on war and revolution. Its materials are of all types—documents, newspapers, manuscripts, journals—and from all parts of the world; they are particularly useful for those working on subjects such as the causes and consequences of twentieth-century war, revolutionary resistance and underground movements, and propaganda and public opinion.[17] The Director of the Institution since 1960 has been W. Glenn Campbell, formerly Director of Research at the American Enterprise Institute for Public Policy Research and former research economist with the U.S. Chamber of Commerce.

Though the primary function of the Hoover Institution is to preserve and organize materials on war and peace, it also supports research and a publication program on subjects directly bearing on the defense and national security. This work has been directed since 1961 by Dr. Possony, aided by a staff of research associates. With funds from its own endowment, from the University, from the sale of its books, and from foundations and gifts, the Institution prepares and publishes collections of important documents as well as original studies. Within this publications program, the Institution in 1963 arranged for the publication of the proceedings of the first conference held by the Georgetown University Center for Strategic Studies in January of that year.[18]

Established late in 1962 with Admiral Arleigh Burke as Director, the Georgetown Center has two basic functions: "(1) To inventory specific research efforts in university and research centers, and to catalogue study papers, testimony, and reports from governmental and Congressional sources; and (2) to identify research and information gaps, and to initiate and encourage research efforts where needed."[19] Admiral Burke works with a four-man Executive Board which includes W. Glenn Campbell of the Hoover Institution and William J. Barody, the President of the American Enterprise Institute for Public Policy Research and a trustee of the Hoover Institution; the other two members are the Dean of the Georgetown Graduate School and the Chairman of Georgetown's Department of Government. The Center also has an Advisory Board made up of public figures like Neil H. McElroy, Senator Hugh Scott, Admiral Arthur Radford, General Nathan F. Twining, and Senator George A. Smathers. Leading scholars and teachers in the field are conspicuously missing.

The first conference sponsored by the Center for Strategic Studies took as its subject "National Security: The Demands of Strategy and Economics in the Decade Ahead," and brought together a large number of scholars and practitioners, including those who had worked closely with the Foreign Policy Research Institute. The first paper at the conference, by Dr. Strausz-Hupé on "Soviet Strategy 1962–1970," and the last paper, by W. Glenn Campbell on "Assuring Primacy of National Security," taken with the introduction by Admiral Burke in the published proceedings, emphasize the Communist threat and the need for western unity and American military strength. The second conference, held in May, 1964, was on "NATO: Problems and Prospects." Those who gave papers included Dr. Strausz-Hupé, Philip E. Mosely, Stefan Possony, W. Randolph Burgess, Milorad M. Dradikovitch (of the Hoover Institution), Karl Brandt, the German Vice Admiral Frederick Ruge, and several other European experts.

The connection between the Foreign Policy Research Institute, the Hoover Institution, and the Center for Strategic Studies lies in the general agreement on basic working assumptions. The principal participants emphasize the ideological motivations in Communism, and they are more prepared to accept military solutions to difficult situations than are most scholars or policy-makers. (Their closest ties are not with scholars and professors, but with the military departments and a segment of the business community.) The effort to present these views to the "opinion elites" in and out of government has been a particularly conscious policy of the most active of these three organizations, the Foreign Policy Research Institute, but what the effect of this effort has been is difficult to judge. Certainly, the view it espouses of the nature of the Communist threat and the program it has developed for meeting that threat are widely accepted, though there are reservations in many quarters.[20] There may also be reservations about how far a scholarly enterprise should go in influencing policy and opinion. Of all the academic programs, the Institute hovers closest on that thin line that separates research from advocacy, and that sets the limits to an acceptable role for the scholar engaged in policy-oriented studies. In its determination to examine policy issues within a fairly rigid analytical framework, the Institute stands in contrast to a group such as the Washington Center of Foreign Policy Research, where national security studies are approached no less realistically, but with less preoccupation with the threat of Communism and with more understanding of the complexities of the international system.

The Behavioral Approach

If one were to arrange the centers and institutes concerned with national security studies along a spectrum based on points of view, general approaches, and objectives, one might well place the Foreign Policy Research Institute of the University of Pennsylvania at one end and the Center for Research on Conflict Resolution of the University of Michigan at the other. The Foreign Policy Research Institute is highly structured, tightly organized and centralized, employs group research on directed projects, consists largely of political scientists, and stresses the theme of protracted conflict. The Michigan organization, on the other hand, is loosely organized and decentralized, includes scholars from many of the social sciences, emphasizes the behavioral approach, and is interested more in the resolution of conflict, in theory and practice, than in the means to combat the Communist threat. Both are concerned with the same objective situation, but the Pennsylvania group seeks a prescription for victory, the Michigan group a method for resolving the conflict.

The behavioral approach, which is so important to the work at Michigan, is also essential in the program of Studies in International Conflict and Integration at Stanford and in the work of Charles E. Osgood at the Institute of Communications Research at the University of Illinois. Of the three programs, the Michigan program is the largest. Established by the University in June, 1959, as a unit of the College of Literature, Science and the Arts, support came initially from funds given by a private donor, to which were added grants from foundations for specific projects, and University funds. But the interest and distinctive approach that mark the Center date from an earlier period—to the activity of a group of social scientists at Michigan and several other universities in the general area of international conflict. This interest found expression in the quarterly *Journal of Conflict Resolution*.[21] The first issue, appearing in March, 1957, and carrying on its masthead a distinguished roster of scholars in almost every one of the social sciences, explained the purpose of the journal in the following terms:

> Our main concern is to stimulate a new approach, especially in the direction of the formulation and testing of theoretical models relating to the central problem (the prevention of global war). We are interested also in the improvement of the information processes in this area through quantification, index numbers, or any other means. Our belief in the fruitfulness of an interdisciplinary approach in this area is

based on the conviction that the behavior and interactions of nations are not an isolated and self-contained area of empirical material but part of a much wider field of behavior and interaction.[22]

Taking *conflict* as the key concept in international relations, the editors noted that it could be approached from several points of view —by economists, sociologists, psychiatrists, psychologists, anthropologists, and political scientists—and could be applied to a variety of situations—family relationships, labor-management negotiations, political parties, and finally, relations among nations. The study of conflict in one area might, therefore, have application to the others. After all, they said, price wars resembled arms races, and jurisdictional disputes of labor the territorial disputes of states; frustration had the same effect on individuals as on groups; and the patterns of mediation and negotiation were much the same in economic disputes and international rivalries.

The Center is, in effect, the result of three years of planning by the same group of social scientists at Michigan that founded the Journal. The organization of the Center is informal and loose, though it has become somewhat more structured in recent years. Originally, it had no director and no staff other than that required for administration and secretarial support. Supervision of the program was exercised by an Executive Committee appointed by the Dean of the College and consisting of members of the founding group of the Journal. The first chairman was Robert C. Angell, Professor of Sociology and a former President of the American and International Sociological Associations. Later, Professor Kenneth Boulding, a leading economist, became co-director of the Center with Professor Angell. Both Professor Angell and Professor Boulding are committed to working for a peaceful world, a commitment that is also evident among others in the group that founded *The Journal of Conflict Resolution.*

The Michigan Center not only represents a truer interdisciplinary approach to the problems of the cold war than any other program in the field, but also is more theoretical and less policy-oriented than most other centers and institutes. Its main interest is to stimulate a new approach to the problems of national security, but it is not unaware of or indifferent to the practical aspects of the pursuit of knowledge, and expresses a frank preference for research that is relevant to the urgent problems of the cold war. Conflicts in family, economic, or political disputes are important, and in many cases findings would be applicable to international politics; by drawing on the study of conflict in all these fields, the Center hopes to devise what it termed "an intellectual engine" that will make possible the prevention of war. The same engine might solve other conflict problems, and this would be helpful. But such problems as individual and industrial conflict, it observes, "threaten us with inconvenience, with distress, with losses. War threatens us with irretrievable disaster."[23] Thus, the Center expresses the hope that the research it fosters will be utilized not only by scholars but also by public officials in the United States and elsewhere in their efforts to resolve international conflicts.

The Center does not maintain a full-time, permanent research staff, although it sometimes supports the research of members of the Michigan faculty and employs graduate students as research assistants. The Center attempts to create interest in its objectives and approach among social scientists at other universities in the United States and in other countries, and to support their research without separating them from their institutions. In this way, it hopes to have a wider impact on both teaching and research than it could have with a staff concentrated in one place. The function of the Center under this arrangement is to stimulate research, act as a clearing-house for projects within its area of interest, provide assistance in securing financial support, and publish research in progress in *The Journal of Conflict Resolution*.

The program of the Center consists in general of two distinct but related activities: the first consisting of conferences and seminars; the second, research and training. The Center organizes its conferences in terms of their purposes and the problems discussed: one to deal with the development of theory, another with programs of action groups striving for peace, a third with public-opinion leadership, and a fourth with government policy. In May, 1960, for example, the Center, in cooperation with the Political Science Department of the University, conducted a symposium on the place of theory in the conduct and study of international relations. In 1963, the Center was instrumental in convening an International Arms Control Symposium under the joint auspices of the University and the Bendix Corporation. While, in the first meeting, scholars talked to scholars, at the second conference (which was repeated in 1964), scholars, government officials, industrial executives, and foreign observers were brought together in an ambitious program that dealt with both the theoretical and "hardware" issues of arms control.[24] The symposiums represent an effort by members of the Michigan Center and the Bendix Corporation to make Ann Arbor an important center of work done on arms control and to explore methods by which research on the means for resolving international conflict can be utilized by government and private groups.

The research and training activities of the Center include a variety of research projects, a plan for predoctoral and postdoctoral fellowships, and the establishment of research professorships for peace research. Research projects are of three types: those that deal with the implications of permanent peace, with studies in conflict resolution and peace-making, and with quantitative international studies. In the first category, the Center has already completed a project (supported by a grant from the Carnegie Corporation to Professor Boulding and Emile Benoit of Columbia) on the economic consequences of disarmament, the purpose of the study to demonstrate how economic dislocations brought on by a reduction in defense spending could be met without fear of permanent disruption.[25] A second research project, entitled "A Comparative Study of the Social Psychology of Nationalism," conducted by Professors Daniel Katz and Herbert Kelman, considered the psychological components of nationalism in the United States and in certain countries that have only recently become sovereign nations. Other studies were concerned with such questions as: What would be the effect of lasting peace on the forces holding together the diverse groups in a nation? What are the political implications of peace? What effects would a permanent peace have on human beings?

The Center's projects for the study of conflict resolution and peace-making are designed to throw light on the processes by which nations settle issues between them, and on the reasons for their inability to do so more frequently. The first, undertaken jointly by Professor Angell and J. David Singer, deals with the relationship between the values held by decision-makers and influential groups in the United States and the Soviet Union, and their respective foreign policies.[26] The second project resulted in a book by Professor Boulding, *Conflict and Defense*, in which he develops a general theory of conflict that is applicable, within varying limits, to different situations.[27] A third project was an analytic study of *Fights, Games and Debates* by Anatol Rapoport. Dr. Rapoport's thesis was that, "once we understand conflicts, we may prevent a fight by turning it into a game (even such a dangerous game as a cold war), or turn the game into a debate, the most civilized and only productive form of conflict."[28] Another project included the analysis of positive and negative influences affecting communication in groups in which the members have strong ideological differences. In all these studies, the basic purpose is to learn more about human behavior in order to control human conflict.

The third category of projects is concerned with studies of the systematic means of gathering and weighing quantitative data on the state of international relations. The perfecting of an information-processing mechanism that will provide information on the direction in which the international conflict system is moving and how close it is to war will be based on the collection of quantitative data relevant to the political system. Professor Karl Deutsch of the Yale Political Science Department completed one exploratory study in this field. The investigator collected comparable, quantitative information on 1,000 variables in ninety countries. The variables are all "objective ones concerned with such national characteristics as population, income, form of government, literacy, and also with international interaction variables such as exchange of mail, tourists, trade, currency, etc."[29] A second study, conducted by Robert Hefner, attempts to provide comparable information from many countries on public opinion as it affects a country's behavior in international affairs.

The training program of the Center seeks to attract young scholars to the study of conflict resolution—by offering fellowships and by dramatizing its own work and initiating a new movement in the social sciences (comparable, it is hoped, to the movements of the 1930's in the field of race relations). Whether or not this goal is finally achieved, the Center has already made a real impact in the field and is firmly established as one of the more important groups whose strongly interdisciplinary approach holds out the promise of important and interesting results. *The Journal of Conflict Resolution* is required reading for all students of the subject, and the Center has been an important element in the application of the behavioral approach to national security studies at other institutions. It is, for example, directly related to another academic program with a behavioral approach—the program at Stanford University.

The Stanford program was actually started in 1957, when the Department of Political Science organized the Conflict Study Project (the name was later changed to Studies in International Conflict and Integration) as a faculty seminar composed of political scientists, historians, economists, psychologists, and sociologists with a common interest in the behavior of nation states "in both conflict and community building situations."[30] A small grant permitted the group to initiate research on a pilot project—a day-by-day, hour-by-hour study of the six weeks between the assassination of the Archduke Franz Ferdinand and the outbreak of World War I. The choice of this situation was undoubtedly influenced in large part by sources available in the library of the Hoover Institution.[31]

On the basis of the hypotheses on conflict derived from this chronology and a series of working papers on the behavior of states in crisis, the seminar drew up plans for a series of studies utilizing the materials already assembled, as well as other data available at the Hoover Institution. A five-year grant for $250,000 from the Ford Foundation in 1960 gave substance to these plans and made possible the expansion of the Project. It has two broad purposes: first, to produce a systematic analysis of the nature, processes, and effects of international conflict; and, second, to provide a training program in international relations for advanced graduate students. The program is interdisciplinary, with representation from a wider group of disciplines and fields than is usually found in such centers. Faculty members and graduate students work together in pairs or small teams, thus combining the functions of research and training.

The Project is administratively attached to the Political Science Department of Stanford and is directed by Robert C. North, a member of the department. Other than the faculty and students engaged in research, the Project has no regular staff. The research has two purposes: to develop concepts and theories concerning the elements of conflict; and to test specific hypotheses against empirical data. In each of these areas, the Project has supported a number of studies. For example, to test hypotheses of international conflict, various conflict situations—such as the Bosnian Crisis of 1908, the Arab-Israeli conflict, Hitler's decision to invade Poland, and the Quemoy-Matsu crisis of 1958—were examined. Some ended in violence, others did not, and the research is designed to explore the reasons for these and other differences.

The second type of research includes studies on international communication in crises and how diplomats perceive their role. Additional studies have been initiated on Sino-Soviet relations, on conflicts within the Communist world and variations in the response of the member nations to international crises, on Communist ideology and organization, on the behavior of underground organizations, and sects and sect-like organizations in Africa and elsewhere. Finally, since the Project has access to a unique collection of about half a million feet of German newsreel for the period 1940 to 1943, it is using its resources to analyze the content, form, and function of this film.[32]

The work done at Stanford is reflected in several books, in many articles, and in special government studies. In the latter category, for example, members of the staff published a manual of methodology, and the Project has had several contracts with the Naval Ordnance Test Station at China Lake, including one to assess the Sino-Soviet controversy on the basis of the techniques and conceptual framework developed for the 1914 crisis study.[33] Invited by *The Journal of Conflict Resolution* to prepare a special issue on the general theme of "Decision-Making in Crisis," the Stanford group organized a two-day conference in 1962 and later published selected conference papers that dealt with a number of historical crises.[34] Members of the Stanford group have also contributed to research in national security policy in an advisory and consultative capacity for both government and private agencies. They have been active, for example, in the Committee for the Application of the Behavioral Sciences to the Strategies of Peace, set up in San Francisco.

The emphasis in both the Michigan and Stanford programs in the area of what has been called "peace research" is noteworthy. It is fair to say that this reflects a general trend among the programs dominated by social scientists who follow a behavioral approach. This generalization is reinforced by the work of someone like the psychologist Charles E. Osgood at the University of Illinois and by the number of behavioral scientists (as opposed to more traditional social scientists) who are involved with the various peace groups. It would be an over-simplification, however, to divide all social scientists into two camps and relate the degree of behaviorism in their methodology to the policy direction of their research. The problem is more complex and less susceptible to one-factor analysis. Nevertheless, the desire to be able to understand human behavior leads to a desire to be able to predict and, from there, to the use of this predictive ability for certain goals and values. For the more traditional social scientist, trained in history and looking for evidence in the history of man's experience rather than in the psychology of man's makeup, the prospect of change in human behavior seems less probable.

IV

Government and Private
Research Programs in National
Security Affairs

10

The Education of Government
Executives

ACADEMIC PROGRAMS in national security affairs reveal one measure
of the response to the cold war; they demonstrate how American
higher education has sought to develop intellectual resources in national security affairs and thus meet the triple challenge of providing
professional training, general education, and scholarly research. Another measure can be seen in how the expanding knowledge of national security affairs is brought to bear on the policy-making process
of government. We have already suggested that this problem is being
solved by increasing the continuity and expertise of political executives, by assigning to the career executive in government a larger role
in the formulation of policy, and by developing procedures for contracting out special projects and studies to research groups. The roots
of this process of developing and applying intellectual resources lie
largely in the colleges and universities, but there is a constant interplay between development and application, between the academic
world, government agencies, and private research organizations.

The relations between and contribution of the political executive,
the career government official, and the scholar to the determination of
policy in national security affairs are complex, and there is no clear-
cut division of labor among the three. The effectiveness of the first,
who is responsible for policy, may be limited by political vulnerability,

by presidential prerogative and style, and by personal pressures to return to private life. The contribution of the scholar consulted outside the government is also limited. He cannot affect the policy-making process directly; he has no way of ensuring that his work is used; and he does his research within a framework developed by the government executives. In the total process, it is the career government executive who supplies the long-term continuity and stability within which public policy evolves, wins approval, and is accepted. His contribution may be limited by his relations with his political superiors; but if relations are good, the career executive can be the critical participant.

An examination of the preparation of career government executives in national security affairs is complicated by the fact that the two major career types, civilian and military, have responded so differently. It is now evident that the armed services responded to the intellectual demands of the cold war much earlier than did civilian officials, primarily because national security is the business—the only business —of the military forces, but also because of their training in technical aspects of war, and because of the development of staff training within the armed forces since the turn of the century.[1]

The increase in the educational background of the officer corps is due as much to the expansion of the recruitment base as to conscious policy decisions to upgrade the importance of education within the services. While the military-academy system (augmented by the establishment of the Air Force Academy shortly after World War II) continues to supply the core of military officers, the largest single source of long-term officers is now the Reserve Officers Training Corps. The educational background of the officer corps is thus given variety and depth through the influx of young men from many American colleges and universities. Furthermore, the officers who have come up through the ranks and do not have a college education can, through special programs set up by the military services, take college-level courses on a part- or full-time basis. As a result of these efforts, each service is approaching the point where almost all its officers will have a college degree.

But the services have gone far beyond the baccalaureate level in strengthening the educational background of the officer corps. Within their own educational systems and also in civilian universities, they have provided many senior officers with graduate education, often in science and technology—reflecting the technological innovations that have so dramatically changed the nature of war and so drastically altered the services themselves. Many other officers have done graduate work in the social sciences, either at the service war colleges or the joint colleges—the Armed Forces Staff College, the Industrial College of the Armed Forces, and the National War College. In a number of cases, specially selected officers are sent to universities like Princeton, Harvard, Columbia and Georgetown, where they work toward a Master's or Doctor's degree in international relations, history, political science, or economics. This military program is of significance for several reasons: It demonstrates how the armed services are using the educational facilities of the nation to meet their training requirements; it brings thousands of uniformed officers into contact with civilian academicians every year; and, by this association, it relates the issues of national security to the work on a number of college and university campuses. Of the three services, the Army and the Air Force use the program most extensively.

Nothing like this system exists for civilian government officers. And, with one exception, they wholly lack the sense of "corporateness," of professional pride and solidarity, that is found in the military services. Yet it is this sense of "corporateness" that provides much of the incentive to develop an educational system that will strengthen their loyalty to the profession and to public service while training them in the skills they need. (The one exception is, of course, the Foreign Service, which, like the military services, has its own history and traditions.) Only recently has the government begun to provide the Foreign and Civil Services with the opportunities for career development and graduate education that military officers have had for so many years.

Staffing the Career Service

Throughout the government, but most dramatically in national security affairs, both specialists and men with a broad policy perspective are needed.[2] For, in national security policy, there is no way of solving problems without specialized knowledge, but this specialized knowledge must be placed in the context of the broad objectives of American policy. Thus we need both the specialist and the generalist, but the same official must often be both at the same time. One way of having both (more easily stated than achieved) lies in a system that elevates young career officers through the normal channels and also attracts experts at mid-career and senior levels; another solution would be a system that provided both special and general training all the way up the career ladder.

The combination of special and general training has been an aim in recent years in certain graduate schools of public administration. There has been a discernible trend—at such institutions as Princeton, Harvard, Syracuse, and Pittsburgh—away from an earlier concern with administrative procedures to a policy approach that requires an understanding of policy-making and politics, of the interdisciplinary nature of contemporary public policy, and of the need for increased knowledge in fields relating to public policy. The reason for this trend was summed up by President Robert Goheen of Princeton: "to augment the flow of well-prepared people into positions of public responsibility, and to set by example new patterns of excellence throughout the nation in education for public service." The response made by graduate schools of public administration to the requirements of the United States' international commitments is exemplified by the broad training provided at the Maxwell School of Citizenship and Public Affairs of Syracuse for service overseas. The Maxwell School offers opportunities for training and research abroad as well as courses at the School given in collaboration with foreign students and public officials brought to the United States for instruction in public administration.

Within this changing context, the schools of public affairs and public administration continue to be recruiting centers and training grounds for young men and women entering government service. The Georgetown University School of Foreign Service has been for many years a primary source of personnel for the State Department, and, more recently, the School of International Service at American University instituted a similar but more broadly conceived program. Princeton, Syracuse, Pittsburgh, and other universities with schools of public affairs provide the student interested in government service with an education in the liberal arts as well as in public administration and policy.

Unfortunately, recruitment into the public service still suffers from the popular image of government as a huge bureaucracy in which the crudest political pressures prevail, career advancement is slow and limited, and the work frustrating. Recruitment procedures have not been able to dispel these impressions entirely. True, applications from college and high-school graduates to enter the Foreign and Civil Services now far exceed the openings available every year. The problem is not so much quantitative as qualitative: how to attract into the public service skilled men and women with the potential to hold positions of high responsibility.[3]

Two major techniques for recruitment into the public service have been used during the past decade: expansion of short-term intern programs in federal agencies; and secondly, and more specifically related to national security affairs, greater professionalization in both general management and specialized programs in defense, economic aid, information and cultural affairs, and foreign relations.

The intern programs take two main forms: a summer student-trainee program; and a cooperative-education program that extends over a longer period. In the former, students work under professional guidance with the specific intent to decide whether to seek permanent employment in the agency after graduation. All the military departments operate such programs for students of science and technology, as does the National Aeronautics and Space Administration. In a slightly modified program, students are assigned to work with professional and technical personnel, not with the expectation that they will remain with the agency but rather with their long-range recruitment into the government in mind. In this category, for example, the Air Force employs assistants in science and engineering, while the Department of State has recently started a program for students of international relations, political science, economics, and business or public administration. The cooperative-education program, usually arranged between federal agencies and educational institutions, provides for study while working on the job. The three military departments and NASA have also embarked on such programs to attract young scientists and engineers into the public service.[4]

In recent years, the summer intern programs have attracted more and more young people, until they now draw several thousand young men and women annually to the federal agencies and the Congress. Each agency has its own orientation program and work pattern, although all of them give each student a broad view of the agency's operations and its role in the government, and all of them permit the student to work closely with the professional staff in an area relating to his academic studies. In 1962, a general program for interns in Washington was organized for the first time; in many ways, it was a short course in American government in action, consisting of lectures by prominent members of all three branches of the government—including the President, the Vice President, a justice of the Supreme Court, and several cabinet officers. These lectures also served as a catalyst for many "seminars" held within agencies and on an inter-agency and inter-collegiate basis.

While in the summer intern programs the emphasis is less on the interns' immediate contributions than on their possible ultimate recruitment, under the cooperative-education programs of the military departments and NASA, there is an immediate contribution to research and development. Students in these programs alternate between classroom work and practical training for four or five years, are paid for their working time, and are promoted as they progress toward a degree. While they perform mostly technical tasks under supervised assignment, they bring a youthful interest to their work and may, on graduation, continue to work for the agency at a more advanced civil-service level than might otherwise have been the case.

The intern programs have advantages and disadvantages in terms of ultimate recruitment objectives.[5] Through various selection procedures, the programs attract students of high motivation and academic standing, and they are shown government at its best, for they are brought into a professional world where decisions of more than "academic" significance are being made. There is thus an excitement of "involvement" which in recent years has been heightened by the increased participation of high-ranking officials, including the President, in the Washington program.

But there are disadvantages: The students become aware of how large the government has become; how easy it can be to get lost in the bureaucracy; how frustrated many career executives are; how distant from their work the area of decision often is; how ferocious the in-fighting of government agencies can be; and how elusive a working concept of public interest is. They are likely to see these problems, moreover, as unique to government, simply because they are in no position to compare their experience against private business.

The difference between excitement and disillusion may depend on the attitude and conduct of the intern's immediate supervisors and associates, for he is likely to reflect the sense of devotion and professional standards that he finds around him. To this extent, the intern programs are no more than opportunities. The real test of whether qualified young people will be attracted into the public service depends in the last analysis on the quality of officer they find in the government.

Within the agencies involved in national security affairs, recruitment has also been enriched by the development of the concept of specialized career services. It is in many ways the application of the Foreign Service or military-corps concept to new fields—like the civilian management of military affairs, economic aid, and information and cultural affairs. In each case, the ultimate objective is to develop a cadre of career executives who can assume responsibility in defense or foreign relations.

The normal route for entrance into the permanent civil service is through the Federal Service Entrance Examination or through specialized examinations for scientific, technical, secretarial, or accounting posts. In recent years, it has also been possible for qualified persons to apply for the Management Intern option of the FSEE, a program with antecedents in the 1930's, developed for college graduates who demonstrate a potential for top-level performance. One such management-intern program in the Office of the Secretary of Defense brings into the Department a small group of "executive trainees" who have been educated in public or business administration, political science, economics, and law. Upon entrance, they participate in a sixty-day orientation in the history, mission, and organization of the Department. Their assignments after the initial period are rotated so that during the first year they work in several different program and administrative units. They are also given the opportunity to take leave to complete their graduate training. Early in their service, they are given positions of progressive responsibility. The program thus is responsive to the needs for both increased specialization and broad policy perspectives.

The Defense Department program began in 1954, with about ten trainees participating that year and each year since then. The rotational tours that follow the initial two months place the trainee in professional work situations. In 1957, for example, a trainee in the Economic and Fiscal Analysis Division of the Comptroller's Office worked on "measurements of the impact of inflation on the Defense Budget, reviews of both the House and Senate Defense Appropriation bills, and an analysis of possible savings resulting from Hoover Commission recommendations." Another trainee, "working in the European Region of International Affairs at the time of the revolution in Hungary, prepared daily summaries of developments for the Assistant Secretary of Defense [for International Security Affairs] . . . and [worked] on recommendations for a top-level review of existing policies to meet new developments in the satellites."[6] Trainees who completed the program were posted in most of the new and expanding units in the Defense Department, including the Comptroller's Office, International Security Affairs, and the Advanced Research Project Agency.

A similar training program, the Overseas Intern Program, was inaugurated in 1957 in the International Cooperation Administration (now the Agency for International Development). The purpose of this program is to facilitate the task of meeting staff requirements of overseas missions with persons with strong qualities for professional growth. Interns had to be between the ages of 23 and 28, and had to be well-grounded in economics, business management, or public administration. The minimal requirement was the bachelor's degree or equivalent, plus two years of working experience. The posts for which the interns were destined involved the planning and coordination of technical programs of economic and social development. Their one-year period of training in Washington thus included work-training assignments at agency headquarters, and the study of the culture and language of the country to which they would initially be assigned. By 1961, more than 100 interns had passed through the program, and a report of the agency noted that "the program has proved to be a valuable resource in attracting junior personnel to careers in the management fields of activity."[7]

The special training programs in defense and economic aid are attempts to develop a high-level career service in new areas of government operation that stem from the challenges of the cold war; they may, therefore, be compared to the career services of the military departments and the State Department. A similar move has also been made by the United States Information Agency in recent years to establish a career basis for work in what is described as "a new arm of diplomacy—to present abroad . . . the life and culture of the people of the United States." The USIA has established its own Foreign Service Career Reserve Corps and adopted a selection procedure similar to that of the Foreign Service. Candidates for USIA must first pass the regular Foreign Service written examination and then, if successful, an oral examination as well. Again, like the regular Foreign Service, USIA officers are initially assigned to Washington for a six-month orientation period before going overseas. The ultimate aim is "a disciplined corps, knowledgeable in world affairs, rich in experience, with appreciation and sympathy for the cultures and mores of peoples of other lands."[8]

The concept of a separate corps has, of course, long been a distinguishing feature of the Foreign Service. The Foreign Service was established as a unified professional corps by the Rogers Act of 1924 and later strengthened by the Foreign Service Act of 1946, which permitted the lateral entry of specialists and high-level "generalists."[9] From the end of World War II until late in the 1950's, however, the Foreign Service experienced a period of a serious demoralization. The reasons were several: New, more specialized agencies like the Defense Department and the aid program (conducted under the Foreign Operations Administration until 1955) competed with the State Department in representing important American interests abroad; the "general" foreign service officer was often unable to cope with the new military and economic problems; attacks on the integrity of the Service came in the wake of harsh domestic criticism of American foreign policy between 1949 and 1954; and, finally, cumbersome administrative practices prevented the Foreign Service from adopting imaginative programs to recruit young officers and attract mature specialists.[10]

The problems of staffing the Foreign Service have since been approached in two ways: through an expansion of the lateral-entry route, and through a broadening of the recruitment base for new officers. Acting on the recommendation of the Wriston Committee, in 1954, the Department integrated its specialized civil-service staff in Washington into the Foreign Service. The move was not without tension. Some felt that the Foreign Service was being diluted, while many specialists resented being sent on overseas assignments where they would not be using their expertise and would, at mid-career, be plunged into a new kind of career pattern. Such objections could be expected during the transition period, but it was assumed they would recede as new recruits came into an integrated Foreign Service.

The State Department, moreover, has continually resisted the lateral entry into the Foreign Service of specialists who have not first gained experience in the Foreign Service Reserve or in other government agencies. The underlying premise is that Foreign Service officers, as practitioners, go through a system of practical training during their first years of service and that anyone entering the service at mid-career should possess an equivalent background.[11] This undoubtedly reflects a preference for "generalists" that has always marked the Foreign Service (as well as the military services) and the belief that morale is weakened by bringing in outsiders rather than promoting from within the career ranks.

The Wriston Committee also recommended in 1954 that the State Department establish a scholarship program for attracting men into the Foreign Service, a recommendation based on the Navy's subsidized Reserve Officers Training Program. The Department of State has never acted on the recommendation or on the more elaborate proposals for a Foreign Service Academy that were submitted from several sources.[12] One reason is that the number of applicants to the Foreign Service far exceeds the number of openings every year—especially since 1955, when examination procedures were simplified to meet another of the Wriston Committee's recommendations. The Department has also argued that both schemes would incur unnecessary costs, and that proposal for an Academy had the danger of developing an inbred elite that would exacerbate the problems of a service already accused of being too exclusive. The Department's efforts have thus concentrated on a rational projection of personnel needs that will permit the assignment of qualified junior officers without delay, and on closer relations with colleges and universities to encourage faculty members, particularly in the social sciences, to recommend the Foreign Service to their most promising students.

The strengthening of the recruitment sources for the Foreign Service is only one part of a wider program of staffing the civilian side of the career service to meet the problems of the cold war. It must be seen in relation to the broad range of intern programs, the projects for attracting young scientists and engineers into public service, and the attempts to increase the professionalism and stature of junior officers in the information and aid programs and among civilians in the defense establishment. At the same time, all these programs must be related to advances in in-service training, since recruitment and career development are but two parts of the same problem. Successful recruitment brings into the public service men who have the qualities that permit them to develop with training. By the same token, programs of career development provide an attraction to qualified and ambitious men who are looking for careers that offer opportunities for advanced training and, in turn, promotion into positions of high responsibility.

Programs of Career Development

Among the many in-service development programs in national security affairs now available to career officers, the most important are the several war colleges and the State Department's Foreign Service Institute. Before examining these programs in detail, however, it would be well to review the broad expansion of training that has taken place in government since World War II.

There are in general four methods of career development in the federal government: (1) educational programs, usually college and university extension programs, in which careerists enroll on their own initiative; (2) training activities conducted by a department or agency for its own staff; (3) inter-agency programs organized by the government; and (4) educational programs in universities and private organizations to which federal employees are assigned for training purposes. All these programs have expanded in recent years.[13]

The career-development program at the Agency for International Development illustrates this general growth.[14] The program actually begins with projects like the overseas intern training, which is a bridge between recruitment and career development. There are, however, other more modest orientation programs that prepare technical advisers for their first assignments; they comprise background lectures and seminars on American foreign policy, the aid program, and the area of assignment. AID has also found it necessary to provide refresher training and new technical instruction for staff officers who have been on overseas assignments. Sometimes this refresher training is done while an officer is on duty in Washington, or else in short programs offered by arrangement with universities, other government agencies, and private groups. All these orientation and refresher courses have two important objectives: to permit the staff, particularly the technical advisers, to maintain a high level of expertise, and to develop an awareness of the problems involved in using their expertise for the benefit of the developing nations.

For the core of the new career service in economic and social development, AID also provides mid-career programs involving "comprehensive systematic training in the programming of technical and economic assistance." One such program is carried out through the School of Advanced International Studies (SAIS) of the Johns Hopkins University, located in Washington, and another, concerned solely with African affairs, was conducted by the African Research and Studies Program of Boston University from 1959 to 1962. Under the arrangement with Johns Hopkins, the Institute on ICA Development Programming (since renamed the Institute for International Development) was established in 1958. The decision to establish this Institute at the School of Advanced International Studies was made largely because the program would thereby be close to agency headquarters, with access to its top staff and program materials.

The program at the Institute lasts for twenty-one weeks (there are two sessions of twenty students each per year), during which the student attends two lecture courses—one on the economics of development programming and the second in the culture and politics of economic development—augmented by workshops, guided reading, and individual work assignments. The course in economics meets three times a week and that in culture and politics twice a week. Each class session usually consists of a one-hour lecture or panel discussion followed by a discussion period of one or two hours. The workshops, in which teams of students meet two or three afternoons a week, provide practice in applying the principles and theories of the two courses to specific situations, and demonstrate various aspects of the development process. Finally, each participant undertakes an individual study assignment on a newly developing country or a comparative analysis of a problem area. This kind of project is, in fact, little different from the analysis and reporting an officer might do as part of his regular duties. The student, however, is free of operational pressures, can try new approaches, and work within a broader framework.

The original contract with Johns Hopkins (for three years, but it was later extended) stipulated that SAIS provide a director and three faculty members to give full time to the Institute. The contract also provided for administrative support and guest lecturers from government and academic life. By mid-1962, a total of almost 200 members of the AID agency staff had attended the Institute. Their assignments after completing the program were almost always to a higher post in an overseas mission or a program division at headquarters.[15]

The African-studies program at Boston University was a mid-career course that at first sought to achieve similar objectives as the SAIS Institute but that concentrated on a continent about which relatively little was known. In initiating the course in 1959, International Cooperation Administration took advantage of one of the few African area-study programs already in existence. The training course was limited to twenty ICA officers, and the first session lasted for seven months—six months of actual training and one month for travel and evaluation. The training period was divided into three phases: orientation at the African Research and Studies Center at Boston University; study of African development with experts in Europe; and field study in Africa. Because of the increased need for men to staff American missions in Africa, the training sessions were cut back in 1960 to enable larger numbers to participate. Each session was then conducted wholly in Boston, and consisted of four weeks of intensive orientation on African anthropology, culture, geography, politics, economics, and linguistics. An additional three-week seminar was organized for selected persons who were to be assigned major program responsibilities in tropical Africa. Operational requirements, in effect, forced a change that made the program much more a preparation for the next assignment than the development of analytical skills and understanding for higher posts of responsibility.

In addition to mid-career training programs conducted by specific agencies, the federal government provides many opportunities for inter-agency training.[16] Foreign Service Officers may participate in the SAIS Institute, and the Foreign Service Institute provides training in foreign languages and world affairs for members of other departments. Limited numbers of civilians from all these agencies and departments may also be assigned to the service war colleges, the Industrial College

of the Armed Forces, or the National War College. This kind of training in the program of another agency is usually considered a step up
the ladder, suggesting that a career executive is well-grounded in his
own agency's work, that he can view his work from a variety of different perspectives, and that he is beginning to see government—and
policy—as a whole.

In addition to inter-agency programs run by individual agencies or
departments, there are those conducted by the Civil Service Commission—including the Executive Seminar Center—and the Executive
Leadership Institutes of the Brookings Institution. The former was
established in the fall of 1963 at Kings Point, New York, for senior,
high-ranking civil servants. The total registration of the first seminar
was thirty-six, and the course lasted twenty weeks, divided into ten
two-week courses in three areas: administration, domestic programs,
and national security and world change.[17] Among the courses related
to national security were "Implications of International Conditions,"
"Effects of Technological Development," and "The National Defense
Establishment." In addition to a small faculty, the work of the
seminar was conducted by leading scholars, business executives, and
government officials brought in to discuss special topics.

The Brookings program is of particular importance, for it not only
concerns top-level executives, but it has the advantage of being organized and conducted by a private institution that is itself deeply
involved in foreign-policy and defense research.*

The initial Brookings conferences for federal executives were held
in 1957; after two years of successful experiment, they were made
permanent. The conferences, which may last from two days to two
weeks, are broadly conceived "to develop approaches and attitudes
leading to more effective administrative decisions and actions, to
broaden the participants' understanding of department-wide and
government-wide aspects of policy-making and administration, and to
enlarge their knowledge of the relationship between government and
society and the impact of government action on the Nation's social
and economic development."[18] These general aims have been applied
in depth in one area that is closely related to national security: the
role of science and scientists in government. Beginning in 1958, a
series of conferences have been arranged by Brookings for administrators and scientists nominated by the Atomic Energy Commission,
the Defense Department, the National Science Foundation, the
National Aeronautics and Space Administration, and other scientific

* For a description of the activities of the Brookings Institution, see below,
Chapter 12, pp. 278–81.

agencies—in order "to promote better understanding of scientific endeavor on the part of administrators and fuller comprehension of governmental and administrative processes on the part of scientists."[19]

The executive conferences are part of a broader program conducted by Brookings whose purpose is to develop an informed leadership in public and private life. The Advanced Study Program provides an opportunity each year for about 500 officials drawn from business, labor, the professions, and all levels and branches of government to explore issues of public policy with each other and with scholars and experts. Brookings also offers about ten Federal Executive Fellowships each year to senior government officials to spend six months to a year in study and research.

Since the passage of the Government Employees Training Act of 1958, all federal agencies have the authority, previously limited largely to the defense establishment, to send civilian career executives to private colleges and universities for specialized training not available in the government. During the fiscal year ending June 30, 1961, for example, more than $14 million was spent for such training. Sixty-four per cent of the total, however, was spent by the Department of Defense, most of it in scientific and engineering fields; an additional 15 per cent was expended for technical training for employees of the Federal Aviation Agency.[20]

The demand for advanced training of government officials in universities has by and large been met by the expanded graduate schools of public affairs. We have already noted the programs for career executives at the Woodrow Wilson School at Princeton and the Harvard Graduate School of Public Administration. Career federal employees on training assignments to these schools, or to the Maxwell School at Syracuse or the School of Public and International Affairs at Pittsburgh, also gain the experience of working with government officials from foreign countries. (At Pittsburgh, for example, there is a Foreign Specialists Program, conducted for the State Department, which brings students from Africa, Asia, and Latin America to the University.) Many government officers who are not sent on long training assignments can study at one of the universities in the Washington area, often with government support. The School of International Service at the American University is one such institution, which offers not only regular graduate courses but also special programs for government agencies, including a Program in Overseas Industrial and Labor Relations for State Department personnel and an Army program to train military officers for assignments in Africa.

In addition to the many government-financed training postgraduate programs, two major career-development programs—one old and one new—are financed from private sources. The newer program, the Career Education Awards Program, was established early in 1962 and is supported by a grant from the Ford Foundation. It enables young career executives with four to six years of government service to attend selected universities for a year of graduate study.[21] Candidates must be nominated by their agencies with selections made by the National Institute of Public Affairs in cooperation with the Civil Service Commission. (Originally set up by the Rockefeller Foundation in 1934 to administer an early government intern program, the National Institute of Public Affairs was reactivated to administer the new program.[22]) The original grant from the Ford Foundation amounted to $1.25 million for a five-year program for fifty participants each year, with an equal amount set aside to continue the program if it proves successful. The participants are kept on government salary, with the Ford money used to cover tuition, personal expenses, and costs the universities incur in preparing special courses and materials for the students.

The distinctive feature of the Career Awards Program is that it is designed for *young* federal employees. One of its objectives is to encourage bright young men and women, many of whom plan to go on to graduate school, to enter public service immediately after graduation from college with the hope of graduate study under government sponsorship. The opportunity for advanced study is also considered to be an incentive for remaining in government service. Since it comes early in their careers, the program tends to identify the young executives who are especially qualified. But beyond these aims, the program is a major step in developing closer relations between the government and colleges and universities in meeting the broad problems of staffing and career development, and it will undoubtedly influence the universities' public-service activities.[23] At the same time, the fact that the executives in the program are not much older than most graduate students should enable them to act as unofficial recruiters in the normal course of their social and academic meetings.

Rockefeller Public Service Awards, in contrast, are made at a later stage in career development—to executives between the ages of 35 and 50.[24] The objective is related less to the recruitment and retention of promising young public servants than to the broadening and refreshing of those already in government service. The awards, first made in 1952 in an effort to counteract demoralization in the Civil Service by giving special recognition to about ten outstanding career executives each year, are made by a committee of the Princeton

University Board of Trustees on the nomination of government departments and agencies. Administered through the Woodrow Wilson School at Princeton University, the awards originally covered salary, tuition, and personal expenses for six months to a year of formal education or educational travel. The programs have varied from a year of study at universities in the United States and abroad to a "program of independent research to attempt to develop a method for analyzing the total military program and budget in terms of basic factors."[25]

In 1960, when the original purpose had been met, the nature of the award was changed. Still administered by Princeton, it is now an outright prize of $5,000 each awarded to five persons recognized for their outstanding accomplishment in the federal service in five areas of government activity, including foreign affairs and science, technology, and engineering. But the winners can still take time off from their work for research, writing, or study, and if they choose to do so will receive additional funds.

While the opportunities for career development for civilians are numerous, they are less focused than similar programs within the military services. The military services are more highly structured than the civilian services, and education and training are closely related to the whole system of selection and promotion. Certain courses must be passed before given levels of promotion can be reached, and assignment to schools is often preliminary to assignment to higher positions. The system, of course, frequently breaks down, particularly when commanders refuse to release their best officers for further training or higher education. But the relation of military education to personnel practices is, for all its lapses, infinitely more important to the career structure of the military than anywhere in the civilian system.

Within the Foreign Service, new educational opportunities have been created in response to the pressures, particularly from Congress, to follow the lead of the military services in more closely relating training with the practices of personnel advancement and assignment. Progress was slow at first and has only begun to accelerate in recent years.

The Foreign Service Institute

Immediately after World War II, it became evident that the Foreign Service had to be revitalized. Not only had the national sources of recruitment been closed to it during the war years, but it now had to meet new and specialized problems for which it was not wholly prepared. It was determined at an early stage that in-service training should be a major part of this revitalization, and the Foreign Service Act of 1946 thus made provision for a Foreign Service Institute within the Department of State. In recommending the Institute, the House Foreign Affairs Committee noted that "no training worthy of the name has been administered until very recently" and suggested that "if the highly selected talents of the future Service are to be kept from atrophy a continuous program of in-service training must be directed by a strong central authority drawing on the best educational resources of the country."[26]

The Institute was initially planned to be "comparable to the Army and Navy command schools and staff colleges," its Director to be "an educational leader of distinction in his field," and its staff to include "the best scholars that the universities of the country can furnish."[27] The Institute actually built on several existing educational programs in the Department—programs that included special training in difficult languages, orientation courses for entering officers in the Foreign Service Officers' Training School, and assignments to universities for instruction in economics and to the military staff colleges. These efforts were hardly adequate to meet the new demands, however, and the Institute represented an attempt to deal with the problems of staff development and specialization through an expansion of the training program of the Department.[28]

During its first ten years, the Institute accomplished very little. This failure is perhaps best summed up in the harsh criticism of the Wriston Committee in 1954:

> Here . . . was an important idea . . . one for which the pattern had been set in other Government services; one relatively easy of attainment; one which had the support of the Congress and the interest of many citizens across the land. Yet it is dying of neglect. The Department has never developed a clear concept of the training requirements for the officers of the Foreign Service, just as it has never had a program of career planning and development. It has not supplied the Institute with the kind of Director the Congress stipulated. It has not staffed the Institute with the sort of faculty that was expected. It has not assigned to the Institute students of the grade capable of taking full advantage of the kind of facilities that the Congress intended to supply.[29]

Part of the dismal record of the Institute—a "pedestrian preoccupation with job mechanics," according to the Wriston Committee—was undoubtedly related to the grave demoralization of the Foreign Service to which we have already referred. But part of it was also the result of the State Department's traditional preference for the general political officer.

The Wriston Committee's criticism was difficult to evade. In response, the Department started on a major expansion of the Institute. Against actual obligations of less than $800,000 for fiscal year 1954, plans were developed for an annual program of slightly over $5 million. Progress was nevertheless still slow, and the Institute did not reach the projected spending rate until 1962.[30] In 1956, for example, an *ad hoc* group at the Council on Foreign Relations found that "the importance of training still tends to be underrated or imperfectly understood by the Department" and recommended that "sights should be set higher."[31] Similarly, a Brookings Institution study completed for the Senate Foreign Relations Committee in 1960 reported that "the training skeleton is there, but meat needs to be put on the bones if the future requirements of the Foreign Service are to be met."[32]

The Brookings report was a measure of the improvements in the years since the Wriston review, as well as of the continued inadequacies of the Foreign Service Institute. The Wriston Committee had found that little was going on in the Institute beyond short orientation courses in formal procedures for new officers, and language instruction for staff from the State Department and other government agencies. The Brookings survey, on the other hand, found vastly expanded and improved courses in orientation and language training, and some advanced work in foreign affairs for mid-career and senior officers. Its criticism was directed rather at the continued difficulty in freeing officers for such training, and at the quality of the instruction. "Much of the teaching is done as a gesture of good-will by governmental employees taking time off from their regular duties, by single appearances of experts from outside the government, by nonprofessional educators drawn from the Foreign Service, or by ill-paid tutors with little job security."[33]

While the State Department agreed in substance with the Brookings study, it had definite goals for its career-development program and definite plans for achieving them. The goals were:

(1) General introduction to the Service and its operations for all new junior officers; (2) preparation where necessary in the language and culture of the country of next assignment for all officers; (3) preparation where necessary in the function to be performed in the next assignment for all officers; (4) broadened awareness of the world situation for mid-career officers; and (5) deepened understanding of national security affairs and of policy formulation for selected officers at the senior level.[34]

To achieve these goals, the Department planned to expand the Foreign Service and to release more officers from active assignments for training. At the same time, more assignments would be made to universities and private institutions, especially for specialized training in geographic areas and in traditional disciplines such as economics. But the heart of the Department's program continued to rest on an expanded and improved Foreign Service Institute.[35]

The Institute is divided into two schools: the School of Languages and Area Studies and the School of Foreign Affairs. The former received a particular stimulus in 1960 when the Congress wrote foreign-language requirements into the Foreign Service Act, specifying that Foreign Service officers should have "a useful knowledge of the principal language or dialect of the country in which they are to serve, and knowledge and understanding of the history, the culture, the economic and political institutions, and the interests of such country and its people." While the language of the law left room for administrative interpretation, the intent of the Congress was clear. Moreover, the immediate background to Congressional action had been considerable public criticism and newspaper investigation of the inadequate preparation of American representatives serving in the new nations of Asia, Africa, and the Middle East.[36]

The School of Languages and Area Studies now offers full and part-time training in not only European but also Asian and African languages. Altogether, sixty different languages are taught; in 1961–62, almost 10,000 students attended language courses.[37] And in addition to studying languages at the Institute in Washington prior to their assignment overseas, officers can take part-time language instruction at some two hundred overseas posts. The Institute also conducts field schools in Taiwan, Tokyo, and Beirut. In building its language program, the Institute has used all the modern techniques of language instruction.

The area studies complement the language courses by offering instruction on the history and institutions of particular areas; it is thus equally responsive to the Congressional policy set out in the 1960 amendment to the Foreign Service Act. Area studies are actually of two kinds: concentrated, three-week courses for officers about to be posted to areas with which they are not familiar; and longer training periods for officers who expect to specialize in an area. In 1961, the Institute initiated short programs on Eastern Europe, the Near East, South Asia, Southeast Asia, China, Northeast Asia, Latin America, and Africa.[38] The longer specialist training lasts from ten to thirty months and may include enrollment in selected universities or the field schools in Taiwan, Tokyo, or Beirut, as well as at the Institute itself.

Usually the total course is divided into two periods of ten to twenty-four months, with several years of actual service intervening.[39] For many Foreign Service Officers, area specialization thus becomes a means for advancement at a crucial period in their careers, and the development of area specialists makes for a better balance between "generalists" and "specialists."

The program of the School of Foreign Affairs may be roughly divided into four broad categories: general orientation; functional training; general seminars in problems of American foreign policy; and general career training. Orientation courses lasting from one to three weeks are available for officers, clerical staff, and dependents upon entering the Department and before moving to overseas posts. Functional training concentrates on problems of administration, finance, and consular affairs, and is usually for men who are about to assume supervisory positions. The seminars, which last from eight days to four weeks, provide information and instruction on current policy areas to officers from all agencies that are involved in the conduct of foreign relations. For example, in 1960, 355 military officers and civilians from the Department of Defense attended the Institute's two-week seminar on Communist strategy. The seminars cover such subjects as the formulation and development of foreign policy, international labor affairs, U.S. diplomacy and the U.N., economic development and political stability, and regional organization in western Europe.[40]

The most important courses at the School of Foreign Affairs comprise the general career training of the Foreign Service. The first, the Basic Foreign Service Officer Course, is given to officers who have just entered the corps. Lasting eight weeks, it is both an introduction to the Department and to government in general and a broad survey of the major problems of American foreign policy. The Mid-Career Course, for those with seven to twelve years' service, lasts for twelve weeks and concentrates on the development of analytical skills in preparation for more responsible assignments and on an over-view of the internal and external factors of American foreign policy. Both courses are directed by Foreign Service Officers on the staff of the Institute and include lectures, briefings, and informal discussions. In the past, the Mid-Career Course has relied heavily on outside lecturers from the government and universities. Indeed, in the fall of 1959, students had to attend lectures or briefings almost every day of the twelve-week period, a procedure that had been noted by the critical authors of the Brookings study. A course so completely dependent on outside speakers not only risks losing all sense of unity, but it does not help the students to develop creative conceptual skills of their own.

The Senior Officers Course is the highest instruction offered by the Institute. Organized in 1958, the course represented a direct response to the Wriston Committee's charge that the State Department did not offer advanced training for those ready to assume responsibilities at a policy-making level. The course lasts nine months and has the advantage of being limited to a small number. (In 1962, for example, the class totaled twenty-five.) In addition to Foreign Service Officers, the class usually includes an officer of colonel rank from the Army, Air Force, and Marine Corps, a Navy captain, and several officers from other agencies, particularly the Central Intelligence, AID and Information agencies. The length of the course, its size, and the composition of the class combine to offer an unusual opportunity to develop, in theory and through association, a sense of the multidimensional nature of national security affairs. Indeed, in recent years, the final exercise of the course has been a policy-planning exercise in which the students are actually sent to overseas posts to conduct on-the-spot investigations and draw up a policy study which they then review with officers from other agencies.[41]

The senior course, like the mid-career course, focuses on both internal and external factors of American foreign policy. But in the former, the analysis is much deeper, several sections of the course being devoted to the trends in American life that influence the formulation and execution of foreign policy. This emphasis undoubtedly reflects the traditional concern of the State Department for the continual "re-Americanization" of Foreign Service officers and a growing realization of the limits that domestic pressures impose on foreign policy. The study of American life is supplemented by "field trips enabling the participants to sharpen their acquaintance with relevant political, economic, and social conditions in different regions of the United States."[42] The remainder of the course is largely taken up with current policy issues, ending with the policy-planning exercise. While the course requires considerable reading and research by the students, it relies heavily, like the mid-career course, on lecturers from a variety of professions and fields.

In range and scope, the curriculum of the Foreign Service Institute has now sufficiently expanded to conclude that there is some "meat" on the "bones." The work in language and area studies is advancing most rapidly and is being related to area studies in universities.[43] But, in other fields, the Institute has still some distance to go, and one may still maintain with justice that it has been slow to respond to the intellectual challenges of the cold war. The early Congressional intent, stated in 1946, that the Foreign Service Institute be headed by "an educational leader of distinction," has not been realized. The Director appointed shortly after the Wriston report was published was Harold B. Hoskins, a businessman whose organizing ability was undoubtedly helpful in the period of expansion but who could not meet the requirement for educational leadership. When Mr. Hoskins resigned in early 1961, the Institute was left in the hands of a series of Acting Directors for almost a year and a half, until George A. Morgan was appointed in June, 1962. A professor of philosophy before joining the Foreign Service, and formerly a member of the Department's Policy Planning Council, Mr. Morgan at least brought an academic background to the Institute, although he had not held an academic post for many years.

Moreover, problems of course direction and teaching, especially with the mid-career and senior courses, remain serious. One alternative to the present practice of leaving the supervision of the course entirely to Departmental staff was suggested in June, 1962, when a new seminar was offered in "problems of development and internal defense." Touched off by President Kennedy's concern with our inability to deal with the complex problems of internal violence in new states, the five-week seminar was devised by the Institute's staff, with the assistance of a team from the M.I.T. Center for International Studies headed by Max Millikan.[44] The M.I.T. group, experienced teachers who had done advanced research in economic and social development, not only helped to give the material a unifying conceptual framework, but taught the first two weeks of the course, thus eliminating any further need of outside "experts." The course, then, came close to meeting the requirement that, in the language of the 1946 Act, the Institute be staffed by "the best scholars that the universities of the country can furnish." But while men like Max Millikan might be willing to cooperate in starting such a course, it is less likely that they would be willing to resign from their academic posts to run the program permanently, at least under the present organizational arrangements of the Institute.

The program at the Center for International Affairs at Harvard, in which Foreign Service Officers are enrolled for a nine-month assignment is an alternative to participation in the senior seminar in foreign policy with two advantages: First, it takes officers out of Washington and thus relieves them of the inevitable pressures of internal departmental politics that persist within the Institute itself; secondly, it combines advanced training for the Foreign Service with opportunities for advanced research in long-range foreign policies in an institution independent of direct government supervision, making the Harvard Center more attractive to scholars.

A private institution could perhaps be set up on a contract basis, separate from the government as well as any established university. The disadvantage for the government of such an arrangement, of course, is that the State Department would not control the program. This is a point that the military departments have been keenly aware of in their resistance to any move to broaden the directing authority of their own educational institutions. It is more than a matter of jurisdiction. It involves the need to relate training to the Department's mission and operations, to have access to classified information, and to evaluate the students' performance—if their training is to be related to their promotion and selection for higher responsibility. It is true that some educational institutions might be willing to set up courses under State Department or Defense Department supervision and specifications, but universities willing to do this would probably not have "the best scholars" in the country on their faculties. All of these problems underscore the real difficulties of staffing educational programs in government, no matter what the intent of Congress may be.

A major change, substantially affecting many of the issues discussed here, may come from the study compiled in late 1962 by a committee headed by former Secretary of State Christian Herter. The Herter Committee recommended the establishment of a National Foreign Affairs College to replace the Foreign Service Institute, and for two reasons. First was the need for training in economic development and information services, and for a more conscious integration of these services with the Foreign Service. The report, for example, speaks of "a family of compatible services governed by uniform statutory provisions regarding personnel management." The new College would, in effect, be a training institution for the three services without the "parochialism" the Committee found in the Foreign Service Institute and the advanced training programs of the AID and Information agencies.

The second reason was that the Herter Committee felt it imperative to strengthen the professional quality of advanced training in foreign affairs. To achieve the needed academic excellence, the Committee insisted that the College "be a semi-autonomous educational institution" with a Chancellor appointed by the President on nomination from an independent Board of Trustees. The teaching staff would be a "small, permanent core faculty" supplemented by specialists on assignment from government agencies and professors on leave for one to three years' service. The Committee also recommended more extensive use of the nation's universities for foreign-affairs instruction, in much the way they have been used by the military services.

Unwittingly perhaps, the Herter Committee recommendations resemble the structure of military education: the National Foreign Affairs College is like the National War College with each of the basic services—diplomatic, aid, and information—maintaining nonprofessional and staff training programs in much the same way the individual military services now do. The difference would be in the independent status of the College. The key to the success of the Herter plan, however, lies in recruiting a "core faculty" of men with "that rare mixture of high academic standards and rich exposure to the practical world of foreign affairs." Under the best of circumstances, it would be difficult to secure the services of leading scholars for an institution established under government auspices, however broad its mandate and independent its charter.

The recommendations of the Herter Committee confirm the basic trends in staffing and training which we have discussed. They call for greater quality, professional competence, diversity in talents and skills, and broader perspective in foreign-affairs personnel. They seek to gain these objectives through better recruitment, more use of lateral entry, and broader and stronger training programs.

Civilian Executives and Military Education

One of the major functions of the Foreign Service Institute, in terms of the education it offers in national security affairs, is to bring military officers and civilian executives into close association. This is a function also performed by some of the military colleges, and it is of major significance in developing the habits of cooperation that are so crucial to effective policy formulation and execution in national security affairs. Civilians and military officers must be sensitive to and appreciate each other's perspectives; joint educational programs provide one of the few ways by which they can gain this understanding. In 1960, another step was taken to achieve this same objective when the Departments of State and Defense began an exchange program under which selected civilians and uniformed officers took over posts in each other's department for a two-year period. Appropriately enough, three of the seven Foreign Service Officers assigned to the defense establishment in 1961 were graduates of one of the military colleges.[45]

For a number of years, the State Department, as well as other civilian agencies such as the AID and intelligence agencies, have sent students to the service war colleges, the Armed Forces Staff College, and the Industrial College of the Armed Forces, and usually have been represented on the faculty of these colleges. For example, one year, twenty-one civilians from twelve different agencies were among the 141 graduates of the Industrial College.[46] The civilian representation at the National War College is substantially larger, equal in fact to that of each of the services. About one-fourth of its students are civilians and more than half of these are Foreign Service Officers; the others are from the Office of the Secretary of Defense, CIA, USIA, the Bureau of the Budget, and the Department of Commerce.[47] The State Department nominates a member of the civilian faculty as well as one of the three Deputy Commandants of the National War College; the other two and the Commandant represent the three military services, with the top post rotating among the three. Three other members of the faculty are civilians, usually professors on leave from their own institutions.

Despite the large civilian contingent, the program at the National War College is no less dominated by the military than that of the other military colleges. Not only are military students in the majority and the top direction always in military hands, but organizationally, the College (and the Industrial College, too) is under the direct supervision of the Joint Chiefs of Staff. The administrative structure of the College reflects this line of command by subordinating all civilians on the staff, both from the State Department and from academic faculties, to military supervision.[48] Military dominance is also reflected in the curriculum: Priority is given to the military requirements of national security policy, and instruction in political, social, and economic affairs is given at a level more suitable for the military officer than for the more experienced civilian.

The Industrial and National War Colleges are at the summit of the military education system. Though their curriculums have tended to overlap in recent years, the mission of the Industrial College was originally limited to the economic problems involved in wartime mobilization. In 1960, a new directive issued by the Joint Chiefs of Staff broadened the Industrial College's objectives to provide training in the more complex economic problems posed by situations ranging "from cold war to post-attack recovery in a nuclear war."[49] The curriculum of the Industrial College had in fact already evolved to include more instruction in the political and social aspects of national security, and the new charter only confirmed what was coming to be practice.[50]

The curriculum of the Industrial College is divided into a series of units, such as National Security Objectives and Requirements, Resources, Material Management, Economic Stabilization, Contemporary International Politics, Economic Capability for International Conflict, International Field Studies (including visits abroad), and Plans and Readiness (an appraisal of the preparedness of the United States). A detailed syllabus is prepared for each unit giving a day-by-day listing of the lectures and discussion sections, as well as the scope to be covered in any single presentation and the objective to be sought in any specific section of the course. This amount of detailed preparation is typical of military education on all levels. The students know exactly what is expected of them, readings and work loads are assigned, and the aims are explicitly stated to give guidance and a basis for later evaluation of the program. Compared to a university situation, however, the preparation seems unduly elaborate and the opportunities for creative work by the students restricted. Indeed, the framework within which it operates tends to weaken the otherwise broad and comprehensive Industrial College program.

On its establishment in 1946, the National War College was instructed to devise a curriculum reflecting the many dimensions of national security policy to prepare officers for high-level command and staff functions. The curriculum has developed over the years as a nine-month program broken down into ten courses, which broadly divide into three parts: an analysis of the elements of national power, with particular emphasis on the United States; the study of geographic areas in which the United States has interests; and the development of American policies for selected areas of conflict and commitment.[51] Like the Industrial College, the National War College prepares a detailed outline of each course. The one for the course on "The Western Hemisphere and Free Europe" given in 1960 is illustrative. The course included a study of American relations with major countries and an analysis of general problems, such as European integration and economic development, and military strategy in the European theater. The syllabus included a background statement on each topic, and on the scope and purpose of the section, suggested questions for consideration by the students, and gave a list of assigned and collateral reading. The issues to be considered were thus spread out for the students beforehand; they had guidelines to cling to, clues as to the important factors to be considered, and were even supplied with questions to ask the speakers.

Instruction at the National War College, like that at other military colleges and at the Foreign Service Institute, relies heavily on outside lecturers. Both the Industrial and National War Colleges have civilians on the faculty—at the first, a full complement under civil service status, and at the second, a small number on a rotating basis on loan from colleges and universities—but neither they nor the military faculty do any teaching in the conventional sense. The "teaching" is done almost entirely by visiting speakers, and on a "do-it-yourself" basis through committees and discussion groups in which the students prepare joint reports and individual analyses for criticism. The function of the faculty is to maintain a general oversight of committees and annually review the curriculum—with the civilians usually in a minority position if they dissent from the military consensus.

Much of the criticism of military education reflects, of course, a basic criticism of the framework within which it operates. The only way to eliminate fragmentation and parochialism completely is to offer instruction that is free of departmental interests and within an organization that is administered by experienced teachers and scholars. But the broad achievements in military education since World War II should not be minimized, or the positive value to civilian participants denied. There is no lack of evidence that association within programs of military education has been advantageous for both civilians and military officers who have gone on to positions of increasing responsibility.[52] Indeed, there is a community of war-college graduates who, for all their differences, recognize that their common experience gives them a starting point for effective cooperation.

Since 1945, proposals have repeatedly been made to establish a high-level national security college that would not operate under an individual department but would be government-wide in its administration and scope. At times, the proposal has been framed within a broader plan for a senior staff college concerned with the full range of public affairs.[53] On the other hand, proposals for a Freedom Academy are limited to the challenge of the cold war, and have as their aim to develop an "integrated cold war operational science . . . the training of government personnel, private citizens, and foreign students in this science," and informing the public "of the dimensions and nature of the global struggle between freedom and communism."[54]

Interest in training geared to the problems of the cold war was also the basis for a proposal made to President Eisenhower just before he left office by the President's Committee on Information Activities Abroad. The Committee recommended "the establishment of a National Security Institute . . . under the National Security Council . . . to provide high-level training in the interrelated economic, political, informational and military aspects of the present world struggle, for . . . the top officers of agencies dealing with international and security affairs."[55] A most recent proposal has been for a National Academy of Foreign Affairs, made to President Kennedy in December, 1962, by an advisory panel headed by James A. Perkins, then Vice President of the Carnegie Corporation and now President of Cornell. The purpose of the Academy would be to provide "leadership required for the training, education, and research needs of our foreign operations."[56]

Yet if the existing joint war colleges and the Foreign Service Institute are not accomplishing their own tasks well enough, the solution is not to establish another school for high-level training, but to improve the intellectual quality of the existing ones. Furthermore, it is difficult for a career executive to develop a broad perspective on national security policy and programs if he has spent the better part of his career within a system that virtually forces parochialism on him through the pressures of the promotion system, a confining administrative environment, limits on his ability to transfer within the government, and limits on the quality and breadth of his training. The time for acquiring new knowledge is during a man's formative years, when he can move easily from operational responsibilities to academic study.

There may still be a need for an advanced institute of national security affairs, the aims of which, like those of the initial Rockefeller Public Service Awards, would be to broaden and refresh executives within a collegial environment. It would be attached to no department; it would be small and highly selective; it would be geared not so much to formal instruction as to offering an opportunity to senior civilian and military officers to reflect, talk, and refresh themselves intellectually in an atmosphere completely free of staff duties. Valuable as such an institute might be for the participants and for the more effective high-level staffing in national security affairs, it alone would not provide better policy-makers at the top of the career development system. That can be achieved only by better staffing and training throughout the public service.

11

Advice by Contract

THE EDUCATION of career officials for their increasingly important part in the policy-making process is only one aspect of the larger problem of how to bring to bear on national security issues the highest degree of analytical skills, technical knowledge, and wisdom in the ordering of human affairs. To assist elected officials in the difficult policy decisions they must make, one must provide the best advice available, whatever the source. Traditionally, this advice has come from appointed political executives, who drew on career government officials and experts for the technical knowledge they needed. But the government has also utilized outside sources, such as the universities, the business community, and the church, in special cases where detachment or special information not available within the government was required. Before World War II, however, this practice was the exception rather than the rule.

World War II and the cold war drastically altered the function of private groups in the formulation of national security policy. Today, their contribution to the development of weapons systems and to the policy process is a significant aspect of our national life. The government needs all the help it can get—technical, analytical, scientific, engineering, and industrial—to meet the problems of the cold war. It has employed various methods to get this assistance: special commissions, *ad hoc* committees, grants to colleges and universities to foster research and scientific study; and contractual arrangements with outside institutions to develop, test, and evaluate weapons systems, to analyze these systems by the most powerful intellectual tools available and to conduct studies as to how and under what circumstances they could be utilized most effectively. In some cases, these contractual services have included studies of alternative strategies or policies, and of issues of political and social as well as military consequence. All these methods have one purpose—to utilize the best talent of the nation in the solution of the great problems of our time.

Federal Support of Private Organizations

The nature and extent of federal support to private organizations for research and development in national security affairs, and the problems created by this support, can be understood most readily by analyzing the federal expenditures in this field during the past decade. In 1950, the total amount of money spent by the federal government for research and development (the greatest part of which went for research in the physical sciences and for the development of weapons systems), was slightly more than $1.1 billion; by 1953, this total had tripled, and, by 1960, it had increased sevenfold.[1] Expenditures in 1961 were about $9.3 billion, and, for 1963, about $12 billion—almost twice the amount spent by the federal government for all purposes in 1934, at the height of New Deal emergency spending.[2] By far the largest part of these expenditures was for the national defense, $7.7 billion in 1961 and $8.6 billion expended in 1963, most of it spent by the Department of Defense, NASA, AEC, the Department of Commerce (Weather Bureau), and the National Science Foundation.

The amount spent is not the only startling feature of the phenomenal growth in research and development. Equally significant is the fact that the federal government now supports more than two-thirds of all the research and development in the United States, but spends in its own laboratories only 20 per cent of the amount it appropriates. The rest goes to private industry, universities and research centers, and nonprofit institutions. Thus, out of a total national expenditure for research and development of $12.6 billion in 1960, $8.3 billion represented the contribution of the federal government, $4 billion that of industry, and $200 million that of universities and research centers. In contrast, the federal government spent only $1.8 billion on research and development in its own laboratories and by its own scientists, as compared to $9.6 billion by private industry and $1 billion by universities and affiliated centers. Private, nonprofit institutions contributed $100 million to the total national expenditure but spent two and a half times that sum.[3]

These statistics, impressive as they are, do not tell the whole story. The chief recipients of the federal funds in recent years have been not the older industries (automotive, shipbuilding, steel, and oil) that traditionally supplied the government, but the newer industries specializing in nuclear and space technology. These industries, which have little to sell in a competitive, open market, find that their best and sometimes only customer is the federal government. Thus, the military sales of General Motors in 1958 was 5 per cent of its total production; those of the Martin Company (aircraft and missiles), 99.2 per cent.[4]

The universities, which have always done some research for the government, now find that more and more of their funds for research come from federal agencies.[5] More than 70 per cent of all research conducted by colleges, universities, and associated research centers is financed by the federal government, with such well-endowed institutions as Harvard, M.I.T., Princeton, Stanford, and California Institute of Technology receiving more than half their research funds from that source. Actually, universities finance less than 10 per cent of the research they conduct, receiving contributions not only from the government but from private industry and foundations as well. Nor are these sums distributed evenly among the nation's colleges and universities. In 1953-54, 178 institutions received federal funds, but of these, fourteen received more than half the total amount. Four years later, the percentage had dropped somewhat, but twenty universities still received more than half of the federal money. It was these institutions, too, that received the bulk of nongovernmental funds for research.[6] The geographical distribution of funds is also significant. Except for two or three schools in California, the institutions receiving the largest amounts of outside funds were located in the northeastern and north central United States. The problems created for the universities themselves, as well as for the government, by these developments are readily apparent and are the subject of increasing concern and study.[7]

Since 1950, United States national security has depended less on the nation's productive capacity and the ability to stockpile large quantities of weapons than on its ability to make technological break-throughs in both weapons systems and defense. Federal research and development funds, therefore, have tended to concentrate in the areas of science and technology directly related to these needs.[8] As much as 90 per cent of budgeted academic research in the physical and life sciences is financed by the federal government, which provides only slightly less than that percentage for research in engineering, while the social sciences get less than half their funds from the government—most of what they do have going to the behavioral sciences. (It is instructive also to compare the amounts spent in each of these fields by the universities and their associated research centers: physical sciences, $262.3 million; life sciences, $251.5 million; engineering, $186.4 million; social sciences, $35.6 million.[9]) Though this disparity is more apparent than real, the imbalance is still there between the sciences and engineering on the one hand, and the social sciences and humanities on the other. The latter, with limited funds for research, are increasingly in an unfavorable situation vis-à-vis their scientific colleagues; there is growing dissatisfaction and, in some cases, a real morale problem on the campus.

The phrase "research and development" covers activities that range from basic research in the physical and natural sciences to operational analysis and policy studies. Obviously, different organizations, as well as disciplines, are required to perform these varied activities. Colleges and universities provide the most suitable intellectual environment for basic research and for some aspects of applied research. Private industry possesses special advantages in technology and in organization for development and testing. Both have generally met the demands placed on them by government, though not without considerable adjustment and modification of their internal organization. The scope of federal programs, as well as new techniques of analysis and methods of research which are not readily adaptable to the traditional academic patterns, have resulted in new institutional arrangements at the universities, and in the creation of entirely new organizations (popularly referred to as "think factories") with some of the characteristics of a university and some of private industry.

In recent years, there has also been a growing recognition of the need to apply systematic analysis to the problems of arms control, particularly since the establishment of the U.S. Arms Control and Disarmament Agency (ACDA) in 1961. The creation of the ACDA made available new funds for arms-control investigations and encouraged many industrial and private centers to begin research in this area. Some of the ACDA's research is for projects primarily undertaken through the Defense Department and the Atomic Energy Commission—such as the work done on verification of nuclear testing. But ACDA has developed other research areas that the Defense Department had largely ignored and the State Department had been unable to pursue. In its first year of operation, 1961–62, for example, ACDA (in addition to its own research) signed contracts for research on the inspection of restrictions on missiles, techniques for monitoring missile production, political control of an international police force, political and strategic implications of civil-defense programs, and stable military environments. These contracts were given to Sylvania Electric, Aerospace Corporation, the Institute for Defense Analyses, the Hudson Institute, Raytheon, Bendix Systems, the Peace Research Institute, and the American Academy of Arts and Sciences, among others. Since 1961, the area of ACDA's research interests, and the number of its contracts, has greatly increased.

The creation of special institutes for research and development is one way the universities have responded to the needs of the federal government and to the changes of the postwar world. Sometimes, these institutes are affiliated with one or more universities and draw their consultants and staff from their various departments; sometimes, they are entirely independent, with only the most distant relationship to their academic parents. In either case, they are organizational entities able to conduct analytical studies or basic and applied research on a large scale, without regard for the traditional division of specialties in a university and without the necessity of fulfilling the usual duties of an academic department. Examples of such centers are the Lincoln Laboratory, established by contract between M.I.T. and the Air Force; the Jet Propulsion Laboratory, associated with the California Institute of Technology and under contract to the Army and NASA; the Radiation and Los Alamos Scientific Laboratories of the AEC under contract with the University of California; and the Human Resources Research Office of George Washington University. A variant of this arrangement is the government-owned, privately operated facility such as the Brookhaven National Laboratory, owned by the AEC and operated by the nine universities composing the Associated Universities. The hallmark of these organizations, of which there are about twenty, is that they are large operations, financed entirely by government funds; they engage only in research and development that fall within the broad framework of the sponsoring agency's interests; and they operate outside the federal bureaucracy, generally under the direction of university officials or their representatives, free of government personnel regulations and salary restrictions.[10] But these research organizations also differ widely among themselves; even within each type or category of contractor (university, industry, or independent nonprofit), there may be more differences than similarities.

Private industry also operates research centers or laboratories owned by the federal government. Thus, the Knolls Laboratory was set up by the General Electric Company under contract with the AEC, and Union Carbide runs the AEC's Oak Ridge National Laboratory. In addition, private industry has set up laboratories such as Boeing's Aero-Space Division, where much of their government research is done. In terms of staff, plant, and operating expenses, these centers are larger than most of the ones affiliated with universities, but, like them, they work almost entirely for the federal government on programs related to national security and space technology.

A new kind of organization is the private corporation specifically created to provide the government with services not usually available in the universities or in private industry: the Aerospace Corporation in Los Angeles, formed from a subsidiary of Thompson Ramo Wooldridge to perform research and development in space technology for the Air Force, is representative. Also working for the Air Force is the Mitre Corporation, which is concerned mainly with the development of electronic systems for air defense and tactical operations. The largest of this type of private enterprise is the Systems Development Corporation, which employs about 900 scientists and engineers.

Operations Research

Although most of the funds spent by the federal government for research and development have gone into the science and technology of new and improved weapons systems, much has also been spent for operational and policy research on the choices of weapons available to policy-makers, the strategies these weapons should support, and the most effective methods of using them. The military planner and policy-maker, faced with problems of unprecedented size and complexity, needs advice from specialists accustomed to dealing with intricate data and armed with computers and the latest techniques of analysis and scientific measurement. The problems these experts must work on are indicative of the difficulties facing an official such as the Secretary of Defense when he must choose among weapons systems, each costing billions of dollars and still years from actual production. One writer compared this difficulty to that of mixing an unnamed cocktail with millions of ingredients, many of them unknown and not yet distilled, intended for unknown customers, at an unspecified time and place, which might or might not be served.[11]

The application of science and of analytical techniques to the solution of military problems is not new: History provides numerous examples of scientists contributing to the military art. By the turn of the twentieth century, the intimate relationship between technology and war was thoroughly appreciated, if not effectively organized and coordinated. World War II witnessed a massive research effort, initiated largely by civilians, in which the scientific manpower of the nation was for the first time harnessed to the needs of the government. As Vannevar Bush, head of the wartime Office of Scientific Research and Development, pointed out, World War II "was the first war in human history to be decisively affected by weapons unknown at the outbreak of hostilities."[12]

With the modern application of science to war came the application of modern scientific techniques to military problems—an activity that came to be called operations research. Operations research makes use of theoretical models, mathematical concepts, scientific techniques, and, where appropriate, detailed experiential data in order to improve a given activity or system. It is neither science nor technology, nor any of the special activities involved, but all of these in combination—requiring, as one writer put it, "the ability to reason abstractly, to organize generalities, and to distinguish between the construction of a *superior* mousetrap (which is technology) and the improved use of an *existing* mousetrap (which is the goal of operations research)."[13]

Operations research may be done by individuals or several men in the same field, but its characteristic feature is "team research" by a group of specialists in different fields.[14] In determining the most effective bomb pattern, for instance—a familiar problem for operations analysts in World War II—scientists, engineers, and social scientists worked with military men to arrive at a solution that would "optimize" the operation. All relevant information was assembled, a "model" created, and, with the aid of mathematical techniques and time-saving devices such as computers, all possible patterns were examined. In this way, the course of action seeming to offer the greatest advantage and least disadvantage could be discovered; that it was actually the ideal solution did not necessarily follow, but at least the method opened up a number of possibilities for those who had to make the decision, and examined these possibilities as realistically and accurately as possible.

Although this method of research and analysis captured the public imagination, it is by no means a magic formula for the solution of all problems. It can be applied only to certain types of problems, and even then the chances of success are not always high. In relation to Army operations, it has been estimated that only one out of ten operations research studies will lead to significant improvements.[15] Since most of the studies performed for the government are classified, and only those that are successful are usually mentioned, it is difficult to judge the accuracy of this estimate. But it is important to note the limitations of the method. It relies heavily on test data, but often the data are not available and sometimes may be inaccurate; it makes assumptions about future actions that cannot always be tested and may be invalid; it is concerned with an area in which opportunities for experimentation and validation are rare; and it is not suited to non-quantitative problems whose solutions depend more on leadership, judgment, and intuition than on scientific analysis; finally, these studies, especially the more ambitious ones, may take from one to two years to complete, and their usefulness is therefore limited to long-range problems.

Operations research came into its own during World War II. Utilized first by the British in connection with radar, it was adopted by the Americans and applied to problems ranging from tactical studies on antisubmarine warfare and bombing accuracy to strategic studies of methods of warfare. The Navy and Army Air Forces developed their own operations research organization; by the end of the war, these had so proved their worth that plans were made to continue them in peacetime. Since then, these organizations have been greatly expanded. New groups have been formed, and the range of problems they have been called upon to solve has greatly increased.

The success of operations research in military affairs has led to its application to nonmilitary areas in both private industry and government. So quickly did this occur after the war that in November, 1952, a national organization, the Operations Research Society of America, was formed and began publication of a quarterly journal.[16] It also became recognized in some universities as a regular field of study. M.I.T. led the way in 1948, with a course in the nonmilitary application of operations research, given in collaboration with the Navy. Columbia and Johns Hopkins Universities followed M.I.T. a few years later, and the Case Institute of Technology went even further when it established a course of study in operations research leading to the Master of Science degree.

Like the study of national security, the status of operations research as a field of study is still undetermined. Some feel that operations research is a profession for which students can and should be trained, a new discipline deserving a separate place in the curriculum. Others see it as a combination of the methods of many disciplines, and believe the best preparation for it would be in a basic discipline, preferably mathematical or scientific.

In general, social scientists had avoided operations research because of their lack of familiarity with the scientific, engineering, and mathematical concepts employed in it. Many social scientists viewed it with real skepticism and doubted that it could be applied to social and political problems. Thus the wartime operations research units had few historians and social scientists. But, since the war, there has been a recognition of the contribution they could make, and most operations research and analysis organizations employ more and more social scientists, particularly economists and psychologists. New techniques of operations research have also been developed since the war that utilize the advances made in the social sciences. Indeed, in its present form, operations research is much more than a method of attacking operational problems; it is an intellectual tool for the analysis of all kinds of problems, including those of strategy and policy.

The application of operations analysis to defense and security problems has become increasingly common. The military services have been the greatest consumers of the products of operations analysis, but civilian agencies, such as the Office of Civil and Defense Mobilization, the AEC, NASA, ACDA, and even the Congress, have utilized it to help solve particularly difficult and complex problems: the most effective tactics for an infantry battalion in battle, alternative location of Strategic Air Command bases overseas, or Minuteman missile sites in the United States, choices among weapons systems still in the blueprint stage, the cost of billion-dollar programs, the behavior of Soviet leaders, and arms control, inspection, and nuclear-testing policies.

Because of the nature of the work and the special skills required, operations research and policy analysis are largely performed in specially created organizations. Like the great scientific laboratories such as Lincoln and Los Alamos, these organizations are financed by government funds and are of two types: university-affiliated groups and private, nonprofit corporations, with the latter the more common type. The private, nonprofit corporation, free from government control and the profit motive, has proved most useful for analytical groups, since apparently it best provides for essential independence and objectivity. The best-known and most widely publicized of these organizations is the Research and Development Corporation (RAND), working largely for the Air Force. Others are the Research Analysis Corporation (RAC), recently established to serve Army needs; the Institute for Defense Analyses (IDA), set up by a consortium of five universities to handle Department of Defense contracts; and, finally, the Hudson Institute, formed in 1961.

These are the major systems-analysis groups serving the government. Other, smaller organizations, supported largely by government funds and providing similar or related services, are Operations and Policy Research, Inc., of Washington, which contracts out the assignments it receives from the government to more than 100 consultants, mostly social scientists; United Research, Inc., of Cambridge, a private corporation formed by a group in the Harvard Business School, with a staff of 100 and paid consultants drawn from Harvard and M.I.T.; and Analytic Services, Inc., a nonprofit organization with about forty-five scientists and engineers on its staff. A larger organization of this type is Arthur D. Little, Inc., of Boston. Established originally to solve management and engineering problems for industrial concerns, the company has moved recently into the military field and taken on contracts for the government. The appointment of General James Gavin as Vice President, after his resignation as Chief of Research and Development in the Army, is an indication of the company's growing interest in military problems. The government also utilizes management consultant firms, such as McKinsey, Cresap, and others, in connection with national security activities from time to time.

Finally, many of the major defense contractors in private industry maintain operations and problems analysis groups of their own in order to advise them on such future developments in strategy and policy as might affect their contracts for government work. Some of these, such as Boeing and the Douglas groups, operate as an integral part of the company and are located in the company's plant. Others are separate operations of the company in an environment designed to encourage creativity and objectivity.[17] General Electric not only has its own group of analysts and consultants, but also publishes the *General Electric Defense Quarterly* with articles by leading scholars in the field.

The Army and the Navy: OEG, ORO, and RAC

The oldest of the operations research organizations in the United States is the Navy's Operations Evaluation Group (OEG). Established by the Office of Scientific Research and Development in May, 1942, under a contract with Columbia University, the group was known initially as the Antisubmarine Warfare Operations Research Group. The name derived from the fact that at the time of its first assignment, when German U-boats were threatening to cut the Atlantic supply line, it was instructed to study methods of antisubmarine warfare, utilizing the methods developed in Britain to combat the Luftwaffe. The results were highly successful; the arrangement was continued and expanded to cover a variety of operational problems throughout the war.

An example of the method employed is shown in a study the group completed on ways to combat kamikaze attacks. The analysts were asked whether a vessel under attack should maneuver violently to avoid being hit or continue on direct course in order that its antiaircraft guns could aim at the oncoming plane. Working with data secured from 450 attacks, they concluded that a large vessel should maneuver violently and a small one more slowly, and suggested the particular manner and direction in which ships about to be struck by a kamikaze plane should turn. The results were most positive: Vessels that followed their recommendations were hit only 29 per cent of the time; those that did not were hit 47 per cent of the time.[18]

The group was a small organization, working directly under the Chief of Naval Operations, and, like other organizations at the time, it was virtually unknown to the public. At first, it consisted of seven men, headed by Philip M. Morse of M.I.T., but, by the time the war was over, it had grown to more than seventy—including mathematicians, physicists, chemists, biologists, radar experts, geologists, statisticians, and one chess champion.[19] From the beginning, it functioned as a single unit under central control in Washington, but usually as many as one half of its men were organized in teams attached to various operational commands in the field for special assignments. This organizational pattern continued after the war.

In 1946, the Operations Research Group was changed to the Operations Evaluation Group, and its tasks outlined in a new contract drawn up between the Office of Naval Research and M.I.T. Designated Op 34H, its staff was organized into teams for work on specific problems—such as antisubmarine doctrine and tactics, antiaircraft gunnery, guided missiles, radar, and atomic warfare. These teams, each headed by a project leader, continued to work under the Office of the Chief of Naval Operations, thus enjoying considerable freedom for research while having easy access to all levels of command in the Navy. Like its wartime predecessor, the OEG has continued to function almost as an integral part of the Navy. Its offices are in the Pentagon; its members work only for the Navy, usually on classified projects; they rarely talk publicly about their work, as do members of other groups, and they rarely publish their findings. For the scholar, the physical location and secrecy are distinct disadvantages, but the OEG's effectiveness within the Navy may be enhanced by these very qualities. Still, its members are active in professional organizations, and occasionally publish their work in unclassified form.

(A standard work in the field, *Methods of Operations Research*, was originally an OEG Report.[20])

The OEG, so far as is known, does no policy analysis, and offers no advice on grand strategy or political problems affecting the Navy. Its primary contribution was to the solution of operational problems, although its range of activities was broader than it had been at the end of the war. In 1961, the Navy established, under contract with the Institute for Defense Analyses, an Institute of Naval Studies in Cambridge, Massachusetts, to work on long-range, high-level problems. This new organization served also as a technical support group of the Navy's Long-Range Study Group at the Naval War College in Newport. It consisted of civilian scholars and senior Navy and Marine officers working together under the direction of a naval officer and civilian research director.

By 1962, the Navy had various operations research groups, working under different direction and in different locations. To secure a "broader spectrum of analytical counsel," it decided to place these activities under consolidated management, and, on July 1 of that year, completed a contract with the Franklin Institute by which the latter assumed responsibility for management, technical direction, and support of both the Institute of Naval Studies and the Operations Evaluation Group. These two were placed in a specially created Center of Naval Analyses, with a staff of about 250 persons organized as a division of the Franklin Institute, and charged with the task of conducting "analyses of immediate and long-range naval warfare problems, operational and logistical," and serving the fleet "by interpreting advances in science and technology in terms of naval hardware, weapons systems, long-range logistics, and long-range strategic planning."[21] But both the OEG and the Institute of Naval Studies continued in their present locations and with their usual operational procedures. The OEG's Naval Warfare Analysis Group, formed several years ago, which supports the Long-Range Objectives Group in the Office of the Chief of Naval Operations, and a small Marine Corps Operations Analysis Group responsible to the Commandant both share the common scientific staff and directorate of the OEG and coordinate their research programs. More recently, the OEG established an Economics Division, thus giving the social scientist a regular place in its organization for the first time.

The Institute of Naval Studies continues unchanged, too. One of its major projects is a continuing study of "Naval Task Analyses," to make assumptions about the course of events over the next decade as a guide to naval planning. The project aims, first, to set up a model of the international environment; second, to map out the tasks the Navy would be called on to perform in the model constructed; and, finally, to analyze these tasks in order to provide guidance for long-range naval planning.

In contrast to the Navy, the Army's ground forces made almost no use of operations research and analysis during World War II. General Marshall had been impressed with the work done for the Army Air Force, and, in 1943, had suggested to theater commanders that they use analysis teams, also, but the reaction was disappointing. It was only toward the end of the war that an effort was made to apply the technique in the Pacific theater, and this was only a token effort.[22] The Army was simply not interested in operations analysis, despite the fact that its own air elements and the Navy were using its techniques with great effectiveness. Thus, when the war ended, the Army was the only service that did not have the nucleus for a peacetime organization for analysis and research.

For three years, the Army did nothing. Finally, in September, 1948, under the urging of Vannevar Bush and General McAuliffe, head of the Army's research and development program, it established the Operations Research Office (ORO) under a contract with Johns Hopkins University. Initially located at Fort McNair, in Washington, close to the National War College, the ORO was entirely a civilian organization, free from military control and administratively a part of the University. Ellis A. Johnson, a physicist and one of the pioneers in operations research, was the director; for his chief assistants, he selected three physicists, an astrophysicist, and a political scientist—a fairly accurate reflection of the importance of the different disciplines to operations research. None of these men was a member of the Johns Hopkins faculty, nor was the professional staff, which included mathematicians, chemists, electronics and communications engineers, geologists, meteorologists, social psychologists, anthropologists, sociologists, economists, and historians—in fact, men from all the academic disciplines.[23] The decision to locate the ORO at Fort McNair instead of on the Johns Hopkins campus had stemmed from the belief that if it were physically a part of the university, "the intense jealousy of academic freedom and the insistence on complete, comprehensive study might hinder the quick achievement of practical results."[24] But the location at Fort McNair did not prove entirely satisfactory either, and in 1951, the ORO moved into separate quarters just outside Washington.

Under the terms of the contract between the Army and Johns Hopkins, the ORO was to handle exclusively military problems. Provision was made, though not with complete success, to keep it free from military control, allowing it to make studies on its own initiative and to refuse those it did not feel it could or should perform. (About half the studies it prepared were proposed by the Army.) Its function was purely advisory; its role ceased with the completion of a study embodying its recommendations for policy or action. It was up to the Army to accept, in whole or in part, or reject its recommendations.

The internal organization of the ORO roughly resembled the organization of the Army's general and special staffs. There were nine divisions: Strategic, Tactics, Operations, Intelligence, Air Defense, Management Systems, Electronics Laboratory, Computing Laboratory, and Basic Research. In each of these, a variety of specialists were grouped in basic project sections, and, for any particular assignment, special teams were established. The ORO also employed special consultants, officers assigned by the Army, and retired officers who could provide the military expertise the others lacked. Finally, it functioned as a prime contractor, farming out almost half of its research to universities and industries.

The problems on which the ORO worked were varied, and virtually all were classified.[25] The first assignment it had was to study foreign military aid and advise the Army whether to recommend such aid, and if so, what kind, when, and to which countries. The resulting analysis of the political, economic, social, and military aspects of the problem recommended that the Army favor an aid program, while it pointed to some of the dangers involved and suggested measures to overcome them. Another early study, conducted largely by social scientists, dealt with the question of the segregation of Negro troops and apparently contributed to the decision to integrate Negro troops into white units.

The Korean War provided the Army with a host of new problems, and the Operations Research Office was soon sending teams to the battlefield to study such subjects as the effectiveness of antitank weapons, close air support for ground troops, psychological warfare, and the load the soldier carries. Altogether, the ORO sent to Korea eight teams totaling forty men—including physicists, chemists, economists, historians, and engineers. When the Chinese intervened in November, 1950, the ORO asked S. L. A. Marshall, military analyst for the Detroit *News* and author of many works on military subjects, to make a study of Chinese tactics.

In September, 1961, after 13 years of operation, the ORO was dissolved and the Army's contract with Johns Hopkins ended. This move did not imply that the Army lacked confidence in operations research and analysis or that it did not have the funds to continue the work, but simply that the Army and the University were mutually dissatisfied with existing arrangements. Almost immediately, the Army negotiated a five-year contract with a new organization, the Research Analysis Corporation (RAC), formed specifically for the purpose of performing operations research for the Army.[26] The RAC took over the quarters and almost the entire staff of the ORO—140 professional analysts, 15 research assistants, and a supporting staff of more than 150 persons. Unlike the Operations Research Office, it was a private, nonprofit organization; it may well be that the Army and the analysts had decided that this form was better suited to the kind of services being performed. Replacing Ellis Johnson as director is Frank A. Parker, a former Assistant Director of Defense Research and Engineering in the Office of the Secretary of Defense, with a record of successful experience dating back to 1941. Under the terms of its charter, the new organization is free to do work for agencies other than the Army, and, by the end of 1962, it had contracts with the Advanced Research Projects Agency of the Department of Defense and others.

It is difficult to evaluate the contribution of organizations like the OEG and ORO; there is no yardstick to measure their achievement and no way to relate their little-known activities to decisions actually made by the Army and Navy. The situation now is different from what it was during World War II or the Korean War. Then, the problems were fairly concrete, data were available, and the results could be observed. In the cold war, the situation is different, as a result of the enormously complicated technology of modern weapons systems. The development of new techniques and theories has made it possible to solve some of the new problems, and the method has undoubtedly proved itself, for both the Army and Navy continue to employ operations and policy analysts, not only for studies and reports but also informally as members of committees and as consultants. And even if the work of the analyst does not pay off immediately, it may have value by providing additional background, new ideas, a broader understanding of the problem, and increased confidence in existing practices. And in the ever-continuing battle for appropriations and favor in Washington, the work of the analyst sometimes offers valuable ammunition to an agency fighting for a program. Some have even claimed that its greatest usefulness lies in providing such support, and in defending decisions already made.

The Air Force: RAND

In contrast to the Army, the Air Force enthusiastically accepted operations research early during World War II, perhaps because it was a young service and because many of its weapons and methods had not been fairly tested in war. By the end of 1942, an Operations Analysis Division had been established at Army Air Force headquarters, with one group assigned to the Eighth Bomber Command in England.[27] Additional groups were formed as the need arose—the Radiation Laboratory at MIT and the Princeton University Station providing trained analysts—and, by the end of the war, virtually every major command in the Air Force had its operations analysts.

Unlike the Navy's program, the AAF program was decentralized: Each of the sections in the field worked directly under the local commander on problems assigned by him, while the Washington headquarters functioned largely as a training and recruiting center. When the war came to an end and the various commands were reduced or disbanded, many of the analysts left the Air Force, although operations research was not entirely discontinued. In 1946, on the initiative of General Ira C. Eaker, operations analysis was reorganized on a peacetime basis. An Office for Operations Analysis was established in the Air Staff, and Operations Analysis sections were assigned to each Air Force command.[28] This provided the Air Force with an integrated, decentralized operations analysis system.

Useful as this system was to study immediate operational problems, it was scarcely suited for long-range, high-level studies on future developments in air warfare. To meet this need, General Henry H. Arnold established Project RAND, under a three-year, $10,000,000 contract with the Douglas Aircraft Company. The name RAND, an abbreviation for Research and Development, was actually a misnomer, for RAND was from the start a research organization only. The idea behind it was to obtain the best scientific talent in the nation—whether in the universities or in private industry—to assist the Air Force in its future development. The charter of Project RAND, prepared originally in 1946, when General Curtis LeMay was Chief of Air Staff for Research and Development, called for "a continuing program to assist the Air Force in improving its efficiency and effectiveness by furnishing information and independent, objective advice derived from selected research and analysis of airpower problems of interest to the Air Force." RAND studies, it was hoped, would point the way to "preferred methods, techniques and instrumentalities" that help "in the formulation and implementation of Air Force plans, policies and programs."[29]

To the Air Force, it seemed evident, in contrast to the Navy's view, that men of the caliber they wanted would be unwilling in peacetime to leave their civilian posts as they had during the war. A purely military organization, then, would not do, since civilian scientists would not work effectively under such an arrangement. A purely academic organization, on the other hand, presented problems of military security for the Air Force, which also believed that academicians would not wish to work under security restrictions. The task was to reconcile academic freedom with military security; the RAND contract with Douglas seemed at the time to be the best solution.[30]

As part of the Douglas Aircraft Company, Project RAND reflected to a large extent the outlook of the aircraft industry. Its advisory council consisted of top executives of four aircraft companies (North American Aviation, Northrop, Boeing, and Douglas), and its first staff was made up largely of scientists and engineers oriented to industry. Academic scientists, mathematicians, and, later, social scientists joined in sufficient number to fulfill General Arnold's hopes for a group combining the best academic and industrial brains to advise the Air Force.

But, it turned out, the status of Project RAND as an integral but somewhat alien element within Douglas Aircraft was neither congenial for the many academic people who joined it nor effective for the kind of studies they wanted to do. Besides, RAND gradually outgrew its place in Douglas; it was decided, therefore, to make it an independent and permanent organization that could conduct research on national security problems not only for the Air Force but for other public and private groups as well. The Ford Foundation provided $100,000 (an interest-free loan) as working capital. This made it possible to establish credit with the banks and to qualify for a contract with the Air Force for about $4 million annually for three years.

Thus, in 1948, the RAND Corporation was formed as a private, nonprofit organization for the stated purpose of promoting "scientific, educational, and charitable purposes, all for the public welfare and security of the United States of America." The Air Force contract provided funds sufficient for several years of operations, but these were specifically earmarked for studies of interest to the Air Force. This amount has been increased since, so that the annual Project RAND contract is about $13 million. The Ford Foundation loan was increased in a few years to $1 million and, in 1952, was converted into an outright grant to finance research in national security problems other than those done for the Air Force. The only condition of the grant was that RAND provide an equal amount from its own funds for independent research. RAND also has received funds under contracts with such agencies as the AEC, NASA, and the Office of the Secretary of Defense. It has received grants also from Rockefeller, Carnegie, and the National Science Foundations, but roughly 80 per cent of its funds still comes from the Air Force. The Air Force, it must be noted, is not entirely convinced that RAND should work for other organizations or conduct its own research projects.

From the first, the RAND Corporation enjoyed a phenomenal success.[31] Not only was it financially secure from the outset, but it was strongly supported in influential civilian and military circles. Its top officials initially came from the aircraft industry (the president, Franklin R. Collbohm, was a Douglas engineer); its funds came from the Air Force, whose senior officers were deeply committed to its success. (In 1954, General Nathan Twining established a RAND Military Advisory Group—since renamed the Air Force Advisory Group—of high ranking officers to meet twice a year to hear about present and future projects, to keep him informed of the progress of research at RAND, and to advise him on Air Force policy toward the RAND Corporation.) Important officials and scientists had helped to shape RAND (Karl Compton and Donald K. David of the Harvard Business School had, in 1948, persuaded Henry Ford II to suggest the original RAND loan to the Ford Foundation Trustees). This combination of interests—industrial, academic, and governmental—is reflected in the composition of the Corporation's Board of Trustees, which has included public officials, foundation executives, officers of some of the largest corporations in America, university presidents, directors of large research institutes, and outstanding scholars and scientists.

The RAND Corporation is located in Santa Monica, California, close to the Los Angeles industrial and academic complex. Its quarters, consisting of two connected buildings completed in 1952 and 1962, cost about $4 million, and are large enough to house the entire staff in 770 separate offices. The building is heavily guarded, contains a library, a major computing facility, a simulation laboratory, and thirteen conference rooms—the last apparently an essential feature. RAND also maintains offices in Dayton, Ohio, near the Air Force Aeronautical Systems Division at Wright-Patterson Air Force Base, and in Washington, where one of its vice-presidents is permanently located to provide continuous and direct contact with the high command of the Air Force and other government agencies RAND serves.

Altogether, there are about 600 professionals on the RAND staff, of whom about 270 are Ph.D.'s; thus, it has as large a staff as many colleges have. In addition, RAND employs as consultants some of the most eminent scholars, scientists, and engineers in the country, as well as a small group of senior Air Force officers, usually colonels, who work in civilian clothes as regular members of research teams. The professional staff is organized into eleven technical departments, including economics, systems operations, cost analysis, logistics, computer sciences, and social sciences. (The last numbers about twenty-eight political scientists, historians, psychologists, and sociologists.) A Research Council of five senior men representing the major disciplines (physics, engineering, economics, mathematics, and social sciences) is entrusted with the surveillance of research and the review of long-range plans as well as current programs.

The RAND organization, therefore, is based on professional skills rather than categories of military operations, a system that facilitates recruitment, provides flexibility, and gives each discipline represented on the staff a home, much like the department of any academic institution. This organization is, however, purely an administrative convenience. When work begins on a project, specialists from the various departments often join together in a team; the arrangements are as flexible and fluid as possible, crossing organizational and disciplinary boundaries. Project leaders report to management either directly or through the heads of the departments, on whom they may call for supporting studies. The departments may also sponsor studies of their own, lying entirely within their own field; at the same time, their members may be on several teams working on different projects. A completed study—a staff-report, research memorandum, or technical report—is carefully reviewed before it is submitted, and, if it is an important one, the director of the study briefs the agency that commissioned it. RAND considers these briefings most important (sometimes they are given to audiences in the Department of Defense, the Joint Chiefs of Staff, and other federal departments), and they are thoroughly rehearsed and criticized in advance.

The quality of the professional staff at RAND is largely responsible for its reputation and for its accomplishments. But how has RAND managed to compete successfully with industry and the universities for the best talent? The answer lies not wholly in the remuneration it offers, since government and academic salaries for similar persons now compare favorably. But so great is RAND's prestige and so liberal are its policies on professional and publishing activities, leave, travel, etc., that it is able to draw many able people from the universities, especially younger men without tenure. Those men it cannot persuade to work full-time, it employs as consultants or for limited periods of time on short projects. Whether scholars working in the RAND environment do as good or better work than they would in an academic environment is not certain, however, despite RAND's great success.

One of the attractions of RAND is the opportunity for new research. Many of the staff members choose their own projects and are relatively free to pursue their own interests. They can have their work read by colleagues in their own or different disciplines, for there is easy and frequent interchange of views among the different departments. Many RAND members teach part-time at neighboring colleges and universities and are also granted sabbatical leave to teach full-time or do research when the opportunity arises. They hold office in professional societies, read papers, and attend professional meetings, conventions, and special study programs; they serve as editors and members of editorial boards of professional journals; and they sit on a great number of official committees and research groups in the State and Defense Departments, and on *ad hoc* committees such as the Killian and Gaither Committees. Some even supervise Ph.D. theses at distant universities.

Another reason for RAND's attractiveness is its policy on publishing RAND material. Although much of RAND's work is classified and unavailable to the public—which concerns some RAND scholars—about half of its work is free for publication. In its first fifteen years, RAND prepared about 7,000 reports, research memoranda, and papers. Unlike most other analysis groups, RAND makes every effort to declassify these products and distribute them as widely as possible—through free distribution mechanisms, publication in scholarly journals, and in commercial book form. RAND also provides about forty-two depository libraries in the United States and seven abroad with copies of all its unclassified publications, numbering more than 2,000 titles. The number of books written by members of the RAND staff and representing or resulting from work done at RAND is impressive indeed. Close to eighty titles could be listed—on subjects ranging from Soviet military policy to linear programming and economic analysis—including some of the most important ones in the entire field of national security.[32]

The major activity at RAND has been and continues to be assisting the Air Force to solve the problems involved in improving its existing weapons systems and selecting the most effective weapons systems and strategies for the future. RAND uses in this work the latest methods and tools of research and analysis—such as linear and dynamic programming, Monte Carlo and game theory, and the technique that has come to be called "systems analysis." An extension of operations research, systems analysis is simple in concept but extremely complex in application. In essence, it is a scientific method of arriving at a decision by seeking the particular response that in its combination of the elements is distinctly better than alternative responses to a problem. Since it involves many skills—scientific, technical, political, economic, and military—it is usually conducted by a team, as is operations research. The idea is that no single person is an expert on the problems facing a modern policy-maker in matters of national security, and that group research must therefore be substituted for individual judgment and expertise. "Systems analysis," said one writer, "is understood in sixteen different ways by sixteen different people, and yet they all do it together like a jazz band playing around an unexpressed four-four beat."[33]

The early RAND enthusiasm for systems analysis, which was first hailed as an almost magical method for solving virtually any complex problem, has somewhat abated. RAND analysts now use it with more caution and make fewer claims for its infallibility, although they still regard it as a valuable and even necessary method for dealing with problems—such as determining the relation between weight and thrust of rocket systems—whose complex solutions require the use of mathematics and computers. But questions of strategy and policy, they feel, do not lend themselves so readily to systems analysis. Uncertainty and unpredictability are the constants of the real world, and, though systems analysts with their new tools—computers, war gaming, game theory, Monte Carlo, and linear programming—may reduce this uncertainty, they cannot eliminate it. As a consequence, RAND studies have become increasingly realistic, and the contributions of social scientists and historians, who lack the scientist's precision tools but who do deal with the real world, have correspondingly increased.

Although RAND emphasizes problems of interest to the Air Force, it also does work on a range of military conflicts such as limited war and counterinsurgency—in which the Air Force would play only a minor role. But RAND's major effort is still in strategic studies. RAND was among the first to foresee the possibility of missiles, and as early as 1946 studied the problems involved in space launching. It has made extensive studies of strategic bombing systems, vulnerability, air defense, tactical air operations, and logistics. In the social sciences, it has explored a variety of political and social factors affecting national security, nonmilitary defense, Soviet political behavior, the strategy and tactics of Communist organizations, political warfare, and manpower resources. In all of these areas, its staff has made important contributions.

In the public mind, RAND is the archetype of the new analytical organization that has come to loom so large in national security affairs. The names of some of its members are widely known through their writing and public utterances. They move in and out of Washington briefing government officials; sit on some seventy different government committees; attend national and international conferences; teach at universities across the land; and lecture at the war colleges and service academies. Their books and articles are considered indispensable for government officials and students of national security, and no meeting to discuss U.S. or cold-war strategy is complete without a representative from RAND. From it and from other research centers throughout the country there issues a stream of distinguished consultants who, wrote one British critic, "move freely through the corridors of the Pentagon and the State Department, rather as the Jesuits through the courts of Vienna and Madrid, three centuries ago."[34]

The Defense Department: The Weapons Systems Evaluation Group and the Institute for Defense Analyses

Like the separate services, the Secretary of Defense and the Joint Chiefs of Staff have their own organization for analysis and evaluation. This organization, initially the Weapons Systems Evaluation Group (WSEG), was created in December, 1948, by Secretary of Defense James Forrestal on the advice of a special committee formed for this purpose, and formally established early in 1949 with Lieutenant General John E. Hull as Director and Philip Morse of M.I.T. as Technical Director. Its mission was much the same as that of the service research groups but, in addition, it was to review the studies made by the OEG, ORO, and RAND, whose conclusions became data for the WSEG evaluations.

At first, the WSEG was entirely a government operation. Located in the Pentagon with its senior officer reporting to the Joint Chiefs of Staff, it consisted of military officers and professional civilians integrated in a single group. The officers came from all three services; the civilians, all of whom were civil-service employees, represented a wide variety of disciplines. The military officers clearly predominated; the heads of the various sections were military, and there were more officers than civilians on the staff. With the passage of time, this imbalance was somewhat redressed. The number of civilians was increased until it was almost equal to the military (about twenty-five), and the civilian Research Director, who was also the Deputy Director, took a more active role.[35]

Organizationally, the WSEG was closest to the Air Force Operations Analysis Division, which was responsible for operational studies for the Air Force, but it dealt with a range of problems more nearly like those handled at RAND. Nevertheless, it failed to attract and retain the kind of professionals that were required for such studies, for its civilian professionals were subject to the restrictions of civil-service pay, leave, and work hours. In 1955, therefore, Secretary of Defense Charles Wilson and the Joint Chiefs of Staff appealed to the universities to help to strengthen WSEG. The first result was a contract under which M.I.T. assumed responsibility for WSEG's technical and professional civilian staff—who thereupon became employees of M.I.T. although they sat at the same desks and did the same work as before.

This arrangement lasted only a short time. In April, 1956, while M.I.T. moved to strengthen the civilian component of WSEG, five universities—the California Institute of Technology, Case Institute of Technology, M.I.T., Stanford, and Tulane—joined in creating a new, non-profit organization called the Institute for Defense Analyses (IDA) whose purpose was to provide the machinery for employing the intellectual resources of the nation for the analysis and evaluation of problems facing the Secretary of Defense and the Joint Chiefs of Staff.[36] The following month, the Ford Foundation granted IDA $500,000 as working capital and, subsequently, as support for studies to increase the usefulness of IDA to university research programs in national defense and operations research. On September 1, IDA accepted a contract to furnish the scientific and technical services needed by WSEG.

The status of WSEG as an organization serving the Secretary of Defense and the Joint Chiefs of Staff was not at first altered, except in a minor way, by the creation of the IDA. Its professional civilian staff, increased to eighty-five, now constituted a division of IDA, but continued to work in the Pentagon under a military chief and with officers from the three services on projects assigned by the Joint Chiefs or the Director of Defense Research and Engineering. The nature of its work did not change, but the staff was now large enough and of a high enough quality to perform the tasks it had been set up to do. More recently, WSEG operations have been revised so that military officers are in an advisory position, leaving to the IDA the responsibility for assigning projects and for the results achieved.

Like RAND, WSEG utilizes the most up-to-date tools of analysis and operations research, and faces the same imponderables and uncertainties. Almost all the work it does is classified; most of it is extremely sensitive, and rarely does it reach more than a handful of officials whose business it is to act on the problems with which it is concerned. For these officials, the studies may be of real value in reaching a decision, or they may, as one observer noted, merely provide the support for a course already decided on; for WSEG is in the difficult position of having to make recommendations on problems that other services have already studied or that may be in dispute between the Defense and State Departments.[37] This sensitive position in the jungle of interservice and interagency conflict only increases the necessity for secrecy and for objective and comprehensive evaluation.

When the Institute for Defense Analyses was formed in 1956, WSEG constituted its sole activity. Since then it has acquired additional responsibilities and tasks, so that today WSEG is only a part of its total program, though the largest part. In 1957, it gave support to the work of the Gaither Committee, which had been commissioned by the National Security Council, and, early in the next year, it assumed responsibility (similar to that it had for WSEG) for the Advanced Research Projects Agency (ARPA). This agency, which was responsible for research done on a wide range of technical problems—including antimissile defense systems and the military applications of space flight—was part of the Office of the Secretary of Defense.

Thus, in 1958, IDA, consisting of two divisions, WSEG and ARPA, had a total capital of $650,000 (of which half was used as working capital), and it was already considering expansion into other areas, including establishment of a laboratory for the study of cryptology. It was also planning to strengthen its ties with the academic community. In recent years, IDA has continued to grow in size and in additional responsibilities. To the original five founding members were added four new universities—Chicago, Columbia, Michigan, and Pennsylvania State. Each of these institutions added to its resources not only in the physical sciences and engineering, but also in the humanities and social sciences. Their joining signaled an increased awareness on IDA's part of political and social factors bearing on questions of national security.

With the addition of the four new members, IDA became a consortium of nine universities governed by twenty trustees who represent the member institutions or are prominent in science and in public life. Successive Chairmen of the Board of Trustees have been Dr. James R. Killian, Jr., Dr. T. Keith Glennan, and William A. M. Burden. Policy direction is in the hands of an Executive Committee appointed by the Board from among its members, and a Professional Committee, which advises it on professional matters. The President and the Vice President direct IDA's operations, and the latter, as Director of Research, is assisted by two associate directors, each of whom is also head of one of the seven divisions into which IDA is organized. IDA headquarters are in Washington but one division of IDA works on the Princeton campus, another is located in Cambridge, and the members of a third meet from time to time at different places. IDA also maintains small offices in London and Paris.

Some measure of the size, but not the nature, of IDA's operations may be gained from its financial reports. The working capital, it will be recalled, was provided by a grant of $500,000 from the Ford Foundation, and the first contract was with the Office of the Secretary of Defense for work done by the Weapons Systems Evaluation Group. At the end of the first six months, its expenditures totalled almost $600,000, of which 80 per cent was for salary and personnel services, and its gross revenues were $540,000. In March, 1961, five years later, IDA had capital resources amounting to $1,164,000 and a working capital of $700,000. Its assets were over $1.5 million and its gross expense was $7,113,800. Expenditures for salaries alone in 1961 were over $3 million, not including such indirect personnel costs as employee benefits, travel, and fees for consultants. The total number of employees, which in mid-1956 had been less than 100, was more than 360 five years later, and more than 200 of these were professionals. Gross revenues equalled expenses, and of this amount more than $6 million represented reimbursement for direct contract costs, as compared to $1,600,000 in March, 1957. But large as this amount is, it is only about half the budget of RAND—an indication of the extent to which analysis and operations research has grown since World War II.

The growth of IDA reflects the increased tasks it has assumed since its inception. It has or has had contracts with other agencies, in addition to the Office of the Secretary of Defense and the Joint Chiefs of Staff, including the Navy Department and the Arms Control and Disarmament Agency.[38] From a single division, IDA has grown to seven divisions; the Research and Engineering Support Division, financed by a separate contract with OSD, does work which differs from that of the Weapons Systems Evaluation Group in that it is concerned less with the evaluation of existing or possible weapons systems than with impartial scientific judgment of issues facing the Director of Research and Engineering. The Communications Research Division, established in 1958 and located at Princeton, conducts basic research in communications theory and in problems in cryptanalysis, interception, and interruption of communications. Since much of its work is in fundamental theory and technology, in mathematical and linguistic concepts, there is little need for secrecy.

One problem facing IDA, as well as other research organizations and the government itself, is the shortage of professionals who are trained and experienced in the tasks set by the nation's defense needs. It was in part to meet this need that IDA, in 1959, organized its Jason Division. Initially, this was an informal group of about twenty young physicists from university faculties and research institutions who met from time to time under IDA sponsorship to explore the application of their special fields to national security. Started as an experiment, the Jason Division has since become a regular part of IDA, but it is still a fluid group whose members work in teams on problems to which they feel they can contribute. The entire group meets occasionally for discussion and, in the summer, for concentrated work on a single problem. In this way, young and promising scientists are exposed to national security problems and may contribute to their solution while continuing their academic careers.

From the start, IDA, like other research and analysis organizations, planned to sponsor studies of its own, and, in 1960, one was launched on arms control. In it, more than in most IDA projects, there were ample opportunities for social scientists and historians, and when a special studies group (later changed to the International Studies Division) was formed, it included a number of people in those disciplines. Even before the arms-control study was completed, the State Department sponsored it as an official project.

The IDA also has a special projects division that performs special tasks from time to time. The first of these came in 1957 in connection with the report of the Gaither Committee, and the next year with the Draper Committee on the Mutual Security Program. Not only did IDA assign its own men to the Draper Committee staff, but it brought into the project about thirty other people from universities and private agencies, and subcontracted for separate studies with the Foreign Policy Research Institute of the University of Pennsylvania and the Washington Center of Foreign Policy Research. Other special projects on which IDA has worked include the disarmament study conducted by Charles A. Coolidge for the Defense and State Departments, the Glipar Study on technical problems of the intercontinental bombing system, and Professor Oskar Morgenstern's study (supported by a grant from the Carnegie Corporation) of the application of game theory to strategic problems. Finally, IDA, on contract with the Office of the Secretary of Defense, sends some of its men to NATO countries each year to give two-week courses on new techniques of scientific analysis and evaluation at selected universities and technical schools. The purpose is to encourage the use of operations research in NATO nations. IDA has also agreed to send experienced analysts to these countries on request, to assist in the formation of operations research organizations.

As an institution created and largely controlled by the academic community, IDA has always placed education high on its list of objectives. It has recognized its obligation not only to make available to the government the best minds in the universities, but also to increase the number of people trained in scientific methods of analysis and to "feed back" through the universities a greater understanding of the problems of national security. These objectives it accomplishes in various indirect ways—through the Jason Division, through its consultants, subcontracts, and staff rotations. But it acts directly too, although its financial resources are limited. It annually awards two graduate fellowships in mathematical physics as well as postdoctoral fellowships for work in operations research and analysis; it also supports those of its staff who wish to continue their formal training in subjects that relate to their work at the IDA.

Since most of IDA's work is classified, it can show little of it to the public. Yet IDA attracts high-caliber persons, for its personnel and work policies, like RAND's, are relaxed. It commands large resources and undoubtedly exerts influence at the highest levels in the Pentagon, though the extent of this influence is difficult to measure. But it is little known beyond the government and the small body of national security experts, whereas RAND is well known to a large public. IDA is more highly structured than RAND, with its activities organized in general around particular government contracts, while RAND, organized on the basis of professional interests and related disciplines, seems to adapt better to a great variety of studies. And though IDA is much more a creature of the academic world, it seems to have less impact on the universities than RAND. Even its educational activities and its independent research program are modest by comparison with RAND's achievements. RAND had the marked advantage of developing at a time when needs were great and it was the major organization of its kind.

Nonaffiliated Organizations: The Stanford Research Institute and the Hudson Institute

Although most of the research-analysis groups considered thus far have been private nonprofit corporations, free to accept contracts from anyone who can afford them, each has close ties with one of the military services or with the Defense Department. And these groups were in fact created to meet the needs of a service or office. But the military and civilian agencies of the government also use other research groups which offer similar services and use the same scientific and intellectual methods. And large industrial companies maintain such groups, primarily for their own use but also available for special assignments on government contract. Industrial management concerns such as Arthur D. Little, Inc., which draws heavily on M.I.T. and Harvard scientists, also work on national security problems for the Pentagon. The Systems Development Corporation, a nonprofit offshoot of RAND and now much larger than the parent organization, has large contracts with the Air Force.

The Stanford Research Institute (SRI) is typical of these independent analysis organizations. Despite its name, it is only nominally a part of Stanford University and maintains its own separate full-time staff. Organized in 1946 by a group of prominent West Coast business and industrial leaders in cooperation with the trustees of Stanford to meet the needs of industry on the West Coast, it now also serves the government and individuals. Its staff has increased from three to more than 2,000, and its contracts now amount to about $26 million annually, about two-thirds of which represents research done directly or indirectly for the government; the remaining third is done for industry, foundations, and individuals. Most of this research is nonmilitary: SRI is not an analysis group like RAND or the Research and Analysis Corporation; its basic orientation is toward scientific and economic research programs. Interdisciplinary military studies at the Institute draw their strength from this base and may be regarded almost as a dividend on the work done on other programs. The main office of the SRI is in Menlo Park, California, but it maintains a laboratory in South Pasadena, offices in various parts of the country and overseas in Zurich, and representatives in Tokyo, Milan, and elsewhere.[39]

The Institute has a Board of Directors, elected annually by the University trustees, who also serve as general members of the Corporation. The President of the University is chairman *ex officio* of the Board and of its Executive Committee, and the Vice President is a member of both. Research is organized under four headings: Life Sciences, Physical Sciences, Economics and Management Sciences, and Engineering. Under each of these are various divisions, each with a staff organized into appropriate groups corresponding to the major research areas. For example, under Engineering are three divisions, one of which, the Operational Technology Division, does most of the nontechnical research relating to national security. The Operational Technology Division, in turn, has three subordinate elements: the Defense Analysis Center, the Naval Warfare Research Center, and the Operations Analysis Department. The first is sponsored by the Navy Department's Office of Naval Research and conducts research on such long-range naval problems as antisubmarine warfare, logistics, anti-aircraft warfare, and weapons systems for amphibious operations. Specialists from all over the Institute—engineers, operations analysts, mathematicians, and scientists—are assigned to the Center, which also draws on the faculty of Stanford and other universities for advice on specific problems.

The research methods used at the SRI are similar to those employed by other research and analysis groups. Its approach is completely interdisciplinary, which it claims gives it a great advantage over academic communities, organized into traditional areas of study that impede rather than facilitate research on defense problems. The SRI applies this interdisciplinary approach to various strategic problems facing the United States. The results can be observed in a report it prepared for the Senate Committee on Foreign Relations on the possible effects of scientific advance on foreign policy.[40]

Since its establishment, the SRI has put more and more of its effort to "research in the public service," a theme reflecting the Institute's objective "to contribute to the peace and prosperity of mankind."[41] Much of this work is scientific and technical, related to the research and development programs of the armed forces, but, at the request of the Pentagon, the Institute has also completed studies on the long-range defense posture of the United States. One of its programs was in the field of economic development, and it prepared studies for several of the emerging nations of Southeast Asia and the Middle East on various industries.

Most of the nontechnical research the SRI performs under contract for the government is assigned to the Operational Technology Division and its three subordinate elements. One of these, the Operations Analysis Department, uses techniques of operations research and systems analysis, and employs economists, operations analysts, geographers, industrial engineers, and cost analysts in combination with scientists and engineers. The problems worked on have been concerned with civil defense, the cost of future weapons systems, the allocation of research and development funds among competing programs, the determination of strategies and tactics for various types of warfare, the selection of weapons systems in terms of their technology and cost, and logistical support systems for mobile, dispersed forces. The Operations Analysis teams also design, conduct, and interpret experiments carried out by the Army's Combat Development Experimentation Center at Fort Ord, a unit of about 3,000 men that conducts experiments to test new concepts of organization, doctrine, and tactics.

The Stanford Research Institute's interest in national security extends to other activities. It publishes a quarterly, the SRI Journal,[42] and in April, 1960, it conducted a National Strategy Seminar for selected reserve officers, similar to the one given at the National War College the previous summer by the Institute for American Strategy. The course chairman, Richard B. Foster of the Institute, had as his assistant Colonel William R. Kintner of the University of Pennsylvania's Foreign Policy Research Institute, which had organized the curriculum and largely directed the first National War College course. The Asilomar Conference, as it was called, lasted one week and consisted of lectures and discussion groups. An abstract of the proceedings was later published and distributed to the participants.[43]

The Stanford Research Institute, like most analysis and evaluation groups, is oriented to the physical sciences, mathematics, and engineering. It, of course, gives token recognition to history and the social sciences, and employs professionals in these disciplines, most of them economists whose expertise is particularly helpful in determining cost factors involved in national security decisions. But history and the other social sciences, whose relationship to systems analysis and strategic studies is not so clear, are weakly represented in the "think factories." The Stanford Research Institute has only a few social scientists; IDA employs historians and political scientists in its newly formed International Division; and at RAND, the Social Science Division has about thirty professionals on its staff.

The presence of historians and social scientists in these organizations, though their numbers are small and their direct influence not great, is an encouraging sign of a broader approach to the solution of problems heretofore considered primarily scientific and technological. More and more, it is being recognized that certain problems are not susceptible to quantification and scientific analysis. One sign of this development is the criticism of systems analysis by some of the foremost practitioners of the technique at RAND, by the two leading British scientists, P. M. S. Blackett and Sir Solly Zuckerman, by critics of a national security policy based on deterrence, and by a growing number of senior military officers. Criticism from such diverse sources has little in common except opposition to the professional civilian military analyst. Albert Wohlstetter, for an example of the first group, is as concerned with the limits of the technique as with its potential, and warns against expecting magical results from its use.[44] Blackett, one of the originators of operations research, is highly skeptical of the uses to which it is now being put. Military officers like General Thomas D. White and Admiral George W. Anderson, alarmed at the influence that civilian analysts from RAND and elsewhere have in the Department of Defense, emphasized the importance of military experience and judgment and warned against the growing tendency to minimize it.[45] Finally, the various advocates of peace research and the opponents of a deterrent strategy view the military analysts as rationalists of nuclear war and paid servants of the vested interests. "Their most important function," wrote Marcus Raskin, formerly a member of the staff of the National Security Council, "is to justify and extend the existence of their employers."[46]

Herman Kahn, whose book *On Thermonuclear War* brought down on him the full wrath of everyone opposed to the professionalization of military analysis, also expresses concern with the narrowing emphasis on systems analysis at the RAND Corporation. In 1961, he resigned from RAND in order to establish a new organization in which history and the social sciences would be emphasized. The Hudson Institute took form in July, 1961, as a private, nonprofit corporation with headquarters at Harmon-on-Hudson, about thirty miles north of New York City.

The Hudson Institute offers an interesting contrast to other nonprofit research groups. One-third of its directors, for example, are professors; and "ownership" of the Institute, as in a cooperative, resides in its members, to whom the trustees are responsible. Membership is of three kinds: Public, Fellow, and Employee. Public members, with seven-year terms, are community leaders; fellow members, with five-year terms, are scientists and scholars, many of whom are consultants to the Institute; employee members are chosen from the senior professional staff of the Institute. Each of these groups elects its own new members and one trustee each year for a four-year term, so that the board will ultimately consist of fifteen members—twelve elected by the members plus the three principal officers of the Institute, *ex officio*—Donald G. Brennan, President; Herman Kahn, Director; and Max Singer, Counsel.[47]

The first list of members, published in March, 1962, showed that they represented a wide diversity of interests. Among the Public members were representatives of the major research organizations in national security affairs; distinguished intellectuals like Raymond Aron,

Sidney Hook, Reinhold Niebuhr, and John Strachey; industrial leaders and public figures such as William A. M. Burden, John W. Irwin, II, Thomas J. Watson, Jr., and William Webster. Fellow members included many of the social scientists who have contributed to the study of national security, as well as physicists, mathematicians, engineers, and lawyers. The social sciences were most heavily represented by economists and political scientists. There were only two philosophers, three professors of law, one psychologist, and one historian in the group; sociology, social psychology, and anthropology were not represented at all.

In outlining their aims and purposes, the founders of the Hudson Institute expressed their concern with problems not only of national security but also of international order—the issues of peace and war, freedom and international justice, and the relationship of these to economic, social, and political development. They considered their task, like that of other similar groups, to provide the environment in which "high-quality minds" could work most effectively. Their further aim was to refine and develop the methods of analysis, and to create and establish a vocabulary and a set of concepts, for the study of national security—so that men from many disciplines could work and communicate with each other more effectively.

The founders of the Institute were well aware of the problem of recruiting and keeping first-rate scholars. Their answer was the familiar one—a liberal personnel policy, pay comparable to that of similar positions in the government, and working conditions resembling those of the academic community. To these they added the challenge of the task and the opportunity to contribute to peace and the establishment of a world order. Individual scholars would sign their own work and reach their own conclusions; the role of the Institute would be only to assure a uniformly high quality of work and to encourage free discussion. The Institute's organization would be along the lines of academic disciplines, and members of the staff would be encouraged to do independent research in their own fields, attend professional meetings, and publish the results of their research whenever possible. When the Hudson Institute was established in 1961, the staff numbered only six—including the director and the acting president, but, by the end of 1963, the number had risen to about eighty, of whom one-third were senior research analysts, with a larger number of "research aides," who combine research with secretarial duties.

The Institute, it was expected, would work primarily for the government on the immediate problems facing decision-makers. Initial contracts were with the Department of Defense, the Arms Control and Disarmament Agency, Office of Emergency Planning, Air Force,

Atomic Energy Commission, Martin-Marietta Corporation, Systems Development Corporation, IBM, and the Mitre Corporation. In addition, the Hudson Institute had retainer agreements to act as consultant on national security matters with the AVCO Corporation, Boeing, Martin-Marietta, and North American Aviation. But it planned also to devote part of its energies to other kinds of issues—on the political and moral implications of military technology and strategy—which had in the past been given less attention and been analyzed less rigorously than the scientific and technological problems of national security. In an admirable statement of their credo, the founders of the Hudson Institute affirmed their belief "that the existence of large numbers of readily deliverable H-bombs and an active arms race make it necessary to devote serious, detailed, informed thought to such things as disarmament and world government."

In itself, this view is not surprising. Other analyst groups also concern themselves with arms control and international politics. What is unusual is the Hudson Institute's degree of commitment to this objective. It is also the reason why the Institute emphasizes the social rather than the physical sciences, for the basic issues of disarmament and world government, it believes, are not technological but political and moral. "While such things as game theory, war gaming, modern mathematical techniques, high speed computers, and operations research have valuable uses," the Institute stated, "they are not the essence of the kind of intellectual effort that needs to be made on the problems of national security and international order." Since this effort would be primarily in the social sciences, the Institute expected that most of its professional staff would be social scientists and that physical scientists and engineers would play only a supporting role.

The studies done at Hudson naturally reflect the interests of the contractor, the agency or corporation that pays the bill. But the Hudson staff tries also to work on studies that reflect its own interests and those of its widely divergent members—including both Edward Teller and A. J. Muste. For the Department of Defense, it has prepared a study on "A Framework for the 1965–1975 Strategic Debate," but it has also worked on "Crises and Arms Control" and "Eleven Worlds of the Early 1970's"—the latter an attempt to probe the future for the Air Force. At an approximate cost of $1 million, it had produced in two years about a dozen studies whose value, like those by other groups, is frankly speculative.[48]

The Hudson Institute's educational activities also differ from those of most other organizations—possibly as a result of Herman Kahn's experiences at RAND. They consist primarily of a six-day course in national security which is given several times a year on a fee basis to a variety of groups—government officials; executives of defense industries; newspaper, radio, and television men; professors and researchers in national security affairs; and representatives of public groups interested in promoting disarmament and world organization. Dealing with such topics as foreign and military policy, strategy, and arms control, the course is given in both a classified and unclassified version. The faculty consists of the senior members of the Hudson Institute's staff. Through it, the Institute hopes to play a significant role in national security affairs, reach a larger public than is ordinarily available to research and analysis groups, and at the same time finance its other operations.

The total impact of these many research and analysis activities on the policy-maker is extremely difficult to assess. As we have already noted, the work of the groups is not generally open to inspection; often, even the nature of the problems they deal with is a closely guarded secret. The claims made in the press for the decisive influence of such organizations as RAND are undoubtedly exaggerated, but it is clear that at least to the government officials faced with the complex issues of national security, the work of these groups fills a vital need and has real value. It is for them a rare commodity—an objective and informed judgment by highly-trained first-rate minds—and they are willing to pay dearly for it.

Few major decisions in national security affairs are made today without a study of the issues by one or more of the analysis groups. As a result, the influence of the national security analyst has increased greatly during the past decade. Like his academic colleague, he belongs to the community of scholars who are frequently consulted by public officials and whose views often have a real effect on strategy and policy. His business is advice, and nowhere inside the government can the policy-maker find groups organized to provide this advice so well. Nor, in the opinion of many, would it be desirable, even if it were possible, to establish analysis groups within the bureaucracy to fill this need. It might be less expensive to do so, but it is doubtful that the objectivity, freedom of expression, and range of activity that characterize the work of outside groups would survive. The private research and analysis organizations are a significant new development in American life. They are a product peculiar to the cold-war period, and until the problems that gave them birth disappear, they are likely to remain. Advice has become a major industry of our time and an active instrument of government in the nuclear age.

12

National Security and Private Research

Our analysis thus far has moved from the broad academic base for the intellectual response to the cold war through two of the channels through which knowledge and rigorous analysis are directly brought to bear on national security policy: staffing and training the career service, and providing for outside research through contractual arrangements. We turn now to those private research institutions that contribute both to the development of intellectual resources and to the application of these resources to policy, and which play an important role in crystallizing public opinion on the issues of national security. Each of these organizations is interested in a different set of problems, and each has its own approach, method, and distinctive organization.

There are eight organizations that are representative of the group in range of activity, influence, and method of operation—the Carnegie Endowment for International Peace, the Council on Foreign Relations, the Twentieth Century Fund, the Brookings Institution, the Institute for International Order, the National Planning Association, the Center for the Study of Democratic Institutions, and the Institute for Strategic Studies (the latter a British organization, but with a significant American membership and a growing influence in the United States). The Carnegie Endowment is the oldest, having been founded in 1910. The Council, the Twentieth Century Fund, and Brookings were established in the decade after World War I; the National Planning Association is an inter-war development; and the others are more recent. The Center for the Study of Democratic Institutions, an offshoot from the Fund for the Republic, dates from 1959, the Institute for International Order from 1949, and the Institute for Strategic Studies from 1958.

Of the eight organizations, four—the Carnegie Endowment, the Council on Foreign Relations, the Institute for International Order, and the Institute for Strategic Studies—are directly concerned with problems of national security. The interest of the others is indirect. It was not until 1946, almost twenty years after it was formed, that the Brookings Institution inaugurated a Foreign Policy Studies Program to supplement its existing programs of Economic and Governmental Studies. The Twentieth Century Fund and the National Planning Association were concerned almost exclusively with domestic economic and social problems until the early 1950's, when both initiated projects in national security affairs. The Fund for the Republic, established in 1952 by the Ford Foundation, initially made grants for research in areas in which it had an interest. After a few years the Fund established its own research program, the Basic Issues Program, to study six areas or institutions basic to the democratic system; of these six, one, "The Common Defense," was related to national security.[1] When the Fund for the Republic organized the Center for the Study of Democratic Institutions, the Basic Issues Program became the core of the activities of the Center which maintained its interest in military institutions.

The entrance of these private organizations into the field of national security affairs derives in part from their recognition of the importance of these problems in the nuclear age and in part from the relation of their special area of interest to national security issues. Thus, the Brookings Institution, always concerned with economics and government, developed an interest in national security because of its concern with foreign affairs and with the recruitment and training of professional and executive personnel in government service. Like the Brookings Institution, the Twentieth Century Fund had a long-standing interest in economics and public education. The basis for its interest in the field of national security was its recognition that, in the postwar period, "the area of mutual concern between civilian and military was virtually coextensive" with the entire area of governmental activities.[2] As a result, the Twentieth Century Fund embarked on a research program that had as its objective a better understanding by the public of the problems of civil-military relations. The Center for the Study of Democratic Institutions, less concerned with governmental activities and foreign threats than with the effect of domestic threats to democratic institutions, approached the field of national security through a study of the impact of military factors on American society.[3]

All these organizations except the Institute for Strategic Studies related their programs in national security to broader, existing programs. Their decisions to establish the programs were made because of their conviction that the problems of national security were so fundamental and so pervasive, and so likely to continue indefinitely, that they would fail to achieve their objectives if they did not give adequate attention to them.

Like the academic centers, though not to the same extent, the private research organizations rely on foundations for support. The Council on Foreign Relations, for example, received about 35 per cent of its income in 1962–63 from foundation grants. The Fund for the Republic received its funds from a grant of $15,000,000 from the Ford Foundation, and it is this endowment that supports the Center for the Study of Democratic Institutions. (The Center is now seeking additional funds from other sources since it exhausted its part of the original endowment.) The Ford Foundation has also supported the Institute for Strategic Studies and the Brookings Institution, which receives support from other foundations as well. Least dependent on foundation support is the Twentieth Century Fund, itself a foundation subsisting largely on income from the endowment of its founder, Edward A. Filene.

Though these organizations differ in their organization and administration, they are similar enough to warrant a generalized description. All of them are private, nonprofit corporations that conduct research and educational programs with professional staffs. General policy is in the hands of a Board of Trustees, which establishes broad guidelines for programming, makes funds available, and approves major projects and budget allocations. Administrative control is exercised by the officers of the corporation, supported by an administrative staff.

Direction of specific programs of research or of a particular activity is separate from administrative control and is lodged with a study or program director. Subject to the broad guidelines of the trustees and the policies established by the President and officers, the study director organizes his program, allocates responsibility to his staff for specific topics, supervises their activities, and is responsible for the entire program. As one would expect, these study directors are usually drawn from academic life and have had experience directing large research programs. Their staffs, too, are composed of academicians, some of whom accept these posts for short periods and others who for one reason or another prefer this kind of career to teaching. Often the officers of these organizations also come from universities, but when they do, it is usually as much because of their administrative as their scholarly attainments. The Boards of Trustees may include a college president, dean, or eminent scholar, but usually their membership sounds the roll of finance, industry, law, and public life. The academic figures, scholars, administrators, and influential men of affairs who set the policies and direct the research of these organizations provide a close link to the universities, the foundations, and the government.

The Quest for Peace

Of the private institutions, two—the Carnegie Endowment for International Peace and the Institute for International Order—were organized basically because of the aspirations of their founders to find alternatives to the use of force in resolving international conflict. Both may be viewed as representative of the many groups concerned with the development of a peaceful world.

The Carnegie Endowment was established by Andrew Carnegie in 1910 "to hasten the abolition of international war." Unlike other organizations with similar idealistic purposes, the Endowment never engaged in direct political action. Its main activities, from the beginning, were in education and research, though the focus of its efforts shifted during the years. In its early years the Endowment sought to strengthen the contribution of international law to peaceful settlement and to assist in the development of international relations as an academic discipline. Among the institutions it helped to create are the Hague Academy of International Law, the Association of International Relations Clubs, with groups on many college campuses, and the Institute of International Education, which has now become the chief United States clearing-house for all student and teacher exchanges.

Over the years, the general aim set down by Mr. Carnegie has been reinterpreted in the light of changing conditions. After World War II, international organization became a principal focus of the Endowment's work.[4] On the fiftieth anniversary of the Endowment in 1960, its president, Dr. Joseph E. Johnson, noted that interest in the United Nations was consistent with the original objectives, but that immediate peace was not "at the top of the scale of values of most statesmen or even of most thoughtful persons in the world. I should imagine that most people place something else, such as justice or freedom or the right to worship, higher than they place peace. Nevertheless, in this nuclear age a threat to the peace is a threat to all the other values that we hold in high esteem."[5] Headquarters of the Endowment is in New York, in a building constructed by the organization facing the United Nations and also housing the World Affairs Center and the main offices of the Foreign Policy Association.

The Endowment's operations are under the general guidance of a Board of Directors consisting of statesmen, outstanding scholars, and distinguished professional men. Dr. Johnson, the President, is a former professor of history at Williams College, and the vice president, Lawrence S. Finkelstein, a political scientist who served on the State Department staff that planned the United Nations. Income from the original endowment continues to cover the major operating expenses (which run to about $1 million a year), but grants from other foundations support specific projects undertaken by the staff or through facilities made available by the Endowment.

The Carnegie Endowment serves as a foundation sponsoring research by others, though it conducts some research on its own. Its grants are usually made not for general purposes but for a project that has been planned within the organization itself. It initiated research, for instance, in the changing role of force, for which were commissioned five case studies of conflicts resolved after 1945: the Franco-German dispute in the Saar; the Franco-Moroccan dispute that led to Moroccan independence; the Cyprus dispute; the Anglo-Iranian oil dispute; and the Yugoslav-Italian dispute over Trieste. The project was placed under the general direction of the director of the Endowment's European office in Geneva, John Goormaghtigh, and each study was entrusted to the direction of a European scholar.[6]

The case study method has also been followed in a study of Cuban-United States relations undertaken by Roberta Wohlstetter, the author of a recent prize-winning study of the attack on Pearl Harbor who was on leave from RAND. The study, it is anticipated, will illustrate the limits that "exist on the capacity of a great power to bring its superior military strength to bear upon a recalcitrant smaller state."[7] Arms control is another subject to which the Endowment is turning, with particular emphasis on the implications of arms control for small and middle powers. The subject is of particular interest to Vice President Finkelstein, who spent the year 1961–62 on leave as a Research Associate at the Center for International Affairs at Harvard.

The Endowment also arranged for Jerome H. Spingarn of the National Planning Association's arms-control project to prepare a general analysis of approaches to arms control. This latter study was then published by the Foreign Policy Association in its "Headlines Series."[8]

Problems of national security have also been the subject of many issues of the Endowment's periodical *International Conciliation*, now in its 58th year of publication. One issue a year is devoted to an analysis of items to appear on the agenda of the U.N. General Assembly and each of the other four issues to study of a particular problem by a single author. Among these in recent years have been "The Governance of Berlin" by Bruce L. R. Smith, "The Diplomacy of Disarmament," by Joseph Nogee, "The United Nations and the Use of Force," by Inis L. Claude, and "Communist China in the World Community," by H. Arthur Steiner.[9] The Endowment has also sponsored a series of studies published on behalf of the Endowment by the American Council on Education, on the impact of world affairs on American universities. Among these have been *World Affairs and the College Curriculum*, by Richard N. Swift of New York University, and the final report of the series *American Higher Education and World Affairs*, by Howard and Florence Wilson.[10] Mr. Wilson was formerly a member of the Endowment staff and is now Dean of the School of Education at the University of California, Los Angeles.

The program of the Carnegie Endowment is illustrative of the wide variety of projects undertaken by private institutions; it includes not only the projects described above, but also programs for visiting scholars and diplomats, conferences on international law and organization, studies on regionalism, investigation of the implications of science and technology on international relations, and many others. But the Endowment also illustrates how an organization over a period of years can adjust its program to meet new problems as they arise. If Andrew Carnegie's hope for peace is ever realized, his own foresight in setting up the Endowment must certainly be counted as a major aid in developing the intellectual resources for dealing with the conflict. But just as important is the realism and wisdom of the staff and board that developed the program with a sense of worldly experience and an understanding of what issues are truly relevant to the quest for peace.

The objectives of the Institute for International Order are very similar to those of the Carnegie Endowment: to further peaceful settlement of international disputes, and to gain support for international law and the United Nations. Founded in 1949, the Institute conducted a minimal program for several years until Earl D. Osborn, retiring president of the Edo Corporation, was elected president and assumed personal responsibility for the Institute's financial support in 1954. At first concerned solely with public information and education, the Institute gradually shifted its emphasis to research and study, seeking to break new ground and open new fields. In order to maximize its limited resources, it makes small grants to initiate programs, leaving the task of supporting long-range programs to the larger foundations. Some of the projects it supported in its early years include an exhibit on the Eisenhower "open-skies" plan for arms control; a Disarmament Studies Project in Washington, headed by Jerome H. Spingarn (this was eventually replaced by the National Planning Association's Committee on Security through Arms Control); and an arms-control seminar at Fairleigh Dickinson University, also conducted by Mr. Spingarn.

In 1959, the Institute decided to make a major effort to achieve its objective of furthering research for peace. The Institute's Research Director, L. Larry Leonard, reviewed the work being done on problems of peace and war and recommended that the Institute undertake two major projects. The first was to support research surveys by qualified scholars of work already done, studies in progress, and problems that still needed investigation in six specific areas: (1) *The Technical Problems of Arms Control*, by a committee of the American Academy of Arts and Sciences headed by Bernard T. Feld; (2) *Economic Factors Bearing Upon the Maintenance of Peace*, by Kenneth Boulding and others at the University of Michigan; (3) *The International Rule of Law*, by Arthur Larson of the Law School at Duke University; (4) *National and International Decision-Making*, by Richard C. Snyder of the Government Department at Northwestern University; (5) *Communication and Values in Relation to War and Peace*, by Ithiel de Sola Pool of the Political Science Section of M.I.T.; and . (6) *Psychological Factors of Peace and War*, by Charles E. Osgood of the University of Illinois.[11] Published by the Institute, these programs of research (each containing a basic bibliography) are most valuable. Like other Institute projects, the research programs are regarded as seeds from which more fruitful harvests will grow, for they have actively called the attention of scholars and the larger foundations to the opportunities catalogued in them.

Leonard's second major project for the Institute for International Order was the publication of *Current Thought on Peace and War*, a semi-annual digest of the literature and of the research in progress. The first issue of *Current Thought*, a pilot effort, appeared early in 1960. Books, articles, unpublished manuscripts, research in progress, and general research programs were abstracted, arranged in categories and cross-references. Also included was a resumé of the activities of the major institutes, centers, and foundations concerned with research in the field. In 1961, when Dr. Leonard left the Institute and moved to Durham, North Carolina, where he was associated briefly with the World Rule of Law Center at Duke University, he continued to publish *Current Thought* privately.

The program of the Institute for International Order has several categories, of which research is only one. A second is concerned with adult education to increase public understanding and support of the United Nations, and to give financial aid to organizations such as the Foreign Policy Association with similar aims. Another major interest of the Institute is international law; to date, several volumes, including Grenville Clark and Louis Sohn's *World Peace Through World Law* and John B. Whitton and Arthur Larson's *Propaganda: Towards Disarmament in the War of Words*, have been supported.[12] The Institute also briefly published a bulletin entitled *Peace Opportunities* designed to interest foundations and other donors in supporting scholarship and action in the field.

In 1961, the Peace Research Institute was established, with the assistance of the Institute for International Order, to sponsor basic research activities. The new organization had a long list of advisers, most of them scholars in national security affairs, and a small staff headed by Donald N. Michael. It did not itself conduct research, but sought to stimulate studies by bringing together subjects that needed research and men qualified to work on them; by disseminating information about research in progress or completed; and by acting as a "prime contractor."

The sponsors of the Peace Research Institute contrasted it with other research organizations by emphasizing its concern in finding an alternative to the strategy of deterrence. Like the Conflict Resolution Center at the University of Michigan and the informal academic discussion groups which have been organized at universities throughout the country, the Peace Research Institute was committed to exploring the possibilities of establishing stability on something other than the uneasy balance of arms.[13] While the subjects undertaken reflected this commitment, it is significant that responsible scholars and scientists find it necessary to apply the most rigorous kind of analysis to national security problems, whether they are interested in developing maximum efficiency or exploring the limitations of a system of deterrents.[14]

In 1963, the Peace Research Institute was dissolved and its small staff joined a new organization, the Institute for Policy Studies, located in Washington. The new Institute, like the Washington Center of Foreign Policy Research, was frankly designed to encourage research on key problems of public policy, but under conditions that would avoid both too close and too distant a relationship to the policy-making process. These conditions the Institute sought to achieve by its physical location, close to the center of government policy and operations, by financial independence, and by association with universities and colleges that would be a continuing source of academic talent and financial support. Under this arrangement, each associated university contributed $2,500 annually to the Institute and agreed to pay full salary to one of its faculty members while in residence at the Institute. In return, the Institute provided facilities for the visiting faculty member and was prepared to accept a limited number of graduate and undergraduate students from the associated university and to try to place some students in government offices. It also agreed to furnish notes of the seminars held at the Institute and to provide its Fellows as lecturers to the associated universities. At the time of its establishment, the Institute expected to have associated with it about a dozen universities. Income from this source was obviously not adequate for an organization that estimated its annual budget at about $200,000; additional support was provided by a number of individuals and small foundations, and more was expected from others.

The policy of the Institute was set by a Board of Trustees consisting of scholars and others interested in public issues, especially those of foreign affairs and national security. The co-directors of the Institute are Marcus Raskin and Richard J. Barnet. The small permanent staff, or faculty, as it is called, initially numbered five, but the trustees expected it to reach a total of about a dozen part-time Associate Fellows and ten full-time Resident Fellows, the former to include government officials and public figures as well as scholars—to provide a link to policy-makers similar to that provided by the Washington Center of Foreign Policy Research. The number of Visiting Fellows at the Institute at any one time varies; in 1963–64, there were three, but more are expected as other universities join and additional funds become available. It is expected that when fully operational, the Institute will number thirty-two Fellows.[15]

The Institute does not have a comprehensive research program, but provides the physical facilities and intellectual environment in which Visiting Fellows can pursue their own research interests. The only restriction on them is that they may not accept any paid relationship with the government while at the Institute. By the end of 1963, eight studies were in progress, several of which dealt with arms control or foreign affairs. Within a month or two of its establishment, it was already conducting regular seminars for its own members and interested government officials—one on the economic structure of the United States, another on education, and a special seminar, given under the auspices of the Federation of American Scientists and chaired by Donald Michael, on problems of control of chemical, bacteriological and radiological warfare. Two more seminars were scheduled before the end of 1963—science and government, and changing power relationships in government—and four more were projected for the following years. One of these was on "National Security Institutions and Disarmament," conducted by the co-directors and Arthur Waskow. Additional research projects included studies of arms control and disarmament, and U.S. relations with supranational institutions such as the World Court and the United Nations.[16]

The Center for the Study of Democratic Institutions presents an interesting contrast to the various organizations we have just discussed. Growing out of the Fund for the Republic's interest in "the traditional rights and liberties of the American people," the Center seeks to clarify and promote discussion of the issues of a free society. It is less concerned with the solution to problems faced by American society today than with the identification of these problems. Describing itself as an educational organization, the Center stresses that it is not an action group except insofar as action may result from the ideas it generates and the public discussion it stimulates. The nature of its program stems from the present world crisis, and its aim is to re-examine democratic institutions and ideas in the light of changed conditions. National security, quite naturally, is the focus for much of the work done at the Center.

With its establishment in 1959, the Center moved from the New York office of the Fund for the Republic to Santa Barbara, California, where there were facilities for a larger staff and more full-time participants and where it could accommodate visitors for extended periods. There it could also share in the intellectual and scientific community of the University of California at Santa Barbara. Several of the consultants to the Center in that first year, including George N. Schuster, retired President of Hunter College, spent considerable time launching the Center's program. Altogether, several hundred scholars and experts, including John Kenneth Galbraith, Herman Kahn, Aldous Huxley, Allan Nevins, Mortimer J. Adler, and Sir Charles Snow, have since participated in the program at the Center for varying periods of time.[17]

The Center's staff is small: In addition to Robert M. Hutchins, President of the Center as well as of the Fund for the Republic, and other administrative officers, the staff includes seven staff directors, each of whom is responsible for a particular area of study in the Basic Issues Program, and a small number of full-time scholars. For the study of war and democratic institutions, the staff director is Walter Millis; for the study of the influence of technology on world affairs, Carl F. Stover of the Stanford Research Institute served as staff director and was aided by Center consultants I. I. Rabi, Scott Buchanan, Harrison Brown, and Sir Robert Watson-Watt.

In addition to the studies prepared under the Basic Issues Program, the Center conducts other activities related to the issues it regards as central to our times. In September, 1961, following the Conference on Science and World Affairs (an outgrowth of the Pugwash conferences) at Stowe, Vermont, the Center invited five Soviet scientists to Santa Barbara to discuss problems of disarmament and scientific cooperation, as set out in papers prepared by Harrison Brown and Walter Millis. The following January, the Center sponsored a conference on "Democracy and the Emerging Nations," chaired by Dean Zelman Cowen of the Faculty of Law, Melbourne University, and including scholars from American and foreign universities. That same month, it conducted a seminar on "Technology and World Problems" at the request of the U.S. Civil Service Commission, for the chief scientists of government installations on the West Coast. Some months later, together with the Board of Editors of the *Encyclopaedia Britannica*, it sponsored another conference, on the Technological Order. The Center has also tried to stimulate public discussion through a television program on a commercial network, programs on educational television stations, and adult-education programs. In 1963, the Center experimented with major conferences featuring internationally prominent speakers in Chicago, New York, and Los Angeles.[18]

In its few years of existence, the Center for the Study of Democratic Institutions has already made a substantial contribution to the intellectual life of the nation and to the study of important world problems. It has not only attracted men of the first caliber from a variety of fields; it has published half a dozen volumes and many pamphlets, papers, and reports. It has made a distinctive contribution also in its methods. "If we have done nothing else," said Mr. Hutchins, in appraising the results of the Center's operations in 1962, "we have shown how narrow are the usual channels of thought in this age of specialization. We have reached a point where a man with a good mind, superior education, and a deserved reputation in his own field may be appallingly ignorant of the world—and it is the world we must now be concerned with."[19]

Under the earlier Basic Issues Program, an excellent start was made on the study of "The Common Defense," later retitled "The Study of War and Democratic Institutions." Most of the work has been done by Walter Millis, who has had available to him the advice of the Program's consultants.[20] Millis's first publication for the Program was a pamphlet published in 1957, entitled *Individual Freedom and the Common Defense*; the second, in 1959, was *The Constitution and the Common Defense*. In addition, in 1958, the Fund for the Republic published separately two papers, one by Millis and the other by Father John Courtney Murray, together with a discussion of the papers by the consultants, under the title *Foreign Policy and the Free Society*.[21] At the present time, Millis is working on an ambitious study of the problems involved in the abolition of war and "war systems." The first installments of the study, published by the Center as *A World Without War* and *Permanent Peace*, have been combined in a book under the former title.[22]

Interestingly enough, from 1961 to 1962, Millis's work was supported by a grant from the Rockefeller Foundation to the Carnegie Endowment for International Peace, though he remained a staff member of the Center.[23] This arrangement illustrates the interlocking relations and close sense of community among the groups interested in national security and foreign affairs and the emphasis placed on the individual scholar and his work, no matter how intricate the committee and panel systems become.

National Security and Programs of Public Affairs

Problems of national security affect almost every aspect of national life. It is thus not unusual that organizations concerned with the broad problems of American society and economy should sponsor research in the field. The National Planning Association (NPA) is one of these. Established in 1934, NPA brings together leaders of agriculture, business, labor, and the professions in order to focus the resources of diverse groups on national problems.

The NPA had been interested in national security problems for some years when, in the mid-1950's, it moved actively into the field. In 1957, it set up a Committee on Security through Arms Control with Richard S. Leghorn, President of Itek Corporation, as Chairman, and as Secretary Jerome H. Spingarn, a Washington lawyer who subsequently joined the Arms Control and Disarmament Agency. The membership was made up of academic people, newspaper and magazine editors, scientists, businessmen, and others—Archibald Alexander, David F. Cavers, Norman Cousins, Klaus Knorr, David Riesman, Amrom Katz, and Harrison Brown. The Committee produced four short reports that the NPA published: *1970 Without Arms Control* (1958); *International Control of Nuclear Explosions* (1959); *The Nth Country Problem* (1960); and *Strengthening the Government for Arms Control* (1960). In each case, a draft was prepared by Mr. Spingarn in consultation with a small subcommittee, subjected to review and discussion by the full Committee, and published as a Committee effort with individual members commenting in footnotes on points with which they disagreed or on which they wished to elaborate. In the last report, the Committee was primarily concerned with effective government machinery and with key considerations in planning new approaches to arms control. The report, subsequently printed as a Senate document, was helpful in the establishment of the Arms Control and Disarmament Agency in 1961.

The National Planning Association has also dealt with security problems through its International Committee, headed by Frank Altshul, through study projects in civil defense, and through a study of the economic impact of disarmament prepared by its chief economist, Gerhard Colm. As a subsidiary activity, the NPA Committee on Security through Arms Control sponsored occasional seminars for the purpose of permitting an exchange of views among scholars, government officials, and journalists on disarmament problems. The most notable, which took place in January, 1961, brought together State and Defense Department officials, scholars, and incoming officials of the new administration for a discussion of methods of organizing the government to deal with arms control problems.

The Twentieth Century Fund, whose primary interest has always been in domestic economic and social problems, in recent years turned its attention, like the NPA, to the field of national security. In 1952, the directors of the Fund asked a group of scholars for advice on the kind of national security program the Fund should adopt. Several meetings were held and a variety of possible approaches considered.[24] The one finally adopted was an examination of the effect of military considerations on national policies in a series of specific cases—a study on the basis of which it was hoped to derive generalizations about civil-military relations. It was to be a three-year, three-part project: first, a general historical survey of civil-military relations during the past two decades; second, a study in depth of about a dozen specific cases to illustrate how decisions are made; and third, an analytical discussion of civil-military relations based on the material assembled in the survey and case studies. The results would be published as books directed to a general rather than a specialized audience.[25] Dr. Harold Stein, former Deputy Director of the Office of War Mobilization and Reconversion and editor of a series of case histories in public administration, was to head the project and write the historical survey himself. Stein chose to locate the project at Princeton, and he received a titular appointment in the Woodrow Wilson School of Public and International Affairs.

Under the original plan, Stein was to write the historical survey himself. Because of his serious illness, the task was eventually assumed by Walter Millis, who had recently left *The New York Herald Tribune* to become Staff Director on the Common Defense for the Fund for the Republic, and Harvey C. Mansfield, Professor of Political Science at Ohio State University. From this association came *Arms and the State*, a nontechnical, historical survey of civil-military relations and their effect on national policy from the mid-1930's to the mid-1950's.[26] Work on the case studies got under way almost immediately. Under Professor Stein's direction, a group of young and promising scholars at various universities began to assemble the materials for these studies, which were published late in 1963, bringing the project to a close.[27]

In 1960, the Twentieth Century Fund entered the field of arms-control studies in a limited way by supporting a summer study group that had been formed on the initiative of the Cambridge Chapter of the Federation of American Scientists.[28] The group, led by Professor Bernard T. Feld of the Physics Department at M.I.T. and a steering committee—which included Donald Brennan of the Lincoln Laboratory, Professors David Frisch, Max Millikan, and Jerome Wiesner of M.I.T. and Paul Doty and Thomas Schelling of Harvard—met at M.I.T. during the summer of 1960 for a series of sessions on arms control. Altogether, about fifty persons from various universities and research organizations participated in the sessions; from the meetings came a number of papers and seminar notes that were distributed in limited quantities, as well as several larger projects that were continued under Fund support until the end of the year. In terms of results, the Fund's contribution to this pioneer study of arms control was most gratifying. Two important volumes on the subject were the direct result of this program, and a third was based in part on it.[29]

The Brookings Institution supports a broader program than either the National Planning Association or the Twentieth Century Fund and contributes to the study of national security problems through research, education, and publication. Established in 1927 by the merger of the Institute for Government Research, the Institute of Economics, and the Brookings Graduate School, Brookings has been from the start strongly oriented to economics and government, and to education for the public service. For many years it maintained a program leading to a Ph.D. degree, as well as a fellowship program, and has granted 74 Ph.D.'s and more than 300 fellowships. In addition, Brookings sponsors special seminars and conferences; makes studies for the government on request; conducts its own research programs; and, since 1954, has held an annual series of Brookings Lectures on research and policy questions. In 1960, it moved into its new $4 million building, financed by income from investments, private donors, and philanthropic institutions including the Ford Foundation. With larger quarters, it was able to provide facilities for visiting scholars and expand its program to make the Brookings Institution a center for research and study in the nation's capital.

Since 1946, when it began programs concerned with American foreign policy, Brookings has shown an increasing interest in problems of national security. The original objectives of the Foreign Policy Studies Program—to aid in the development of an informed and responsible public opinion and to contribute to the training of specialists in international relations—have enlarged, and the emphasis on the program has increased as the importance of national security issues for foreign and domestic policy has grown.

Begun by Leo Pasvolsky and headed by him until his death in 1953, continued by Robert W. Hartley, and most recently by H. Field Haviland, Jr., the Foreign Policy Studies Program moved steadily forward. Its publications in the field of foreign policy included an annual review of the major problems of U.S. foreign policy published for several years but since discontinued, and a series of volumes on the United Nations. In addition, the Foreign Policy Studies Program, with assistance from outside scholars, prepared for the Senate Committee on Foreign Relations a study on "The Formulation and Administration of United States Foreign Policy" in 1959. Under Pasvolsky, the group had conducted a series of five national and seven regional seminars for scholars, government officials, military officers, businessmen, and others to consider particular problems of U.S. foreign policy. The Brookings staff prepared background papers on these problems in advance, and altogether more than 1,000 people participated in these conferences. Finally, the Brookings Lectures for 1956 dealt specifically with foreign policy. Focused on the theme

"The Changing Environment of International Relations," they included lectures on "Science, Technology, and International Relations" by Harrison Brown; "Emerging Requirements for an Expanding World Economy," by Edward S. Mason; and "Asian Cooperation with the West," by Harold H. Fisher.[30]

In the expanded program of the Institution's Center for Advanced Study, made possible by a $5 million grant and inaugurated in November, 1960, national security was given an important place. Among problem areas marked out for research in the Foreign Policies Studies were relations with developing countries, U.S. policy toward Communist countries; and the United Nations.[31] Although the focus is clearly on international relations, much of the research in this large program is clearly related to national security, and several bear directly on problems of defense and defense organization. Among the works produced to date under this program are Bernhard G. Bechhoefer's *Postwar Negotiations for Arms Control*; *The Turkish Revolution 1960–1961: Aspects of Military Politics*, by Walter F. Weiker; *The United States and the Sino-Soviet Bloc in Southeast Asia*, by Oliver E. Clubb, Jr.; and Max Beloff's *The United States and the Unity of Europe*.[32] Further, this program deals specifically with policy issues, and has as one of its aims improvement of the organization and procedures in the field of foreign policy. Thus, it may be considered a policy-oriented program utilizing scholarship, research, meetings, and a large publication program to identify problems, stimulate public discussion, improve the caliber of public servants, and secure the adoption of specific reforms in organization and adjustment in policy to meet these problems.

The research program of the Economic and Governmental Studies groups at Brookings includes a wide variety of subjects, some of which are clearly of interest to the student of national security problems and to government officials. In economics, these would include foreign investments, the impact of governmental spending, the tax structure, and studies in international trade. The governmental studies include research in leadership and management in the public service—where Brookings has already made a notable contribution—the legislative process, and national defense. Six specific lines of research are laid down in this last subject: a redefinition of the problem of national defense since 1945; civil defense; administration, including the role of the Secretary of Defense; the military budget; manpower requirements; and the implications of defense contracting policy. Many of these studies are carried out under government contract.[33]

Research and publication are only two of the methods Brookings uses to promote public discussion and improve the public service. Now operating with an annual budget of over $2.5 million, it also has a program of advanced study to bring together the university scholar, the public official and the civic leader for discussion of policy issues; research conferences and seminars; a research fellowship program; visiting professorships and lectures. The Advanced Study Program encompasses a variety of activities—present and planned—special programs for government officials and career executives, roundtable discussions, study groups, conferences for teachers and the press, seminars for management interns in government, and briefing sessions for new political appointees. Many of these conferences deal with administration and management problems rather than with policy issues, but they draw on high-level officials from agencies concerned with the formulation of defense policy, and they thereby may affect, however indirectly, national security policy. The periodic meeting in Williamsburg of career government executives in the highest grades is one such program, and in 1959–60, a series of conferences brought together scientist administrators from various agencies such as the Atomic Energy Commission and the Departments of State and Defense to discuss common problems.[34] Finally, Brookings hopes to publish a journal of public affairs that would appeal to both a scholarly and general audience and provide a forum for discussion of national problems.[35]

An International Program: The Institute for Strategic Studies

The Institute for Strategic Studies in London is different from the organizations we have already discussed in two ways: It has an international membership, and it is directly responsive to the strategic problems of modern warfare. Established in 1958, the Institute seeks "to promote on a non-party basis the study and discussion of . . . the influence of modern and nuclear weapons and methods of warfare upon the problems of defense strategy, disarmament and international relations."[36] It is incorporated under British law as a company limited by guarantee, and received its funds initially from the Ford Foundation under a three-year grant for $50,000 a year. Since then, a large number of British firms, including the Nuffield Foundation and the Leverhulme Trust, have also helped to support it, and it has greatly increased its membership. At the end of 1961, its annual budget stood at about $70,000, and the prospects for the coming year were for additional income from European as well as British and American sources, and for an expanded program.[37]

The Institute is a lineal descendant of the "Brighton Group," a loosely organized group of clergymen, academicians, publicists, and military men who were concerned with the need for rational defense planning. The Reverend Alan Booth maintained a modest central office for the Brighton Group, from which papers and articles were circulated among the members. Admiral Sir Anthony Buzzard, one of the leaders of the Group, approached the Ford Foundation and urged that it support an organization that could carry on and extend the work of the Brighton Group. The proposals were acted on favorably, and Alastair Buchan, defense analyst and former Washington correspondent of *The Observer*, was selected as director when the Institute began operations in November, 1958.

Membership in the Institute is limited to persons with a serious interest in strategic problems. At the end of 1963, there were almost 500 members, of whom about half were British or from the Commonwealth, about 100 from the United States, and the same number from Continental Europe. The Institute is governed by a Council composed entirely of British subjects (because of company and tax laws), but its International Advisory Council is composed of leading authorities on defense in different countries of the free world. The active direction of the Institute is in the hands of the Director, Alastair Buchan, and a Deputy Director, an executive committee of the Council, and the administrative staff. Membership is of three types: regular, associate, and corporate—the latter also being international in character. The American members of the Advisory Council in 1963 were Robert R. Bowie, Director of the Center for International Affairs at Harvard; General Cortlandt van Rensslaer Schuyler, formerly Chief of Staff at SHAPE; and Albert J. Wohlstetter of the RAND Corporation.[38]

The program of the Institute supplements that of the British Royal Institute of International Affairs, which had failed to respond promptly to the need for work in the field of national security studies. In Europe, where there is less contact between official and nonofficial groups and little or no use of private individuals as consultants or researchers for the government, the Institute attempts to foster a closer relationship between government officials responsible for defense policy and individuals outside the government. This it does in a variety of ways: by inviting officials to join the ISS as Associate Members (designed for those who hold official positions) and attend meetings for informal exchanges of views; by publications; by offering seminars and courses for business executives and other interested persons; and by other means. The results have apparently been excellent, and a number of British and NATO officials attend these meetings frequently. Moreover, in keeping with its international character, the Institute embarked on joint study projects with French and German research institutes. One advantage of these projects is that the Institute serves as a clearing house for European and American ideas.

In addition to small informal meetings, the Institute also conducts larger meetings from time to time at which distinguished speakers address the group. In 1962, there were nine such meetings, with speakers drawn from various countries; two Americans who addressed the Institute were Paul Nitze and Henry Kissinger. Further, whenever foreign experts visit London, they are invited to come to the Institute to talk informally to the members. Such sessions have been held with Raymond Aron, Walter Lippmann, Robert Bowie, Arnold Wolfers, Raymond Garthoff, Herman Kahn, Henry Kissinger, Robert Osgood, Louis Sohn, and Paul Kecskemeti. The Institute members are also briefed from time to time by government officials and others on important defense topics. Briefings during 1959 included those by the Air Ministry and the Admiralty, a joint meeting with church leaders at Lambeth Palace to discuss the moral issues of a nuclear strategy, and another with the Institute of Race Relations on the strategic importance of Africa. In 1962, the briefings included talks by General Norstad and the British Ministers of Defense, Air, and State for Foreign Affairs.

Finally, the Institute has an active program of conferences. Some of the most successful have been organized in conjunction with other organizations. Thus the European-American Assembly, organized jointly by the Institute and Columbia University's American Assembly, and held at Burgenstock, Switzerland, in July, 1961, saw thirty leading Europeans discussing disarmament with a similar number of eminent and specially qualified Americans. In May, 1962, another meeting brought eighty Americans and Europeans together in Brighton to discuss the political, economic, industrial, and strategic implications of man's activity in space.

But the conferences that constitute the Institute's most significant contribution to international intellectual cooperation are those held in conjunction with its own annual program of studies. These studies are produced according to a highly successful formula in which a draft of each study is prepared by an expert working with an international study group over a period of nine months to a year. The draft is then discussed at the Annual Conference of the Institute, and finally published in book form.

For its first subject in 1959, the Institute chose "The Implications of Interdependence within NATO." All NATO countries were represented at the Annual Conference, and in a book completed after the meetings, Alastair Buchan proposed a number of measures to increase participation by the European countries in NATO policymaking. The 1960 study group provided opportunities for discussion of Hedley Bull's book, *The Control of the Arms Race*, a clear and perceptive analysis of the problem of disarmament and arms control. The 1961 study, *World Order and New States* by Peter Calvocoressi, was an examination of the internal and external stability of the new nations and was of particular interest to those concerned with the political and economic development of Africa.[39]

The 1962 study on *Arms and Stability in Europe* was the most ambitious project on which the Institute had yet embarked.[40] Conducted in collaboration with the Centre d'Études de Politique Étrangère in Paris and the Deutsche Gesellschaft für Auswartige Politik in Bonn, the study examined the relationship between political stability and military policy in Europe. It was an attempt to discern those measures which might be taken by agreement or unilaterally to lower tension in Europe without jeopardizing security, in the hope that such measures might lead eventually to a more normal system of coexistence between Eastern and Western Europe. The Annual Conference at which preliminary draft papers on this subject were discussed was held at Bad Godesberg; 150 experts and men of affairs came from all over Western Europe and the United States. The fifth Annual Conference was held at Cambridge in September, 1963, on the subject of "The Evolution of NATO and the Control of Western Strategy." The principal speakers at that meeting were Dean Acheson, Fritz Erler, Maurice Schumann, and Harold Watkinson.

The Institute's research program is necessarily a limited one. Since it cannot equal the resources of American groups such as RAND, the Institute has wisely decided to concentrate on practical rather than theoretical problems, and to clarify existing policies rather than suggest new ones. Since 1961, the Institute has aimed at producing, in addition to its annual study, one purely research study. The first of these research studies was a comparative analysis of military manpower systems by Michael Foot. The second, on *The Spread of Nuclear Weapons*, was by Leonard Beaton and John Maddox, who visited the United States, Canada, India, Israel, Sweden, Switzerland, Germany and France in the course of preparing it.[41] A third study deals with strategic mobility, a fourth with the security of Southeast Asia, and others are planned for the future.

A third aspect of the Institute's program is to provide its members and other students of defense problems with reference materials and information that will help them to keep abreast of writings in the field. It accomplishes this aim in two ways: (1) by a library consisting of the most important recent books published, and selections from about seventy serious journals and magazines from all over the world; and (2) by publishing a bi-monthly magazine, *Survival*. Aside from the book reviews, the magazine contains no original material; its value lies in reprinting in convenient form a variety of articles and statements from different countries, including the Soviet bloc, on military problems. The Institute also publishes annually "The Military Balance," a detailed and authoritative analysis of military forces of virtually every country in the world; and, in 1961, it initiated a series of informal papers called Adelphi Papers for circulation to members.

The Institute exerts influence through its membership, its meetings, and its publications. By promoting public discussion of the issues of defense, by providing an international forum for exchange of views among policy-makers, military men, scholars, newspaper men, and others, and by seeking to clarify issues that face all the Western nations, the Institute for Strategic Studies makes an important contribution to public understanding of national security problems and, indirectly, to the policies adopted to meet these problems.

Other activities in England that relate to international security, in addition to the Institute, include an international quarterly journal, *Disarmament and Arms Control*, organized in 1963. Edited by the British journalist Wayland Young, it has a mixed British-American editorial board that includes Henry Kissinger, Donald Brennan, Bernard Feld, and Alastair Buchan. The close British-American connection here, as well as in the Institute for Strategic Studies, is undoubtedly the result of several factors: the leadership taken by the Americans in the field, the traditional cultural and linguistic ties, and the closeness that has marked the relationship of the two countries in academic, military, and scientific fields during and since World War II. But it is also because, among the United States' allies, Britain has had a "special relationship" with America in dealing with broad strategic problems which, until very recently, America had not shared with other nations. As the nature of the NATO alliance changes and its member states assert greater independence within the alliance, it is possible that there will be greater interest among Europeans in the intellectual problems of the cold war. There is already evidence for this in the expanding participation of Continental countries in the activities of the Institute since 1962.

The Council on Foreign Relations

Probably the best known of the private research groups in the United States is the Council on Foreign Relations. Organized immediately after World War I by a small group of men who "thought the United States had an important role to play in the world and [who] resolved to try to find out what that role ought to be," the Council through its members has been close to policy-makers in the government and to scholars in the academic world.[42] From the original organizing committee that met in Paris during the Peace Conference, the Council has grown to a membership of 1,400, half of whom come from New York or its environs. It could undoubtedly be much larger, but has been kept to this number to avoid unwieldiness and fragmentation.[43]

The members of the Council are leaders in public and private life and include present and former Presidents and Secretaries of State, leading public officials, college presidents, editors and commentators, scholars, businessmen and industrialists, and others. Linked by a common interest in foreign policy, these men, through their individual associations and positions, exert perhaps more influence on the policies of the United States than any other single private group. One writer called the Council a "School for Statesmen," and credited it, on the basis of one of its special wartime projects, with many of the basic decisions taken in the post-World War II settlement.[44]

The Council is an association rather than an institute. Chartered as a nonprofit organization, it is governed by its membership through a rotating board of twenty-one directors, elected officers, and standing committees. A staff of about ninety, supplemented by visiting scholars, organizes and directs its various activities, carries out research projects, and performs the necessary administration. The Council occupies its own building in New York, and derives its funds from income on its own invested assets ($3,450,000 in 1959), dues, foundation grants, and receipts from sales. Its budget for 1963 was $1,315,600; its income, $1,298,100 as compared to $100,000 in 1927. About $125,000 came from membership dues, $452,500 from foundation grants, $103,000 in income from investments, and almost $300,000 from publications, including Foreign Affairs.[45]

The major purpose of the Council "is the study and clarification of significant questions of foreign policy which confront the United States in the contemporary world."[46] It seeks to achieve this purpose by research, conferences, lectures, grants, study groups, and an extensive publications program. Basically, its activities are of two types:

educational and research. Because of the methods it employs and the audience it reaches, its activities are more effective than those of almost any other organization in the field.

The Council's primary activity and the one for which it is best known is its Studies Program. Under the direction of a standing committee, the Studies Program is designed to bring the resources, knowledge, and experience of the Council's members to bear on important problems related to the foreign policy of the United States.[47] Suggestions for subjects suitable for study may come from the Director of Studies, from the standing committee, from the members, or from scholars throughout the country. Generally the topics selected reflect issues of current or possible future significance, including many related to national security.[48] The subjects are intended to be timely, but not so immediate as to preclude proper analysis and discussion because of the difficulty of dealing with day-to-day operations or because the material is classified. What is sought is objectivity and perspective, "often more easily obtainable in such privately sponsored endeavors than within the government itself."[49] In each case, the study is expected to result in publication of a book.

Once the subject is selected, a study group is formed—consisting of a chairman, who is a Council member with some special interest or knowledge in the field; a study director, who may be one of the professional members of the staff or a research fellow (usually an outstanding scholar) brought in for the purpose; and a varying number of regular members invited to participate in the study. The study director is the key person in the group. It is his task to do the research and write the book; responsibility for the book is the author's. But he can derive great benefit from the group since its members read portions of his manuscript as it is written, provide advice and responsible criticism, meet periodically to discuss the issue, and sometimes invite outsiders with special competence to discuss it with them. For example, the study group on Communist China and U.S. policy in Asia held seven meetings in 1958–59 to discuss papers prepared by the study director, A. Doak Barnett. Discussion leaders at these sessions included: Robert R. Bowie, former Assistant Secretary of State; John C. Campbell, Director of Political Studies for the Council; Major General Paul W. Caraway, a member of the Joint Strategic Survey Committee; Paul M. A. Linebarger, of the Johns Hopkins School of Advanced International Studies; and Dean Rusk, then President of the Rockefeller Foundation. These meetings were confidential, so that there could be the kind of full and frank expression of views that would be most helpful to the author in analyzing present and future problems of U.S. policy in the Far East.[50]

The process by which a book is produced under this arrangement was described by Gordon Dean and Henry A. Kissinger, chairman and study director of the group from whose discussions emerged Kissinger's book *Nuclear Weapons and Foreign Policy*.[51] The group was first organized in 1954 simply to explore the problem. It included, in Dean's words, "Framers of our military and foreign policy, experts knowledgeable in the effects of modern weapons, persons in responsible positions in government, persons who had held such positions in the past, persons . . . who brought to us the benefit which comes from reflective thinking, within the confines of our universities."[52] Some time later, Dr. Kissinger was appointed study director, and after about eighteen months, the group ended its deliberations. To Kissinger, who by now was thoroughly familiar with the views of its members, was left the task of writing the book. How much he owed to the discussions of the group and to the facilities of the Council he makes clear in his preface.

> An author who is invited by the Council on Foreign Relations to work under its auspices, is in a fortunate position. He can draw on the experience of an extraordinary group of individuals who have been exposed to the practice of the problem with which he is dealing. . . . Their deliberations gave me a sense of the dimensions of the problem and of the considerations on which policy is based; this I could have acquired in no other way.[53]

The work of the study groups often has results that go far beyond the production of a scholarly work. For it may influence the Council members and their guests, many of whom are public officials whose views may affect the policies finally adopted by the government. Furthermore, it is not unlikely that some of the members would be appointed to public office for the same knowledge and experience that made them members of the study group in the first place. Finally, as influential private citizens, they are often in a position to present their views on the highest level, and to secure wide public discussion of the problems they have considered.

In addition to the study groups, the Council also conducts a series of discussion groups. The two groups are similar in almost every respect, with the one important difference that the discussion groups do not have as their aim a published book. Their purpose is rather to explore a problem, define its limits and the issues involved, and to determine whether it should be made the subject of more formal study. (The discussion group in 1959 on "Political and Strategic Problems of Deterrence" led to the organization of a study group the following year on "Strategic Deterrence and Foreign Policy," with Albert Wohlstetter as director and James A. Perkins as chairman.) The discussion group has a secretary, usually a member of the Council or its staff, who organizes the meetings and assists the chairman in preparing the agenda. Not all discussion groups lead to study groups; some are abandoned because of lack of interest, declining importance of the problem, or inability to find a competent scholar willing to undertake the assignment of writing a book on the subject. Others are continued for several years as a means of keeping the members informed about a particular problem, and then either are dropped or develop into a study group.

The number of discussion groups in any single year varies, but it is rarely more than five. The topics, like those for the study groups, reflect the Council's interest in problems of immediate or future importance for the foreign policy of the United States. Prominent among these problems is national security, and each year, one or more of the discussion groups devotes itself to this aspect of foreign policy, and others deal with it as part of a larger problem. One year, a group was formed to consider the problem of strategic bases and their relation to alliances, with James A. Perkins as chairman and Melvin Conant of the Council staff as secretary. The following year, two groups were formed to discuss national security problems, both chaired by Mr. Perkins, with Henry A. Kissinger as secretary. One dealt with the interaction of power and policy and the other with the political implications of changing strategies. At both, members of the RAND Corporation, high-ranking military officers, and present and former officials of the Defense and State Departments participated.

These small study and discussion groups are central to the Council's other activities—its publications, lectures, special seminars, and meetings. The publications program of the Council includes a quarterly journal, three annuals, and a series of special studies on foreign policy, which together reach a wide and influential audience. The special studies series is the tangible result of the study groups and includes some of the most notable contributions to the study of foreign and defense policy.[54] The annual publications consist of *Political Handbook of the World*, published continuously since 1927; *The United States in World Affairs*, and *Documents on American Foreign Relations*. All are standard reference works for public officials, journalists, teachers, and students.

The major publication of the Council is *Foreign Affairs*, edited by

Hamilton Fish Armstrong, a quarterly journal with authoritative and timely articles by leading political figures, diplomats, and scholars. *Foreign Affairs* is so highly regarded that it has been called required reading for statesmen and diplomats.[55] Established in 1922, *Foreign Affairs* had a circulation of about 5,000 at the end of its first year, 27,000 in 1959, and in 1963, about 57,000. Its great prestige, however, comes not from the number but the kind of people who read it, and from its distinguished roster of contributors. About two-fifths of its articles have been by foreigners, including Lenin, Churchill, Khrushchev, Bevan, Gaitskell, Adenauer, Tito, Senghor, Eden, Nkrumah, and Nehru. Among American contributors, to name only a few, are Dean Rusk, George Kennan, Hubert Humphrey, J. K. Galbraith, and the late President Kennedy. Its articles are frequently cited, reprinted in other journals and books, and reproduced for teaching purposes.[56]

Foreign Affairs, like the Council, devotes a good deal of attention to national security problems as they affect international relations. Articles on such subjects are sometimes prepared by the Council staff in connection with a discussion or study group. High-ranking military officers, officials of the government, journalists, and scholars also find an effective outlet in *Foreign Affairs*. A list of such authors would include McGeorge Bundy, Klaus Knorr, Edward Teller, Herbert Dinerstein, Malcolm Hoag, Henry Kissinger, Max Millikan, General Lucius Clay, Walt Rostow, Lincoln Bloomfield, Townsend Hoopes, and Albert Wohlstetter. In addition to its articles, *Foreign Affairs* contains reviews and summaries of recent books on international relations and most of the material published on national security, prepared by Henry L. Roberts, and a summary of published source material.

Another series of Council volumes originates with the Elihu Root Lectures, commemorating the former Secretary of State who was one of the founders of the Council. This lecture series was inaugurated in 1957 with Thomas K. Finletter's lectures on the aims and conduct of foreign policy, which were published in 1958 under the title *Foreign Policy: The Next Phase*, to become the first of what promised to be an important new series. The second Root lectures, dealing with problems of leadership in U.S. foreign policy, were delivered by Dean Rusk in the winter of 1960. The importance of the lectures was underscored by Rusk's subsequent appointment as Secretary of State, although his taking office required the cancellation of publication plans. (One of his lectures was published in the April, 1960, *Foreign Affairs*.) The following year, the Root lectures were delivered by Caryl P. Haskins, President of the Carnegie Institution of Washington, on the subject

"American Foreign Policy and the Forces of Science and Technology"; in 1963, by Professor Edward S. Mason of Harvard on the subject of "U.S. Foreign Aid Policy."[57]

In 1961, the Council inaugurated another series of volumes, the Policy Books, designed to cover timely and important topics in brief compass and inexpensive format. They were to be written by statesmen and scholars already familiar with the subject. The first of these volumes, by former Ambassador Ernest A. Gross on the United Nations, was published early in 1962; others have since been published, and the Council plans four or five a year.[58] "It is hoped," the Council reported, "that the quality of these books combined with their brevity will mean that they are read by top government officials and other leaders who cannot find the time for standard length books."[59]

Another of the Council's activities that is widely influential and serves to keep its members informed on foreign affairs is the extensive program of meetings. These are of two kinds: small round-table discussions by experts in a particular field; and larger meetings at which the general membership has the opportunity to hear an outstanding national or international figure whom the Council invites to address the group. The subjects discussed at both often deal with questions of national security, and, like the discussion groups, are off the record. Many of the meetings deal with specialized problems in a particular part of the world, and sometimes a special series of meetings is devoted to aspects of a single problem or area, such as the Soviet Union, the Middle East, national strategy, or foreign aid.

The list of speakers at the large meetings is impressive, and more than one Secretary of State or other responsible official has used this forum to announce an important development in foreign policy. Kellogg launched the policy that led to the Kellogg-Briand Pact at a Council dinner in 1927, and Dulles did the same in 1954 with his speech on massive retaliation. The round-tables, which meet usually in the afternoon, also have speakers, some of them as distinguished as those that address the larger groups. The subjects, however, are more specialized and the audience composed of members with special competence in the field. Invitations are issued on the basis of information supplied by each member indicating the geographical area and general subject (Economics, Finance, Military Affairs, Culture, Law) in which he is interested.[60]

All of these meetings are held at the Council headquarters in New York. But the Council also has affiliated groups, Committees on Foreign Relations, in about thirty cities, with a membership of about

2,000. These committees meet throughout the year (more than 200 meetings were held in 1962–63) and the Council assists by providing speakers. There is no formal connection between the Council and the committees—each is an independent organization—but once a year, representatives of the committees meet for two days to discuss some broad problem with Council members and a group of invited experts in the field. These meetings are made possible by a grant from the Carnegie Corporation of New York.[61]

In support of its research and publication program, the Council each year offers a small number of fellowships. These fall into four groups. First are the Research Fellowships in connection with a Studies Program. These are awarded for one year to a recognized scholar to enable him to devote all his time to his study. During this year, the research fellow works at the Council headquarters and is encouraged to participate in all the Council's activities. Selection of these fellows is based on the relationship of the applicant's project, which must deal with some significant aspect of U.S. foreign policy, to the Council's program of studies. Among the grants awarded in recent years were those to Melvin Conant, for a study of U.S.–Canadian defense relationships, and Albert Wohlstetter, for a study of the requirements of a strategic deterrence.

The Council offers three other fellowships each year. One is to an American foreign correspondent to broaden his knowledge of a particular area or subject by study at a university and use of the resources of the Council for a year. The second is the Senior Council Fellowship, inaugurated in 1961. This fellowship is designed for men who have had long and wide experience in the making of policy and who wish to record their experience in a published study. The first appointment under this program was James Phinney Baxter, 3rd, former president of Williams College and author of the Pulitzer Prize-winning book *Scientists Against Time* and other works, and for more than twenty years active as participant and adviser in national security and foreign-policy problems. The third fellowship, for an especially qualified Air Force colonel to participate in the Council's activities, was established "on the suggestion of the Air Force" in 1962.

One final activity of the Council deserves brief mention because of its relationship to public discussion and education in national security affairs. This is the Corporation Service, offered by the Council to financial, industrial, and other organizations engaged in international trade or concerned with international affairs. This program provides an opportunity for rising business executives to become familiar with some of the major issues of foreign policy—by use of the Council library, subscription to *Foreign Affairs* and the Council's other publications, briefings by the staff, and seminars for young business executives. These seminars are held twice a year, and each devotes five or six meetings to a single theme, using members of the Council and outside experts as speakers. Usually one of the seminars deals with some aspect of international trade or investments; the other with some broad problem in U.S. foreign policy—with one or more of the meetings given over to its military aspects.[62]

There is little doubt that all the private institutions discussed in this chapter have and will continue to have a considerable influence on civilian education and public understanding of the problems of national security. This influence is felt in many ways, directly through publication and discussion, and indirectly through research and sponsored programs. Their interest in national security affairs, combined with the support of the foundations, has given the field of national security studies recognition and standing as a proper subject for scholarly inquiry, and has encouraged research and teaching in the universities. Further, through their individual members, these organizations have been able to arouse public interest and even to influence policy. Though one may disagree with their particular points of view or programs, there is little doubt that they are generally more effective in directly shaping public attitudes toward defense issues than the university programs.

The most tangible contribution of these programs to education is the body of literature on national security they have produced or for which they have been responsible. Much of it is in the form of articles or pamphlets, but the number of books published as a result of their activities, as well as their quality, is a considerable achievement. This body of literature has served two purposes: It has enlarged the knowledge of the field; and it has provided the materials around which courses on the subject can be built. In 1950, anyone wishing to teach the subject of national security would have had virtually to create his own materials. This is no longer true, and as source materials and texts have become available, the number of courses has increased.

The private organizations have served the cause of education in still another way—by providing the kind of nonstructured, interdisciplinary environment that is particularly suited for work in national security studies. Academic institutions are organized departmentally and provide no opportunity except under special programs for the scholar whose primary interest is national security or military affairs. Whether he is an economist, political scientist, or historian, such a person may have more in common with men in other disciplines interested in national security than with his own departmental colleagues. And his teaching opportunities are likewise limited in a department that regards him with skepticism or, perhaps, suspicion. The private organizations provide both the environment for productive work and, on occasion, young scholars serving as assistants who may take the place of graduate students. In this way, they not only further research, but in some cases provide the kind of training that universities with their departmental organizations cannot or will not provide.

Independent research organizations, by providing the resources for long-term comprehensive programs, make it possible for scholars interested in national security to engage in research, free from their time-consuming teaching activities. And they do not draw their talents from the universities alone; government and industry employ perhaps the largest number of experts in the field and contribute significantly to the programs of these research organizations. Such arrangements not only provide for the pooling of diverse talents and experience in an interdisciplinary environment, but also facilitate the flow of ideas and personnel among the universities, industry, and government. But in terms of the people involved, this movement is largely one-way. Few experts from government and industry receive academic appointments, partly because national security is not a recognized field, partly because the academic hierarchy is rigidly structured and jealously guarded, and partly for financial reasons. None of these is an insurmountable obstacle, and if the study of national security increases in the universities, then the number of appointments of academically qualified scholars from private research organizations and government should also increase. In the meantime, organizations like the Carnegie Endowment, Brookings, and the Council on Foreign Relations provide an essential bridge between the world of scholarship and the world of the policy-maker.

V

Perspectives on the Intellectual
Response

13

Problems for Government and Education

The issues of war and peace are no longer essentially military. With the revolution in military technology and in the United States' role in world politics, national security has become a matter of deep concern to civilians, and scholars and scientists have been called on to participate in the determination of national policies. The problems involved in this intellectual response to the cold war are several: how to stimulate the professional interest of scholars and scientists in the issues of national security; how to develop methods of communication and organization to enable their findings to flow into the policy-making process; and how to protect their objectivity and professional integrity while applying their competence and expertise to key issues of public policy in which they may be deeply and emotionally involved as citizens.

There has been no planned development and application of intellectual resources; there has been instead an unorganized, free interplay between agencies of government, higher education, private philanthropy, and research groups. As a result of this interplay, intellectuals have become more important in the formulation of national security policy, and have broken the monopoly of the military profession in the field of strategy and the almost exclusive hold which lawyers and businessmen had on political appointments. They have done this by serving in various roles—as advisers within the government, as government executives, as teachers and writers whose work is the primary source of instruction in national security affairs, and as experts supplying specialized information and analysis through contractual arrangements.

Taken together, the institutional programs described in this book comprise a significant experience in American intellectual history. There are lessons in this experience, lessons that might be applied to other areas of national interest and that involve the complex relationship between education and public policy. They can be summed up in terms of the three issues we discussed earlier in this book and to which, in conclusion, we can now return: focus, financing, and the risks of orienting research to public policy.

The Problems of Focus and Financing

Whether the increased participation of intellectuals in positions affecting national security policy is desirable or not, the fact is that scholars and scientists are called upon because national security issues demand the kind of knowledge and ability they possess. But the scholar or scientist must still relate his work in the field to his own discipline. Clearly, national security is not a discipline in the same sense as history or economics or biology. It does not have a distinctive method, theory, set of concepts, and body of knowledge. Instead, it uses the methods of many disciplines and encompasses a variety of interests and fields of knowledge—ranging from the conduct of individual soldiers under the stress of combat to the organization of the Defense Department or the American contribution to NATO. The study of national security and military affairs, then, cannot be said to be the prerogative of any single discipline.

But without a clear focus and too broad to fit into any of the established disciplines, it remains largely undefined and unclaimed. If the study of national security affairs is not a discipline, where then does it belong within the academic structure? The answer is that, as a policy field like social welfare or urban studies, it belongs to any discipline whose subject matter coincides with the problems faced by the policy-maker. The real task for the academician is to integrate the revelant elements into his own discipline and to apply the methods and concepts of his training to those aspects of national security in which he is interested. Thus, the organizational aspects of defense would be included in a course in public administration; the economics of national security or military history would be the province of the economist or historian.

The reluctance of the established disciplines to incorporate national security as a continuing area of intellectual interest is undoubtedly related to the narrow definition of the field that has been generally accepted by many academicians. As a policy field, national security has often been conceived as stemming from the particular confluence of political and technological problems at this period of history. Even when it is acknowledged that these problems are intellectually challenging and worthy of scholarly study and analysis, they are frequently viewed as temporary. And, indeed, much of the research and writing on the subject, often polemical and transitory, has tended to give substance to this view; so has the way scholars and scientists have been drawn into the decision-making process of government and forced into compromise and commitment at the expense of objectivity.

There is, nonetheless, little reason to believe that men will not have to continue to be concerned with the relation of military force to national goals. This is not to say that the basic elements in the present situation—the nation-state system, the monopoly of force by the state, and national rivalries and competition—will remain unchanged. But the problems of security, of resolving conflict between competing interests, and of making decisions about the role of force in relation to individual and group goals, have occupied men since organized society began and will probably continue to do so for some time to come. Indeed, even under a world government, the use and control of force will pose problems. Certainly there are distinctive features to the present set of problems, but there is a difference between understanding these distinctions and regarding national security as a time-bound set of problems that have little to do with the future. It is only when this more fundamental concept of national security is accepted that the study of it will find a place among the continuing problems of man and society that are the concern of historians and social scientists.

The organization of scholars in an interdisciplinary program on a single policy area such as national security has real advantages, especially when the field is new. Many of these advantages are evident in the development of the centers and institutes described in this book. The range of national security studies is wide and beyond the competence of any single individual; many problems can therefore be dealt with most effectively on a "team basis." At the same time, each scholar must be familiar with the work and published material of the other disciplines that relate to national security. Association and communication with men in different disciplines greatly ease this problem. For they provide information, stimulus, criticism of work in progress, and confidence born of a community of interests and activity. And, in the process, they define the relation of the various disciplines to the policy area.

Although the existence of a center or institute on a campus may encourage work in national security affairs and facilitate research and teaching in the field, it is not at all certain that such a center is an essential prerequisite to scholarship. Nor does the absence of a formal program necessarily imply a lack of interest in the faculty. Yale University, for example, has no organized program, yet considerable work is done in areas directly related to national security in several departments, and there are as many members of the faculty engaged in research, consultation, and other activities as at any university with a center or institute. Why, then, does Yale not organize a program? It was one of the pioneers in national security studies, and its assets for establishing a successful center are numerous: It has a strong tradition of public service; it has an outstanding faculty, including specialists in the field; it has a great library, especially rich in military literature; and it has one of the largest endowments in the country. It has not done so in the belief that the training of government officials and the preparation of students for public careers are not the tasks of a university but rather of the government. The university's function is research and teaching, and these, it is held, can go forward without special programs or organizations, and with funds provided by the university rather than by a foundation or the government—a refreshing point of view, but one that only the most richly endowed institutions can afford.

There also does not seem to be any necessarily direct relationship between the quality of the results obtained in research and the degree of financial support, organizational structure, or administrative support available to the scholar through a center or institute. We have noted in the case of Ohio State University a program in a strong financial position and with an assured future but with little to show for its efforts. Its impact on the University has been small and its contribution to the study of national security affairs marginal. On the other hand, Duke University and the University of North Carolina, with no outside financing and little or no organizational and administrative support, have succeeded in making the study of national security a meaningful intellectual activity on both campuses. The reasons for this difference can be found in the focus of the programs, the faculty's experience and participation, and the relevant academic tradition and interest.

The most important element in any research effort is the quality of the scholars who do the work. All that a formal structure can do is provide the conditions that make creative scholarship possible. As we have seen in examining the centers at Princeton and Columbia, creative scholars often do their best work when they are given the opportunity to investigate problems that interest them in an atmosphere conducive to free exchange of ideas. A highly organized hierarchical structure may repel scholars or inhibit their creativity.

For senior scholars who have achieved academic status, work in national security affairs and participation in a center's program is an opportunity for advanced study and research, although the extent of their involvement may be limited by departmental considerations. Through the center, they may get outside support for research as well as a chance to become involved with government agencies through consultantships or contracts for outside research. Once a scholar has established a reputation in the field, the demand for his services increases rapidly, and by association with others in similar posts he finds himself able to influence, in subtle and indirect ways, the formulation of policy. As directors or staff members of their centers, the leading scholars in national security affairs share a community of interest that brings them together frequently for both formal and informal discussion. Equally at home in Washington and on the campus, they acquire information not available to the public and filter it through the interested academic community. Their number is small, but as a group their influence is large when it is brought to bear on a single issue on which there is agreement. In an informal way, they serve as a bridge between the world of scholarship and the world of policy-making.

Though they offer many benefits, special seminars, research institutes, and interdisciplinary centers do not train or place the graduate students who must staff the colleges and universities throughout the country or who will serve as public officials, responsible for clarifying and interpreting issues of national security. This training is provided by the graduate departments of a fairly small number of universities and colleges across the nation. And the centers are at a disadvantage in competing for the best young men, when the centers' staffs are not integrated in some measure with the departments. Since virtually all permanent appointments are in departments, and they usually oppose lateral entry, the center may be only a temporary assignment for a young scholar and may be an interruption in his career, even though it offers the opportunity to do uninterrupted research. This problem is compounded in the research corporations like RAND, which must accept the fact that despite the excellent working facilities, high salaries, and fringe benefits they offer, it is the university that remains the more prized home for scholars.

Within the structure of the academic world, promotion and status derive from standing in an academic department and are most often the reward for work done in established fields of inquiry. In the final analysis, then, the strength of national security studies in the universities depends on acceptance by the traditional departments. The acceptance, moreover, must be wholehearted. A single course offering in deference to the peculiar interests of a colleague is not sufficient. There will undoubtedly always be a few men who will pursue their special interests, regardless of the professional hazards. But to survive and grow as a field of academic inquiry, national security affairs must become a recognized specialty for graduate study, firmly rooted in the appropriate disciplines and attracting young men of promise who can pursue their interests without losing career opportunities. To date, few history or social science departments, with the possible exception of political science, have recognized national security affairs as a special field in their disciplines, or encouraged their best students to specialize in it.

The difficulties in staking out a new field of inquiry, integrating it into the traditional academic structure, and training sufficient students to fill the need are not to be minimized. Strong forces, however, favor the continued support of national security studies in the academic community. The first of these is the need of the government policy-maker; the second is the public's concern with questions of war and peace in the nuclear age. There are still large gaps in our knowledge of military institutions and behavior; the political, economic, and social consequences of the enormous change in the nature of warfare are as yet only partially perceived; and the great role of the United States in world affairs calls for new and imaginative policies. In all these, the scholar is of assistance to the policy-maker.

Despite the prevalent view of national security as an important but temporary phenomenon, the need for encouraging young scholars in the field has not gone unanswered. The Social Science Research Council, as one example, has given concrete expression to the need for professional development through its Committee on National Security Policy Research and has tried to stimulate interest in military affairs among social scientists and historians through its program of grants. The Committee, like some foundations and private research groups, has also tried to exert a unifying force in the development of the field by bringing together historians, political scientists, economists, sociologists, and natural scientists to exchange views on research and teaching on national security problems. The first of two general conferences was held at Dartmouth College in 1957, and the second at West Point in 1959. During the summer of 1958, the Committee sponsored a summer seminar in which some of the most promising scholars participated, and while each was working on his own research, they all met as a group regularly to discuss national security as a field of research.[1] And in 1962, the Committee co-sponsored a series of meetings with Columbia University's Council for Atomic Age Studies on the role of the scientist in national security affairs.

The attempts by the SSRC Committee and the foundations to encourage research and bring together men and materials from different disciplines has paid large dividends, but national security studies still lack a strong unifying force. One way suggested to compensate for this lack is to develop stronger professional ties, particularly by establishing a professional journal devoted exclusively to national security affairs.[2] Such a journal, it is argued, could provide an outlet for scholarly articles that cannot be published in existing professional journals, publish important documents and information on work in progress in and out of the government, and provide an annotated bibliography on a regular basis of published material. The journal could possibly also serve as the basis for a new professional association that would give even more impetus to the development of a unified field of study and research.

Articles on national security affairs are now mainly published in the scholarly journals, the military journals, and a group of publications primarily concerned with problems of public policy. Among the scholarly journals, the *American Political Science Review* and the *American Historical Review* are generally receptive to articles on national security. But their space is limited and they must publish articles in many special fields within their disciplines. The military journals present a different problem. Supported by active organizations and by industrial advertising, they are monthly magazines devoted entirely to questions of national defense. But each of them—*Army*, *Air Force*, and the *Proceedings* of the U.S. Naval Institute—has its own special viewpoint of national security affairs. They emphasize the military aspect of national security, openly support the causes espoused by the services they represent, and print many technical articles of interest mainly to their professional military readers.

Journals devoted to public policy, especially in the field of foreign affairs, have been by far the most significant source of national security articles. Four of the five major journals in this category are attached to research organizations—*Foreign Affairs* to the Council on Foreign Relations, *World Politics* to the Princeton Center of International Studies, *Orbis* to the Foreign Policy Research Institute at the University of Pennsylvania, and *Conflict Resolution* to the Center for Research in Conflict Resolution at the University of Michigan. The fifth, the *Bulletin of the Atomic Scientists,* is the uniquely successful enterprise that began in Chicago in 1946 with those scientists who had worked on the Manhattan Project. The *Bulletin* is mainly concerned with science and technology in relation to national security, and *Conflict Resolution* is largely devoted to a behavioral approach. *Foreign Affairs, World Politics,* and *Orbis,* on the other hand, regard defense as an important aspect of current foreign policy but give scant attention to the domestic implications of defense, the complexities of the defense establishment itself, and historical studies.

While there is no single journal, then, that treats the many aspects of the field, it is not at all certain that the bulk of published material already facing the policy-maker and scholar should be increased, or that a professional journal is what is most needed to unify and strengthen the field. The quantity of research is no longer a problem, and the problem of bibliography, which is central, has been alleviated in several ways. Both the *American Political Science Review* and *Foreign Affairs* now list books, articles, and documents in their sections of book notes and bibliography. So does *Military Affairs,* which carries a bibliography of military publications. Extensive lists of current literature and research-in-progress on problems of war and peace have been published in *Current Thought on Peace and War;* similar lists are available through the State Department's Bureau of Research and the historical offices of the military services. Finally, the British Institute for Strategic Studies reprints documents and some of the most significant articles on national security from all over the world in its bi-monthly publication *Survival.*

Certainly scholars should strengthen their professional bonds, but this is no longer the crucial step toward further development of national security studies. It is the colleges and universities that must assume major responsibility for this development and guarantee stability to the field. Until now, financial support has come primarily from the private foundations and from government contracts. Government-sponsored projects are particularly weak support for long-range development of the field, since they are drawn up largely to serve the immediate needs of the contracting agency or policy-maker. Operating in a quasi-official capacity, a scholar may enjoy access to classified information and the satisfaction of knowing that his work will be used by a government agency and may affect important national policies. But these advantages may be offset by security restrictions on publication and, even under the most liberal policies, a sense of obligation to undertake research on "bread-and-butter" projects which hold no interest within his field and no real opportunity to develop national security studies within his institution.

The major source of support for university-based centers and institutions, however, has been the private foundation. The contribution of the universities has usually been limited to facilities and minimal services, and there is little indication that they are willing to assume a greater financial burden. Indeed, it may be said that as a matter of policy, college and university trustees refuse to support national security research as long as the possibility of foundation support exists as an alternative. Since, in almost all cases, foundation support is only for a limited period of time, the future of most of the national security programs is often in doubt, and their tentative financial status then affects the strength of national security studies within the academic structure.

The reliance on outside funds, whether foundation or government, also generates heavy competition for grants among the colleges and universities, and places control over the broad lines of research development in the hands of a small group of foundation executives or government officials. For the most part, they have wielded their power with a high sense of responsibility. The public official dispensing contracts has a limited choice in selecting areas of research, and the foundations have been increasingly sensitive to their role and intelligent in the administration of their bounty. They have consulted each other to avoid confusion and duplication; they have sought the advice and counsel of educators and statesmen; and some foundation officials, such as Kenneth Thompson at Rockefeller and James Perkins at Carnegie (until 1963), have contributed to the field in their own right. They certainly are concerned for the quality of research and are aware of the dangers that exist in the prevailing system of financing.

It is to be expected that these influences—professional, governmental, and foundation—will continue to be important in the growth of national security as a field of study. Professional association is important to academicians; policy-makers need the help of scholars and scientists; and the government and the foundations do not seem ready to abandon the responsibility they have assumed, even though foundation interest has shifted to other areas in recent years. The groundwork has been laid for making national security an accepted part of the regular academic program: for military history to take its place with intellectual and social history; for the economics of defense and disarmament to take its place with labor and agricultural economics; for military sociology to take its place with the study of the family and population problems. A literature now exists, and a professional community of scholars from the various disciplines is developing. It remains for institutions of higher education, particularly the graduate schools, to give the field depth and security by assuming responsibility for integrating national security studies into the disciplines and by providing the necessary financial support.

The Role of the Scholar and Scientist in Policy-Making

The problems of focus and financing relate primarily to the institutional means of maintaining and strengthening intellectual resources to assure a continual flow of talent—scholars and scientists—to staff the academic programs, research centers, research corporations, and government agencies that deal with national security affairs. A particular set of problems arises in the actual application of these resources to the needs of government in formulating and executing policy.

A major problem has been how to bring scholars and scientists into government. The personnel policies of the civil service make it difficult to recruit the kind of men who are needed, and the bureaucracy creates an environment that most academicians and intellectuals find restrictive. For these reasons, special arrangements—such as consultant contracts, ad hoc committees, the establishment of supergrades, special pay benefits, and advisory positions—are made to secure their services. But professors are still reluctant to leave regular academic or research posts except on a temporary basis, because to do so would deprive them of tenure and prejudice their professional standing. In a sense, the government-affiliated, nonprofit institutions like RAND and the Institute for Defense Analyses, which contract to do research and studies for the policy-maker, come closest to meeting the needs of both the government and the scholar. Working in a simulated academic environment, with high pay and liberal personnel policies, the scholar is freed from the traditional disciplinary organization of the university and is offered greater flexibility in approaching the complexity of national security problems. Yet, there is no assurance that their obligation to perform directed research provides the most fruitful atmosphere for scholarly or scientific creativity.

At the same time, the development of contract research and other special devices to utilize the best brains of the nation in the interests of national security has created problems of its own. With so much of the federal government's research performed by private agencies, the necessity for effective management and supervision of contracts becomes increasingly important—and more difficult to achieve. Moreover, contracting makes it even more difficult for the government to recruit the men it needs within the federal service; it creates a competitor for the services of men of talent and provides the funds that make it possible for the competitor to outbid the government or draw scholars away from the academic environment in which they may do their most creative work. More than that, the government supports a number of contract organizations that do similar work and may even work on the same projects. And each organization bids not only against the government and the universities, but against each other.

Clearly, the government must develop both the resources and the organization to carry out systematic analysis within its own agencies. The heavy dependence on outside consultants and organizations has been, in one way, evidence of the inadequacies of the career services to cope with cold war issues. This is not to say that all studies should be undertaken within the official departments and contract research be eliminated. The advantage of divergent viewpoints should be retained, not only to see that all feasible alternatives are examined, but also to insure that official views are continually challenged. It is the high proportion of contracted research, the inability of the government to absorb the fruits of research in the most effective way, and the effects of such research as well as huge government expenditures on independent scholarship and teaching that must be questioned.

Providing a favorable climate for research and reflection within the government is a continuing problem. Good minds are at a premium in any situation, and the press of operating requirements is such that men of intelligence and talent are always needed to help "put out the fires." This has been the history of the State Department's Policy Planning Council at various periods and, to some extent, of the secretariat developed to service the National Security Council. The problem can never be entirely solved since the primary function of government is essentially operational. The requirements of planning and evaluation are, however, more deeply understood than they were immediately after World War II, as, indeed, are the advantages. Nevertheless, experiments in organization for planning and evaluation will have to continue, as will recruitment and training for career officials to staff the agencies that are responsible for such functions.

We have already reviewed the increased sense of professionalism in national security affairs within the civilian career services. It would be no exaggeration to say that the challenges of the cold war have been among the major reasons for the expansion of government recruitment and training programs. Nor is it surprising that among the principal innovations in civilian preparation for advancement have been instruction in the issues of war and peace. Better planning organization, recruitment, and training are all part of the quest for greater professionalism in national security affairs in government. But the result will mean more than a development of an "in-house" capacity to deal with the flow of contracted research. Where there are government officials who are trained in the complexities of national security, there is bound to be a greater sense of understanding between the policy-maker and the scholar and greater appreciation of the limits of the scholar's role. Where government officials are not trained to deal with these problems, there is likely to be tension between the "doer" and the "thinker"; and the scholar is more apt to be drawn into taking a position or projecting his analysis beyond the evidence if there is no one in government who can interpret his objective findings in terms of the policy issue involved.

Increased professionalism among government officials in national security affairs will not itself completely clarify the role of the scholar or scientist in policy-making. The scholar or scientist in government, whether he serves as political appointee, temporary consultant, or even career official, will continue to have to distinguish between his role as expert and his part in the policy process. The role of the expert is to clarify choices, and the role of the policy-maker is to participate in the process through which choices are made. The line between "clarifying" and "making" choices is often difficult to maintain, and one of the important features of national security policy has been the extent to which expertise is brought directly into the political process and heavy reliance placed on technical analysis in the choice of objectives and strategies. In this kind of situation, it is of little value to caution the intellectual and the policy-maker to respect each other's role and limit their own involvement to prescribed functions. More often, the functions overlap and the objectivity to which the scholar and the scientist rightly attach so much importance visibly diminishes with personal involvement. By force of engagement and commitment, scholarship can easily become mixed with value judgments and subconscious biases and be molded to fit preconceived attitudes and notions.

These dangers of personal commitment are as evident in research conducted outside government as they are among intellectuals who find themselves in positions of political sensitivity. The pressures of the problems being what they are, there is a strong tendency for national security research to be oriented to current policy issues and for the product of the scholar, whether he intended it or not, to be used in support of policy. Where the scholar deliberately chooses to work on current policy in an effort to influence a decision, he is stretching his role as expert dangerously. Moreover, if he is not working under government sponsorship, he is attempting to write authoritatively about policy without the data available to the responsible officials. The result may be neither scholarly nor useful. Yet, cloaked in the garb of scholarship and backed by academic respectability and even distinction, the work may carry more weight than it deserves. Fed into the policy process, it may have an unfortunate effect on the choice of policies adopted; or, in the political process, it may be used for partisan purposes with the same result. Such research, therefore, can be a disservice to both policy and scholarship.

But these dangers do not nullify the function of scholarship in national security affairs, any more than they suggest that the solution is to bar intellectuals from influencing policy; they only underscore the importance of objectivity and careful selection of appropriate areas of research. The contribution of the intellectual to policy rests not only on his objectivity and accuracy, but also on the quality of his mind and level of his analysis. The scholar or scientist who enters into a direct relationship with government must, however, recognize that, at some point, he is likely to find himself more an "advocate" than an "expert," caught up in the process of "making" choices.

The private and university-based centers and institutes that have developed since World War II have had to deal with the temptations of competing with the policy-maker, of trying to make policy for the government. Many have sought to avoid this temptation by defining their role in terms of the long-range issues and forces affecting national security and by avoiding the immediate crises. In dealing with these fundamental factors, there is less press of time and less dependence on privileged information. They are thus more appropriate subjects for scholarly inquiry, though the results may still help the policy-maker by defining the broad limits within which decisions must be made.

We have already described the approach and general areas of research of the major centers and institutes throughout the country. Some, like the Michigan Center for Research on Conflict Resolution, emphasize the development of a distinctive methodology, and others, like the Princeton Center of International Studies, encourage a variety of approaches in their fields of interest, from policy issues to theoretical advances. The published results of their scholarship in the field of national security are diverse also. They may be said to fall into four general groups, two that are policy-oriented and two more oriented to theory and process.[3] First are those works that deal with the larger problems of national security in their immediate context and may advocate one or more policies or strategies. The writings of Henry Kissinger and Herman Kahn are examples of this type. Each has dealt with the immediate problems of integrating nuclear weapons and long-range delivery systems into strategic doctrine, but has encompassed a broader canvas than could be covered in a staff study written under operational stress. Special policy studies, as distinguished from general policy studies, constitute a second type. Such studies focus on a particular aspect of national security and treat it in more detail, usually within its historical setting. Examples of this type are the work of Harry Ransom and Roger Hilsman on intelligence operations and Raymond Garthoff and Herbert Dinerstein on Soviet military policy.

Scholarship in the two remaining groups is less related to policy. Studies of strategic theory, for example, represent an effort to abstract and generalize strategy in much the same way that economists develop economic theory by generalizing experience. The works of Thomas Schelling of Harvard and Morton Kaplan of Chicago illustrate this type. Finally, there are the studies that deal with political processes by which policy is made, that is, with the institutions, groups, and attitudes that shape national security policy. The scholarly work that falls under this group—for example, the work of Huntington and Janowitz—includes purely historical studies and analyses of a single decision by the case-study method. For many, these last two approaches are the most appropriate ways for scholars to contribute to a better understanding of national security policy. They deal with subjects that are "researchable" and for which data are usually available and open; they avoid special advocacy; and they explore basic concepts, relationships, and forces rather than immediate issues.

The study of theory and process deals, in effect, with the same forces with which the policy-maker must contend, but it avoids being caught up in controversy and politics. It is in his work on policy issues, however, that the scholar can most effectively contribute as a critic, and the role of critic is particularly important in the light of the nature of American politics. National parties are fragmented and decentralized, and political programs have no doctrinal base. They are thus dealt with in a pragmatic fashion, and it is difficult, if not impossible, within the party and legislative systems, to develop a broad strategic program in opposition to Administration policy. Opposition leaders in Congress can criticize, modify or sometimes defeat particular programs, but more is needed to offer policy alternatives. The national security debate during the Eisenhower Administration is illustrative. Opposition to the policy of "massive retaliation" came from two major sources: from certain elements within the executive branch, particularly the Army; and from groups of research scholars, journalists, and other intellectuals, many of them members of study centers and institutes. The opposition from the Army was part of the legislative struggle within the government. The Army could not, however, develop a firm theoretical basis for its position nor a broad base of public support. This was the task of the outside critics, and their efforts were highly influential in the change to a more flexible strategy by the early 1960's.

One of the most immediate and penetrating attacks on the massive retaliation doctrine was contained in an essay entitled "The Requirements of Deterrence," by William W. Kaufmann. Originally published as a monograph by the Princeton Center of International Studies, it was later included in an influential book written by several scholars at the Center and edited by Kaufmann himself.[4] In 1957, two books were published that continued the attack in depth. The first, *Limited War*, by Robert E. Osgood, was written under the auspices of the Center for the Study of American Foreign and Military Policy at the University of Chicago. Osgood, through reference to historical situations and through careful analysis, demonstrated the need to limit war as the only way to insure what he called "the principle of political primacy." In the months following its publication, Osgood's book was frequently quoted in the influential column of Hanson Baldwin, military analyst for *The New York Times*. The second book, *Nuclear Weapons and Foreign Policy*, by Henry A. Kissinger, was the product of a study group of the Council on Foreign Relations. Its publication had already been anticipated by the appearance of several chapters as articles in *Foreign Affairs*. The scope and forcefulness of the analysis, and the authority and prestige of its sponsorship, made it an extraordinarily important contribution to the debate on national strategy.

To the influence of the Council on Foreign Relations there was shortly added that of the Rockefeller Brothers Fund. The Rockefeller study group had been set up by Nelson Rockefeller shortly after he left the Eisenhower Administration in 1957. Rockefeller was concerned that the dominant forces in the Administration were imposing arbitrary financial restrictions on strategic programs and ignoring the non-military aspects of national security policy. He therefore decided to use the Fund to organize a group to take a hard look at America at mid-century. Like the Council project, the panel brought together by Rockefeller included an important group of citizens, among them Adolf A. Berle, Jr., Arthur F. Burns, John W. Gardner, and Dean Rusk. The executive secretary for the study program was Kissinger, who was again in an extraordinary position of influence. One of the first reports issued by the panel was on "International Security: the Military Aspect." Like Kissinger's volume, it called for a balanced strategic program that provided for a variety of conflict situations. And like all of the earlier works, it raised the problems of national security to a high level of intellectual and political debate.[5]

The entry of the scholar into what was once regarded as the domain of the military profession marks a significant change in the role of the civilian in the formulation of national strategy. Since there is no experience with nuclear warfare and only very limited opportunities for testing new weapons systems, much of the thinking about future warfare is of necessity theoretical. And because of the complexity of translating military power into political terms, the greatest use must be made of any intellectual tools that can ease the task of making difficult choices. These conditions place a premium on the talents of the scholar who more than any others in our society is skilled in theoretical analysis and the use of intellectual tools. Thus, the decade of the 1950's witnessed the increased importance of the intellectual in strategy-making and an accompanying decline in the once predominant role of the military in this field. The work of Kissinger, Osgood, Brodie, Huntington, and others provides ample testimony of the importance of scholarship in national security affairs.

The utility of national security studies is, of course, no testimony to their scholarship. Many are polemical, written in haste to capitalize on superficial trends rather than important underlying issues. Moreover, the responsibility of political utility can be a serious burden to a scholar. The success of scholarship may come to depend on its timeliness and impact in the policy process. In order to be sure that his work comes to the attention of those in positions of influence, the writer may resort to techniques of exploitation that are inconsistent with scholarly research. Certainly scholars in important fields of public policy cannot afford to live in ivory towers—for their sake and for the sake of society in which they live—but their own role is apt to be debased and made less unique and meaningful if their standards deteriorate under the pressures of short-range policy-making.

Again, this expression of dangers should not be construed as an argument against the involvement of scholars and scientists in the total process of decision-making in our society—and by the "total process" we mean the development of public opinion, the influence of interest groups, and the legislative struggle, as well as the policy machinery of the executive branch. It is difficult to specify, in time and participation, when and how major shifts in national security policy have occurred since 1945. But certainly, as in the case of the acceptance of a doctrine of limited war, intellectuals have played an important and even critical role in the process of articulation, debate, and persuasion through which change must occur in an open society. This was equally demonstrated in the development of the concept of arms control and its acceptance as a major aspect of American policy.

Like limited war, arms control has been a response to changes in the international system, in the relative power of the Soviet Union and the United States, and in the technology of war. But the process of conceptualization was an essential contribution that scholars and scientists made. Their motives were varied. Some started from an emotional disillusionment with a strategy of deterrence and an urge to contribute to peace; others began from an intellectual understanding of the limits and dangers of deterrence under conditions of parity with the Soviet Union and a diffusion of power in the world. Different motives and different assessments of the international situation have not prevented intellectuals from agreeing on the need for controls, for encouraging more research in the problems involved, and for creating both the intellectual and political atmosphere for a new kind of public receptivity for arms control as part of official policy. It is difficult to say whether the theories of limited war and arms control would have developed and been accepted without the contributions of scholars and scientists, just as it would be difficult to assert that scholars and scientists were responsible for their growth and adoption. It is enough to note the great part played by intellectuals and the significant change that this participation suggests in their involvement in our society.

The dangers of policy involvement are closely related to the need to integrate national security studies into the traditional disciplines of history and the social sciences. The needs of the policy-maker will be met if national security becomes part of the contemporary development of these fields. The literature will continue to grow in scope and wisdom; educational and training material will be available; young civil servants and the attentive public will be confronted, in a systematic way, with the issues of war and peace; and the intellectual framework within which decisions must be made will be continually refined and clarified by scholarly research. If, on the other hand, national security affairs becomes little more than an area for government-sponsored policy studies and polemical journalism, there will be little growth within the processes of education or research to meet these continuing and deeper purposes. The fact is that the most effective way to serve policy is by the development of intellectual resources, and intellectual resources will develop most richly and well if national security studies respond to the highest kind of scholarship —not merely to the changing crises of policy.

Notes

Introduction

1. See Bureau of Intelligence and Research, Department of State, *Arms Control and Disarmament*, ACD-1, May, 1963; *Current Thought on Peace and War*, I, No. 1 (Winter, 1960); and Colonel W. C. McDonald and Captain L. J. Larsen, *National Security Policy: Some Observations on Its Place in the American University* (mimeographed; Boulder: U.S. Air Force Academy).

2. U.S. Arms Control and Disarmament Agency, Agency Circular No. 8 (Revised), *Guide for the Submission of Proposals for and Administration of Research Grants*, July 25, 1963.

Chapter 1: National Security: Challenge and Response

1. For a discussion of the prewar decade and World War II, see Walter Millis, with Harvey C. Mansfield and Harold Stein, *Arms and the State* (New York: Twentieth Century Fund, 1958), especially Part I, by Mansfield and Stein. For the interwar period, see also Louis Morton, "War Plan Orange: Evolution of a Strategy," *World Politics*, XI, No. 2 (January, 1959), 221 ff.

2. Commission on Organization of the Executive Branch of the Government, *The National Security Organization, A Report to the Congress*, February, 1949, pp. 2–3.

3. *Report of the Rockefeller Committee on Department of Defense Organization*, Committee on Armed Services, U.S. Senate, 83d Cong., 1st sess., 1953, p. 1.

4. For a discussion of the "civilianization" of the military and the "militarization" of the civilian, see Gene M. Lyons, "The New Civil-Military Relations," *American Political Science Review*, LV, No. 1 (March, 1961), 53–63.

5. Lyons, *loc. cit.* Another reflection of this changing relation is the broadening character of the military profession. See John W. Masland and Laurence I. Radway, *Soldiers and Scholars* (Princeton, N.J.: Princeton University Press, 1957); Gene M. Lyons and John W. Masland, *Education and Military Leadership* (Princeton, N.J.: Princeton University Press, 1959); and Morris Janowitz, *The Professional Soldier* (Chicago, Ill.: The Free Press of Glencoe, 1960).

6. For the relevance of history to present problems of national security, see Louis Morton, "Historia Mentem Armet," *World Politics*, XII, No. 2 (January, 1960), 155 ff.

7. For an early and critical analysis of the doctrine of massive retaliation, see William W. Kaufmann, "The Requirements of Deterrence" in William W. Kaufmann (ed.), *Military Policy and National Security* (Princeton, N.J.: Princeton University Press, 1956), pp. 12–38.

8. The complexity of the limited war problem is underscored by Henry A. Kissinger's reappraisal of his earlier advocacy of limited nuclear war. "Limited War: Conventional or Nuclear? A Reappraisal," *Daedalus* (Special Issue on Arms Control), Fall, 1960, pp. 800–817. See also Louis Morton, "The Twin Essentials of Limited War," *Army*, XI, No. 6 (January, 1961), 47–49.

9. See the interview with President Kennedy reported by Stewart Alsop, "Kennedy's Grand Strategy," *Saturday Evening Post*, March 31, 1962.

10. The case for increased invulnerability has been stated most completely by Oskar Morgenstern, *The Question of National Defense* (New York: Random House, 1959). Arms control has been the subject for a number of books in recent years. Among them are: *Daedalus* (Special Issue on Arms Control); Thomas C. Schelling and Morton H. Halperin, *Strategy and Arms Control* (New York: Twentieth Century Fund, 1961); David H. Frisch (ed.), *Arms Reduction: Program and Issues* (New York: Twentieth Century Fund, 1961); Hedley Bull, *The*

Control of the Arms Race (New York: Frederick A. Praeger, 1962); Richard J. Barnet, *Who Wants Disarmament?* (Boston: Beacon Press, 1960).

11. The *Hearings*, Subcommittee on National Policy Machinery, Committee on Government Operations, U.S. Senate, 86th Cong., 2d sess., and 87th Cong., 1st sess., 1960 and 1961, offer a clear description of the operations of the National Security Council and its subordinate units. See particularly Parts IV, V, and VI.

12. *Ibid.*, communication from McGeorge Bundy, Part IX, pp. 1335–38.

13. E. R. Piore and R. N. Kreidler, "Recent Developments in the Relation of Government to Science," *The Annals of the American Academy of Political and Social Science*, Vol. 327 (January, 1960), especially pp. 15–18. See also *Science Organization and the President's Office*, Subcommittee on National Policy Machinery, Committee on Government Operations, U.S. Senate, 87th Cong., 1st sess., 1961. In 1962, President Kennedy recommended that an Office of Science and Technology be established; while the President's Special Assistant would become Director of the office, the role of the PSAC would not be changed (Reorganization Plan No. 2 of 1962).

14. The Kennedy Administration sought to solve the first of these problems by establishing a Disarmament Administration within the State Department in 1961. For a critical analysis of the situation until that point, see the report by the National Planning Association, Special Project Committee on Security Through Arms Control, *Strengthening the Government for Arms Control*. Reprinted as 86th Cong., 2d sess., Senate Document 123, 1960.

15. It is important to note that most top-ranking scientists are quite aware of how unrealistic it can be to try to separate the scientific and political strands of controversial issues. See, for example, the testimony of Dr. James B. Fisk before the Subcommittee on National Policy Machinery, Committee on Government Operations, U.S. Senate, 86th Cong., 2d sess., 1960, Part II, pp. 304 ff.

16. For a broad review of the organization and administration of the Department of State, see *The Formulation and Administration of United States Foreign Policy*, prepared by the Brookings Institution at the request of the Committee on Foreign Relations, U.S. Senate, 86th Cong., 2d sess., 1960.

17. Gene M. Lyons, "The New Civil-Military Relations."

18. For perceptive statements on the policy process, see Richard E. Neustadt, *Presidential Power: The Politics of Leadership* (New York: John Wiley & Sons, 1960); Samuel P. Huntington, "Strategic Programs and the Policy Process," *Foreign Affairs*, 38, No. 2 (January, 1960), 285–99; and Roger Hilsman, "Congressional-Executive Relations and the Foreign Policy Consensus," *American Political Science Review*, LII, No. 3 (September, 1958), 725–44.

19. For a summary of possible innovations, see Walter Millis, *The Constitution and the Common Defense* (New York: Fund for the Republic, 1959), pp. 33 ff. For a specific proposal that seems to reflect the opinion of a number of important scholars in this field, see Roger Hilsman, "Planning for National Security: A Proposal," *Bulletin of the Atomic Scientists*, XVI, No. 3 (March, 1960), 93 ff. See also Senator Jackson's final statement in the study by the Subcommittee on National Policy Machinery, Committee on Government Operations, U.S. Senate, 87th Cong., 1st sess., 1961, p. 2.

20. See Henry A. Kissinger, *The Necessity for Choice* (New York: Harper & Brothers, 1961), pp. 340 ff. Also Max F. Millikan, "Inquiry and Policy: The Relation of Knowledge to Action" in Daniel Lerner (ed.), *The Human Meaning of the Social Sciences* (Gloucester, Mass.: Peter Smith, 1959).

21. For a discussion of the variables in the appointment process as applied to

Cabinet posts, see Ralph F. Fenno, Jr., *The President's Cabinet* (Cambridge: Harvard University Press, 1959), especially Chapter 2, pp. 51–67.

22. This evidence is based on interim findings by the Brookings Institution in its study of the selection of federal political executives. See also Dean E. Mann, *Federal Political Executives: Problems and Processes of Selection*, prepared for delivery at the International Conference on Public Personnel Administration, October 23–27, 1960 (mimeographed).

23. For a discussion of the difference between "presidential" and "program" responsibility, see Wallace S. Sayre, *The Political Executive in the National Government: The Constitutional and Political Setting*, prepared for the Conference on the Political Executive, Woodrow Wilson School of Public and International Affairs, Princeton University, 1956, pp. 23–24 (mimeographed).

24. Several essays that are pertinent to this topic can be found in Joseph E. McLean (ed.), *The Public Service and University Education* (Princeton, N.J.: Princeton University Press, 1949), especially those by Donald Stone, George Kennan, Paul Appleby, Rowland Egger, and James Forrestal. Note also the second Hoover Commission's recommendations for a "senior civil service": Commission on Organization of the Executive Branch of the Government, *Report of Task Force on Personnel and Civil Service*, 1955.

25. In developing the concept of the expert in national security affairs, no attempt is made to suggest that national security is a "policy science" in the Lasswellian sense. Our efforts are more modest. Nevertheless, like many others, we have found the "policy science" thesis stimulating. See Daniel Lerner and Harold Lasswell (eds.), *The Policy Sciences* (Stanford, Calif.: Stanford University Press, 1951).

26. See Gabriel A. Almond, *The American People and Foreign Policy* (New York: Harcourt, Brace, 1950). (Republished with a new introduction in 1961 by Frederick A. Praeger, New York.) The terms "general mood" and "attentive public" are borrowed from Almond.

Chapter 2: The Growth of National Security Research

1. Harold Lasswell, *World Politics and Personal Insecurity* (New York: McGraw-Hill, 1935). It was, perhaps, a sign of the times that this book was republished in 1950.

2. Quincy Wright, *A Study of War* (2 vols.; Chicago, Ill.: University of Chicago Press, 1942; abridged ed., 1964).

3. See Sir Halford J. MacKinder, *Democratic Ideals and Reality* (New York: Henry Holt, 1942), for a complete statement of his views.

4. Nicholas J. Spykman, *America's Strategy in World Politics* (New York: Harcourt, Brace, 1942); George T. Davis, *A Navy Second to None* (New York: Harcourt, Brace, 1940); Arnold Wolfers, *Britain and France Between Two Wars* (New York: Harcourt, Brace, 1940).

5. Hans Speier and Alfred Kahlir (eds.), *War in Our Time* (New York: W. W. Norton, 1939).

6. Edward Meade Earle (ed.), *Makers of Modern Strategy* (Princeton, N.J.: Princeton University Press, 1943); Harold and Margaret Sprout, *The Rise of American Naval Power, 1776–1918* (Princeton, N.J.: Princeton University Press, 1939) and *Toward a New Order of Sea Power* (Princeton, N.J.: Princeton University Press, 1940); and Bernard Brodie, *Sea Power in the Machine Age* (Princeton, N.J.: Princeton University Press, 1941).

7. Grayson Kirk and Richard Stebbins, *War and National Policy: A Syllabus* (New York: Farrar & Rinehart, 1942).

8. E. Pendleton Herring, *The Impact of War* (New York: Farrar & Rinehart, 1941).

9. *Civil-Military Relations: Bibliographical Notes on Administrative Problems of Civilian Mobilization* (Chicago, Ill.: Public Administration Service, 1940). The bibliography was brought up to date in 1954 by the SSRC Committee on Civil-Military Relations Research: *Civil-Military Relations: An Annotated Bibliography, 1940–1952* (New York: Columbia University Press, 1954).

10. J. D. Clarkson and Thomas C. Cochran (eds.), *War as a Social Institution* (New York: Columbia University Press, 1941).

11. For a review of activities on the management of the war effort, see *The United States at War* (Washington, D.C.: Bureau of the Budget, 1946); for a review of the planning for the United Nations, see Harley A. Notter, *Postwar Foreign Policy Preparation, 1939–1945* (Washington, D.C.: U.S. Department of State, 1949).

12. Among the editors during the early years were Leland M. Goodrich (chairman), Rupert Emerson, William T. R. Fox, Edgar S. Furniss, Grayson Kirk, Charles P. Kindleberger, John W. Masland, Norman J. Padelford, and Walter R. Sharp.

13. On the development of research in national security, see William T. R. Fox, "Civil-Military Relations Research: The SSRC Committee on Its Research Survey," *World Politics*, VI, No. 2 (January, 1954), 278–88; Laurence I. Radway, *The Study of Military Affairs*, prepared for delivery at the 1958 Annual Meeting of the American Political Science Association (mimeographed); and the *Summary of Proceedings* (mimeographed) of two conferences held under the auspices of the Committee on National Security Policy Research of the Social Science Research Council, the first on June 24–26, 1957, at Dartmouth College, Hanover, New Hampshire, and the second on June 17–19, 1959, at the U.S. Military Academy, West Point, New York. For a review and evaluation of research on foreign policy, see Philip E. Mosely, "Research on Foreign Policy," in *Research for Public Policy* (Washington, D.C.: Brookings Institution, 1961).

14. William T. R. Fox, *The Super-Powers: The U.S., Britain, and the Soviet Union—Their Responsibility for Peace* (New York: Harcourt, Brace, 1944); Bernard Brodie (ed.), *The Absolute Weapon* (New York: Harcourt, Brace, 1946).

15. For a description of the role of scientists, see Robert Gilpin, *American Scientists and Nuclear Weapons Policy* (Princeton, N.J.: Princeton University Press, 1962).

16. *Military Situation in the Far East*, Committee on Armed Services and Committee on Foreign Relations, U.S. Senate, 82d Cong., 1st sess., 1951, Parts I–V; *Hearings on S. Concurrent Resolution 8 Relative to the Assignment of Ground Forces . . . to the European Area*, Committee on Foreign Relations and Committee on Armed Services, U.S. Senate, 82d Cong., 1st sess., 1951; U.S. Atomic Energy Commission, *In the Matter of J. Robert Oppenheimer; Transcript of Hearings before Personnel Security Board*, Washington, D.C., 1954.

17. Some of the books published by this group were: George F. Kennan, *American Diplomacy, 1900–1950* (Chicago, Ill.: University of Chicago Press, 1951); Louis Halle, *Civilization and Foreign Policy* (New York: Harper & Brothers, 1955); Charles B. Marshall, *The Limits of Foreign Policy* (New York: Holt, 1954); Dorothy Fosdick, *Common Sense and World Affairs* (New York:

Harcourt, Brace, 1955); John J. McCloy, *The Challenge to American Foreign Policy* (Cambridge, Mass.: Harvard University Press, 1953); Thomas K. Finletter, *Power and Policy* (New York: Harcourt, Brace, 1954); and Dean Acheson, *Power and Diplomacy* (Cambridge, Mass.: Harvard University Press, 1958). See also Acheson's foreword to Halle's book for an interesting, if reluctant, acknowledgment of the relation of theory to practice in foreign affairs.

18. This series, published by the government, was under the general editorial direction of Kent Roberts Greenfield during this period.

19. Although the Gaither Committee's report was never made public, the essence of its findings (that the United States was not exerting itself in the defense effort as forcefully as it should) was leaked to several sources. See Morton H. Halperin, "The Gaither Committee and the Policy Process," *World Politics*, XIII, No. 3 (April, 1961), 360–84.

20. *Review of Foreign Policy, 1958*, Committee on Foreign Relations, U.S. Senate, 85th Cong., 2d sess., 1958, Parts I-IV.

21. The studies made by these groups were issued by the Senate Committee on Foreign Relations, 86th Cong., 1st sess. (1959) and 2d sess. (1960). See also Jay H. Cerf and Walter Pozen (eds.), *Strategy for the 60's*, a summary and analysis of the studies, with an introduction by Senator J. W. Fulbright (New York: Frederick A. Praeger, 1961). Senator Fulbright points out that "U.S. policies may be strengthened by the Committee [on Foreign Relations] if it is in a position to test these policies against views which may not always correspond to those held by the Department [of State]." Among the groups that participated in this review were: Council on Foreign Relations; Stanford Research Institute; Foreign Policy Research Institute, University of Pennsylvania; Program of African Studies, Northwestern University; Maxwell School of Citizenship and Public Affairs, Syracuse University; Washington Center of Foreign Policy Research; The Brookings Institution; Center for International Affairs, Harvard University; Russian Institute, Columbia University; and Center for International Studies, M.I.T.

22. See, for example, Richard Rovere, *The American Establishment and Other Reports: Opinions and Speculations* (New York: Harcourt, Brace & World, 1962), for a friendly but nonetheless cutting suggestion that these men make up an American Establishment.

Chapter 3: History and the Social Sciences

1. For a summary and bibliography of the literature on national security, see Samuel P. Huntington (ed.), *Changing Patterns of Military Politics* (New York: The Free Press of Glencoe, 1962), pp. 235 ff.

2. This section, with minor modifications, was published separately in *The Mississippi Valley Historical Review*, XLVIII, No. 4 (March, 1962), 599–613.

3. See John Bowditch, "War and the Historian" in H. Stuart Hughes (ed.), *Teachers of History: Essays in Honor of Laurence Bradford Packard* (Ithaca, N.Y.: Cornell University Press, 1954), pp. 322–23.

4. Richard C. Brown, *The Teaching of Military History in Colleges and Universities of the United States* (U.S. Air Force Historical Division, Research Studies Institute, *Historical Studies*, No. 124, Air University, 1955). There is no evidence that the situation had changed much by 1964.

5. Brown, *ibid.*, p. 23.

6. Brown, *ibid.*, p. 15. The three courses were those taught by Professor Gordon B. Turner at Princeton ("A History of Military Affairs in Western Society since the Eighteenth Century"), Professor William R. Emerson at Yale

("War and Western Society"), and Professors Horace Montgomery and Wilbur D. Jones at the University of Georgia ("American Military History").

7. T. Harry Williams, Richard N. Current, and Frank Freidel, A History of the United States (2 vols.; New York: Alfred A. Knopf, 1959).

8. Harry J. Carman, Harold C. Syrett, and Bernard Wishy, A History of the American People (rev. ed., 2 vols.; New York: Alfred A. Knopf, 1960–61); Dumas Malone and Basil Rauch, Empire for Liberty (2 vols.; New York: Appleton-Century-Crofts, 1960); Richard Hofstadter, William Miller, and Daniel Aaron, The American Republic (2 vols.; Englewood Cliffs, N.J.: Prentice-Hall, 1959). Economic history texts are also giving increased attention to the impact of war. See, for example, Seymour E. Harris (ed.), American Economic History (New York: McGraw-Hill, 1961), pp. 207–237.

9. Samuel Flagg Bemis, A Short History of American Foreign Policy and Diplomacy (rev. ed.; New York: Holt, Rinehart and Winston, 1959), p. 695.

10. Julius W. Pratt, A History of United States Foreign Policy (Englewood Cliffs, N.J.: Prentice-Hall, 1955), p. vii.

11. Louis Morton, "Sources for the History of World War II," World Politics, XIII (April, 1961), 435–53.

12. Brown, Teaching of Military History, pp. 15–16. The five graduate courses were: "Problems in the History of World War II," Gordon Prange, University of Maryland; "Military History and Problems," Gordon B. Turner, Princeton University; "Problems of Sea Power," A. E. Sokol, Stanford University; "Military History of the Civil War," Gordon T. Chappell, Huntingdon College; and "The First World War," Hardin Craig, Jr., Rice Institute. Combined graduate-undergraduate courses were offered at Duke University, Temple University, Louisiana State University, the University of Michigan, and the University of Missouri.

13. George L. Gropper and Robert Fitzpatrick, Who Goes to Graduate School? (Pittsburgh: American Institute for Research, September, 1959), Table, p. 49. Of those responding to a questionnaire given to a representative selection of graduate students, 20 per cent of the political science students planned to enter government or business and 66 per cent teaching, as compared to 2 per cent in history and 1 per cent in English who hoped for a career in government and business. Ninety per cent of the graduate students in history and 94 per cent in English planned to teach; only 42 per cent of the psychology graduate students and 38 per cent of the physicists expected to enter an academic career.

14. See Corinne Lathrop Gilb, "Should We Learn More about Ourselves?" American Historical Review, XLVI (July, 1961), 987–93.

15. See, for example, Walter Millis, Military History (Service Center for Teachers of History, Publication No. 39, American Historical Association, 1961), p. 16; and his Arms and Men (New York: G. P. Putnam's Sons, 1958), p. 7.

16. See Louis Morton, "The Writing of Official History," Army, XI (May, 1961), 38–39.

17. See Charles S. Hyneman, The Study of Politics (Urbana, Ill.: University of Illinois Press, 1959); Emmette S. Redford, "Reflections on a Discipline," American Political Science Review, LV, No. 4 (December, 1961), 755 ff.

18. For full discussion of the behaviorist controversy, see Bernard Crick, The American Science of Politics (Berkeley, Calif.: University of California Press, 1959); Heinz Eulau, "Political Science," in Bert F. Hoselitz (ed.), A Reader's Guide to the Social Sciences (Chicago, Ill.: The Free Press of Glencoe, 1959); Robert A. Dahl, "The Behavioral Approach," American Political Science Review, LV, No. 4 (December, 1961), 763 ff.

19. Richard E. Neustadt, *Presidential Power;* Elias Huzar, *The Purse and the Sword* (Ithaca, N.Y.: Cornell University Press, 1950); Robert A. Dahl, *Congress and Foreign Policy* (New York: Harcourt, Brace & World, 1950); Holbert N. Carroll, *The House of Representatives and Foreign Affairs* (Pittsburgh, Pa.: University of Pittsburgh Press, 1958).

20. Among more recent books the following might be noted: James L. Mc-Camy, *The Administration of American Foreign Affairs* (New York: Alfred A. Knopf, 1950); Arthur W. MacMahon, *Administration in Foreign Affairs* (University, Ala.: University of Alabama Press, 1953); Don K. Price, *Government and Science* (New York: New York University Press, 1954); William R. Kintner *et al.*, *Forging a New Sword* (New York: Harper & Brothers, 1958); Paul Y. Hammond, *Organizing for Defense* (Princeton, N.J.: Princeton University Press, 1961).

21. These advances in administrative science and sociology are illustrated by works such as Chester Barnard, *The Functions of the Executive* (Cambridge, Mass.: Harvard University Press, 1938); George Homans, *The Human Group* (New York: Harcourt, Brace, 1950); and the books of Herbert Simon. See Eulau, "Political Science," in Hoselitz, *A Reader's Guide to the Social Sciences*, for a description of these developments.

22. See Harold Stein, *Public Policy and Public Administration* (New York: Harcourt, Brace, 1952).

23. The Twentieth Century Fund cases were published by the University of Alabama Press in 1963. For the Columbia studies, see Warner R. Schilling, Paul Y. Hammond, Glenn H. Snyder, *Strategies, Budgets, and Defense Politics* (New York: Columbia University Press, 1962). See also Samuel P. Huntington, *The Common Defense* (New York: Columbia University Press, 1962).

24. Among these studies are: Burton M. Sapin and Richard C. Snyder, *The Role of the Military in American Foreign Policy* (Garden City, N.Y.: Doubleday, 1954); Samuel P. Huntington, *The Soldier and the State* (Cambridge, Mass.: Belknap Press, 1957); Walter Millis, Harvey C. Mansfield, and Harold Stein, *Arms and the State;* John W. Masland and Laurence I. Radway, *Soldiers and Scholars;* and Morris Janowitz, *The Professional Soldier.*

25. Robert K. Carr, *et al.*, *American Democracy in Theory and Practice* (New York: Henry Holt & Co., 1951; rev. ed., 1961).

26. James M. Burns and Jack W. Peltason, *Government by the People* (Englewood Cliffs, N.J.: Prentice-Hall, 1952; rev. ed., 1960).

27. Frederick Schuman, *International Politics* (New York: McGraw-Hill, 1933); Edward H. Carr, *The Twenty Years' Crisis, 1919–1939* (New York: St. Martin's Press, 1939).

28. Richard N. Swift, *World Affairs and the College Curriculum* (Washington: American Council on Education, 1959), pp. 113–14. Swift relies heavily on Grayson Kirk's 1947 study on the teaching of international relations.

29. *Ibid.*, pp. 118–19.

30. Hans J. Morgenthau, *Politics Among Nations* (New York: Alfred A. Knopf, 1948; rev. ed., 1960).

31. For a criticism of "ambiguity," see Stanley H. Hoffmann, *Contemporary Theory in International Relations* (Englewood Cliffs, N.J.: Prentice-Hall, 1960), pp. 30–38; for the criticism that Morgenthau's power concept condones the use of force, see Frank Tannenbaum, *The American Tradition in Foreign Policy* (Norman, Okla.: University of Oklahoma Press, 1955).

32. See Quincy Wright, *The Study of International Relations* (New York:

Appleton-Century-Crofts, 1955), for a complete analysis of the problems and progress of the study of international relations.

33. Wendell C. Bennett, *Area Studies in American Universities* (New York: Social Science Research Council, 1951). Other discussions may be found in Marshall K. Powers, "Area Studies," *Journal of Higher Education*, XXVI, No. 2 (February, 1955), 82–89; J.-B. Duroselle, "Area Studies: Problems of Methods," and Hans J. Morgenthau, "Area Studies and the Study of International Relations," *International Social Science Bulletin*, IV, No. 4 (December, 1952), 636–55; L. Gray Cowan, A *History of the School of International Relations* (New York: Columbia University Press, 1954); Harlan Cleveland, "The Vices and Virtues of Area Studies," paper read at the 46th National Foreign Trade Convention, November, 1959.

34. *International Social Science Bulletin*, IV, No. 4 (December, 1952), 63.

35. Department of State, Bureau of Intelligence and Research, *Foreign Affairs Research: Projects and Centers: External Research Report*, ER-44, November, 1960.

36. The description of Huntington's course is based on the syllabus for the autumn term, 1959–60; of Greene's course, on the syllabus for the spring term, 1960–61.

37. Henry Kissinger, *Nuclear Weapons and Foreign Policy* (New York: Harper and Brothers, 1957); John Spanier, *American Foreign Policy Since World War II* (New York: Frederick A. Praeger, 1960).

38. Klaus Knorr, *The War Potential of Nations* (Princeton, N.J.: Princeton University Press, 1956), p. vii.

39. Max F. Millikan and Donald L. M. Blackmer (eds.), *The Emerging Nations* (Boston: Little, Brown, 1961), p. v.

40. Arthur Smithies, *The Budgetary Process in the United States* (New York: McGraw-Hill, 1955).

41. See Kenneth E. Boulding, *et al.*, *Economic Factors Bearing Upon the Maintenance of Peace*, Program of Research No. 2, Parts I-V, The Institute for International Order, 1961. In Part II, Professor Benoit sets out a program of research on the "Economic Adjustments to Disarmament." He and Professor Boulding then continued their research under a grant from the Carnegie Corporation of New York to the Center for Research in Conflict Resolution at the University of Michigan (see Chapter 9 for a description of the Center).

42. Thomas C. Schelling, *The Strategy of Conflict* (Cambridge, Mass.: Harvard University Press, 1960).

43. Social Science Research Council Conference, *Economic Research on National Security*, A *Report* (mimeo.; New York: 1958).

44. Charles J. Hitch, "National Security Policy as a Field for Economic Research," *World Politics*, XII, No. 3 (April, 1960), 436 ff. See also Charles J. Hitch and Roland N. McKean, *The Economics of Defense in the Nuclear Age* (Cambridge, Mass.: Harvard University Press, 1960).

45. See Horace Taylor, "The Teaching of Economics," in H. W. Ehrmann (ed.), *The Teaching of the Social Sciences in the United States* (Paris: UNESCO, 1954), pp. 39–54.

46. Klaus Knorr, "Economics and International Relations: A Problem in Teaching," *Political Science Quarterly*, LXII, No. 4 (December, 1947), 552–68. The problems Knorr set out immediately after the war are still far from solved.

47. Paul A. Samuelson, *Economics* (2d ed.; New York: McGraw-Hill, 1951), pp. v-vi. The first edition appeared in 1948.

48. Hitch, *op. cit.*, p. 436.

49. See William E. Dougherty, in collaboration with Morris Janowitz, *A Psychological Warfare Case Book* (Baltimore, Md.: Johns Hopkins University Press, 1958), especially pp. 126–45.

50. Samuel A. Stouffer *et al.*, *The American Soldier* (Princeton, N.J.: Princeton University Press, 1949–50); Eli Ginzberg, *The Ineffective Soldier* (New York: Columbia University Press, 1959).

51. Morris Janowitz, *Sociology and the Military Establishment* (New York: Russell Sage Foundation, 1959), p. 15.

52. Presented at a working session of the Inter-University Seminar on Sociology and the Military Establishment held at the University of Chicago, March, 1962.

53. Kenneth Boulding, *Conflict and Defense* (New York: Harper & Row, 1962).

54. *Ibid.*, Chapters 13 and 14.

55. *Ibid.*, Chapter 2.

56. Lewis F. Richardson, *Statistics of Deadly Quarrels*, ed. Quincy Wright and C. C. Lienau (Chicago, Ill.: Quadrangle Books, 1960), p. viii; and by the same author, *Arms and Insecurity*, ed. N. Rashevsky (Chicago, Ill.: Quadrangle Books, 1960).

57. Anatol Rapoport, *Fights, Games and Debates* (Ann Arbor, Mich.: University of Michigan Press, 1960). For a valuable summary of the contributions of mathematics to national security, see Richard R. Fagen, "Some Contributions of Mathematical Reasoning to the Study of Politics," *American Political Science Review*, LV, No. 4 (December, 1961), 895–97.

58. Thomas C. Schelling, *The Strategy of Conflict*; also Thomas C. Schelling and Morton Halperin, *Strategy and Arms Control*.

59. For a summary of Osgood's views, see Charles E. Osgood, "A Case for Graduated Unilateral Disengagement," *Bulletin of the Atomic Scientists*, XVI, No. 4 (April, 1960), 127 ff.

60. "Strengthening the Behavioral Sciences," reprinted in *Science*, Vol. 136, No. 3512 (April 20, 1962), 233 ff.

61. Social Science Research Council, *Annual Report 1960–61*, pp. 1–2.

Chapter 4: Scientists, Lawyers, and Businessmen

1. A. Hunter Duprée, *Science in the Federal Government* (Cambridge, Mass.: Belknap Press, 1957).

2. See Robert Gilpin, *American Scientists and Nuclear Weapons Policy* (Princeton, N.J.: Princeton University Press, 1962).

3. Almost all of these issues were discussed during the Oppenheimer hearings. See *In the Matter of J. Robert Oppenheimer*. For analysis of the H-bomb controversy, see Warner Schilling, "The H-Bomb Decision," *Political Science Quarterly*, LXXVI, No. 1 (March, 1961), 24 ff. On the continental defense issue, see James R. Killian, Jr., and A. G. Hill, "For a Continental Defense," *The Atlantic Monthly*, CXCII, No. 5 (November, 1953), 37–41.

4. The Office of the Science Adviser had been first established in 1950 but was short-lived. See *Science and Foreign Relations*, Department of State Publication 3860, General Foreign Policy Series 30, May, 1950.

5. Quoted in W. I. B. Beveridge, *The Art of Scientific Investigation* (rev. ed.; New York: W. W. Norton, 1957), p. 57.

6. *Ibid.*, especially Chapter X, "Strategy"; see also James B. Conant, *On Understanding Science* (New Haven, Conn.: Yale University Press, 1947).

7. Statement of the Committee on Science in the Promotion of Human Welfare, American Association for the Advancement of Science, *Science*, Vol. 132, No. 3419 (July 8, 1960), 69.

8. For an outstanding example, see Norbert Wiener, "A Scientist Rebels," *The Atlantic Monthly*, CLXXIX, No. 1 (January, 1947), 46.

9. The objectives of the Federation of American Scientists have been along these lines, as have been those of the *Bulletin of the Atomic Scientists*.

10. For a clear statement of the philosophic rationalization of this position, see Jacob Bronowski, *Science and Human Values* (New York: Julian Messner, 1956).

11. See James G. Crowther and Richard Whiddington, *Science at War* (London: His Majesty's Department of Scientific and Industrial Research, 1947). The American experience is described in James Phinney Baxter, 3rd, *Scientists Against Time* (Boston: Little, Brown, 1946).

12. See Chapter 11.

13. For examples of the broad interests and achievements of the RAND staff in the social sciences, see *A Selected List of Unclassified Publications of the Social Science Department, The RAND Corporation 1948–1962* (Santa Monica, California).

14. The following section summarizes in part the editorial comments made during the past few years by the editor of the *Bulletin*, Eugene Rabinowitch.

15. See Eugene Rabinowitch, "Berlin and Beyond," *Bulletin of the Atomic Scientists*, XVII, No. 7 (September, 1961), 258–62.

16. The discussions of these meetings have been reported in the *Bulletin of the Atomic Scientists*; see, for example, the report of the seventh conference in XVIII, No. 1 (January, 1962), 15–30.

17. Mr. Eaton financed the first three conferences, but the scientists in 1959 turned to other support in view of Mr. Eaton's controversial role in political affairs. See "Letter to the Editor" submitted by Harrison Brown, Bentley Glass, and Eugene Rabinowitch, *Bulletin of the Atomic Scientists*, XVI, No. 8 (October, 1960).

18. Letters in *The New York Times*, December 18 and 30, 1960.

19. Herman Kahn, *On Thermonuclear War* (Princeton, N.J.: Princeton University Press, 1960). For illustrations of the viewpoints discussed here, see the reviews by James Newman, *Scientific American*, Vol. 204, No. 3 (March, 1961), 197–200; by H. Stuart Hughes, *Commentary*, XXXI (March, 1961), 185–92; by Walter W. Marseille, *Bulletin of the Atomic Scientists*, XVII, No. 4 (April, 1961), 157 ff.; and by Donald Michael, *Science*, Vol. 133, No. 3453 (March 3, 1961), 635. See also Kahn's reply to his critics in *Thinking About the Unthinkable* (New York: Horizon Press, 1962).

20. "Science and Human Survival," *Science*, Vol. 134, No. 3496 (December 29, 1961), 2083; for a contrary view, see the editorial in *Science*, Vol. 135, No. 3498 (January 12, 1962), 69.

21. See Part III.

22. See the recommendations of the Association's Committee on Science in the Promotion of Human Welfare, *Science*, Vol. 132, No. 3419 (July 8, 1960), 72.

23. See Social Science Research Council, *Items*, Vol. 15, No. 1, Part 2 (March, 1961), 6.

24. In addition to Don K. Price's *Government and Science* and James L. Mc-Camy's *Science and Public Administration*, previously cited, books on science and public policy include J. Stefan Dupré and Sanford A. Lakoff, *Science and the Nation* (Englewood Cliffs, N. J.: Prentice-Hall, 1962), and Dael Wolfle, *Science and Public Policy* (Lincoln, Neb.: University of Nebraska Press, 1959).

25. See Donald R. Matthews, *The Social Background of Political Decision-Makers* (Garden City, N.Y.: Doubleday, 1954); also Joseph A. Schlessinger, "Lawyers and American Politics," *Midwest Journal of Political Science*, I, No. 1 (May, 1957), 26 ff.

26. For a general view of legal education, see Albert P. Blaustein and Charles O. Porter, *The American Lawyer* (Chicago, Ill.: University of Chicago Press, 1954) and Albert J. Harno, *Legal Education in the United States* (San Francisco: Bancroft-Whitney, 1953). See also Esther L. Brown, *Lawyers, Law Schools, and the Public Service* (New York: Russell Sage Foundation, 1948), and Julius Stone, *Legal Education and Public Responsibility* (Columbus, Ohio: Association of American Law Schools, 1959).

27. For recent surveys of business education, see Frank C. Pierson and others, *The Education of American Businessmen* (New York: McGraw-Hill, 1959), and Robert A. Gordon and James E. Howell, *Higher Education for Business* (New York: Columbia University Press, 1959). For a general review of mid-career programs, see Peter E. Siegle, *New Directions in Liberal Education for Executives* (Chicago: Center for the Study of Liberal Education for Adults, March, 1958).

28. For a criticism of legal education as preparation for policy-making, see Henry A. Kissinger, *Nuclear Weapons and Foreign Policy*, p. 434. As a general rule, law schools are noncommittal on what subjects students should major in during their undergraduate years. The largest number of law students, however, have majored in the social sciences. See Arthur T. Vanderbilt, "A Report on Prelegal Education," *New York University Law Review*, XXV, No. 2 (April, 1950), 200 ff.; also Charles H. Russell, *Liberal Education and the Law* (mimeo.; New York: Columbia University Teachers College, Institute of Higher Education, 1957).

29. See Edward H. Levi, *4 Talks on Legal Education* (Chicago, Ill.: University of Chicago Law School, 1952).

30. "How Should Lawyers Be Educated? A Report on the Yale Law Curriculum," *American Bar Association Journal*, Vol. 37, No. 9 (September, 1951), 655–58.

31. *Bulletin of Yale University Law School for the Academic Year 1958–1959*, Series 54, No. 16 (August, 1958), 26.

32. See Columbia University School of Law, *Bulletin*, 1960–61, Series 60, No. 12 (March 19, 1960), pp. 10–11; and *Columbia University Bulletin*, International Fellows Program, 1960–61, Series 60, No. 20 (May 14, 1960).

33. *A Survey of Courses offered in Law Schools of the United States in International Law and Related Subjects*, prepared by the American Bar Association, Special Committee on World Peace Through Law (mimeo.; Washington, D.C., February, 1960).

34. The Ford program is described in *Architects of Order* (New York: Ford Foundation, 1959).

35. *Official Register of Harvard University*, The Law School, LV, No. 4, Catalog for 1958–59 (April 1, 1958), p. 13. For a summary of the first seven years of the program, see Harvard Law School, International Legal Studies, *Report of the Director, 1954–1961* (Cambridge, Mass., 1961).

36. Milton Katz, "International Legal Studies: A New Vista for the Legal Profession," *American Bar Association Journal*, Vol. 42, No. 53 (January, 1956), 55.

37. American Bar Association, "Report of Special Committee on World Peace Through Law," 35 (mimeo.; Washington, D.C., February, 1960).

38. Elihu Root, "Public Service by the Bar," *American Bar Association Journal*, II, No. 4 (October, 1916), 740.

39. Harvard Law School, *Dean's Report*, 1959–60, pp. 5–6.

40. For a discussion of the changing relation of government and industry, see Walter Hamilton, *The Politics of Industry* (New York: Alfred A. Knopf, 1957).

41. Leonard S. Silk, *The Research Revolution* (New York: McGraw-Hill, 1960).

42. Following the outbreak of the Korean War, the Committee for Economic Development revised its research program to take account of national security as a continuing problem of American society. Since then, their Statements on National Policy have included the following: *Economic Aspects of North Atlantic Security*, 1952; *Taxes, National Security and Economic Growth*, 1954; *Economic Development Assistance*, 1957; and *The Problem of National Security*, 1958. Many other statements have focused on international problems closely connected to security affairs.

43. The management problems of the Defense Department have never attracted the attention of the business schools to the degree they merit. During World War II, the Harvard Business School trained military officers and it still gives a course in "Military Management" for armed-services personnel. But the major problems of defense administration have been scrutinized by students of public rather than business administration.

44. For full analyses of the continuing progress and problems of business education, see Pierson, *The Education of American Businessmen* and Gordon and Howell, *Higher Education for Business*.

45. School of Industrial Management, Massachusetts Institute of Technology, 1961–1962 *Sloan Fellowships in Executive Development*.

46. See Kenneth R. Andrews, "University Programs for Practicing Executives" in Pierson, *The Education of American Businessmen*.

47. See Hamilton, *The Politics of Industry*, pp. 141–42; also *The Private Citizen and the National Service*, Study of the Subcommittee on National Policy Machinery, U.S. Senate, 87th Cong., 1st sess., 1961.

Chapter 5: The Education of the Public

1. Kahn, *On Thermonuclear War*; Bernard Brodie, *Strategy in the Missile Age* (Princeton, N.J.: Princeton University Press, 1959). See also the RAND Corporation Study, *Report on a Study of Non-Military Defense*, Report R-322-RC, July 1, 1958; it is significant that this report was directed by Kahn and was sponsored by RAND with its own funds.

2. Office of Civil and Defense Mobilization, Executive Office of the President, *The National Plan for Civil Defense and Defense Mobilization* (Washington, D.C., October, 1958). See also *Civil Defense Shelter Policy and Post Attack Recovery Planning* (House Report No. 2069), Twenty-first Report by the Committee on Government Operations, House of Representatives, 86th Cong., 2d sess., 1960.

3. For excerpts from the Defense Department statement outlining civil-defense proposals, see *The New York Times*, December 15, 1961. For the text of the

information pamphlet and a description of the trials and tribulations of drawing it up, see *The New York Times*, December 31, 1961. A number of academic groups took sharp issue with the premises of the shelter program; see the "Open Letter to President Kennedy and Governor Rockefeller" published by members of academic and research institutions in the New York area in *The New York Times*, December 19, 1961.

4. *Intercom*, III, No. 3 (May, 1961 [New York: Foreign Policy Association]), 13.

5. Bernard C. Cohen, *Citizen Education in World Affairs* (Princeton, N.J.: Princeton University Center of International Studies, 1953), pp. 117 ff.

6. See Merle Curti, *Peace or War: The American Struggle 1636–1936* (New York: W. W. Norton, 1936), especially Chapter 9, "The Struggle Renewed Again, 1918–1936," pp. 262 ff.

7. Foreign Policy Association, *Twenty-Five Years of the Foreign Policy Association, 1918–1943* (New York, 1943), pp. 4–5.

8. Foreign Policy Association, *Annual Report*, 1961–62.

9. *Ibid.*, p. 2.

10. Fund for Adult Education, *Continuing Liberal Education*, 1957–59, pp. 67–73.

11. The Foundation was first named the American Foundation for Political Education, but the name was changed in 1959, when its program was expanded to general cultural as well as political areas. The following discussion is based largely on the Foundation's *Annual Report* for 1956–57 (also a summary of the first ten years of operation) and for 1957–59.

12. American Foundation for Continuing Education, *Programs and Publications* (Chicago, 1962).

13. For an analysis of the peace movement, and of SANE in particular, see Nathan Glazer, "The Peace Movement in America—1961," *Commentary*, XXXI, No. 4 (April, 1961), 288–96.

14. *Sane World*, Vol. 1, No. 7 (April 15, 1962). *Sane World* is published twice a month.

15. See Wendell Bell, Richard J. Hill, and Charles R. Wright, *Public Leadership* (San Francisco, Calif.: Chandler, 1961), a study prepared for the Fund for Adult Education to examine the relevance of social-science research on leadership to the aims and techniques of adult education.

16. Ilo Remer and June Barlow, "A Tentative List of Colleges and Universities Offering Russian, Fall, 1960," *Slavic and East European Journal*, New Series, V (XIX), No. 1 (Spring, 1961), 46 ff.

17. For information on the Association see the section "News of the Profession" in the Association's quarterly, *Slavic Review*.

18. Raymond L. Garthoff, *Soviet Military Doctrine* (Chicago, Ill.: The Free Press of Glencoe, 1953) and *Soviet Strategy in the Nuclear Age* (New York: Frederick A. Praeger, 1958; rev. ed., 1962); Herbert S. Dinerstein, *War and the Soviet Union* (New York: Frederick A. Praeger, 1959); Arnold Kramish, *Atomic Energy in the Soviet Union* (Stanford, Calif.: Stanford University Press, 1959); B. H. Liddell Hart (ed.), *The Red Army* (New York: Harcourt, Brace & World, 1956). *Soviet Military Doctrine* and the books by Dinerstein and Kramish were all sponsored or initiated by the RAND Corporation.

19. See *The New York Times*, January 28, 1962, for a description of the seminar held in St. Louis on January 27, 1962.

20. *Instruction on Communism and Its Contrast with Liberty Under Law* (Chicago, Ill.: American Bar Association, 1962).

21. Introductory pamphlet, *Freedom vs. Communism*, Chamber of Commerce of the United States, 1961. For a condensed adaptation of the material in the course, see "What You Can Do About Communism," *Nation's Business*, Vol. 50, No. 1 (January, 1962), 32 ff. Quotations are taken from this adaptation.

22. The work of the Christian Anti-Communist Crusade has been widely covered by *The New York Times*, following the publication of an article by Cabell Phillips on May 21, 1961; see particularly the article on the financing of the Crusade, June 24, 1962, and the profile of Schwarz, June 29, 1962. For information on the Crusade, see Fred J. Cook, "Juggernaut: The Warfare State," *The Nation*, October 28, 1962, and "The Ultras," *The Nation*, June 30, 1962. The discussion that follows is also based on Schwarz' book *You Can Trust the Communists* (Englewood Cliffs, N.J.: Prentice-Hall, 1960).

23. Harry Schwartz, "Many School Courses Tell Only 'Evils' of Communism," *The New York Times*, July 4, 1962; see also a companion article by Fred Hechinger, *The New York Times*, July 3, 1962.

24. "Communism Study in Depth Urged," *The New York Times*, July 4, 1962.

25. For a journalistic review of the "brainwashing" investigations, see Eugene Kinkaid, *In Every War But One* (New York: W. W. Norton, 1959).

26. Samuel P. Huntington, *The Soldier and the State*, p. 397.

·27. *The New York Times*, April 7, 1962.

28. See *Military Cold War Education and Speech Review Policies*, Hearings before the Special Preparedness Subcommittee, Committee on Armed Services, U.S. Senate, 87th Cong., 2d sess., 1962, Parts I and II.

29. *The New York Times*, April 1, 1962.

30. See Hanson Baldwin, *The New York Times*, January 12, 1962.

31. See Senator Fulbright's memorandum, *Congressional Record*, Vol. 107, August 2, 1961, 13436–42.

32. *Military Cold War Education and Speech Review Policies*, Part 1, p. 6.

33. See John W. Masland and Laurence I. Radway, *Soldiers and Scholars*, Parts V–VI.

34. This description of the National Security Seminar is based on catalogs of the Industrial College of the Armed Forces, Washington, D.C., and on personal observation.

35. The discussion that follows is a condensed version of Gene M. Lyons and Louis Morton, "School for Strategy," *Bulletin of the Atomic Scientists*, XVII, No. 3 (March, 1961), 103–106.

36. The Chairman of the Board of the Institute was Lenox R. Lohr, Chicago Museum of Science and Industry; the Chairman of the Board's Executive Committee was Edwin A. Locke, Jr., President, Union Tank Car Company. Other members of the Executive Committee were: Frank Barnett, Research Director of the Richardson Foundation; Thomas H. Coulter, Chief Executive Officer, Chicago Association of Commerce and Industry; John M. Fisher, Chairman of the Board, American Security Council; Robert E. Wood, retired Chairman of the Board, Sears, Roebuck and Co.; Ivan Hill, Executive Vice President, Cunningham & Walsh, Inc.; Edwin W. Rawlings, Gen. USAF (Ret.) and Financial Vice President, General Mills, Inc.; and Leonard Spacek, Managing Partner, Arthur Anderson & Co.

37. For a list of such activities, see "Instances of Education and Propaganda

Activities of Military Personnel," attached to Senator Fulbright's memorandum, *Congressional Record*, August 2, 1961, pp. 13438–39.

38. The Association was, in fact, a consolidation of a number of branch associations such as the Infantry and Field Artillery Associations. The Secretary's memorandum on the Association was printed in the Association's publication *Army*, December, 1956, p. 79.

39. *The Security of the Nation*, A Study of Current Problems of National Defense, Association of the United States Army (2d ed.; Washington, D.C., 1959).

40. Major General A. J. Drexel Biddle, "The President's Report," *Army*, XI, No. 2 (September, 1960).

41. "Needed: A National Alert," *Air Force*, Vol. 44, No. 11 (November, 1961), 8–9.

42. This discussion is based on a series of articles in the 1961 *Air Force Almanac*, published as a special issue of *Air Force*, Vol. 44, No. 9 (September, 1961), 59 ff.

43. See, for example, Cabell Phillips' article "Right Wing Officers Worrying Pentagon," *The New York Times*, June 18, 1961; also Waldemar A. Nielsen, "Huge, Hidden Impact of the Pentagon," *The New York Times Magazine*, June 25, 1961, pp. 9 ff.

Chapter 6: *The Pattern of Early Programs*

1. For a review of Professor Dunn's work and his impact on the research program of the Center, see William T. R. Fox, "Frederick Sherwood Dunn and the American Study of International Relations," *World Politics*, XV, No. 1 (October, 1962), 1–19.

2. Princeton University, *General Catalogue*, 1960–61, p. 285.

3. Center of International Studies, Princeton University, *Announcement of Publications*. Among these works were: Peter Paret, *Internal War and Pacification: The Vendee, 1789–96* and George Modelski, *The International Relations of Internal War.*

4. William W. Kaufmann (ed.), *Military Policy and National Security* (Princeton, N.J.: Princeton University Press, 1956); Glenn H. Snyder, *Deterrence and Defense* (Princeton, N.J.: Princeton University Press, 1961); and Klaus Knorr and Thornton Read (eds.), *Limited Strategic War* (New York: Frederick A. Praeger, 1962).

5. Some of the studies in these series published by the Center of International Studies, Princeton, N.J., include: Morton A. Kaplan, *The Strategy of Limited Retaliation* (1959) and *Some Problems in the Strategic Analysis of International Politics* (1959); Arthur Lee Burns, *Power Politics and the Growing Nuclear Club* (1959) and *The Rationale of Catalytic War* (1959); Glenn H. Snyder, *Deterence by Denial and Punishment* (1959); Thornton Read, *A Proposal to Neutralize Nuclear Weapons* (1960); Zara S. Steiner, *Present Problems of the Foreign Service* (1961); Morroe Berger, *Military Elite and Social Change: Egypt Since Napoleon* (1960); William Ebenstein, *Church and State in Franco Spain* (1960); Arnold S. Feldman and Klaus Knorr, *American Capability in Basic Science and Technological Invention* (1960); and Thornton Read, *Command and Control* (1961).

6. The course was prepared by Gordon R. Turner under an Advisory Committee consisting of Professors Gordon A. Craig, Wesley Frank Craven, and

Peter A. Isely. A special text was prepared—a collection of readings edited with an introduction by Professor Turner, *A History of Military Affairs Since the Eighteenth Century* (New York: Harcourt, Brace & World, 1962). See Chapter 3, p. 53.

7. *Woodrow Wilson School, Graduate Program, Official Register of Princeton University,* August, 1960, p. 15.

8. L. Gray Cowan, *A History of the School of International Affairs and Associated Area Institutes* (New York: Columbia University Press, 1954), p. 22.

9. See Chapter 4 for relation to professional education in law and business. Also, International Fellows Program, 1961–1962, *Columbia University Bulletin,* Series 61, Number 35 (September 2, 1961).

10. General Eisenhower delivered the first lecture in the series established in 1950 to bring eminent leaders in international affairs to Columbia to speak on the general subject of international peace and understanding. Dwight D. Eisenhower, "World Peace—A Balance Sheet," *The New York Times,* March 24, 1950.

11. The American Military Institute, a private organization devoted to the study of military history, was established in 1933 and has been publishing *Military Affairs* since 1936. The effort to bring it to Columbia is described in *Military Affairs,* XIV, No. 3 (Fall, 1950), 133–63.

12. See L. Gray Cowan, *A History of the School of International Affairs,* p. 91.

13. Columbia University, *Institute of War and Peace Studies, 1952–1962* (New York: 1962).

14. Kenneth Waltz, *Man, the State and War* (New York: Columbia University Press, 1959); Alfred Vagts, *Defense and Diplomacy* (New York: King's Crown Press, 1956).

15. See William T. R. Fox, *Theoretical Aspects of International Relations* (South Bend, Ind.: University of Notre Dame Press, 1959). Research in this area has been carried out with the support of the Rockefeller Foundation.

16. Research Associates or Research Fellows of the Institute have included Paul Y. Hammond, Samuel P. Huntington, Daniel Lerner, Hans Morgenthau, Benjamin Nimer, Katherine Organiski, E. L. Katzenbach, William W. Marvel, Seymour Melman, Miss Jimmye E. Kimmey, Reinhold Niebuhr, David C. Rapoport, Warner R. Schilling, Glenn H. Snyder, and Kenneth Waltz.

17. William T. R. Fox, "Civil-Military Relations Research," p. 284.

18. Warner R. Schilling, Paul Y. Hammond and Glenn H. Snyder, *Strategies, Budgets and Defense Politics* (New York: Columbia University Press, 1962).

19. Samuel P. Huntington (ed.), *Changing Patterns of Military Politics;* David C. Rapoport, *Praetorianism: Government Without Consensus* (Berkeley, Calif.: University of California Ph.D. thesis, 1960); Zbigniew Brzezinski and Samuel P. Huntington, *Political Power USA/USSR* (New York: Viking Press, 1964).

20. Seymour Melman (ed.), *Inspection for Disarmament* (New York: Columbia University Press, 1958).

21. Warner Schilling, "The H-Bomb Decision."

22. The following description is based on the *First Report of the Council for Atomic Age Studies,* January, 1957–June, 1959 (mimeo.). No formal reports have since been published, and information on recent activities has been gained through interviews.

23. *Bibliography of the Writings of Hans J. Morgenthau* (mimeo.; Chicago: Center for the Study of American Foreign and Military Policy, 1959). The list was eleven pages long and included ten books.

24. These volumes are: Hans J. Morgenthau, *In Defense of the National Interest* (New York: Alfred A. Knopf, 1951) and *Dilemmas of Politics* (Chicago, Ill.: University of Chicago Press, 1958); Robert E. Osgood, *Ideals and Self-Interest in American Foreign Policy* (Chicago, Ill.: University of Chicago Press, 1953), *Limited War* (Chicago, Ill.: University of Chicago Press, 1957), and *NATO: The Entangling Alliance* (Chicago, Ill.: University of Chicago Press, 1962); Gerald Stourzh, *Benjamin Franklin and American Foreign Policy* (Chicago, Ill.: University of Chicago Press, 1954); Leon D. Epstein, *Britain—Uneasy Ally* (Chicago, Ill.: University of Chicago Press, 1954); George Liska, *The New Statecraft: Foreign Aid in American Foreign Policy* (Chicago, Ill.: University of Chicago Press, 1960); and Tang Tsou, *The Embroilment Over Quemoy: Mao, Chiang and Dulles* (Salt Lake City, Utah: Institute of International Studies, University of Utah, 1959).

Chapter 7: The Cambridge Complex

1. Leach was a Brigadier General in the U.S. Air Force Reserve. During World War II he was Chief, Operations Analysis Division, Army Air Force, and after the war served as consultant to the Secretary of the Air Force. W. Barton Leach, *Memorandum to the Deans of the Faculty of Arts and Sciences, Law School, Business School, Graduate School of Public Administration, Harvard University,* February 14, 1955, pp. 1–5.

2. *Newsweek,* March 21, 1955, p. 96.

3. Leach, *Memorandum to the Deans,* p. 6.

4. Harvard Graduate School of Public Administration, *Report to the Ford Foundation on Grant for Harvard Defense Studies Program,* 1955–56, p. 1.

5. *Ibid.,* p. 5.

6. Leach, *Memorandum to the Deans,* pp. 2–3.

7. Harvard Graduate School of Public Administration, *Report to the Ford Foundation on Grant for Harvard Defense Studies Program,* 1956–57, p. 1.

8. Harry H. Ransom, *Harvard University Defense Policy Seminar,* 1957–58, Series 116, May 27, 1957.

9. Timothy W. Stanley, *American Defense and National Security* (Washington, D.C.: Public Affairs Press, 1956); Harry Howe Ransom, *Central Intelligence and National Security* (Cambridge, Mass.: Harvard University Press, 1958). Morton H. Halperin's works include *A Proposal for a Ban on the Use of Nuclear Weapons* (Washington, D.C.: Institute for Defense Analyses, 1961); *Limited War in the Nuclear Age* (New York: John Wiley & Sons, 1963), *Arms Control and Inadvertent General War* (Washington, D.C.: Institute for Defense Analyses, 1962); Halperin and Thomas C. Schelling, *Strategy and Arms Control;* and *China and the Bomb* (New York: Frederick A. Praeger, 1965).

10. *Report on Grant for the Harvard Defense Studies Program,* 1956–57, p. 14.

11. Ransom, *Harvard University Defense Policy Seminar,* 1957–58.

12. Harvard University, Center for International Affairs, *Program,* 1958, pp. 3–4.

13. *The New York Times,* May 20, 1962.

14. Don K. Price, *Government and Science* (New York: New York University Press, 1954), pp. 200–203.

15. From 1961 to 1963, Professor Kaysen was on temporary leave to work on the White House staff. In 1962, other responsibilities forced Professor Bruner to

leave the committee directing the program, though he continues to be a consultant.

16. Massachusetts Institute of Technology, *Report of the Committee on Educational Survey* (1949), p. 49.

17. *Ibid.*, p. 50.

18. *Ibid.*

19. Norman J. Padelford and Robert C. Wood, *Science and Public Policy: A Range of Issues*, Report on Endicott House Conference, M.I.T., November 28–30, 1958 (mimeo.; Massachusetts Institute of Technology, 1959).

20. Center for International Studies, *Twelfth Annual Report*, 1964, pp. 31–39.

21. Center for International Studies, *Eighth Annual Report*, 1960, pp. 42–43.

22. *Ibid.*, p. 33.

23. *Ibid.*, p. 37.

24. *Loc. cit.*

25. See Max F. Millikan, "Inquiry and Policy: The Relation of Knowledge to Action," in Daniel Lerner (ed.), *The Human Meaning of the Social Sciences*, pp. 158–82.

26. Walt W. Rostow, *The United States in the World Arena* (New York: Harper & Brothers, 1960).

27. Lincoln Bloomfield, *The United Nations and U.S. Foreign Policy* (Boston: Little, Brown, 1960).

28. William Griffith, "European Communism and the Sino-Soviet Schism," *Annals of the American Academy of Political and Social Science*, 439 (September, 1963), 143–52; "The Decline and Fall of Revisionism in Eastern Europe," in Leopold Labedz (ed.), *Revisionism: Essays on the History of Marxist Ideas* (New York: Frederick A. Praeger, 1962), Chapter XVI; *Albania and the Sino-Soviet Rift* (Cambridge, Mass.: M.I.T. Press, 1963); *The Sino-Soviet Rift* (Cambridge, Mass.: M.I.T. Press, 1964); and *Communism in Europe* (Cambridge, Mass.: M.I.T. Press, 1964). See also Edgar H. Schein, with Inge Schneier and Curtis H. Barker, *Coercive Persuasion* (New York: W. W. Norton, 1961); Alexander Korol, *Soviet Education for Science and Technology* (Cambridge, Mass.: M.I.T. Press, 1957).

29. Center for International Studies, *Publication List No. 10*, April, 1964.

Chapter 8: The State University

1. President Kennedy appointed Professor Runge Assistant Secretary of Defense for Manpower, Personnel, and Reserve Affairs in 1961; he returned to the University in mid-1962.

2. The first prospectus of the National Security Studies Group Seminar, "Military Policy and Administration," stated frankly that the course would use a considerable amount of material prepared at Harvard and that members of the Harvard group would be invited to Madison during the year to lecture to the Seminar.

3. University of California, *Bulletin*, General Catalogue, Part I, pp. 159–62.

4. Richard N. Rosecrance (ed.), *The Dispersion of Nuclear Weapons* (New York: Columbia University Press, 1964).

5. The following discussion is based on *A Duke–University of North Carolina National Security Affairs Program*, August 1, 1960, as well as on interviews and correspondence with participants.

6. Quoted in a speech delivered by Ohio State University Vice-President Frederick W. Heimberger, *Mershon Program for National Security*, Columbus, Ohio, January 15, 1959; mimeographed.

7. *The Uniform on the Campus, Final Report of the Ohio State University– Air Force ROTC Instructor Program* (1957). Periodic reports on various aspects of the program were published. (See *The Uniform on the Campus*, p. 13.) During the period of the study, a number of significant changes were made in the AFROTC program, many of them presumably a result of the work carried on at Ohio State.

8. Colonel T. N. Dupuy, *Final Reports of the Director of the Course to the President, Ohio State University* (October 10, 1956; September 9, 1957). Attached to the reports are the outlines of the course, lists of students and faculty, bibliography, and the results of a questionnaire given to the students.

9. These are fully described in the announcement of the Defense Studies Committee, Ohio State University, "Defense Related Courses and Seminars."

10. Defense Studies Committee, Ohio State University, *Proposal to the Board of Trustees for Use of Civilian-Military Half of Mershon Income*, February 7, 1958.

11. Robert Nordstrom to the Faculty, undated letter with enclosure, "Procedures and Guides for Selection of Mershon National Security Projects."

12. John Phelps to Mershon Committee, Memorandum: *National Security Policy Studies 701*, undated, presumably December, 1959, or January, 1960.

13. For the paper presented in the Civil-Military Relations Conference, see Harry L. Coles (ed.), *Total War and Cold War* (Columbus, Ohio: Ohio State University Press, 1962); for the 1960 ROTC conference see Mershon National Security Program, *Role of Colleges and Universities in ROTC Programs* (1960).

14. The volume accepted for publication in 1960 was Gene M. Lyons, *Military Policy and Economic Aid: The Korean Case, 1950–1953* (Columbus, Ohio: Ohio State University Press, 1961). In 1961, the prize was awarded to George Stambuck of Indiana University for *American Military Forces Abroad: A Postwar Pattern in International Relations* (Columbus, Ohio: Ohio State University Press, 1962); in 1962, J. David Singer, *Deterrence, Arms Control, and Disarmament* (Columbus, Ohio: Ohio State University Press, 1962).

15. Frederick Heimberger, *Mershon Program for National Security*.

16. Social Science Faculty Seminar, *A Proposal to Establish a Social Science Center for National Security Policy Studies at The Ohio State University*, June, 1960. The chairman of the committee was Harvey C. Mansfield of the Political Science Department. Two of its members had served on the 1959 Seminar and on the Defense Studies Committee.

17. *Ibid.*, p. 2.

Chapter 9: Policy and Behavior

1. Washington Center of Foreign Policy Research, *Statement of Purpose and Method*, Fall, 1958.

2. The Advisory Council to the School of Advanced International Studies includes: Christian A. Herter, Jr. (Chairman), Frank Altschul, C. Douglas Dillon, Allen W. Dulles, William McC. Martin, Jr., George C. McGhee, Paul H. Nitze, Lewis L. Strauss, McGeorge Bundy, and William C. Foster. Mr. Herter, Mr. Martin, and Mr. Nitze are also on the Board of Trustees of Johns Hopkins University.

3. Washington Center of Foreign Policy Research, *United States Foreign Policy: Developments in Military Technology and Their Impact on U.S. Strategy and Foreign Policy.* Prepared for the Committee on Foreign Relations, U.S. Senate, 86th Cong., 2d sess., Committee Print, 1959; Washington Center of Foreign Policy Research, *East-West Negotiations* (Washington, D.C., 1958) and *Military Policy Papers* (Washington, D.C., 1958); Arnold Wolfers, *Alliance Policy in the Cold War* (Baltimore, Md.: Johns Hopkins Press, 1959), and *Discord and Collaboration* (Baltimore, Md.: Johns Hopkins Press, 1962); Ernest W. Lefever (ed.), *Arms and Arms Control* (New York: Frederick A. Praeger, 1962).

4. Foreign Policy Research Institute, University of Pennsylvania, *Report on Operations, May, 1958,* p. 5.

5. *Ibid.,* p. 6.

6. *Ibid.,* p. 7.

7. *A Four-Part Program for the Foreign Policy Research Institute,* 1960–62, p. 18.

8. *Report on Operations, May, 1958,* pp. 24–28. Among the Associates have been William Y. Elliott, H. Field Haviland, Henry A. Kissinger, Hans Kohn, Stefan T. Possony, and Arthur Smithies.

9. *Ibid.,* p. 10.

10. Robert Strausz-Hupé, William Kintner, Alvin J. Cottrell, James E. Dougherty, *Protracted Conflict* (New York: Harper & Brothers, 1959).

·11. The countries visited were: Japan, Korea, Formosa, Japan (Okinawa), Hong Kong, Cambodia, Thailand, Vietnam, the Philippines, Burma, India, Pakistan, Iraq, Israel, Cyprus, Egypt, Lebanon, Libya, Tunisia, Algeria, Morocco, France, Germany, Austria, Finland, and Sweden. Strausz-Hupé *et al., Protracted Conflict,* p. viii.

12. *Ibid.,* p. xv.

13. Robert Strausz-Hupé, William Kintner and Stefan T. Possony, *A Forward Strategy for America* (New York: Harper & Brothers, 1961).

14. Strausz-Hupé *et al., Protracted Conflict,* p. xiv.

15. *A Four-Part Program for the Foreign Policy Research Institute,* 1960–62, p. 1.

16. These studies include: *U.S. Foreign Policy: Western Europe,* Committee on Foreign Relations, U.S. Senate (Washington, D.C.: U.S. Government Printing Office, 1959); "The Military Assistance Program in Underdeveloped Areas," Annex, II, *Report of the President's Committee to Study the Military Assistance Program* (Washington, D.C.: U.S. Government Printing Office, 1959).

17. Stanford University, *Official Bulletin, Courses and Degrees,* 1964, pp. 447–48.

18. David M. Abshire and Richard V. Allen (eds.), *National Security: Political, Military, and Economic Strategies in the Decade Ahead* (New York: Frederick A. Praeger, 1963).

19. Center for Strategic Studies Conference Program, *National Security: The Demands of Strategy and Economics in the Decade Ahead,* Georgetown University, January 23–25, 1963.

20. See, for example, Lyons and Morton, "School for Strategy."

21. The *Journal* was first published by the Department of Journalism, University of Michigan, and is now published by the Center for Research on Conflict Resolution. The Editorial Board includes representatives from the Sociology, Economics, Political Science, Psychology, Geography, History, Mathematics, Biology, and Law Departments of the University. Among the Associate Editors were foreign

and American scholars including Harold Lasswell, Paul Lazarsfeld, Hans Morgenthau, David Riesman, and Quincy Wright.

22. Editorial, *The Journal of Conflict Resolution*, I, No. 1 (March, 1957), 1.

23. *Ibid.*, p. 2.

24. Proceedings of the International Arms Control Symposium were subsequently published in a special joint issue of the *Journal of Conflict Resolution*, VII, No. 3, and the *Journal of Arms Control*, I, No. 4 (Fall, 1963).

25. See Emile Benoit and Kenneth Boulding (eds.), *Disarmament and the Economy* (New York: Harper & Row, 1963).

26. Robert C. Angell and J. David Singer, *Value Systems, Foreign Policy, and Soviet-American Coexistence: Description of Project*, Center for Research on Conflict Resolution, Summer, 1960.

27. Kenneth Boulding, *Conflict and Defense: A General Theory* (New York: Harper & Brothers, 1962).

28. Anatol Rapoport, *Fights, Games and Debates* (Ann Arbor, Mich.: University of Michigan Press, 1960).

29. See Karl W. Deutsch and J. David Singer, "Multipolar Power Systems and International Stability," *World Politics*, XVI, No. 3 (April, 1964), 390–406; Karl W. Deutsch, *The Nerves of Government* (New York: The Free Press of Glencoe, 1963) uses his exploratory work to suggest looking upon government "somewhat less as a problem of power and somewhat more as a problem of steering." See also Karl W. Deutsch, *The Integration of Political Communities* (Philadelphia, Pa.: J. B. Lippincott, 1964).

30. Stanford University, *Brief Description of the Conflict Study Project*, March, 1960, mimeographed.

31. A summary of the propositions derived from the World War I study can be found in Robert C. North, Ole R. Holsti, M. George Zaninovich, and Dina A. Zinnes, *Content Analysis: A Handbook with Applications for the Study of International Crisis* (Evanston, Ill.: Northwestern University Press, 1963).

32. Stanford University, *Report to the Ford Foundation, September 1, 1961– August 31, 1962*. The work and methods of the Stanford Studies in International Conflict and Integration are described in "Crisis & Crises," *Stanford Today*, Series 1, No. 4 (March, 1963).

33. R. C. North *et al.*, *Content Analysis*.

34. *Journal of Conflict Resolution*, VI, No. 3 (September, 1962).

Chapter 10: The Education of Government Executives

1. See John W. Masland and Laurence I. Radway, *Soldiers and Scholars*, and Gene M. Lyons and John W. Masland, *Education and Military Leadership*.

2. The following discussion has profited greatly from Don K. Price, "Administrative Leadership," *Daedalus*, Vol. 90, No. 4 (Fall, 1961), 750–63.

3. See the testimony of John R. Macy, Chairman of the Civil Service Commission, *Independent Offices Appropriations for 1962*, Part I, Committee on Appropriations, House of Representatives, 87th Cong., 1st sess., 1961, pp. 167–71. For a summary of the findings of a Brookings Institution survey, see *Civil Service Journal*, II, No. 3 (January–March, 1962), 16–20.

4. U.S. Civil Service Commission, *Summer Employment in Federal Agencies*, Pamphlet 45 (Washington, D.C.: U.S. Government Printing Office, January, 1962). For a description of the Army's Cooperative Education Program, see

James M. Pride, "Cooperative Education Program," *Army Information Digest* (December, 1958).

5. The following is, *inter alia*, based on experience gained in the administration of a student intern program at Dartmouth College. See Dartmouth College Public Affairs Center, *Dartmouth in the Public Service*, summary of Conference Proceedings (mimeo.; Hanover, N.H.: April 14–15, 1962).

6. Lee Huff, Tenney Johnson, and Alan Rosenthal, "Executive Trainee Program of Office of Secretary of Defense" (October 1, 1958). The three authors were all trainees.

7. International Cooperation Administration, *Career Development Training Programs, Fiscal Years 1959 through 1961* (mimeographed), p. 5.

8. United States Information Agency, *Career Opportunities for Young People in the USIA Foreign Service* (Washington, D.C., 1962).

9. For a review and critique of the Foreign Service, see the Brookings Institution, *United States Foreign Policy: The Formulation and Administration of United States Foreign Policy*, study for the Committee on Foreign Relations, U.S. Senate, 86th Cong., 2d sess., 1960, pp. 121–38. For more recent recommendations, see the report of the Committee on Foreign Affairs Personnel, *Personnel for the New Diplomacy*, Carnegie Endowment for International Peace, December, 1962. (Hereafter referred to as the *Herter Report*.)

10. See the report by the Secretary's Public Committee on Personnel, *Toward a Stronger Foreign Service*, U.S. Department of State, June, 1954. (Hereafter referred to as the *Wriston Report*.)

11. See, for example, the testimony of Loy W. Henderson, then Deputy Under Secretary of State for Administration, *Recruitment and Training for the Foreign Service of the United States*, Committee on Foreign Relations, U.S. Senate, 85th Cong., 2d sess., 1958, pp. 8–81.

12. For a discussion of these proposals, see the Brookings Institution, *United States Foreign Policy*, pp. 132–34.

13. See, for example, *Training of Federal Employees*, Committee on Post Office and Civil Service, House of Representatives, 85th Cong., 2d sess., 1958. These hearings were held on a bill that was later passed as the Government Employees Training Act of 1958.

14. See the statement on training plans by the Deputy Director for Management, ICA, before the Subcommittee on Manpower Utilization, Committee on Post Office and Civil Service, House of Representatives, 86th Cong., 1st sess., 1959, pp. 72–74; also International Cooperation Administration, *Career Development Training Programs, Fiscal Years 1959 through 1961*, mimeographed.

15. See the list of participants through December 31, 1961, with posts on selection and after completion of the program, *ibid.*, Annex 11.

16. J. Kenneth Mulligan, "College Without Campus," *Civil Service Journal*, II, No. 2 (October–December, 1961), 8 ff. For a list of the programs, see U.S. Civil Service Commission, *Interagency Training Programs*, Spring, 1962, and *Annual Report*, 1961, p. 5.

17. *Civil Service Journal*, IV, No. 2 (October–December, 1963), 13.

18. *The Study of Public Problems; A report of the activities of the Brookings Institution, 1954–1961* (Washington, D.C., 1961), p. 87.

19. *Loc. cit.*

20. U.S. Civil Service Commission, *Annual Report*, 1961, p. 58.

21. U.S. Civil Service Commission, *News Release*, January 17, 1962.

22. U.S. Civil Service Commission, *Management Intern Programs*, July, 1957, p. 1.

23. See U.S. Civil Service Commission, *University–Federal Agency Conference on Career Development*, report on Conference held at Princeton University, November 2–4, 1961.

24. For background, see the testimony of John D. Rockefeller, III, *Training of Federal Employees*, pp. 11–40.

25. *Ibid.*, pp. 31–38.

26. *Reorganization of the Foreign Service*, House Report No. 2508, Committee on Foreign Affairs, House of Representatives, 79th Cong., 2d sess., 1946, p. 3.

27. *Ibid.*, pp. 9–10.

28. *Ibid.*, pp. 102–103.

29. *Wriston Report*, p. 47.

30. *Recruitment and Training for the Foreign Service of the United States*, p. 29. For a comparison of costs for the Foreign Service Institute, 1954–62, see *Department of State Appropriations for 1962*, Committee on Appropriations, House of Representatives, 87th Cong., 1st sess., 1961, p. 693. It should be noted that about two-thirds of the Institute's budget includes student salaries; of the total of about $5 million, approximately $1.9 million represented operating expenses for FY 1962.

31. Quoted in *Recruitment and Training for the Foreign Service of the United States*, p. 31.

32. Brookings Institution, *United States Foreign Policy*, p. 134.

33. *Ibid.*, p. 135.

34. U.S. Department of State, position paper reprinted in *Administration of the Department of State*, Committee on Foreign Relations, U.S. Senate, 86th Cong., 2d sess., 1960, p. 195.

35. *Ibid.*, p. 196.

36. See *Improvements in Standards of Language Proficiency and in Recruiting for the Foreign Service*, Committee on Foreign Relations, U.S. Senate, 86th Cong., 1st sess., 1959. One of the most provocative attacks on American diplomats was contained in Eugene Burdick and William Lederer, *The Ugly American* (New York: W. W. Norton, 1958), an admittedly oversimplified but nevertheless pointed attack.

37. *The New York Times*, July 8, 1962.

38. Department of State *Bulletin*, XLIV, No. 1134 (March 20, 1961), 422.

39. Foreign Service Institute, Department of State, *Area Training in the Foreign Service*, June 1, 1959.

40. Department of State Appropriations for 1962, p. 698.

41. For an announcement and brief description of the course given in 1961–62, see Department of State *Bulletin*, XLV, No. 1161 (September 25, 1961), 533.

42. *Loc. cit.*

43. For a description of developing area studies, see above, Chapter 3.

44. For a description of the seminar and Secretary Rusk's remarks on June 11, 1962, at its opening, see Department of State *Bulletin*, XLVII, No. 1201 (July 2, 1962), 41–42.

45. Department of State *Bulletin*, XLV, No. 1150 (July 10, 1961), 92–93.

46. Industrial College of the Armed Forces, *Report to the Joint Chiefs of Staff on Operations during FY 1959* (Washington, D.C., July, 1959), Appendix E-1.

47. This proportion of civilians in the National War College has been fairly constant; see *Directory, Staff and Graduates of the National War College* for a listing of students since 1946.

48. See, for example, National War College, *Organization and Functions*, Circular No. 6, June 1, 1959.

49. *Army–Navy–Air Force Journal*, XCVIII, No. 3 (September 17, 1960). For the full development of the Industrial College curriculum, see Masland and Radway, *Soldiers and Scholars*, pp. 392–415.

50. Industrial College of the Armed Forces, *Catalog*, 1959–60.

51. This description is based on the curriculum for the academic year 1959–60. The ten courses are: (1) The World Setting and Basic Orientation; (2) Elements of National Power and Their Application to the United States; (3) The American Government and the Formulation of National Security Policy; (4) Strategy and Warfare; (5) The Communist States; (6) The Western Hemisphere and Free Europe; (7) Africa and Free Asia; (8) Field Studies—An Appraisal of World Conditions and United States Policies; (9) A National Estimate of the Situation; and (10) The Development of National Security Policy.

52. Masland and Radway, *Soldiers and Scholars*, pp. 370–73, 487–88.

53. For the plan for a Senior Staff College drawn up by the Civil Service Commission late in 1961, see U.S. Civil Service Commission, *University–Federal Agency Conference on Career Development*.

54. *The Freedom Commission and the Freedom Academy*, Report No. 1812, Committee on the Judiciary, U.S. Senate, 86th Cong., 2d sess., 1960, p. 5. A bill to establish such a Commission and Academy passed the Senate in 1960, but did not come up for action in the House.

55. Department of State *Bulletin*, XLIV, No. 1128 (February 6, 1961), 188.

56. *Report of the President's Advisory Panel on a National Academy of Foreign Affairs*, December 17, 1962.

Chapter 11: Advice by Contract

1. The equivalent total figure for the years 1941–45 was only $3 billion.

2. Allowance must be made, of course, for the decline in the value of the dollar. Prior to World War II, total federal research and development programs did not exceed $100 million, most of this going to agricultural research. In 1940, almost all the $15 million spent by the federal government for research in colleges and universities was controlled by the Department of Agriculture. A critical view of expenditures for research and development may be found in David Novick, "What Do We Mean By Research and Development?" *California Management Review*, II, No. 2 (Spring, 1960), 9–24.

3. These data are derived from *Report to the President on Government Contracting for Research and Development* (Office of the White House Press Secretary, April 30, 1962), Annexes 3 and 4. The report was prepared by a Committee consisting of the Director, Bureau of the Budget (chairman); the Secretary of Defense; the Chairman of the AEC; the Administrator of NASA; the Director of the National Science Foundation; the Chairman of the Civil Service Commission; and the Special Assistant to the President for Science and Technology.

4. *Ibid.*, p. 9.

5. Before 1940, the military services made little use of the universities' re-

search resources, although they fully understood the importance of scientific discovery and technological advances. Some use was made of scientists in World War I, and a National Research Council was established in 1916 for the duration of the war.

6. *Report to the President on Government Contracting,* p. 10; Charles V. Kidd, *American Universities and Federal Research* (Cambridge, Mass.: Harvard University Press, 1959), pp. 51–55; Alice M. Rivlin, *Role of the Federal Government in Financing Higher Education* (Washington, D.C.: The Brookings Institution, 1961), pp. 45–50. The distribution of federal funds for research has been the subject of considerable concern, most recently to Jerome Wiesner, when he was the Special Assistant to the President for Science and Technology, and to his successor, Donald Hornig.

7. See Kidd, *op. cit.* and Rivlin, *op. cit.*, as well as Richard A. Tybout, *Government Contracting in Atomic Energy* (Ann Arbor, Mich.: University of Michigan Press, 1956); *Harvard and the Federal Government* (Cambridge, Mass.: Harvard University Press, 1961); and Harold Orlans, *The Effects of Federal Programs on Higher Education* (Washington, D.C.: The Brookings Institution, 1962).

8. Another area of research, which will soon exceed in volume that done for military purposes, is NASA's space program. But this program, too, has military aspects.

9. Rivlin, *op. cit.*, p. 49. These figures included funds spent by research centers. In 1953–54, foundations supplied $4.2 million for research in the social sciences and the federal government provided $3 million, out of a total for university research of $14 million. The largest contributor was the Ford Foundation. Kidd, *op. cit.*, pp. 69, 235–36.

10. These institutions range in size from the Lincoln Laboratory, with fewer than 2,000 employees, to the Los Alamos Scientific Laboratory, with almost 3,500. Operating costs are in some cases in excess of $50 million a year; investment in plants and equipment is close to $400 million.

11. Joseph Kraft, "Rand: Arsenal for Ideas," *Harper's Magazine,* July, 1960, p. 69.

12. Quoted in Rivlin, *Role of the Federal Government in Financing Higher Education,* p. 31. For a history of World War II research and development, see J. P. Baxter, 3rd, *Scientists Against Time.*

13. "ORO: Weapon for Peace," *The Johns Hopkins Magazine,* IV, No. 1 (October, 1952), 5.

14. Joseph F. McCloskey and Florence H. Trefethen (eds.), *Operations Research for Management* (Baltimore, Md.: The Johns Hopkins Press, 1954), Introduction by Ellis A. Johnson, and pp. 97–116; Herman Kahn, *Thinking About the Unthinkable* (New York: Horizon Press, 1962), Chapter 5.

15. Colonel Seymour J. Gilman, "Operations Research for the Army," *Military Review,* July, 1956, p. 7.

16. *International Abstracts in Operations Research.* The Operations Research Society of America also publishes the bi-monthly *Operations Research* and a semi-annual *Bulletin.*

17. Edward L. Katzenbach, Jr., "Ideas: A New Defense Industry," *The Reporter,* March 2, 1961, p. 19.

18. Horace C. Levinson and Arthur A. Brown, "Operations Research," *Scientific American,* March, 1951, p. 16.

19. Jacinto Steinhardt, "The Role of Operations Research in the Navy," U.S.

Naval Institute *Proceedings*, May, 1946, p. 9. See also McCloskey and Trefethen, *Operations Research for Management*, pp. 12–20.

20. Philip M. Morse and G. E. Kimball, *Methods of Operations Research* (New York: Technology Press and John Wiley, 1958).

21. Statement of J. G. Richard Heckscher, August 20, 1962, in *Systems Development and Management*, Hearings before the Subcommittee on Military Operations, Committee on Government Operations, U.S. House of Representatives, 87th Cong., 2d sess., 1962, Part 4, p. 1491; letter of J. H. Engel, Director, OEG, to authors, October 19, 1962.

22. McCloskey and Trefethen, *Operations Research for Management*, p. 17; Colonel Seymour J. Gilman, "Operations Research in the Army."

23. Men from approximately thirty different disciplines were on the staff, 35 per cent trained in mathematics and physics, 16 per cent in engineering, and the rest in other fields.

24. "ORO: Weapon for Peace," p. 8.

25. One of the few projects done by ORO that has been published is William E. Dougherty and Morris Janowitz (eds.), *A Psychological Warfare Casebook* (Baltimore, Md.: Johns Hopkins Press, 1958).

26. Testimony of Frank A. Parker, President of Research and Analysis Corporation, *Systems Development and Management*, Part 4, p. 1433; Frank C. Porter, "Capital Commerce," *Washington Post and Times Herald*, September 1, 1961.

27. McCloskey and Trefethen, *Operations Research for Management*, pp. 12–13.

28. *Ibid.*, pp. 3–35.

29. Air Force Regulation 20–9, quoted in *The RAND Corporation: The First Fifteen Years* (Santa Monica, Calif.: The RAND Corporation, 1963), p. 2.

30. F. R. Collbohm, *Project RAND* (Santa Monica, Calif.: Rand Publications, p. 707, March 24, 1955), p. 2.

31. Many articles and newspaper reports have been written on RAND. The best accounts are: John McDonald, "The War of Wits," *Fortune*, Vol. 43 (March, 1951), pp. 99 ff.; Joseph Kraft, "RAND: Arsenal for Ideas," *Harper's Magazine*, July, 1960; *Business Week*, March 3, 1956, pp. 86–90; *Newsweek*, May 18, 1953, p. 75; *The New York Times*, May 22, 1960. See also R. D. Specht, *RAND: A Personal View of Its History* (Santa Monica, Calif.: Rand Publications, p. 160, October 23, 1958); F. R. Collbohm, *ibid.*

32. *The RAND Corporation: The First Fifteen Years*, pp. 32–33. RAND publications to December, 1962, are listed in a 780–page *Index of Publications* (Santa Monica, Calif.: The RAND Corporation, 1962); supplements are issued bi-monthly.

33. John McDonald, "The War of Wits." An excellent critique of systems analysis is Albert Wohlstetter, *Defense Decisions: Design vs. Analysis*, abstract of paper presented at the Second International Conference on Operational Research, Aix en Provence, France, September, 1960.

34. "The Military Intellectuals," *The Times Literary Supplement*, August 25, 1961.

35. Lt. Gen. Samuel E. Anderson and Charles A. Boyd, Jr., "Are We Making the Most of the Tools We Have?" *Air Force*, July, 1956; John G. Norris, "New Civilian Agency to Evaluate Weapons," *Washington Post and Times Herald*, July 15, 1956; Institute for Defense Analyses, *First Annual Report*, 1957.

36. Institute for Defense Analyses, *First Annual Report*, contains the Certificate of Incorporation and By-Laws. The present account is based on the annual reports of the Institute and other literature issued by IDA.

37. Katzenbach, "Ideas: A New Defense Industry," p. 19.

38. The contract with the Navy Department led to the formation of the Institute of Naval Studies, described above, which operates as a Division of IDA to support the Navy's work on long-range planning.

39. This description of the SRI is based largely on the literature of the Institute, its annual reports, and conversations with staff members.

40. Stanford Research Institute, *Possible Non-Military Scientific Developments and Their Potential Impact on Foreign Policy Problems of the United States*, prepared for the Committee on Foreign Relations, U.S. Senate, 86th Cong., 1st sess., 1959.

41. Stanford Research Institute, "In the Public Service," Statement of the President, *Report of Operations*, 1959.

42. One entire issue, devoted to "The Spectrum of Conflict," won an award from the Institute of American Strategy; *SRI Journal*, III (1959), 198 pp.

43. *Proceedings of the Asilomar National Strategy Seminar*, April 24–30, 1960 (Stanford, Calif.: Stanford Research Institute, 1960). Speakers included Walt W. Rostow, Robert Strausz-Hupé, William R. Kintner, George S. Pettee, Herman Kahn, James King, Klaus Knorr, Richard Foster, Paul Nitze, Allan Belmont, Bernard Brodie, and Admiral Chester Ward.

44. See Albert Wohlstetter, *Defense Decisions: Design vs. Analysis* and the articles by Britain's earliest students of operations analysis: Sir Solly Zuckerman, "Judgment and Control in Modern Warfare," *Foreign Affairs* (January, 1962), 196–212; P. M. S. Blackett, "Critique of Some Contemporary Defense Thinking," *Encounter*, April, 1961, pp. 9–17.

45. General Thomas D. White, "Strategy and the Defense Intellectuals," *Saturday Evening Post* (May 4, 1963); Speech of Admiral Anderson before the National Press Club, *The New York Times*, September 5, 1963.

46. Marcus Raskin, "The Megadeath Intellectuals," review of Robert A. Levine, *The Arms Debate* in *The New York Review of Books*, November 14, 1963, pp. 6–7. See also David E. Lilienthal, "Skeptical Look at Scientific Experts," *The New York Times Magazine*, September 29, 1963, pp. 23 ff.

47. This description of the Hudson Institute is based on conversations and correspondence with Herman Kahn and on the prospectus and other materials published by the Institute.

48. Arthur Herzog, "Report on a Think Factory," *The New York Times Magazine*, November 10, 1963, pp. 30 ff.

Chapter 12: National Security and Private Research

1. The other five are: The Corporation, The Trade Union, The Political Process, Religious Institutions, and The Mass Media. A seventh area, the Influence of Technology on World Affairs, has since been added.

2. Twentieth Century Fund, *Annual Report*, 1958, p. 3; "Study of Civil-Military Relations," Announcement by the Twentieth Century Fund, January 5, 1954, pp. 2–3.

3. Center for the Study of Democratic Institutions, *Report of the President*, 1958–59, p. 1.

4. Carnegie Endowment for International Peace, *Report for 1959–61*, pp. 6–8.

5. *Ibid.*, p. 9.

6. The scholars were: on the Saar, Jacques Freymond of the Graduate Institute of International Studies, Geneva; on the Franco-Moroccan dispute, Stephane Bernard, Institut de Sociologie Solvay, Brussels; on Cyprus, Francois Crouget, University of Lille; on the Anglo-Iranian oil dispute, Sven Henningsen, University of Copenhagen; and on Trieste, J.-B. Duroselle, Fondation Nationale des Sciences Politiques, Paris. The first of these studies resulted in Jacques Freymond, *The Saar Conflict, 1945–1955* (New York: Frederick A. Praeger, 1960).

7. Carnegie Endowment for International Peace, *Report for 1959–61*, p. 28.

8. *Ibid.*, pp. 28–30; Jerome Spingarn, *New Approaches to Arms Control* (New York: Foreign Policy Association–World Affairs Center, 1962).

9. Bruce L. R. Smith, "The Governance of Berlin," *International Conciliation*, No. 525 (November, 1959); Joseph Nogee, "The Diplomacy of Disarmament," *International Conciliation*, No. 526 (January, 1960); Inis L. Claude, "The United Nations and the Use of Force," *International Conciliation*, No. 532 (March, 1961); H. Arthur Steiner, "Communist China in the World Community," *International Conciliation*, No. 533 (May, 1961).

10. Richard N. Swift, *World Affairs and the College Curriculum* (Washington, D.C.: American Council on Education, 1959); Howard E. and Florence H. Wilson, *American Higher Education and World Affairs* (Washington, D.C.: American Council on Education, 1963).

11. American Academy of Arts and Sciences, *The Technical Problems of Arms Control* (New York: Institute for International Order, 1960); Kenneth E. Boulding *et al.*, *Economic Factors Bearing Upon the Maintenance of Peace* (New York: Institute for International Order, 1960); Arthur Larson, *The International Rule of Law* (New York: Institute for International Order, 1961); Richard C. Snyder, *National and International Decision-Making* (New York: Institute for International Order, 1961); Ithiel de Sola Pool, *Communication and Values in Relation to War and Peace* (New York: Institute for International Order, 1961); Charles E. Osgood, *Psychological Factors in Peace and War* (New York: Institute for International Order, 1964).

12. Grenville Clark and Louis B. Sohn, *World Peace Through World Law* (2d rev. ed.; Cambridge, Mass.: Harvard University Press, 1962); John B. Whitton and Arthur Larson, *Propaganda: Towards Disarmament in the War of Words* (Dobbs Ferry, N.Y.: Oceana Publications, 1964).

13. Harold Taylor, former President of Sarah Lawrence College and a director of the Peace Research Institute, in urging that colleges and universities become centers for a concerted drive for peace, pointed out that the Institute stood ready to support efforts in this direction and to serve as a coordinating agency. Harold Taylor, "Peace and War and the Intellectuals," *The Progressive*, July, 1962, pp. 7–10. For a description of the Michigan Conflict Resolution Center, see Chapter 9; for discussion of academic discussion groups, Chapter 5.

14. See, for example, Arthur Waskow, *The Limits of Defense* (Garden City, N.Y.: Doubleday, 1962).

15. Institute for Policy Studies, *Prospectus*, November, 1963.

16. Institute for Policy Studies, *Status Report*, November, 1963, with attached prospectus.

17. Harry Ashmore, Chairman of the Board of Directors' Executive Committee, has written an excellent and highly readable account of the Center, "The

Thinking Man's Shelter," *Esquire*, April, 1962, pp. 109–112; see also the Fund for the Republic, *Bulletin*, November, 1959.

18. Center for the Study of Democratic Institutions, *Report of the President: January 1, 1961–March 31, 1962* (Santa Barbara, Calif., 1962); Center for the Study of Democratic Institutions, *Bulletin*, November, 1963.

19. Ashmore, "The Thinking Man's Shelter."

20. Consultants are: A. A. Berle, Jr., Harrison Brown, Scott Buchanan, Eugene Burdick, William O. Douglas, Rabbi Robert Gordis, Clark Kerr, Henry R. Luce, Father John Courtney Murray, Reinhold Niebuhr, I. I. Rabi, and George N. Schuster.

21. Other Center publications in this area include Harrison Brown and James Real, *Community of Fear* (1960); William O. Douglas, *Rule of Law in World Affairs* (1961); John Graham, *The Universal Military Obligation* (1958). See also, *The Printed Word: A Ten-Year Bibliography of the Fund for the Republic and the Center for the Study of Democratic Institutions, 1954–1963* (Santa Barbara, 1964).

22. Walter Millis, *A World Without War* (New York: Washington Square Press, 1962).

23. Carnegie Endowment for International Peace, *Annual Report for 1961–62*, p. 13.

24. Members of the group included the historians Edward M. Earle, Walter Millis, and Gorden Craig; political scientists William T. R. Fox, George Graham, and Harold Sprout; economists Edward S. Mason and Max Millikan; and Lieutenant General E. R. Quesada, USAF Ret.

25. Twentieth Century Fund, *Study of Civil-Military Relations, An Announcement*, January 5, 1954.

26. Walter Millis with Harvey C. Mansfield and Harold Stein, *Arms and the State* (New York: Twentieth Century Fund, 1958).

27. Harold Stein (ed.), *American Civil-Military Decisions* (University, Ala.: University of Alabama Press–Inter-University Case Program, 1963). Case studies selected for examination included: Robert J. Quinlan, "The United States Fleet: Diplomacy, Strategy and the Allocation of Ships"; Paul Y. Hammond, "Directives for the Occupation of Germany: The Washington Controversy"; Martin Lichterman, "To the Yalu and Back," and Theodore J. Lowi, "Bases in Spain."

28. The American Academy held its own conference on Arms Control in May, 1960, but was not in a position to provide continuing support for a research program. It was out of this meeting that plans for the Summer Study Group came. Papers read at the meeting were published in the Fall, 1960, issue of *Daedalus*, and later were edited by Donald B. Brennan, *Arms Control, Disarmament and National Security* (New York: George Braziller, 1961). The Academy meeting was made possible through the financial support of the Johnson Foundation, Racine, Wisconsin.

29. The two volumes stemming directly from the Summer Study program are Thomas C. Schelling and Morton H. Halperin, *Strategy and Arms Control*, and David H. Frisch (ed.), *Arms Reduction: Program and Issues* (New York: Twentieth Century Fund, 1961). The third volume is Arthur Hadley, *The Nation's Safety and Arms Control* (New York: Viking Press, 1961).

30. The Brookings Institution, *The Study of Public Problems, A Report on Activities of the Brookings Institution, 1954–1961*, pp. 64–73, and A *Proposed Development*, pp. 19–21; Brookings Lectures, *The Changing Environment of International Relations* (Washington, D.C.: The Brookings Institution, 1956).

31. The Brookings Institution, *The Study of Public Problems*, pp. 23–26.

32. Bernhard G. Bechhoefer, *Postwar Negotiations for Arms Control* (Washington, D.C.: The Brookings Institution, 1961); Walter F. Weiker, *The Turkish Revolution 1960–1961: Aspects of Military Politics* (Washington, D.C.: The Brookings Institution, 1963); Oliver E. Clubb, Jr., *The United States and the Sino-Soviet Bloc in Southeast Asia* (Washington, D.C.: The Brookings Institution, 1962); Max Beloff, *The United States and the Unity of Europe* (Washington, D.C.: The Brookings Institution, 1963).

33. Government contracts with Brookings amounted to $280,147 in 1961–62 and climbed to $324,770 in 1962–63. Contracting agencies concerned with national security affairs have included the Atomic Energy Commission, the State Department, the U.S. Office of Education, the National Aeronautics and Space Administration, the Council of Economic Advisors, the National Science Foundation, the Senate Committee on Foreign Relations, and the International Cooperation Administration and its successor, the Agency for International Development.

34. The Brookings Institution, *Current Activities*, 1956; *A Conference Program for Executives in the Federal Service* (Washington, D.C.: The Brookings Institution, 1957). The Brookings Conference program is also discussed in connection with government programs of career development in Chapter 10.

35. The Brookings Institution, *A Proposed Development*, p. 10.

36. Institute for Strategic Studies, *Announcement*, p. 1; *Report of the Chairman of the Council, Annual General Meeting*, February 2, 1961.

37. Institute for Strategic Studies, *Report of the Director*, 1962.

38. *Ibid.*

39. Alastair Buchan, *NATO in the 1960's* (New York: Frederick A. Praeger, 1960; rev. ed., 1963); Hedley Bull, *The Control of the Arms Race* (New York: Frederick A. Praeger, 1961; rev. ed., 1965); Peter Calvocoressi, *World Order and New States* (New York: Frederick A. Praeger, 1962).

40. Alastair Buchan and Philip Windsor, *Arms and Stability in Europe* (New York: Frederick A. Praeger, 1963).

41. M. R. D. Foot, *Men in Uniform* (New York: Frederick A. Praeger, 1961); Leonard Beaton and John Maddox, *The Spread of Nuclear Weapons* (New York: Frederick A. Praeger, 1962).

42. Remarks by Walter H. Mallory made at a Council dinner, May 21, 1959, quoted in Council on Foreign Relations, *Annual Report*, 1958–59, p. 5.

43. Council on Foreign Relations, *Annual Report*, 1962–63, p. 72.

44. Joseph Kraft, "School for Statesmen," *Harper's Magazine*, July, 1958, p. 67. See also Richard H. Rovere, *The American Establishment* (New York: Harcourt, Brace & World, 1962).

45. Council on Foreign Relations, *Annual Report*, 1962–63, pp. 70–71.

46. Council on Foreign Relations, *Announcement of Studies on Foreign Policy*, 1958–1959, p. 1.

47. In 1963–64, this committee consisted of Henry M. Wriston (Chairman), Hamilton Fish Armstrong, Emilio G. Collado, Byron Dexter, John S. Dickey, Caryl P. Haskins, Joseph E. Johnson, Grayson L. Kirk, Alfred C. Neal, and James A. Perkins.

48. Council on Foreign Relations, *Annual Report*, 1962–63, pp. 22–40.

49. Council on Foreign Relations, *Annual Report*, 1958–59, p. 12.

50. *Ibid.*, p. 14.

51. Henry Kissinger, *Nuclear Weapons and Foreign Policy* (New York: Harper & Brothers, 1957), pp. vii–xv.

52. Kissinger, *ibid.*, p. vii. The regular members of the group were: Frank Altschul, Hamilton Fish Armstrong, Hanson W. Baldwin, Lloyd Berkner, Robert R. Bowie, McGeorge Bundy, William A. M. Burden, John C. Campbell, Thomas K. Finletter, George S. Franklin, Jr., Lieutenant General James M. Gavin, Roswell L. Gilpatric, N. E. Halaby, Caryl P. Haskins, James T. Hill, Jr., Joseph E. Johnson, Mervin J. Kelly, Major General Richard C. Lindsay, Major General James McCormack, Jr., Frank C. Nash, Paul H. Nitze, Charles P. Noyes, Frank Pace, Jr., James A. Perkins, Don K. Price, I. I. Rabi, David Rockefeller, Oscar N. Ruebhausen, General Walter B. Smith, Henry De Wolf Smyth, Shields Warren, Carroll L. Wilson, and Arnold Wolfers.

53. Kissinger, *ibid.*, p. xiii.

54. Among the volumes related to national security published during the past few years are: John C. Campbell, *Defense of the Middle East: Problems of American Policy* (New York: Harper & Brothers, 1960); Ben T. Moore, *NATO and the Future of Europe* (New York: Harper & Brothers, 1958); Henry Kissinger, *Nuclear Weapons and Foreign Policy* (New York: Harper & Brothers, 1957); Joseph S. Berliner, *Soviet Economic Aid* (New York: Frederick A. Praeger, 1958); Edwin Lieuwen, *Arms and Politics in Latin America* (New York: Frederick A. Praeger, 1960); A. Doak Barnett, *Communist China and Asia: Challenge to American Policy* (New York: Harper & Brothers, 1960).

55. Kraft, "School for Statesmen." In *The American Establishment*, Richard Rovere, with tongue in cheek, characterized it as having, within its own field, the authority of *Pravda* and *Izvestia*.

56. In 1960–61, *Foreign Affairs* received 157 requests for permission to reproduce articles.

57. Thomas K. Finletter, *Foreign Policy: The Next Phase* (rev. ed., New York: Harper & Brothers, 1960); Dean Rusk, "The President," *Foreign Affairs*, April, 1960, pp. 353–69; Caryl Haskins's lectures were published as *Scientific Revolution and World Politics* (New York: Harper and Row, 1964); and Edward S. Mason's as *Foreign Aid and Foreign Policy* (New York: Harper and Row, 1964).

58. Ernest Gross, *United Nations: Structure for Peace* (New York: Harper and Row, 1962); Adolf A. Berle, Jr., *Latin America: Diplomacy and Reality* (New York: Harper and Row, 1962); John Dreier, *The Organization of American States and the Hemisphere Crisis* (New York: Harper and Row, 1962); Christian Herter, *Toward An Atlantic Community* (New York: Harper and Row, 1962); George N. Shuster, *UNESCO: Assessment and Promise* (New York: Harper and Row, 1963). The Council expects that four or five books in the Policy Book Series will be published each year.

59. Council on Foreign Relations, *Annual Report*, 1960–61, p. 3.

60. At least one-fifth of the meetings can be identified as dealing with an aspect of national security. A large number of additional meetings are clearly related to this subject. Council on Foreign Relations, *Annual Report*, 1962–63, pp. 48–64.

61. *Ibid.*, pp. 45–47.

62. *Ibid.*, pp. 66–67.

Chapter XIII: Problems for Government and Education

1. The seminar was held at Dartmouth. Participants were Lewis Edinger, Martin Goldman, Fred Greene, Abbot Greenleaf, Paul Hammond, Samuel P. Huntington, Louis Morton, Robert E. Osgood, Laurence I. Radway, and Glenn

Snyder. A product of the discussion was a paper by Professor Radway, read at the 1958 meeting of the American Political Science Association Meeting on "The Study of Military Affairs."

2. The most recent effort to establish such a journal was in 1961, and several meetings were held in Washington to discuss the possibility. It foundered, as did previous efforts, on the inability to secure financial support. Colonel Trevor N. Dupuy has been most active in this effort, as former President of the American Military Institute and in a private capacity. Professor Barton Leach of the Harvard Law School and Samuel P. Huntington have at one time or another also pushed this project.

3. The authors are indebted to Professors William T. R. Fox and Samuel P. Huntington for an analysis on which the following is largely based. These groupings overlap and some writings fall into several groups.

4. William W. Kaufmann (ed.), *Military Policy and National Security* (Princeton, N.J.: Princeton University Press, 1956).

5. Rockefeller Brothers Fund, Special Studies Report II, *International Security: The Military Aspect* (Garden City, N. Y.: Doubleday, 1958).

Index